P9-BTO-780

How to Write It

*A complete guide to
everything you'll ever write*

THIRD EDITION

Sandra E. Lamb

TEN SPEED PRESS
Berkeley

Copyright © 1998, 2006, 2011 by Sandra E. Lamb

All rights reserved.
Published in the United States by Ten Speed Press, an imprint of the
Crown Publishing Group, a division of Random House, Inc., New York.
www.crownpublishing.com
www.tenspeed.com

Ten Speed Press and the Ten Speed Press colophon are registered
trademarks of Random House, Inc.

Library of Congress Cataloging-in-Publication Data

Lamb, Sandra E.
   How to write it : a complete guide to everything you'll ever write /
Sandra E. Lamb. — 3rd ed.
      p. cm.
   Includes bibliographical references and index.
1. Commercial correspondence. 2. Business report writing. 3. Technical
writing. 4. Letter writing. I. Title.
   HF5721.L273 2011
   651.7'4—dc22

                                                              2011008717

ISBN 978-1-60774-032-2

Printed in the United States

Design by Katy Brown
Author photo by Mark Bennington

10 9 8 7 6 5 4 3 2 1

Third Edition

CONTENTS

PRINCIPLES

If language is not correct,
then what is said is not what is meant;
If what is said is not what is meant,
Then what ought to be done remains undone.

—*Confucius*

1 GETTING STARTED

We write to be understood. And the fastest and best route to that goal is clear and concise language. It sounds easy enough, and it is, if we use a few simple principles. Learn these, and enjoy the rewards of effective communication.

KNOW YOUR MESSAGE

The first element in getting your audience to understand what you write is knowing what you want to communicate. It sounds easy enough, but this is where most messages get derailed.

Before you begin to write, think your message all the way through. No matter how complex it is, this step will make your job much easier and produce a much better result. It's the best investment of time you'll make in any writing or communicating exercise. And the practice of taking the time to do this will help you develop skills of analysis and organization. Distill your message into a single, simple sentence—a message statement.

Once you have your message statement in mind, use the rest of the steps in this chapter to develop, order, refine, and effectively express it.

WRITE FOR YOUR AUDIENCE

Since the reader is your reason for writing, ask yourself some basic questions:

- Who is my reader?
- What does my reader already know about this subject?
- What does my reader need to know?
- How will my reader respond? Will he or she be receptive? Will he or she object? Will he or she be hostile? Will he or she be indifferent?

Make some notes about your reader, as a guide. This will help ensure that you have your reader firmly in mind, which will, in turn, give your writing the proper focus.

Example: You are going to announce a company open house to department employees and to the general public. So, you have two groups of readers—two audiences. You will need to write two messages. For your department employee readers, the focus and content of what you will communicate will be very different from the focus and content of the announcement for the general public. Think about who each group of readers is, what the group already knows, and then what each group needs to know. Your notes about what to include in the announcement to each group might look something like this:

	General Public	Department Employees
What:	Occasion/Open house	Open house
Why:	New product/background, development, benefits, etc.	New product launch
Where:	Address and directions	Specific instructions about areas to be open and those to be closed to visitors
When:	Date, time	Date, time, complete schedule of employees on duty for specific time slots
Who:	Open to public	Detailed assignments for each employee

Obviously, since you have two very different groups of readers, the best approach will be to complete two written communications. This is why knowing your reader *before* you begin writing is vital to effective communication.

DEVELOP YOUR MESSAGE

The secret to effective writing is knowing precisely what you want to say to the reader before you start. This means getting down to the main elements of your message by asking yourself some basic questions:

- What do I need/want to tell the reader?
- What do I want to accomplish with this message?
- How do I want the reader to respond?
- What do I want the reader to do after reading my communication?

Then crystallize the intent of your message by looking more closely at your own motive in writing. Ask yourself what you want your message to accomplish. Do you want to inform the reader? What information do you want to give? Do you want to persuade the reader? Of what? Motivate the reader to take some action? Apologize to the reader? For what? Or, is the purpose to follow up on or confirm a verbal discussion, or to simply create a written record?

Most of your messages will be to inform and/or persuade; sometimes you will want to motivate. A little work here will help to ensure that your message hits the bull's-eye. So, be very precise. Here are some examples of well-thought-out message statements written in a single sentence:

- You can save $525.00 each month if you use our accounting services.
- The meeting is at 10:00 a.m., Tuesday, in my office.
- Buy our Model 104B Analyzer.
- Please send me complete information on the Model L15 Wicker Whacker.
- We must reorganize our distribution system to be profitable.
- I will not be able to attend the values seminar.
- I recommend we invest $5.2 million in the new analyzer product line.
- I was so sorry to hear about your loss.
- I need 12 volunteers for the dance.
- This plane won't fly!

- I want your suggestions on our lunchtime policy changes.
- We need to hire 40 assembly-line workers.
- You overcharged me $376.50.
- Our Model 650B machining station will help your company make $3.4 million next year.

Distilling your core message into a single, precise sentence gives you a head start. It means you'll be taking the next writing step from a focused, secure position. Your message, when complete, will be strong and clear and undoubtedly shorter than it would have been without this step.

For practice, read through several communications on your desk. What, in a sentence, is the message statement of each? What should it have been? Is the message of each clear? Garbled? Off base? Complete?

Now you know (1) what you want to communicate, (2) who you are communicating with, (3) the main points of what you want to say, and (4) what you want to accomplish with your communication. If you view writing as a two-way conversation, your job will be easier, and the end result will be better. It will also help you to use the correct voice and tone. Make it conversational.

USE CLEAR, LOGICAL PROGRESSION

When you began thinking about writing, you had some ideas in mind. Maybe you even made some notes—a very good practice.

Write down the main points, or parts, of your communication in the most logical order. You can do this in the traditional alphanumeric system (I., A., 1., a.), or in a more stream-of-consciousness form often depicted by a series of connected circles, as shown in the two figures. You can put your ideas into your computer, or you can use index cards and write them out by hand. But start to think about organization, and form your headings in as logical an order as possible. Then list your subpoints: (1) Be consistent with the information and with the background of your reader, (2) order your outline the way your reader most likely thinks about the subject, or (3) order it chronologically or developmentally.

By organizing your thoughts on the basis of what the reader needs to know about the subject and what you want the reader to do after reading your communication, you will make your task much easier. And keep going back to your message statement. It will help you stay on track.

Your points should be lining up under these sections:

Introduction/Statement of Purpose
Why you are writing and/or what you are writing about.

Background/Explanation
Use subpoints to set the stage for communication.

Discussion/Proposal
Make your case and give the for-and-against arguments.

Summary/Conclusion
Summarize your points.

Call for Action/Response
Call for action and/or request the reader's response.

Alphanumeric Outline

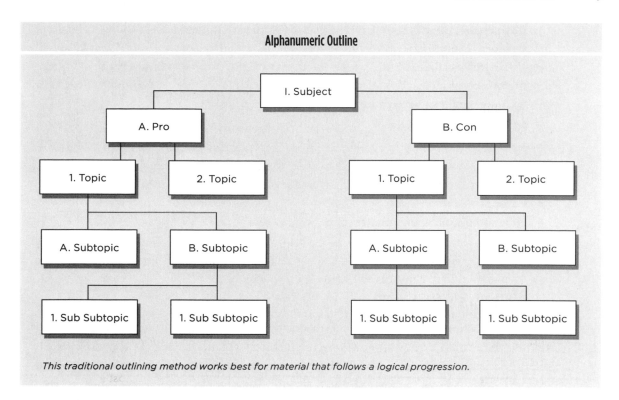

This traditional outlining method works best for material that follows a logical progression.

Stream-of-Consciousness Outline

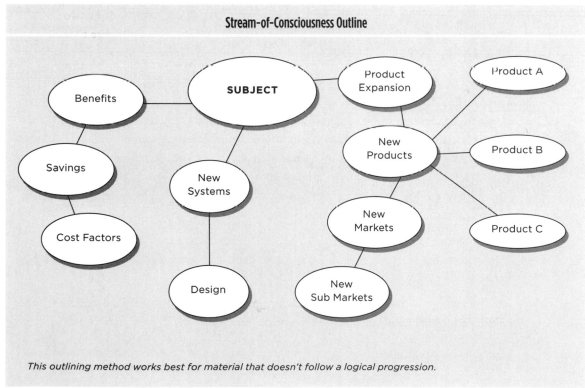

This outlining method works best for material that doesn't follow a logical progression.

As you write, think of your points in terms of occurrence or chronology. This will give order to your ideas. If you are going to define a procedure like running laboratory tests, your ideas will need to be sequential. If you are writing about sales growth over the past five years, your order may be chronological. If your subject naturally orders itself in one of these ways, go with it. Your choices for developing your writing are many:

- Chronological
- Spatial
- Analysis
- Deduction (general to specific)
- Cause and effect
- Decreasing order of importance
- Sequential
- Comparisons
- Division and classification
- Induction (specific to general)
- Increasing order of importance

Think while you write, too, about whether illustrations will make your message clearer and more interesting.

FLESH OUT YOUR OUTLINE

Remember, a strong outline releases you to begin writing. It's like a road map. The complexity of your message, your reader, and your own work methods will dictate when your outline is complete. And remember, too, that the steps are not necessarily sequential: Some of the important steps in the writing process cross over and cross back. For example, during the outlining process, you will probably write some parts of your message, go to the next step, and then return to a previously written portion of your communication.

COMPLETE ANY NECESSARY RESEARCH

You may need a number of kinds of research. At a minimum, you will go to the notes you made during outlining. You may also have to interview others for facts and input, research published sources, and read through special unpublished papers and facts. Or, you may have to do a survey or develop a questionnaire to get your facts and information. Make sure your research is thorough, and if you develop a research instrument such as a survey, use care to create one that will give you valid, objective data (see Questionnaire & Survey, page 242).

Although often this decision is prescribed by your industry or discipline, you will need to fit your message into one of these general categories:

- Formal report
- Memorandum
- Letter
- Informal report
- Proposal

After selecting the format, follow the instructions given in the correct chapter and the conventions of your own organization, industry, or discipline.

WRITE YOUR DRAFT

Let yourself go. Using your outline, notes, written passages, and gathered information, give yourself over to the act of writing. Concentrate on getting all the writing done first, without trying to polish. If you have completed all the other steps, you will be clear on your point of view, methodology, and content. For most writers, the draft is best written in a very concentrated work session, writing without rereading. Let your ideas flow, and get them all recorded.

REVISE

Although writing is hard work, revising is the most difficult task. Clear, precise writing that appears to have been written with ease usually requires hard, intense labor. Here are a few guidelines:

* Be sure you have written a topic sentence for each paragraph. Then pay off in the paragraph by producing the content this sentence has promised.
* Insert headings and subheadings to keep and direct the reader's attention and to make your message clear, easy to grasp, and visually appealing.
* Know that revising is usually a several-times-over process. Be diligent.
* Check for accuracy and completeness. Put on the reader's hat here: what does the reader need to know, and in how much detail?
* Go back to your message statement and write your opening and introduction.
* Keep sentences short, between 12 to 15 words.
* Keep paragraphs at about eight lines.
* Vary sentence length and structure to add interest.
* Think about visual appeal and arrangement as you proceed.
* Check for continuity and create transitions. Does each paragraph build on the one that precedes it?
* Be sure your message is clear. Have others read it and give you input, if possible.
* Check for any word or paragraph problems outlined in the following sections.

Be Clear and Be Brief

It's very easy to get attached to what you write, but in revising, you must be ruthless. Ask yourself whether each word has real meaning, a necessary function. If the answer is no, cut it. Getting rid of the deadwood takes real effort and professional detachment.

Simplify for the General Reader

Use a simple word if it works. Use technical words when they are the best choice—when their meaning is known to your reader and when technical words are the most direct and precise. This doesn't mean that your writing will be dull or simplistic. It will be strong, clear, and easy to understand. Check the examples at the end of this chapter for using direct, simple words instead of pompous, stuffy ones to make your meaning clear.

Make Your Communication Reader-Friendly

Reader-friendly writing means clear and direct writing. It also means an overall visual layout and appearance that invites the reader to read. Use white space so your communication looks open and easy to read, and use headings to catch the reader's attention. Lists, graphs, and charts will make your message visually appealing.

For lists, observe a few rules:

- Start each step with an action verb, but not the same one.
- List each step separately. Don't combine them.
- Make sure each step is in logical sequence.
- Write each step as a full sentence.
- Keep the sentence construction parallel.
- Use an active voice, if possible.

Use Parallel Construction and Consistent Tense

It's amazing how important this principle is. When your ideas are equal, give them equal construction, whether they are items in a list, headings, sentences, or phrases. You can do this by using the same grammatical structure. Like the statements we just listed, each is constructed as a complete sentence, and each begins with an action verb.

USE POWERFUL WORDS

Verbs are your friends. They will happily carry your meaning if you select the correct ones. Verbs enliven your writing and turn passive statements into active ones, if your pick your verbs from the active side of the family.

And don't stop at active verbs; select colorful, precise, and vibrant verbs. Let's try these comparisons:

The hour passed very slowly.
The hour crept by.
The hour inched by.
The hour crawled by.
Time stood still.

None of these sentences is wrong. Some verbs just do more precise work than others. Some create a more vivid picture, and some are more appealing because they don't suffer from overuse. If you write in an active voice, using active verbs, and select them for their precise meanings, you will enliven your communications. Your message will come to life. So, put your subjects to work with active verbs.

The most listless verbs, and often worst offenders, are those in the "nominal" category—verbs turned into nouns by added endings: -ing, -tion, -ment, -ance, -ing, -al, or -ure. Here are a few of those verbs that usually appear with *to* in front of them:

Verb	Nominal	Verb	Nominal
conclude	conclusion	inflate	inflation
direct	direction	assess	assessment
fail	failure	submit	submission
provide	provision	attend	attendance

You can see how important it is to use active verbs whenever possible.

Check the lists in this chapter while writing. The charts that follow provide some more guidelines to help you select simple, powerful words.

To help the flow of your ideas, use words and phrases that work as road signs for your readers.

EDIT, EDIT, EDIT

Writing is really talking on paper, so make your communications talk. Sometimes reading aloud what you've written turns on a light. Listen for stilted words, remoteness, obscurity. You want your communication to sound conversational, more like speaking face-to-face than a speech. That means, of course, that you should look for any hint of talking down to your reader.

There is a place for formal writing, but formal writing isn't pompous, wordy, remote, stilted, or stuffed with polysyllabic words.

Proofread One Last Time

Put what you've written aside for a while, then take one last objective read through it. When you can answer the following questions with a "yes," you've made your communication as clear as possible:

- Did you write to your reader?
- Have you used an active voice whenever possible?
- Have you kept your message simple?
- Have you used specific, not vague, words?
- Have you used present tense whenever possible?
- Have you omitted all the unnecessary and redundant words?

Now, with these principles in mind, turn to the chapter that features the communication you are writing. Each chapter is set up so you can use these steps to make your writing reader-friendly and bulletproof.

Use Transition Words to Help the Reader Understand

To show . . .

sequence	contrast	similarity	an explanation	cause and effect
then	unlike	like	for example	then
in addition	different	the same	one such	as a result
to enumerate	in spite of	similar	for instance	for this reason
number _	on the other hand	close	to illustrate	the result was
first, second, third	on the contrary	likewise	also	then
next	opposite	also	too	what followed
the next in this series	opposing	near	to demonstrate	in response
besides these	however			therefore
	contrary to			thus
	very different			because of
				consequently
				the reaction

Use Simple, Direct Words

Instead of	Use
10 a.m. in the morning	10 a.m.
a substantial segment of the population	many people
above mentioned	these, this, that, those
absolutely complete	complete
absolutely essential	essential
accounted for by the fact that	caused by
achieve purification	purify
activate	begin
actual experience	experience
add the point that	add that
adequate enough	adequate
advise	tell
along the lines of	like
am in receipt of	have
an example of this is the fact that	for example
analyses were made	analyzed
answer in the affirmative	yes
any and all	any, all
are of the opinion that	think that, or believe that
as of this date	today

Instead of	Use
as to whether	whether
assent	agree
assist	help
at a price of $10	at $10
at the present time	now
at the present writing	now
at this point in time	now
attached hereto	attached
attached please find	attached is
attempt	try
attributable	due
basic fundamentals	facts, basics, fundamentals
be desirous of	want
blue in color	blue
came to the conclusion	concluded
cancel out	cancel
category	class
cease	stop
circle around	circle
coalesce	join
cognizant	aware
collect together	collect

Use Simple, Direct Words

Instead of	Use
compensate, compensation	pay
components	parts
concede	admit
conceive	think
conception	idea
conclusion, conclude	end
connect to	connect
consensus of opinion	consensus
consequent results	results
considerable	much
constructive	helpful
deemed it necessary to	[eliminate]
deficiency	lack
delete the most insignificant	delete
deliberation	thought
delineate	outline, draw
demonstrate	show
descend down	descend
despite the fact that	although
determine	find
disappear from sight	disappear
discontinue	stop
during the year of 2008	during 2008
early beginnings	beginnings
effect a change in	change
eliminate	cut out
empty out	empty
enclosed herein	enclosed
encounter	meet
endeavor	try
enter in the program	enter
equitable	fair
establish	set up
evince	show
exactly identical	identical

Instead of	Use
exemplify	show
exhibits a tendency to	tends
facilitate	help
few in number	few
first and foremost	first
following after	following
for the purpose of	for
for the reason that	because
frequently	often
function	use
give a weakness to	weaken
give an indication of	indicate
give encouragement to	encourage
have at hand	have
hold in abeyance	wait
I am of the opinion	I think
I will endeavor to ascertain	I will try to find out
in my opinion I think	in my opinion, or I think
in order of importance	order
in order to	to
in regard to	[eliminate]
in the amount of	for
in the course of	during
in the event of	if
in the event that	if
in the interest of time	[eliminate]
in the majority of cases	most, or usually
in the majority of instances	often
in the matter of	about
in the nature of	like
in the near future	soon
in the neighborhood of	about
in the normal course	normally
in the normal course of our procedure	normally

Use Simple, Direct Words

Instead of	Use
in the opinion of this writer	in my opinion
in the same way as described	as described
in view of the fact that	because
indicate	show
initial	first
initiate	start or begin
institute an improvement in	improve
interpose an objection	object
involve the necessity of	require
is corrective of	corrects
is found to be	is
is indicative of	indicates
is suggestive of	suggests
it appears that an oversight has been made	I [or we] overlooked
it has been brought to my attention	I have learned
it has been recognized that	[eliminate]
it is apparent that	therefore, or it seems that
it is incumbent on me	I must
it is noteworthy that	[eliminate]
it is the intention of this writer to	[eliminate]
it would not be unreasonable to assume	assume
join together	join
large in sample size	large
make a decision to	decide to
make the acquaintance of	meet
may I call to your attention	[eliminate]
may or may not	may
modifications contained herein	these changes
most complete	complete

Instead of	Use
multitudinous	many
mutual cooperation	cooperation
my personal opinion	my opinion
new innovation	new
objective	aim
obligation	debt
of a confidential nature	confidential
on behalf of	for
on the basis of	by
on the few occasions	occasionally
on the grounds that	since
on the part of	by
optimum, optimal	best
owing to the fact that	since
perform an analysis of	analyze
perform an examination of	examine
perhaps I should mention that	[eliminate]
permit me to take this opportunity	I want to
pertaining to	about
preparatory to	before
present a conclusion	conclude
prior to the time of/that	before
proceed	go
proceed to separate	separate
procure	get
prolong the duration	prolong
provide information about	inform
provided that	if
the purpose of this memo	[eliminate]
range all the way from	range from
reached an agreement	agreed
report back	report
secure	get

Use Simple, Direct Words

Instead of	Use
similar	like
state the point that	state that
still continue	continue
structure our planning pursuant	make plans
subsequent to	after
subsequently	later
supplement	add
surrounding circumstances	circumstances
take into consideration, taking this factor into consideration, or take under advisement	consider
tangible	real
terminate	end, stop, dismiss
the committee made an agreement	the committee agreed, or we agreed
the committee made the decision	the committee decided, or we decided
the fact that	[eliminate]
the field of photography	photography
the purpose of this memo	[eliminate]
the question as to whether	whether
the undersigned	I
the writer	I
there is no doubt	[eliminate]
this report is an offering	this report offers

Instead of	Use
to be in agreement with	agree
to have a preference for	prefer
to summarize the above	in summary
total effect of	effect of
transact	do
under date of	dated
under no circumstances	never
undertake a study of	study
until such time as	until
utilize, utilization	use
visualize	see
we deem it advisable	I suggest
what is believed is	[eliminate]
whereas	but
whereby	which
whether or not	whether
with a view to	to
with reference to	[eliminate]
with regard to	about
with the result that	so that
with this in mind, it is therefore clear	therefore
within the realm of possibility	possible
you will find attached	attached is, or here is

2 GRAPHIC DESIGN & LAYOUT

Think visually. Graphic design, layout, and the strategic use of visual aids like chart, graphs, tables, and illustrations can make your communication come alive. It can save you lots of words and make your message immediately apparent. Now, with so much technology at your fingertips, all this becomes much simpler, but you must develop the ability to plan and visualize what you want to convey. Then decide what will appeal to your reader and help his or her understanding of the material.

Plan. Use spacing, indenting, underlining, numbering, boldface type, and different sizes and types of lettering (typefaces) to make your message more understandable and visually appealing. Visual appeal is key not only in its ability to grab the interest of your reader but also to help the reader remember the details of your message. Learn to think in terms of text formats that set off paragraphs; typefaces to denote sections; use of color; and graphs, tables, flowcharts, drawings, and lists that promote your message and reinforce it to your reader. Strategically use bullets and other graphic aids, boldface type, and indentations. You will need to study basic layout and design elements, and learn a few facts about typefaces and type sizes, but the results will be well worth it.

THINK ABOUT CONTENT

Evaluate your content in terms of the following points:

- Know your audience and decide precisely what it needs to know.
- Decide what you want to emphasize to help you focus on how you will create special displays.
- Review the options of the system you will use to produce your communication.
- Use boldface headings in a larger type size to draw the reader's attention and help him or her focus on the subject.
- Use white space to create the impression that your communication is short and easy to read.
- Use underlining, indenting, and varied but consistent spacing to break up the density of the text and help the reader scan for specific information.
- Decide which elements of your communication could or should be reinforced by art, graphs, or charts, and if so, use design graphics that are understandable at a glance by reducing graphics to their simplest, clearest elements.
- Pay special attention to the layout of text and images.

- Remember, the eye focuses first on the upper outside corner of the left-hand page and the lower outside corner of the right-hand page.
- Create a communication in which all the parts look like a unified whole.
- Reader-test your communication whenever possible and make any necessary changes.

ELIMINATE WRONG MESSAGES

Remember that graphics supplement your written message; they don't replace it. Don't create visual "noise" by using too many, confusing, or too varied illustrations, charts, or graphs, and don't make the visuals too complex. This defeats the purpose.

Selecting Type Arrangement

Design and layout can make your communication come alive and make your message immediately apparent. Now, with so much technology at your fingertips, design becomes much simpler, but you must develop the ability to plan and visualize what you want to convey. Then decide what will appeal to your reader and help

Long lines, double-spaced.

Design and layout can make your communication come alive and make your message immediately apparent. Now, with so much technology at your fingertips, design becomes much simpler, but you must develop the ability to plan and visualize what you want to convey. Then decide what will appeal to your reader

Short single-spaced lines, which make use of white space.

Design and layout can make your communication come alive and make your message immediately apparent. Now, with so much technology at your fingertips, design becomes much simpler, but you must develop the ability to plan and visualize what you want to convey. Then decide what will appeal to your reader and help his or her understanding of the material.
   Design and layout can make your communication come alive and make your message immediately apparent. Now, with so

much technology at your fingertips, design becomes much simpler, but you must develop the ability to plan and visualize what you want to convey. Then decide what will appeal to your reader and help his or her understanding of the material.
   Design and layout can make your communication come alive and make your message immediately apparent. Now, with so much technology at your fingertips, design becomes much simpler, but you must develop the ability to plan and visualize what

Type on facing pages should align at top, left, and bottom.

Justified Copy

Design and layout can make your communication come alive and make your message immediately apparent. Now, with so much technology at your fingertips, design becomes much simpler, but you must develop the ability to plan and visualize what you want to convey. Then decide what will appeal to your reader and help his or her understanding of the material.

Design and layout can make your communication come alive and make your message immediately apparent. Now, with so much

Left justified: Lines start at the same position at left.

Design and layout can make your communication come alive and make your message immediately apparent. Now, with so much technology at your fingertips, design becomes much simpler, but you must develop the ability to plan and visualize what you want to convey. Then decide what will appeal to your reader and help his or her understanding of the material.

Design and layout can make your communication come alive and make your message immediately apparent. Now, with so much technology at

Fully justified: Lines start and end at the same position on the left and right, respectively.

Design and layout can make your communication come alive and make your message immediately apparent. Now, with so much technology at your fingertips, design becomes much simpler, but you must develop the ability to plan and visualize what you want to convey. Then decide what will appeal to your reader and help his or her understanding of the material. Design and layout can make your communication come alive and make your message immediately apparent. Now, with so much technology

Right justified: Lines end at the same position at right.

Setting Type in Columns

Design and layout

Design and layout can make your communication come alive and make your message immediately apparent. Now, with so much technology at your fingertips, design becomes much simpler, but you must develop the ability to plan and visualize what you want to convey. Then decide what will appeal to your reader and help his or her understanding of the material.

Design and layout can make your communication come alive and make your message immediately apparent. Now, with so much technology at your fingertips, design becomes much simpler, but you must develop the ability to plan and visualize what you want to convey. Then decide

Two-column grid.

DESIGN AND LAYOUT

Design and layout can make your communication come alive and make your message immediately apparent. Now, with so much technology at your fingertips, design becomes much simpler, but you must develop the ability to plan and visualize what you want to convey. Then decide what will appeal to your reader and help his or her understanding of the material.

Design and layout can make your communication come alive and make your message immediately apparent. Now, with so much technology at your fingertips, design becomes much simpler, but you must develop the ability to plan and visualize what you want to convey. Then decide what will appeal to your reader and help his or her understanding of the material.

Design and layout can make your communication come alive and make your message immediately apparent. Now, with so much technology at your fingertips, design becomes much simpler, but you must develop the ability to plan and

Three-column grid.

Design and layout

Design and layout can make your communication come alive and make your message immediately apparent. Now, with so much technology at your fingertips, design becomes much simpler, but you must develop the ability to plan and visualize what you want to convey. Then decide what will appeal to your reader and help his or her understanding of the material.

Design and layout can make your communication come alive and make your message immediately apparent. Now, with so much technology at your fingertips, design becomes much simpler, but you must develop the ability to plan and visualize what you want to convey. Then decide what will appeal to your reader and help his or her understanding of the material. Design and layout can make your communication come alive and make your message immediately apparent. Now, with so much technology at your fingertips, design becomes much simpler, but you must develop the ability to plan and visualize what you want to convey. Then decide what will appeal to your reader and help his or her understanding of the material.

LAYOUT

Design and layout can make your communication come alive and make your message immediately apparent. Now, with so much technology at your fingertips, design becomes much simpler, but you must develop the ability to plan and visualize what you want to convey. Then decide what will appeal to your reader and help his or her understanding of the material.

Six-column grid: This design consists of two text blocks, the first with four columns of space, and the second with two.

SOCIAL

The difference between the right word and almost the right word is the difference between lightning and the lightning bug.

—*Mark Twain*

ANNOUNCEMENT

An announcement may be good news or bad news, but the form itself is consistent: Get the reader's attention, then give him or her the single message you want to communicate. Be direct, focused, brief, and timely.

ETIQUETTE

Give very careful consideration to the reader when the announcement contains emotional or very personal content. Sometimes your announcement may be of a delicate nature, and in that case require the civility of a human moment—a face-to-face delivery. Use great discretion when this is the case.

DECIDE TO WRITE

Announcements are suitable for many of the events and changes in our lives:

- Change of address
- Anniversary: wedding or business
- Birth or adoption
- Personal life event: graduation, wedding, marital separation, divorce, retirement, or death
- Employee change: resignation, firing, promotion, transfer, special achievement, new employees, job opening
- Opening a business, branch office, or store
- Business changes: new business name, price changes, product recall, new programs, products, policies, hours, practices, contracts, organization buyout, merger, bankruptcy, expansion, acquisition, company layoff, downsizing, closing, or record sales
- Seminars, workshops, or conferences
- Open house for home, business, or school
- Bad news of some sort

THINK ABOUT CONTENT

- Ask yourself *who*, *what*, *when*, *where*, *why*, and *how* to help focus the information you want to communicate and to ensure you make it complete.
- State the information in order of importance.
- Be direct, brief, and concise.

- Check the prescribed format of different kinds of announcements.
- Emphasize the goodwill aspects of your news. If your company is changing working hours, for example, emphasize the greater convenience for employees and customers.
- Use the "need-to-know" guideline in making your announcement. Who needs to know your news?
- When it's appropriate, emphasize the reasons for your news to promote understanding and goodwill.

ELIMINATE WRONG MESSAGES

- An announcement should supply complete, basic information. Leave out lengthy explanations or extraneous facts. Even when the announcement is a hybrid—combined with a sales message, for example—the format and style should strengthen the single message.
- Don't let employees hear or read your organizational information from an outside source first.
- Don't put off a bad news announcement. It is usually best that your bad news be received directly from you rather than from another source. If nothing else, announce the basic news and state that full information will follow.

CONSIDER ANNOUNCEMENT TYPES

- A personal name change is announced by stating that, as of (date) the person formerly known as (name) will be known as (name). No explanation is needed, but written notes to friends and colleagues are desirable.
- Graduation announcements are usually formal and printed but certainly may be handwritten. This announcement has evolved because space at graduation ceremonies is now restricted to only a few invitations per graduate. Send only to close family members and friends. This announcement may be sent with an invitation to a graduation party. "No gifts, please" may be written in the lower left-hand corner.
- Engagement announcements can be handwritten or printed and should be sent to relatives and friends. Because of the rich tradition of this announcement in our culture, a special section has been devoted to it (see page 26; also see Wedding & Engagement Correspondence, page 82).
- Wedding announcements are often printed in a prescribed format. They may also be personal letters or notes (see Wedding & Engagement Correspondence, page 82).
- Birth or adoption announcements are usually made by both parents to friends and relatives. The announcements may be selected either before the birth, and then the final information phoned in after the birth, or commercial cards with blanks may be purchased and then filled in and sent out. Include the infant's sex; birth date (and time, if you wish) or age (if adopted); parents' full names; siblings' names (if you like); and an expression of happiness. Parents may also send an announcement to newspapers and other publications that print this information.

Example:

Roger and Brenda Dell of 344 South Parker Road, Littleton, are delighted to announce the birth of a son, Jared, on August 12, 2007, at Littleton Hospital. They have one daughter, Meredith, four. Mrs. Dell is the former Miss Brenda Sales.

When the couple has been divorced before the birth, the announcement is made by the mother, in the name she now uses. Widowed women may use "Sally and the late Paul Davidson." A single mother should use her chosen title and name. In all cases, personal announcements are in the best taste. Personal birth and adoption announcements should also be sent to close colleagues and work associates.

- Retirement announcements are especially important when the retiree is a doctor, dentist, or other professional. These announcements are usually combined with the announcement of the person taking over the practice or any other changing business information. Printed announcements with a good-news emphasis are important here.

- A death in the family is difficult at best. The immediate family must notify other relatives and friends by telephone and ask that they notify others. If funeral arrangements have been made, this information can be given, eliminating the need for another round of calls. The next step is notifying the attorney of the deceased. Written announcements generally take a number of forms:

    - An announcement may be arranged by the funeral home, or a paid newspaper notice may be placed.
    - An obituary may be written by newspaper staff. Usually the information is verified by a close family member. Information generally included is the complete name of the deceased (including the original family name), date of death, date of birth or age at the time of death, address at the time of death, names of immediate family members and place of residence, hours and location where friends may call on the family, place and time of the funeral, whether the funeral is private, and frequently a request that any contributions be given to a charity (often designated) instead of flowers being sent to the funeral home.
    - A news article describing the achievements and contributions of the deceased may be written by newspaper staff and/or a family representative.
    - Printed announcements may be sent to colleagues and/or out-of-town acquaintances.
    - Handwritten notes may be sent to out-of-town relatives, friends, and acquaintances.

- Legal announcements or announcements with legal implications should be made in conjunction with the proper attorney. Plans to remarry where there are legal agreements in place, adoption of children, and change in payment of debts incurred all come under this category.

- Annulments are very private matters and should be handled with the utmost confidentiality. Generally, only immediate family and close friends are told, and then only on a need-to-know basis. They may be told informally and verbally, or in a personal note.

- Divorce is also the private business of the two people involved and a printed announcement is in very poor taste. Informal notes may be sent as necessary to those who have a need to know. A statement and no explanation is best.

- Good business news is best announced by using a press release. Sending the release to newspapers and other media is a good way to get the word out. Be sure to include a contact person and complete contact information: telephone and fax numbers and an email address (see "Press Release," page 385).

- Business announcements (opening a branch, moving to a new location, introducing a new product, and the like) offer the opportunity to stage an open house. Printed announcements or invitations, a newspaper announcement, and perhaps announcements by other media are the best ways to get the word out.

- Bad business news—if the news is of major public concern—may best be handled by calling a press conference to make a statement. Letting people hear directly from you first gives the organization points for being forthright, open, and honest. This approach also preempts cover-up rumors and/or an unfavorable spin, which can follow when a story originates from the media.

- Board of directors' meeting announcements should follow corporate bylaws, state requirements, and federal laws. Include the date, time, place, reason for the meeting, and who is invited. A waiver of notice or proxy card is enclosed with a postage-paid, addressed return envelope.

- A change of address, status, or mode of doing business should be sent, with only the pertinent information, to the businesses or people who need to know. If this change has legal ramifications, check the particular requirements for making such an announcement or notification.

- A business change should put the information in its best light. State the change; why it's being made; the benefits for employees, customers, clients, and others affected by the change; and any expressions of appreciation to those involved.

SELECT A FORMAT

- Formal personal announcements for an engagement (see page 26; also see Wedding & Engagement Correspondence, page 82), open house, new business, and the like are often printed and mailed directly to the recipients.

- Birth or adoption announcements may be hand-designed, printed, or the blanks of commercially available cards filled in and sent to friends and relatives.

- Inter-office announcements are usually best done in memo format, and may be emailed.

- Changes of address, sales, and new business openings are often emailed, or printed on postcards and mailed.

- Newspaper announcements are best completed after contacting the correct editor and learning exactly how he or she wants the announcement submitted. Most will be by email.

SELECT STRONG WORDS

announce	appointed	call	celebrate
change	delighted	happy	honor
immediate	inform	introduce	notice
open	pleased	promoted	report
start	welcome		

CONSTRUCT EFFECTIVE PHRASES

change in hours	effective immediately	give notice that
located at a new address	open for business	please join us
pleased to announce	to inform you	will open soon

WRITE STRONG SENTENCES

Start with a key verb. Then construct information in concise order of importance:

> We welcome Brian Lee Turner, born August 20, 2011, at 3:36 p.m., weighing seven pounds and six ounces, measuring twenty-two inches, to the family of James and Janice Turner.
>
> Greg and Alice Albright are proud to announce the adoption of a baby boy, Alexander Lee, age seven months, on September 15, 2011.
>
> Our new sales policy will allow you to extend the billing period fifteen additional days for new orders.
>
> We are pleased to announce that Mr. George F. Frommer has accepted the position of Chairman of the Board of Directors at Chances effective June 1, 2011.
>
> We must increase the price of the Model A-455 Diluter from $566 to $625 effective July 1, 2011.
>
> Robert R. O'Malley of Pittsburgh, formerly of Denver, died of leukemia September 12, 2011.
>
> John H. Hadley, formerly of Danbury, a physician and program director at St. Mary's Hospital, died August 30, 2011, in St. Louis.
>
> The "Race for the Cure" breast cancer benefit 5K run will take place at Washington Park's Pavilion on September 29, at 8:00 a.m.

BUILD EFFECTIVE PARAGRAPHS

Focus on an action verb and the essential facts to build strong and effective paragraphs. For example:

> We rejoice at the birth of our beautiful new daughter, Kathleen Kate McNeilly, born at 2:34 a.m., Thursday, May 10, 2006, measuring twenty-one inches and weighing eight pounds, four ounces. Her parents, Ben and Mary McNeilly, and sister, Jennifer, two, welcome her into their hearts and home.
>
> Baby Boom will open its doors in the Tamarac Square Center (next to Lloyd's Jewelry, main floor) Friday, July 15. Bring in this card for your free T-shirt. Store hours will be 10:00 a.m. till 9:00 p.m., Monday through Saturday. Open noon till 6:00 p.m. on Sunday. Sign up to win our $500 shopping spree!
>
> Cooper's sales grew 33 percent this quarter over last quarter. The growth, said CEO Bradley Sandler, was due to the introduction of the new Model Z-560, which sold over 3,000 units.

Quick Lube offers you a full oil change—including filters—for just $24.95 at our new full-service garage on Evans and Orchard. We'll do it in just 20 minutes, while you wait. Bring in this card to receive your free sun visor.

Davis and Company Manufacturing announces the recall of their Model A-7655 Air Conditioner due to defective gaskets found in some units. Leaks from these units may cause nausea due to gases that are not properly sealed in the compressor. Please return all Model A-7655 Air Conditioner units to the place of purchase for a replacement.

Barker, Taylor, and McKenzie are pleased to announce that Harold P. Garon has joined the law firm as a partner. Mr. Garon, who has spent the past five years at Yale and Gates, will head the firm's corporate practice.

Jake Walker Pierce, formerly of Denver, a physician and program director at St. Mary's Hospital, died August 23 in St. Louis. He was 35.

The opening of the Burn Unit at St. Joseph's Hospital will take place Thursday, April 10, at 2:00 p.m. The dedication ceremony will include a speech by the governor and music by the Utah Children's Choir.

Sandra F. Frank, formerly of Schenley Advertising, has joined Marks, Inc. as creative vice president. She will handle all the conceptional aspects of the new Brewer campaign.

Dr. Richard Lewin announces his retirement, effective April 30. His practice will be taken over by his associate, Dr. Stanley Dever.

EDIT, EDIT, EDIT

Pay attention to precise details to insure that your reader gets the message you want to send.

Adoption	Birth
Roger, Delores, Jonathan, *and Allyson Carver* *are proud and happy to announce* *the adoption of a daughter and a sister,* *Jessica Rae,* *born December 10, 2005,* *who arrived from China on* *January 12, 2011.*	*Larry and Lucy Melville* *welcome a beautiful baby girl,*[1] *Melanie Louise,* *who arrived August 12, at 2:30 p.m.* *weighing 7 pounds, 8 ounces; and* *measuring 20 inches.*[2]
	(1) State the good news. (2) Make sure the information is complete.

Divorce

Dear Eleanor,

Regrettably, Dan and I are divorcing.

My temporary address for the next six months will be my parents' home, 144 East Walnut, Detroit 49332. I will stay on at Becker and Becker, and Dan plans to take a position in Los Angeles. I'm sure he will let you know where he settles.

I cherish your friendship, and will be in touch again as soon as I get things settled.

With love,

Jennifer

Formal Professional Announcement

French and French is pleased to announce that

Susan A. Banes

has joined the firm as a partner.
She will be in charge of
Southern Spain Operations.

Obituary

CALVIN LEIGH HOLMES, of Denver, a banking director, died September 12 at his home. He was 68. Private funeral services will be held September 15 at Faith Church in Hampden Memorial Gardens.

He was born January 27, 1943, in Ft. Collins. On September 20, 1974, he married Mary Appleton in Colby, Kansas. She preceded him in death.

Holmes was a banking and agricultural director at Commerce State Bank in Littleton, Colorado, and he was a member of the Farm House Fraternity. He was a lieutenant in the Navy during the Vietnam War.

He is survived by two sons, Steven Holmes, of Denver, and Fred Holmes, of Chile, and a daughter, Margaret Anne Holmes, of Phoenix.

Divorce

Dear Alice,

For reasons I don't wish to discuss, Patrick and I are divorcing after five years. Since we both value your friendship, it makes this separation even more difficult. (Who gets the friends in these situations is always a dilemma, but I hope in our case it will be both of us.)

I will be living with Susan Blake for the next six months, 167 Downing Street, Denver 80233. When we get moved in and settled, I'll give you a ring.

I'm sure Patrick would welcome a call from you. He will be staying in the house.

Talk to you soon.

Yours truly,

Jennie

New Employee

Memo

DATE: (Date)
TO: All Employees
FROM: Cleo Barker
SUBJECT: Mr. William A. Carey Joins
            Glucks as System Sales Vice
            President[1]

We are pleased to announce, effective June 1, that Mr. William A. Carey will join Glucks as vice president in charge of system sales. Bill will handle all Model Lines A, B, and C sales activity, which will be consolidated to our offices from our Seattle and New York offices.[2]

Bill was in charge of automated sales at Z-Rocks for the past seven years and was instrumental in that company's outstanding sales growth of 55 percent during that period.

Please drop by the Sales Department, introduce yourself, and welcome Bill to Glucks.

---

(1) Be precise and complete. (2) State information in order of importance.

New Policy

Memo

DATE: (Date)
TO: Department Managers
FROM: Stewart Collins, VP
SUBJECT: New Lunch Policy

To alleviate the congestion and long lines in the cafeteria between noon and 1:30 p.m., we will serve lunch in three shifts by department:

Preparation Department—11:30 A.M.
Office Personnel and Production
   Department—Noon
Sales and Shipping—12:30 P.M.

Please try to assign employees who need another time equally over the schedule.

I appreciate your cooperation in making this change. Give me a call if you have any comments or questions.

Be sure to address the what, why, when, where, and how.

Professional Office Relocation

(Date)

Dear Patients:

I will move my offices to 1400 Clearwater, Suite 540, on July 8. This is what you have been asking for: a new, larger, and more convenient building.

There is free parking under the building and an elevator directly into our lovely, new reception area. The new office telephone number is 727-555-0123.

I look forward to seeing you on your next visit.

Yours truly,

Dr. Charles Rose

Price Increase

Dear Customer:

Beginning May 1, it will be necessary for Lawer and Frisk to raise our consulting rate from $225 to $250 an hour. We regret that this change is necessary, however, this is our first increase in over 10 years. (Please see the recent survey reported in Denver Business, which indicates that, at the new rates, Lawer and Frisk will still be about 15 percent below the rate structure of similar firms in the area.)

We value the opportunity to serve you, and welcome your concerns and comments. Please contact Julie Reese at 303-555-0123 with any questions about your account.

New Business

Sole Music
is opening in your neighborhood at
433 West Prince Street
(across from Joe's Deli).

If your feet don't feel like dancing,
bring those shoes on in and we guarantee
we'll tune them up!

Bring this card for 25 percent off
your first repair.
10 to 9 Mon. through Fri. • Noon to 9 Sat.
303-555-0123

New Product

John Henry Ford
1335 North Arapahoe Road
is pleased to announce that

THE NEW MODELS HAVE ARRIVED.

Come take a test drive.
Bring this card to receive a free parking lot car locator and register for our Mustang Give-Away.
September 15 to 17, 10:00 a.m. to 9:30 P.M.

ENGAGEMENT ANNOUNCEMENT

Over the past several decades, many factors have influenced the traditional practices of announcing an engagement to be married: the changed role of women in our society; the high rate of divorce and remarriage; same-sex relationships; and the dramatic changes in the ages, career status, mobility, and financial resources of those who are becoming engaged. Although we still cling to some of the traditional, time-honored elements of announcing a couple's engagement, many of the old items of protocol are falling away in favor of announcements that more accurately reflect our changed roles. However, the most important element in the engagement announcement should remain the sharing of the joyous news.

To make the announcement public, it may be printed in newspapers and other publications. Contact the social editor and ask for the desired format. A black-and-white glossy photograph of the engaged couple or just the future bride may appear with the announcement.

Here are some guidelines that are still generally accepted. If a young woman has not been married, her parents usually make the announcement:

> Jack and Julie Bremmer of Cottonwood Manor, Texas, announce the engagement of their daughter, Katherine Anne Bremmer, to Alex James Smerthington, son of John Z. and Lucy Smerthington of Minneapolis, Minnesota. A June wedding is planned.
>
> Ms. Bremmer graduated from Texas A and M and is a communications consultant for Beams and Motes Advertising Agency. Mr. Smerthington graduated from Texas A and M. He is associated with Mickey Advertising Agency in New York City.

If one of the future bride's parents is deceased, the announcement is made by the other:

> Mrs. Barbara Gates announces the engagement of her daughter, Ms. Sandra E. Gates, to Dr. David R. Cole. . . . Ms. Gates is also the daughter of the late Robert Gates.

If a parent of the future groom is deceased:

> . . . son of Mrs. Abigail R. Wright and the late Mr. George B. Wright.

When the engaged woman is divorced or widowed, her parents may make the announcement, using her current name.

A mature woman, single, divorced, or widowed, may make her own announcement:

> The engagement of Miss [Ms. or Mrs.] Deana Turner to Mr. Jacob Die has been announced . . .

When the future bride's parents are divorced, the announcement is usually made by the mother:

> Mrs. Susan Raines announces . . . Ms. Raines is also the daughter of Mr. Julius B. Raines of Boston, Massachusetts.

When the divorced parents are cordial, they may announce the engagement together:

> Mr. John Kelly of Ft. Lauderdale, Florida, and Mrs. Margaret B. Waters of Indianapolis, Indiana, announce . . .

If a remarried mother makes the announcement, it may read:

> Mr. Richard R. and Glenda F. Gaines announce the engagement of Mrs. Gaines's daughter, Ellen Sue Bates. . . . Ms. Bates is also the daughter of Mr. Robert G. Bates of Riverside, New York.

If the engaged woman is adopted, the family that raised her from infancy has no reason to mention this fact. If she joined the family later and has retained her original surname, the announcement should read:

> Mr. Roy and Mrs. Rose Weinstein announce the engagement of their adopted daughter, Ms. Carla Reid, daughter of the late Mr. Carl and Mrs. Trudy Reid.

If the engaged woman is an orphan, the nearest relative, godparent, or dearest friend may make the announcement as may the woman herself:

> The engagement of Daisey Marlys Gibson (daughter of the late Mr. Darrel and Mrs. Alta Gibson) is announced . . .

The parents of the engaged man may make the announcement when the woman is from another country, has no living relatives, or for some other reason has no contact with her family. The man's parents should not make it in their own names, but in the woman's parents' names:

> The engagement of Miss Sutra Batra of Bombay, India, to Dr. Walker Dennis Tabor, son of Dr. Walter and Gloria Tabor of Kentilworth, Illinois, is announced.

The couple may elect to announce their own engagement, either alone or in concert with their parents:

> Louise Albright and Steven Barr join with their parents, Mark and Helen Albright, and Albert and Joan Barr, in announcing the couple's engagement.

If an engagement is canceled, the same persons who received an announcement should also be notified, simply, of this change.

Engagement

*Douglas and Anne Wittenberger
announce the engagement
of Anne Wittenberger's daughter,*

*Elizabeth Sterling Dunning,
to
Robert Townsend Fielder,*

*of New York City.
Miss Dunning is also the daughter of
Larry Dunning of Phoenix.*

Broken Engagement

*Dear Celia,
   David and I have broken our engagement. I am, therefore, returning the lovely teapot you sent.*

*Best,
Josey*

4 CONGRATULATIONS

Nothing makes our accomplishments sweeter than the compliments and praise of others. We've gotten away from the practice of sending personal, handwritten notes and letters of congratulations over the last couple of decades, so if you send one, yours may make a lasting impression. If you email one, that will add to the joy of the person who receives it, too. Send congratulations often, making your words sincere and totally positive. Focus solely on toasting the recipient's achievement or happy event—adding to his or her joy.

DECIDE TO WRITE

Send congratulations for events like these:

- Personal achievements such as graduation, award, promotion, successful speech, publication, winning a competition, receiving a prize, finishing a marathon, completing a course of study, receiving a rating for a hobby or avocation
- Family events like marriage, birth or adoption of a child, anniversary
- Life events like a birthday, retirement, first or new home
- Religious events such as joining a church, baptism, confirmation, first communion, bar or bat mitzvah, ordination, taking vows, becoming elder or deacon
- Business achievements like an award for top or outstanding sales, promotion, new job, new assignment, new title, starting a new business, getting a new contract, having a book published, joining an association, other business success
- Election to office in a club or association, professional society, political post, social club

THINK ABOUT CONTENT

- Write immediately. But if you've heard the news long after the fact, or if you have procrastinated, write anyway, and note briefly why your greeting is late: "Congratulations. I may not be swift, but I'm certainly delighted that you are now a vice president."
- State the occasion for congratulations in the first sentence or two.
- Use the word *congratulations* early.
- Write conversationally as you'd talk to the person. (A note to a friend will be less formal than one to a business associate.)
- Connect the person to the achievement, occasion, or event.

- If appropriate, relate how you learned the news, include a newspaper clipping, or refer to a shared memory.
- Relate something that bears on the occasion or event, but remember to keep your message focused on the recipient.
- Make sure your message has the ring of sincerity.
- Express your best wishes for the person and your expectation for continued success.
- Make sure your congratulations letter has a single focus.
- Make it short. Three to six sentences is usually just right.

ELIMINATE WRONG MESSAGES

- Don't assume a tone improper to the relationship you have with the recipient.
- Avoid being overly flattering. Effusive, unmerited praise is never appropriate. It rings as false.
- Keep your message focused. A congratulations letter should include only congratulations. Use another letter to address other matters.
- Avoid negative phrases like "Who would have believed it?" (This is especially important for occasions like birthdays and anniversaries).
- Watch your language and phrasing. Avoid words and phrases—like, "How lucky can you get?"—that imply happenchance, or anything other than personal merit.
- Don't be insensitive. Know how the recipient regards the event or occasion. For example, if the recipient prefers not to discuss the fact that this is his twentieth year with the company and this promotion should have come ten years ago, it is insensitive to refer to the fact that he or she had been passed over. If the recipient has very negative feelings about the event or occasion, don't send the letter at all.
- If you can't be sincere in your congratulations, don't write. If a friend is, in your opinion, marrying the wrong person, don't write a hypocritical letter of congratulations. If a business associate gets a promotion you feel belonged to another, don't write.
- Don't overuse the congratulations message for such public relations purposes as "Congratulations on opening your new checking account at Fisherman's Bank." A welcome letter is more appropriate.

TAILOR YOUR MESSAGE FOR EXCEPTIONAL SITUATIONS

- Six months after an employee has retired, another congratulations letter that cites some contribution the retiree made to the company, states how the person is missed, and includes continued well wishes will mean a great deal to the recipient. This letter can be signed by all the employees with whom the recipient worked.
- Congratulations on successfully handling a very difficult situation, such as the illness of a family member, divorce, unemployment, or being passed over for promotion, must be handled with great care. Again, such congratulations should reflect a deep personal relationship with the recipient, and if done properly, can be very meaningful.

- Congratulations are often misused as a ploy in sales letters. Be sure your letter doesn't err in intent by mixing these messages.
- Use a public forum to give your greetings when it's appropriate. Many newspapers, for example, have a section for family and friends to print congratulations on an anniversary.
- When using a commercial greeting card to extend congratulations, be sure to make the card personal by writing your own message in addition to the printed one.
- Congratulations on a new family member should be sent immediately. Such greetings have now extended to include even a new pet.
- Tradition no longer dictates that messages to a future bride and groom be different. In this area, at least, we have gained parity. Either the words *best wishes* or *congratulations* apply equally to either person.

SELECT A FORMAT

- Personal congratulations may be handwritten on personal stationery or a card.
- For a birthday or a specific occasion, use commercial cards with a handwritten message.
- For professional associates, a formal typewritten letter is often better than a handwritten note. Base your choice on the relationship you have with the recipient and the importance of the occasion or good news.
- In an informal or casual work setting, you may send an email to congratulate a colleague.

SELECT STRONG WORDS

accomplishment	achievement	admire	applaud
appreciate	asset	celebrate	cheer
commend	compliment	congratulate	contribution
create	debut	dedicate	distinguished
effort	enterprising	esteemed	excellent
exceptional	exciting	extraordinary	feat
fine	future	generous	gift
gratified	happy	honor	imaginative
impressive	incomparable	innovative	inspiring
invaluable	inventive	kudos	leadership
legendary	meaningful	memorable	milestone
momentous	occasion	outstanding	perfect
performance	pleasure	progress	proud
recognize	resourceful	respected	sensational
skills	special	success	superb
superior	talented	thrilled	tidings
tradition	tremendous	tribute	triumph
unforgettable	unique	unparalleled	unsurpassed
unrivaled	victory	vision	visible
vital	well-earned	well-wishers	winning

BUILD EFFECTIVE PHRASES

always admired your	congratulate you on
continued success in	delighted to hear of your award
fine accomplishment	held in the highest esteem
how marvelous to hear	join with you in celebration
offer warmest congratulations	received a well-deserved honor
recognize your accomplishment	what an outstanding job
what a wonderful achievement	wish you every happiness
your contribution to	your vision has never faltered

WRITE STRONG SENTENCES

Start with an action verb that expresses your feelings. Put the verb into a phrase, then a sentence:

Congratulations, you did that job perfectly.
I've just heard your good news and am delighted for you.
Congratulations on your well-deserved promotion.
You certainly earned the high praise the reporter gave you.
No one worked harder on the Keene project than you did.
Take a bow for a job done well.

BUILD EFFECTIVE PARAGRAPHS

Remember, the best notes or letters of congratulations are short. This approach adds impact. These paragraphs may constitute most or all of your communication.

Congratulations on a terrific job! I was delighted, but not surprised, to read your piece in the Wall Street Journal. I've seldom seen a piece so well thought out, and so extensively and soundly researched.

Congratulations on receiving the Expert Skier Award. It is well deserved. You sliced through that powder on Saturday like a real pro.

Our warmest congratulations on the birth of William III. He has selected two of the most wonderful people we know for parents.

Congratulations on an exceptional job in whipping the St. John's Annual Bazaar together. It bore your expert fingerprints, and profits were the best ever.

Before you took over Boy Scout Troop IV, the dropout rate was one in two. Over the past year, we have seen our own son, George, go from dread to anticipation in preparing for the next troop meeting. Congratulations. You have truly performed a great service to these boys.

Meeting an imposed deadline is difficult, but reaching a self-set goal that no one else believes possible is a feat of determination and extraordinary self-discipline. Congratulations on achieving the AAS designation. I'd like to hear all the details during our Thursday luncheon.

EDIT, EDIT, EDIT

Keep your congratulations simple, sincere, and in tune with your relationship to the recipient.

Congratulations on New Business

Dear Jim:

I'm giving you a standing ovation! Congratulations! What a phenomenal accomplishment, winning the Joker account. (I should know; I've bid on it three times and lost all three.) I can hardly wait to see your new ideas rolled out over the coming months.

I've always known you have great creativity, and now it will be showcased on the big stage. What a tremendous and well-deserved achievement!

Best wishes for continued success.

Regards,

Adam

Special Project Congratulations

Sarah:

Two words: you rock! You created the perfect balance of visual and text in your Power Point presentation. It was outstanding.

Cheers,

Sam

Congratulations on a Career Achievement

Dear Jennifer,

Congratulations, Dr. J. E. Jensen. That has a wonderful ring to it. We join you in your happiness; we are so proud of your outstanding achievement. You have demonstrated what determination and hard work can produce, and we know the fruits of your labor will be plentiful.

All the best,
Booker and Alice

Congratulations on a Promotion

Dear David:

I was delighted to hear you will be the First Vice President in charge of creativity. Congratulations. A more deserving or talented partner could not have been selected for the post.

I'm looking forward to seeing many more of the unique ideas that brought you this Gold Pick Award at our agency.

Sincerely,

Winnie Backus

Office Congratulations

Bob:

You've really gotten the Stafford project group off dead center and moving in the right direction. Your approach at the meeting this morning was masterful. Your infectious enthusiasm and charm has even gotten the disgruntled members of the group in a very positive frame of mind. Congratulations!

All the best,

Marc

5 CELEBRATION OF LIFE EVENTS

To share in celebrating a life event of another person increases the joy for both the celebrant and you. Whether it's a christening, confirmation, communion, bar or bat mitzvah, coming out, graduation, anniversary, or retirement—a rite of maturation or a religious rite of passage—this is a unique opportunity to add your voice of support and best wishes. Don't miss it! Notes to those reaching a new phase of life are best infused with personal anecdotes and even quotes from the masters of living life well. Focus carefully on the person to whom you're writing, and do some research to make sure you've hit the exact, right tone. To make it very meaningful and personal, comb through some relevant anecdotes that will enliven your writing and make your message very special.

ETIQUETTE

The best celebrations are those that focus on the person being honored, and the occasion. Make your message positive, and centered on the star.

DECIDE TO WRITE

Send a personal note with good wishes for the future for:
- A baptism, christening, or dedication of an infant or child
- Ceremonies of faith, such as first communion or confirmation
- Bar mitzvahs and bat mitzvahs
- Celebrations and occasions of maturation and entering a new stage of life, like coming-out parties, sweet sixteen parties, quinceañeras, debutante events, and similar occasions
- Family events like reunions and wedding anniversaries (also see Congratulations, page 28)

THINK ABOUT CONTENT

- Focus on the person.
- Reflect on his or her positive growth and development.
- Write a brief, personal, warm, and positive anecdote or story about the person, if possible.
- Conclude with best wishes for the future.
- Include a picture that will add to the celebration (but not be embarrassing), if possible.

ELIMINATE WRONG MESSAGES

- Learn something about the occasion, event, or rite before writing your message, if you're unsure. This will help you avoid writing something inappropriate or offensive.
- Don't let your message go beyond your personal knowledge and true feelings, or it will ring false or insincere.
- Avoid anything that could embarrass the celebrant. Check first, if in doubt.
- Don't mix messages. Keep the message focused on the celebrant and the occasion or event and its importance to him or her. Reserve questions and other subjects for another time.
- Be careful not to refer to others' accomplishments or make comparisons: "When I turned sixteen . . ." Keep the focus on the celebrant.

CONSIDER SPECIAL SITUATIONS

- Do something special for the celebrant. A treasured photo or a handmade bookmark could easily be included in your note.
- Offer to do something that will make the occasion even more special: Include a "love coupon" that features some benefit of the new status being celebrated. Check with a parent or other responsible adult about an appropriate gift: a roadtrip for a now driving-age person or a tea for a young woman coming out.

SELECT A FORMAT

- A handwritten note on your own personal note card is the first choice.
- A greeting card—handmade, computer-generated and printed, or commercial—with your written message included is appropriate.
- If you're sending a gift, write your personal message on a gift card and attach it to the gift.
- You may also want to send an email greeting (even an animated one), but don't let it replace the mailed greeting with a special handwritten message for someone you share a close relationship with.

SELECT STRONG WORDS

accomplished	achieved	celebrate	delighted
feat	grand	happy	honor
impressive	innovative	join	joyful
memories	notice	occasion	praise
record	rejoice	remember	special
success	thrilled	tradition	triumph

BUILD EFFECTIVE PHRASES

accomplished so much
delighted to hear
ready for great things
we are all so proud
what a wonderful thing

achievements like yours
join with the well-wishers
shall always remember
we rejoice with you
with solemn respect

WRITE STRONG SENTENCES

Your whole family is so proud of you as you embark on a whole new phase of your life.

You've turned every life change into an opportunity, and we can hardly wait to see what you do with retirement!

You have demonstrated that you are fully equipped to step up to this next great life adventure and turn it into something spectacular!

BUILD EFFECTIVE PARAGRAPHS

Congratulations on making your first communion. It's a day you will always remember and cherish, as your entire family does, as you take this holy step.

We rejoice with you as you take this giant step into adulthood. You'll be terrific at all you do; you've already demonstrated that you have all the skills.

I'm sure all those things I appreciated about David, the boy, will be some of the same characteristics that will make David, the man, a very, very special person. Best wishes as you set out on this new adventure called adulthood.

EDIT, EDIT, EDIT

Read your message aloud when you've finished to be sure it sounds just right.

A Young Man's Bar Mitzvah

Jacob,

Mazel tov! I remember your grandfather's and your father's bar mitzvahs, and now I am fortunate enough to witness yours. Such a wonderful time and such a wonderful family you have. I know you will become one of the next generation of leaders in our community. You have already demonstrated that you are equal to the challenge, with all the excellent study you've completed to reach this day.

I look forward to sharing some special stories with everyone at your party.

Congratulations, and welcome to this bold, new world.

Uncle Max

Reaching Sweet Sixteen

Dear Maria,

Your world overflows with new possibilities,[1] and we know you have the wisdom and maturity to spin them into gold. We've seen you do it many, many times: that first-grade stage performance; on the soccer field; in the swimming pool; in your vocal trio. [2]

We will watch in amazement to see what you'll do next; and stand ready to help in any way we can. Best wishes for a wonderful seventeenth year.

Aunt Rosa and Uncle Simon

(1) Add to the joy. (2) Make it personal and special.

A Relative Retires

Dear Uncle Hermie,

What a perfect day you must have had on Friday. All your dreams about the years to come are now within your grasp, as you set out on this wonderful new and exciting chapter of your life.

I know all the inventiveness and genius you brought to bear in your workplace at Dinger will now be focused on building that sailboat, New Horizons. I look forward to working with you on Saturdays. I've got the champagne ready for the christening! Congratulations and best wishes for smooth sailing in retirement!

Love,
Randy

On the Birth of Children

Dear Carolyn,

What wonderful news that the twins were born and are doing well. I've heard they were pronounced "perfect" by the pediatrician, and we rejoice with you.

I'm sure you would much rather have brought them straight home from the hospital, but perhaps this will give you a little time to rest up. I'll call you next week to see what you need. In the meantime, please call me if there's any way I may help.

Lovingly,
Marjorie

A Wedding Anniversary

Dear Elizabeth and Frank,

Congratulations! Of course we'll attend your fiftieth wedding anniversary celebration. Jack and I will be proud to relate the story of the weekend on Lake Witless. It remains a favorite in this family.

You two have achieved a unique level of oneness in your marriage that we've long admired. Our best wishes for many, many more years of even more happiness yet to come.

Affectionately,
Katie and Jack

On Marriage

Dear Diane and Kirk,

We were overjoyed to learn you will be married in June. Congratulations. May the love you two now share deepen each day of your lives. Our very best wishes for a wonderful, fulfilling life together.

Love,
Uncle Jasper and Aunt June Bug

6 HOLIDAY GREETINGS

Add to the celebration! That's what makes the seasons of our lives sweeter: cherishing them and celebrating them with others. Don't miss an opportunity to extend special greetings to those in your life. Send a personal communication that will add to their holiday joy and celebration. Businesses, too, can make very good use of holidays to build relationships with their customers, employees, and colleagues. Care should be taken, of course, to keep your communications in tune with the spirit of the season or day. (An overly commercial theme or message for a sacred or religious day will offend many.)

ETIQUETTE

Know the history and traditions of the holiday, and keep your message in step with that.

DECIDE TO WRITE

Before the year begins, record all the holidays you will celebrate and make a list of birthdays, anniversaries, and other special days. Businesses need an annual plan and budget for holiday promotions, and four to six months of lead time to get special items prepared and ready. You may want to note some of the following holidays and seasons observed in the United States (U.S.), Canada (C), Mexico (M), and the United Kingdom (U.K.). Individual country celebrations may not be on the same date.

- New Year's
- Chinese New Year
- Lincoln's Birthday (U.S.)
- Presidents' Day (U.S.)
- Flag Day (M, U.S.)
- Ash Wednesday
- St. Patrick's Day (C, U.S.)
- Benita Juarez's Birthday (M)
- Palm Sunday
- Good Friday
- Easter Monday (C, U.K.)
- Battle of Puebla (M)
- Father's Day

- Martin Luther King Jr. Day (U.S.)
- Anniversary of the Constitution (M)
- Valentine's Day (C, U.K., U.S.)
- Washington's Birthday (U.S.)
- First of Muharram
- Ashura
- First day of spring
- Mothering Sunday (U.K.)
- Passover
- Easter
- Holocaust Remembrance Day
- May Day Bank Holiday (U.K.)
- First day of summer

- St. Jean Baptiste (Quebec)
- Civic Day (C)
- Labor Day (C, U.S., M)
- Independence Day (M, U.S.)
- Rosh Hashanah
- Purim (Feast of Lots)
- Columbus Day (U.S.)
- United Nations Day
- Halloween
- Day of the Dead (M)
- Veterans' Day (U.S.)
- Revolution Day (M)
- Virgin of Guadalupe (M)
- First day of winter
- Boxing Day (C, U.K.)
- Canada Day
- Summer Bank Holiday (U.K.)
- Declaration of Independence (M)
- First day of autumn
- Yom Kippur
- Day of the Race (M)
- Thanksgiving (C, U.S.)
- First of Ramadan
- All Saints Day (M)
- Election Day (U.S.)
- Remembrance Day (C)
- Pearl Harbor Remembrance Day (U.S.)
- Hanukkah
- Christmas
- Kwanzaa

THINK ABOUT CONTENT

- Start by mentioning the holiday you are celebrating.
- Connect the holiday to the recipient(s).
- Give information or the news element of your message.
- End with a statement of best wishes for the recipient(s).

ELIMINATE WRONG MESSAGES

- Don't send a commercial greeting card with only your signature. Be sure to include a personal, handwritten message.
- Don't mix messages or use a holiday as a reason to deliver another kind of message. Use a separate, appropriate communication for the second message.
- In personal messages, like holiday family newsletters, avoid bragging or self-congratulation.
- Be sensitive to your audience. Don't send a letter filled with news about your wonderful new job and great success to a relative who has suffered long unemployment, for example. And don't send religious messages to a general audience or to those of another faith.

CONSIDER SPECIAL SITUATIONS

Holiday Family Newsletter

A wonderful way to keep up with people you aren't able to visit regularly is an annual holiday newsletter. They have become a tradition for many. Here are a few ways to make yours a welcome part of the holidays:

- Organize your newsletter well: chronologically, by topic, or by person.

- Edit it by sub-audiences, if possible.
- Keep it short.
- Include ideas and important information, as well as a very brief list of family achievements and activities.
- Use a single statement and a detail or two to make your newsletter interesting, humorous, and celebratory: "Mindy's Waterford vase was previewed by 43 airport security people before we got it home from Ireland. Here's what we learned . . ."
- Make it artsy and more interesting by including a few photos and copying it on colorful, holiday-themed paper.
- If you print or photocopy your newsletter, still add a handwritten personal message to each recipient.

Year-End Business Newsletter

At the end of the year, share important information about your business with employees, customers, and colleagues. Make your message one of appreciating each of those to whom you are writing. Keep these possibilities in mind as you write:

- Consider what you want to say to each audience. You may decide to send one newsletter to all, or you may find that it's more appropriate to create a different newsletter for each audience.
- Include information about employee achievements, charitable events in which you've been involved, and fundraisers that you've sponsored.
- Announce new products and spell out any noteworthy financial success or new directions your business is taking.

Holiday Sales Notice to Customers

Writing your customers during the holiday season can help them remember you. Express your appreciation for their business. Consider these possibilities:

- Use the holiday sales notice as a very important business tool to help create a loyal customer base.
- Consider a notice advertising a "Before Christmas Preferred Customer Sale." If done annually, the sale may become part of customers' regular pre-holiday shopping routine.

Fundraiser Notices

The holidays offer an unlimited number of ways to draw attention to your organization. Here are a few:

- Create a wonderful newsletter that features people who've been helped by your organization throughout the year, or who receive special assistance during the holidays.
- Announce a special upcoming event.
- Share information on an annual drive with target amounts of donations to be raised.

SELECT A FORMAT

- Holiday greeting cards should always include a personal message and a handwritten signature. If you feel at a loss for words, use an appropriate quote to get you started (and properly attribute it) and then connect your personal message to that quote.
- Make your greeting creative. Use a postcard, flat card, picture card with a greeting, fold-over card, or letter format.
- Always keep your greetings in good taste and in the spirit of the holiday.
- Consider sending animated email greetings, which now have many formatting options. But use this venue wisely. It may, for example, be against corporate policy to create and send official office holiday greetings through email.
- Observe email etiquette. When you communicate with people only through email, it is perfectly proper to send an informal, electronic email holiday greeting. But remember, email is still the equivalent of a very informal memo. For all the people you know off-line, send a greeting by regular mail.

WRITE STRONG SENTENCES

It's a wonderful day for celebrating how very special you are to us.

We can't think about this holiday without realizing the bond we share. Wishing you a wonderful holiday.

Our wish for you is that the spirit and joy of this holiday may be yours for the whole year.

This has been a wonderful year for Harvest House Furniture because of you, our wonderful customers. All of us here join our voices to wish you the very best for the coming year.

As we come again to the end of the year, we realize it is your efforts that have helped us achieve so much. Each and every employee is responsible for our success.

Our best wishes for 365 days of joy and happiness.

Our warmest wishes to you and your dear ones on this very, very special day.

Even though we must be absent on this day, our hearts join with yours as we raise a toast and a wish for blessings in abundance, wisdom, and joy in the coming year.

At this time of year, we count our many blessings, and you—dear, dear friends—are among the most precious.

Near or far away, you are in our hearts and minds as we celebrate this wonderful season.

This day, like every day, we wish you all the best.

Hope you have a joyous holiday season.

It's a great time to count our many blessings of the past year, and number one on that list is good customers like you.

May the joy and richness of this season be yours!

Joy and bountiful blessings to you during this holiday season.

In remembering the historical accounts of this day, may the liberating truth be yours to hold and cherish.

One of the delights of this season is reconnecting with those we don't see often, but who still remain in our hearts; we think of you often and wish you the best in the coming year.

How we wish we could open the door to our home and see your faces, as the door to our hearts always remains open to you.

Again, we want to celebrate the bounty of this year by offering you, special customer, the opportunity to join us for our Pre-Holiday Special Customer Sale.

We've prepared a very special surprise for you, valued customer, at our year-end celebration sale.

BUILD EFFECTIVE PARAGRAPHS

It's that very special time of year again! Our annual Special Customer Spring Fling wouldn't be the same without you. So, please set aside this date to join us for a preview of the very latest in smart women's attire and to take advantage of our preseason prices.

There's absolutely no better time to say how very, very dear you are to us than during this special season. Do you know how much we wish we could be there to celebrate with you and hold you tight?

Our hearts are filled with love for all of you, and this special season just makes them over-flow. May you enjoy the most wonderful of holidays.

Inspired by those first celebratory days of harvest and survival, may that true spirit of thanks-giving be yours on this very special day. We look forward to sharing the bounty with you.

As we celebrate the true meaning of this season, we rejoice at seeing the reality of its pre-cepts in your hearts and lives. And we feel so blessed to be able to share it with you.

From peace in your hearts to peace on earth—what a long journey it seems, yet not too far. Thank you for sharing your peace with us. Our hearts rejoice with yours.

It's a new year, with new goals, new opportunities. May you carry with you into the new year the wisdom and wonder you've demonstrated this year.

It was a perfect delight to receive your newsletter and season's wishes. We're so happy everyone at your house has had such a terrific year. We all send our very best wishes to you.

May your new year sparkle with hope and opportunity. We wish you a year that far exceeds your expectations.

A special person, a special holiday, a special wish. When all of these elements converge, there's bound to be a wonderful celebration! You always make the most of such moments. Add our wishes for a truly wonderful day!

To the traditional wishes for your health and happiness, we'd like to selfishly add our hope of spending some of the holidays with you. (Then, of course, you'll have to add your own hope for the more difficult but cherished attributes: long-suffering and patience!) If you're up for the challenge, we'd love to have you join us while you're in town. Do let us know if you might be available for a luncheon, a day, or a weekend.

EDIT, EDIT, EDIT

Reread what you've written to be sure you've expressed yourself the way you intended. Long or short, you'll want to end your message with the focus on the person(s) you're writing to and your heartfelt good wishes for him or her.

Family Newsletter at Year's End

Yulia says:

The end of December, the beginning of the new year, and it still feels here—as it well may at your home—that our sense of national invincibility is forever lost. I'm sure, like you, it has helped us to hold our families, faith, and country near and dear as never before.[1]

Ah, but this is to be a holiday greeting brimming with good cheer and best wishes!

First, the bittersweet. This fall my father, Ezra, was diagnosed with Alzheimer's disease. Mom, Maria, heroically kept him at home long past the usual dimensions of this disease, until his compulsion to "go home" produced a level of combativeness that required a more secure environment. We miss him. It has been my parents' desire to remain in Mississippi, and the only reasonable choice of facilities for Dad there was the Heritage Home. He still recognizes us, and for this we're thankful, as we are for all the fine examples of how to live an honorable life he provided. He's 75. We're thankful, too, for all the wonderful years he had; and for all the joy and happiness he's brought to those who have known him. He truly enjoyed life and lived it well.

Mom has truly risen to the challenge in every way. She has started driving again after more than a dozen years. She drives 70 miles two or three times a week to visit Dad, taking the dog with her.[2]

Now to the more cheery part. Our three sons are all doing well. We've petitioned to see more of them this year, and remain so thankful to have Peter and Jana still living in Colorado. We keep introducing a contract for their signatures, which commits them to stay here. (No signatures yet.)

Monti says:

Thanks for all your wonderful cards and letters. We really appreciate you keeping us in your hearts.

This year we enjoyed life in our little in-town community of 46 homes. Everything we need or want is conveniently nearby. I especially enjoy living an hour from the best ski areas in the country.

Our visit this year to the beautiful Canadian Rockies (Banff and Lake Louise) was remarkable. The all-day horseback ride, however, created footage fit for *America's Funniest Home Videos*.

Our annual trip took us "down under." Sydney is a beautiful city, with its lush gardens and world-famous opera house. We managed to get tickets to a performance there, and it was a wonderful experience. We cruised the Great Barrier Reef onboard the Coral Princess between Townsville and Cairns, and snorkeling among the myriad varieties of marine life, both coral and tropical fish, was the highlight of our trip.

Our best wishes for a wonderful, healthy, and rewarding new year! Plan to spend a tiny bit of it with us, will you?[3]

With love,

Yulia and Monti

P.S. We'd love to set up a weekend get-together in Vail for February. We have so much catching up to do! What do you think?[4]

---

(1) Connect the holiday to the recipient. (2) Make it personal, newsy, and brief. (3) End with best wishes for the recipient.
(4) Handwrite a personal message at the end.

Thanksgiving Day Family Reunion

Dear McDermott Tribe,

We're sure you're as giddy as we are about this year's lineup for the family pilgrimage and reunion at David and Regina McDermott's home. We have, you must know, 12 new family members (list enclosed) to welcome. We'll be giving them the McDermott baptism in the traditional way. You know your food assignments, of course, and hopefully each of you has your family history contribution ready to recite. We'll be waiting to hear it.

As a reminder, the program this year is being handled by Tom Wright, and if your family has a special musical or other contribution you want to perform, contact him within the next week, so he can finish his program announcement.

For the family history part of the program, Harry McDermott will read the new genealogy he and his family have researched and assembled; Mary Bench will bring the new, updated family "story"; and Lauren Givens has promised to have the family picture album on display. You may order copies of any of these.

See you on Thanksgiving Day, 1:00 p.m. (For all the ongoing discussions, directions, details, and chatter, go to Harry's website, McDermottsUnite.com.)

McDermotts, a clan together again! May the road rise up to meet you, and may you always be well upwind!

Gavin McDermott

Company Year-End Letter

Dear Renolds Family:

We have great reason to rejoice and celebrate as this banner year comes to an end. We surpassed our goal of six million dollars in net profits by $1,565,000! There's only one reason for our great success: the dedication and extraordinary hard work of each and every member of our team. Congratulations!

Each of you, as you know, will share in our financial success. But more important, I believe, is the fact that you have helped to create a supportive atmosphere, a sense of pride in achieving quality workmanship, and a great sense of family. Because of you, Renolds is just a great place to work.

Thank you, each and every one, for making this a banner year.

In appreciation,
William Trasker
President

Pre-Christmas Special Family Charity

Dear Christmas Angel,

You know that last year your sharing the spirit of this season resulted in 2,765 children receiving a Christmas gift. And this year we are aiming to make sure that 3,500 children in our area are greeted with a surprise gift on that special day.

This year on December 5, 4:30 p.m., at Summer's Day Preschool, all of us will bring together the gifts we have collected, and we will all wrap gifts and divide them for distribution by the appointed elves. As usual, this will be a very merry workshop experience and celebration for all of us.

Barry McCullom will lead the music, and La Petite, superb caterer, is supplying box lunches for all of us.

We look forward to seeing you again this year for this very special time of celebration.

Patti Reeves

7 SYMPATHY & CONDOLENCE

It is difficult to express your feelings in writing to someone who is suffering a major problem or loss. Empathy for the person, based on care and respect for him or her, is essential. Focus on the person you are writing to, and let your knowledge of the recipient and his or her relationship to the loss guide you.

The letter of condolence or sympathy, while one of the most difficult messages to write, is undoubtedly one of the most important. It may be written to someone who has suffered the death of a relative, friend, or colleague, or to someone who has experienced some other kind of loss (job, home to fire, an unwanted divorce). Your letter should be brief, kind, and offer concrete help, if that is appropriate.

DECIDE TO WRITE

Compose a personal handwritten message when:

- Death touches the life of a relative, friend, neighbor, business associate, or employee.
- Illness or injury strikes a relative, friend, business associate, or neighbor.
- Loss of finances, property, business, or well-being affects a friend, employee, organization you do business with, colleague, or client.
- It's the anniversary of the death, or other significant date, to the person who will experience, again, the loss.
- Divorce affects a friend or associate.
- Keen disappointment or misfortune—such as not winning an election, loss of a job, or not getting a promotion—occurs in the life of a friend or associate.
- Loss of a pet grieves a friend or family member.
- Relocation of a friend's close relatives or friends creates feelings of sadness and loss.

THINK ABOUT CONTENT

- The first and most essential step is to empathize with the bereaved or distressed recipient. Remember you are writing to him or her.
- Think about the emotions of grief: (1) denial and isolation; (2) anger; (3) bargaining or over-rationalizing; (4) depression; (5) acceptance and healing. Attune your message accordingly.
- Think about what you really feel.

- Write immediately, but if you have just heard of the grief after weeks or months or have put off the task, still write. It's not too late.
- Use your relationship with the recipient to guide your writing.
- Focus on the recipient, and don't misdirect your message toward your feelings. The bereaved or distressed person will understand that you feel sad, so simply say "I was so sorry to hear of your grief."
- Open with a simple and strong message of sympathy, naming the person, loss, or event for which you are extending condolences: "Lansing and I extend our deepest sympathy to you at the loss of your dear Lindsay."
- Be hopeful. Remember that your message must not stray into pity.
- It may be difficult, but be sure to write employees, clients, associates, and colleagues in times of grief or loss.
- Save long messages that reminisce about a loved one for later, when the recipient is better able to reflect upon those memories without such a keen sense of loss.
- Choose your words carefully, using words that relate to the loss, sorrow, or grief of the bereaved. Avoid cold and harsh words like *dead*, *killed*, *deceased*, or *bankrupt*, *broke*, *homeless*, and the like.
- Relate a fond memory you have of the deceased, if appropriate.
- Always consider the religious preference, ethnic mores, family wishes, and organizational customs of the bereaved when writing your message.
- Include a message of sympathy to other family members or associates, if appropriate.
- Make a specific offer of help, indicating when and how you will make the next contact to carry through on your offer.
- Close on a warm note.
- Ask the mortuary what the family has requested if you want to send a memento of your feelings in the case of a death, and/or check the obituary column of the newspaper for this information.
- If you send flowers, write a message to accompany them.
- Inquire verbally of a designated relative or friend, or the mortuary, about any immediate needs the bereaved may have and any service or task for which you may wish to volunteer (for example, serving as pallbearer or planning a special commemorative service).

ELIMINATE WRONG MESSAGES

- Don't use overcharged language. "The worst tragedy" or "The most dire news I've ever received" does nothing to comfort the bereaved. The same rule applies to overly sentimental, effusive statements.
- Do not moralize or include statements or clichés meant to be sympathetic. These may be misinterpreted. Remember, this is a time of extreme grief and vulnerability for the bereaved, and language like "He's in a better place now" is not appropriate.

- Don't let your message fall into a pitying or maudlin tone. There's a fine line here. Read your message through several times to ensure you haven't failed on this point. Sometimes it helps to place your letter aside for at least a few hours, then reread it just to be sure.
- Don't give advice. Your sole purpose is to try to give comfort.
- Avoid empty or vague offers of help. Rather, be specific and offer to take the next step: "I will call Joannie tomorrow to see if there are calls I can return on your behalf, or errands you may need to have run."

CONSIDER SPECIAL SITUATIONS

Take special care in these circumstances:

- Divorce of a friend, associate, colleague, or employee requires keen sensitivity. You should know the recipient very well. Make sure your message is timely, brief, and focused on the recipient.
- The death of a child, a stillbirth, or a miscarriage should all be treated the same. Don't fall prey to attempts at "consoling," which tend to diminish the recipient's grief. If a multiple birth resulted in the loss of a child, offer congratulations on the birth(s) of the surviving child(ren) first. Then, in a separate paragraph, express your sympathy at the loss of the other child(ren), taking care not to connect the two emotions.
- For loss of a home in a natural disaster, loss of employment, or a financial reversal, it's best to give your message the legs of real assistance. Ask what would be helpful, and present your gift or offer of help so it does not take on the character of charity. Empty offers of assistance are insulting in the face of crisis.
- The terminally ill person or the person who has suffered a debilitating injury is in a special category. Take your lead from what the recipient has expressed about his or her illness. Don't mention death unless he or she has discussed it openly. It's appropriate to include fond memories you share and/or aspects of your relationship you treasure. Use "Thinking about you," "My thoughts are with you," or other such messages.
- Suicide or a violent crime that results in death or loss is an especially difficult situation. Unless you know the faith and belief system of the bereaved, your message should simply state "I was so sorry to hear of your loss."
- The death of a pet, especially for an elderly person, can be a great loss. A note to such a person at this time, if sincere, will be greatly appreciated.
- In sending flowers to a funeral home, attach a small card addressed to "David M. Meeks," or to "The funeral of David M. Meeks." The plain, single card (available from the florist) should contain a brief message of sympathy, for example, "Sidney, our thoughts are with you and Ann at this time."
- When contributing to a charity in memory of the deceased, include your name and address, in addition to a brief statement, such as "This contribution is made in memory of Robert C. Walker, 8100 West Chicago, Appleton, WI." This allows the charity to acknowledge that your contribution was received and inform the family of the deceased of your contribution.

- Anniversary dates shared with a person now gone are a good time to send another thoughtful note of sympathy to a relative, friend, or associate who will again grieve. It will be extremely meaningful if your relationship is close. This is often a good time to share a warm memory of the deceased.

SELECT A FORMAT

- Your message of condolence and/or sympathy must be very personal, and that requires that it be handwritten. Use a commercial card only if it exactly expresses your feelings, and then also include a handwritten message. The most popular stationery is a plain, fold-over card, but plain personal stationery (smaller than 8 ½ by 11 inches) may also be used.
- For business acquaintances you did not know well or work closely with—this may include an employee who has lost a spouse, a customer, client, or a colleague—either a handwritten note or a typewritten letter of sympathy is appropriate. Use personal business stationery, preferably smaller than the usual 8½ by 11 inches. A 5 by 7–inch size is a good choice.

SELECT THE RIGHT WORD

affection	bereavement	burden	care
comfort	compassion	concern	consolation
difficult	distress	faith	gift
grief	healing	heartache	heartbroken
heartsick	heavyhearted	hope	lift
loss	mourn	overcome	sad (saddened)
solace	sorrow	suffering	sympathy

CONSTRUCT SENSITIVE PHRASES

a loss for all who knew him

a lovely and true person

a wonderful and rare source of wisdom and wit

deep grief at the loss

extend our sympathies

feelings of loss

he was a very special person

in this time of great sorrow

keep you in our prayers

made so much difference in the world around him

may your wonderful memories add comfort

our deep sympathies are with you

our hearts go out to you

please accept our sincere condolences

saddened to learn

sorry for your loss

there are no words to express

warmest sympathies

we extend our warmest thoughts
well remembered for his deeds of kindness
will always be remembered
will always have fond thoughts of
will be so missed

WRITE STRONG SENTENCES

Words are very inadequate at such a difficult time.

Our sympathy and warmest thoughts are with you.

Our thoughts are with you at this time of loss and sorrow.

Our hopes are set on a full recovery from your accident.

We were so sorry to learn that Martha's courageous battle with AIDS is over; her life was truly an inspiration to all of us.

I'm sorry to hear that you and Jim are divorcing; I know this is an extremely difficult time and my thoughts are with you.

Not everyone understands the joy and companionship a pet can bring, and how it is missed when it's gone; I was so sorry to hear Smoky died.

We shall miss David's smiling presence.

John's smile and laughter will live on in our hearts, even as we mourn with you his absence from our lives.

May God's abiding love give you strength and comfort during this time of deep sorrow.

BUILD EFFECTIVE PARAGRAPHS

I was so saddened to learn Toby is gone from us. Words are never adequate to express the proper sense of loss at a time like this.

May the joy of life that was George's sustain you in this dark time of losing him. We will all remember his exuberance in the smallest and simplest pleasures. And we'll all miss him a great deal.

Please don't despair. When we were robbed, the lingering sense of having been violated was the most difficult part of the ordeal. I'll call tomorrow morning to see if there's anything we have you may want to use until you replace things.

Divorce often feels like the death of hope, and we know you must be feeling a great deal of pain at this moment. Please do know that time really does help the healing process.

Also know that we are here, and our home and hearts are always open to you. I'll call in a few days to see if you might be up to coming over for dinner.

I felt sick for you when I heard that your position has been eliminated by L. L. Greedy and Company. You're one of the best-qualified and most creative people I know, and I'm sure that while it doesn't feel like it today, you'll rise like the phoenix to much greater and better things. I have some ideas about companies that might appreciate a person with your sterling qualifications. I'll call you on Tuesday to see if you're ready to mount a search for a new position.

EDIT, EDIT, EDIT

Use the greatest care to ensure your message is clear and sincere.

To a Friend Who Was Downsized

Elizabeth,

Yes, I do feel sad—so very sad—that management does this. I've read of some of the turmoil at the parent organization level and know from personal experience that such things create a great deal of stress on all levels within organizations. At times it brings out the very worst in some colleagues (the hanging peril of possible axings—if that's a proper word).

I'm equally sure, like you, that Rory must be put in a position of real anguish. Oh dear!

But, at the same time, I have a bud of joy within that this may be your life blessing in disguise, though I'm sure that at this moment it feels like something very different. A person as wonderful and talented as you will only triumph in new and extraordinary ways. My hope, my most sincere hope, is that this is the opportunity of your lifetime. In fact, I feel very, very sure of it. After all, I'm sure you need the concentrated time to finish the bust of Alexander. And write that novel. (I'm looking into writers' colonies myself at the moment to do that very thing. Might this be something you want to do?)

Whatever you decide to do—after, I hope, taking a well-deserved time off—will come up roses! I've heard a number of writers say (for the record) that getting fired from their editorial jobs was the best thing that ever happened to them. (I'm sure that's equally true of downsizings.)

Bless you. I'll be eagerly waiting to hear of your next great adventure.

All the very, very best,
Sasha

Death in a Friend's Family

Dear Rodney and Kris,

We were stricken to learn of Jordan's death. He was a wonderful person, your son, and we know how very close you were to him. Words can't touch the depth of sorrow that is yours, but may the joy the three of you shared help to sustain you during such a bleak time.

We will bring the Buick over tomorrow for you to use for as long as you need it. We would like to help, too, by running any errands you may need completed, or answering your telephone if you care to forward your calls here. Please know you may call on us if there's anything else you need.

We will all miss Jordan deeply.

Your friends,
Alice and Art

Financial Loss

Dear Lea and Alex,

Please accept this gift to help with anything you may need immediately in this difficult time. Not many people have the courage to follow their dreams as you two have demonstrated that you have. We're sorry for this loss, but we know this great disappointment won't defeat you. It's only a temporary setback.

Our hopes and prayers are with you for a very bright future. We know it will be yours. We'll call next week to see how we can help.

Sincerely,
Milli and Wick

Miscarriage

Dear Jill and Jeff,

We were very saddened to hear of your miscarriage. We know how eager you were to have this new member of your wonderful family.[1] There really aren't words at a time like this, but please accept our deepest sympathies. Our thoughts are with you.

With our love,
Ted and Carol

---

(1) Use your relationship with the bereaved to guide your writing.

Loss of an Infant

Bebe and Raoul:

How our hearts ache for you at this time when you've lost this long-awaited baby, Collin. Please know our prayers and thoughts are with you each and every day.

If there is any way we can help, please call us—day or night. And when you feel up to a very short visit, we'd love to stop by or have you come over. Just let us know.

Our love and prayers,
Sargh and Soso

Death of a Business Associate

Dear Martha,

I was shocked to learn of Ruth's death. I'm sure this is both a professional and personal loss for you and many others at Banko Corporation.

My staff and I offer our sincerest condolences to you and your entire department.

Regards,

Dudley

Loss of a Pet

Dear Gerry,

I think Sarge was the smartest dog I've ever known—and the most lovable. We were so sorry to hear about the accident, and we know that you are grief-stricken.

I shall never forget the sight of him climbing that ladder to bring back the monkey to you.

I know he was more than a friend to you, and you, I'm sure, made him one of the happiest dogs that ever lived.

Affectionately,
Sue

To a Friend Who May Be Suffering Physical Abuse

Dear April,

I'm writing this rather than asking you directly because I feel it's less confrontational and will perhaps allow me to register a concern more adequately. You seem to be distant and to be suffering in some un-verbalized way, and I'd like to offer my help.

I won't be shocked, you know, about any type of problem that may exist. My motive for writing you is purely one of a friend who knows, values, and loves you. My door and my heart are always open to you. I'm a very good listener, and anything you share with me will remain confidential, if you like. Please feel you can talk to me about anything that's troubling you.

As always,
Krissie

To a Friend Who Was Sexually Assaulted

Dearest Victoria,

I've just hung up the telephone after our chat, and I wanted to write down a couple of things we discussed. It's true, unfortunately, that bad, bad things happen to the very best people. And I'm so very sorry that this has happened to as wonderful a person as you. At the same time, I'm equally as certain that you will turn something bad into something very, very good.

I can't imagine what you've gone through—not even close. But I do know that given time you will work your way through this. Please do give yourself time, and use all the support that's available.

I'm volunteering for whatever you might need— night or day. You know I'm always available on my cell phone, so please call me. I've also been in contact with some counselors at the Sexual Assault Center (telephone 555-0123), and feel that Denise has a level of humanity and experience you might find helpful. Just tell her you're Sidney's friend.

I value your friendship so much. You are one of the really wonderful people. I'd feel so gratified if you'd allow me to help in any way you may choose.

Love,
Sidney

To a Friend Who Survived an Automobile Accident

Dear Elsa,

It was reassuring to hear your voice on the telephone. We are so sorry you've suffered this severe injury, yet so happy you have survived. And now to the process of healing.

I can't imagine what you've gone through. I can only say, again, I've always admired your strength and derring-do, and am 100 percent confident that you will not only survive, but you will emerge triumphant.

I'd just encourage you to allow yourself time to heal, and also to allow those of us who know and love you to pamper and care for you just a little. You could, for example, spend the summer at the lake with us, where the guest cottage sits waiting to welcome you with as much solitude as you desire, and the main house, with as much camaraderie and conversation as you feel up to. You know I'd be thrilled to handle all the physical therapy things, and the cottage is all set up for that.

I'll check in with you next week after you've had an opportunity to reflect on this. Please call me anytime you feel up to chatting. We're all praying for you daily for God's blessing in getting whole again.

Love,
Tessa

Death of a Neighbor

Dear David,

Ann and I were very saddened to learn of Trudy's death. We respected and admired her, and her contributions to the community, and we will miss her in our neighborhood.[1]

Our heartfelt sympathy to you and the children, James, Rebecca, and Chloe.[2] Please call us immediately if we can be of any help. I'll call next week to see what we may do for you in the weeks ahead.[3]

Sincerely,
Anne and Woody

(1) Choose your words carefully. (2) Empathize with the bereaved.
(3) Offer help, then follow up.

After a Natural Disaster

Dear Doty and Darin:

Who can account for the hurricane making an unexpected right turn? How thankful we are that you weren't injured, yet how we sympathize with you in the loss of your home.

Could we take the children for two weeks so you two can concentrate on all the things you'll need to do to get things back together? We can drive down as early as Wednesday. Or, if there is some other way we can help, you have only to ask.

You remain in our hearts and thoughts.

With love,
Sam and Shorty

8 GET WELL

Offering encouragement when a friend, family member, neighbor, or colleague is ill or convalescing is a wonderful way to build a stronger bond between you and him or her. A get-well greeting carries with it an element of solace and the hope of recovery, and that's what your message should convey. But this is certainly an area where your communication needs to be in keeping with your knowledge of, and relationship to, the recipient.

ETIQUETTE

The get-well note should usually be brief and very positive when the illness or recovery is expected to go well. If you know the person well, a gift that will help entertain—a book or a game—is a good idea, though not necessary.

DECIDE TO WRITE

Send a greeting card or personal note that includes a personal message of comfort, hope, and encouragement when:

- An accident or injury strikes a relative, friend, business associate, or neighbor.
- The relative of a friend, business associate, or colleague is ill or injured.
- A friend, relative, neighbor, or business associate experiences a long convalescence.

THINK ABOUT CONTENT

Write as soon as you hear and confirm the news.

- First and foremost, think about offering encouragement.
- Rely on your relationship with the recipient to direct your message.
- If possible, learn something about how the recipient views his or her situation before writing. Use that, too, to help direct your message.
- Focus on the recipient and don't misdirect your message toward your own feelings.
- Express simply that you were sorry to hear about the accident or illness.
- Make a statement about your concern.
- Try to relieve any possible anxiety about things other than the recipient's recovery.
- Keep the message sunny and upbeat.
- Be short and concise.

- Consider the religious preferences, ethnic mores, family wishes, and organizational customs of the recipient when writing your message; don't include any conflicting ideologies you may embrace.
- Make a specific offer of help, indicating when and how you will take the next step to carry out your offer, but be sure to offer only that which you can, and are willing, to do.
- Combine your message with a small gift of a book or an activity the recipient can enjoy while recuperating.
- For the recovering child, build anticipation of an upcoming event at a time when he or she will be fully recovered, and include some kind of related activity for now.
- If you send flowers or another gift, include a personal note.
- Close on a warm and positive note.

ELIMINATE WRONG MESSAGES

- Don't moralize or include empty clichés or statements meant to be sympathetic. These can be easily misunderstood, as can such "silver lining" comments as "At least you didn't . . ." or "It could have been much worse."
- Omit any hint of pity.
- This isn't the time to offer unsolicited advice. Think only of offering comfort.
- Avoid insincere or empty offers of help. Put legs on any offer by defining a specific task you will take on and the time you'll follow up.
- Avoid dramatic or tragic words and phrases in referring to either the patient or your own feelings. Phrases like your "tragic accident" or the "worst case" aren't comforting.
- Don't indulge in comparative stories such as "Jim's brother had the same operation. . . ." And don't relay any other stories of like treatments or injuries that didn't turn out well.

CONSIDER SPECIAL SITUATIONS

Take special care in these situations:

- The injury or illness will have severe financial repercussions for the recipient. Inquire to learn how best to offer help, but don't let your offer take on the character of charity.
- Don't pry. Be sensitive to the wishes of the recipient and take his or her lead in offering help. If it seems appropriate, you might say something like, "I'd like to help. Would it be useful if I took over the Rogers project for four weeks?" or "I would like to organize a carpool to take you to physical therapy, if you'd allow me."

SELECT A FORMAT

- The most frequently used vehicle is a greeting card. Always write a personal message, too.
- Personal stationery in a 5 by 7–inch size is a good choice for a personal note, or a fold-over card may be used.

- For a business associate you do not know well, use a commercial greeting card, personal stationery, or a fold-over note upon which you write a short personal message. You may also elect to use company stationery in the 8½ by 11–inch size, especially if you are including a message about relieving the recipient of his or her workload or other business.

SELECT THE RIGHT WORD

accident	cheer (cheerful)	convalesce	encourage
heal	health (healthy)	hope	illness
rapid	recovered	recuperate	reinvigorated
relapse	robust	support	unexpected

BUILD SENSITIVE PHRASES

back in healthy form	better than new
completely well again	days of chicken soup and good fiction
encouraging news	fit and robust
good, better, best of health	have every confidence
in our thoughts and prayers	recuperating time will be short
rest and recover	speedy recovery
take time to properly heal	thinking healthy thoughts for you
time to heal	up and about

WRITE STRONG SENTENCES

You are in my thoughts and prayers as you begin your journey toward recovery.

I'm thinking that eight weeks of therapy may put you in fine shape for our annual bird-watching trip to see the sand hill cranes. If it's okay with you, I'm going to put it on my calendar.

I feel certain you'll be dancing the "Electric Cowboy" at the spring cowboy poet's roundup.

We were so sorry to hear about your accident, but were very encouraged to hear that the doctors have put everything back together again.

Recovery seems like the wrong word for all the rehabilitation you have endured.

We shall be ever so happy to hear that you are completely recovered.

There's a fishing trip all planned and ready to go the minute you tell me you are recovered enough to land the big one.

BUILD EFFECTIVE PARAGRAPHS

We were certainly sorry to hear about your accident, but very happy to hear that you are determined to be out of that wheelchair by the holidays. I feel certain you'll be joining us on the slopes next season.

The whole department sends best wishes for a complete and full recovery. I've enclosed a suggested listing of department staff to fill in for you—though no one, of course, can take your place. For the next six weeks, please concentrate on getting up and running at full steam. I'll call and discuss staff substitutes with you next week, if you're up to it.

We know that with your determination you'll make a swift and full recovery. We'd just like to help in some small way. Could we stop by each afternoon at four o'clock and take Toby for an hour?

Your entire fifth grade class is sorry to hear that you will need six weeks to get your leg as good as new. We'd like to organize some visits to help you keep up with your schoolwork. And we'd like to arrange some visits for letting you keep up on the presidents' game. I'll call your mother next week to see how to work it all out.

I'm sure you'll be so happy you've had this procedure once you're completely recovered. Jim says your doctor has said it'll be five weeks of intensive therapy to get up and walking again. I'd like to volunteer for noon to one o'clock outings, Mondays, Wednesdays, and Fridays. I'm suggesting slow trips around the neighborhood if you're up for it. I'll call in a couple of days to see if that will work.

EDIT, EDIT, EDIT

Set your written message aside for a little while, then re-read it to make sure it sparkles with hope and good cheer.

To an Injured Colleague

Dear Sarah,

The entire department was distressed to hear your vacation ended with a bone-breaking fall. But we're encouraged that you had excellent medical help so immediately available.[1]

We've divvied up your assignments here temporarily, according to your assistant's input, and will try to keep all your balls in the air until you get back.[2] As soon as you feel up to it, give a call, and we'll get your direct input through conference calls and email.

Here are our individual wishes for your complete recovery. We're all sure you'll be in fine shape in time for the summer softball league. We certainly don't want anyone else as our pitcher![3]

Best,
Todd

(1) Use your relationship to guide your writing. (2) Offer concrete help. (3) Be sunny and upbeat.

To an Injured Employee

Dear Jamie:

Maggie Orway has just reported that you had an accident yesterday. We all send our best wishes for your recovery. Maggie has promised to keep everyone here updated on your progress, and she will be checking with your family periodically to learn your preference on the best way to do that.

I have notified AA Medical on your behalf, and Mr. Symons will be in touch with your wife in a day or two. Please don't be concerned about insurance coverage or about your workload here. Maggie will distribute assignments to keep your accounts on schedule until you are able to give your own directives.

Our warmest wishes for your good progress. We will certainly miss you here and will stand ready to help in any way possible. We look forward to your return to work.

All the best,

Hal Volkers

To a Sick Child

Robbie,

The Cat in the Hat has asked me to say
I hope you'll be up soon, and ready to play.[1]

It's no fun without you, I'm sure that you know.
There's no baseball party, no pizza to go!

Hurry, hurry, get well, recover real soon.
Baseball starts Thursday, April 20, at noon!

    Your pal,
    Ben

---

(1) Keep your message upbeat.

A Neighbor's Surgery

Daisy,

    I was sorry to hear that your tumor required surgery, but very relieved to learn you will be returning home on Thursday. I'll put your newspaper inside the front door until I see you're out getting it yourself.

    Please let me mow the lawn for you for the next four weeks until we leave for France. And I'll check with Jack to see if you're up to eating one of my chicken delight dinners on Friday.

    Our hope is for your return to that robust, competitive gardening good health.

    Best wishes,
    Jennifer

Medical Tests for a Friend

Gwyndelyn,

    I was so relieved to hear from Hank that the test phase is over, and your doctors are now putting together a treatment plan. I'd like to suggest the Bermuda treatment. We did, after all, plan a two-week dose in those sunny climes before this all started.

    I'm just waiting to hear the good news that two weeks of sun and fun is the surefire cure. I'll keep my bags packed, and look forward to seeing you up and practicing that forehand in a few weeks.

    Love,
    Sissy

Uncertain Future

Ben,

    We were so happy to hear the tests are completed, but sorry you have to wait so long for the results and treatment options. Every day at least one person stops by my office and asks after you. It's amazing the impact you've had here.

    All express their best wishes. We're all pulling for you!

    Best,
    Jim

9 WELCOME

A welcome letter is a great opportunity to start a positive relationship with a new neighbor, a new family member, a new business customer, or a new coworker. Whether business or personal, this letter should be warm and congenial in tone, and it should convey a friendly "glad you're here" message. It may also extend an offer of help—although it's wise to define the limits of your offer.

In business or social correspondence, you may want to tell the reader you are happy in this group (location, social club, work situation, department), and include a suggestion or two about how the person can fit in, learn the ropes, or get oriented.

Your closing statement should reaffirm your welcome.

ETIQUETTE

A welcoming note and a welcoming act are the backbone of the kind of civility and hospitality that used to characterize our society. It's time to bring them back in all of our circles.

DECIDE TO WRITE

Use the welcome letter in response to the following:

- A new person is about to join the family
- A new neighbor moves in
- A new employee starts work
- A new member joins your club, faculty, school, student association, church, temple, fraternity, or sorority
- A new business starts
- A new employee joins a customer's or client's business
- A new business prospect, customer, client, or associate is added

THINK ABOUT CONTENT

- Express your pleasure and enthusiasm in welcoming the new person.
- Keep your message simple and focus on how the other person feels at this time.
- Welcome the person into the organization, family, group, or neighborhood.
- Include, if possible, a complimentary statement about the organization, family, group, club, or neighborhood.
- Generate some enthusiasm about the future.

- State your best wishes for the person, drawing a relationship between him or her and the organization.
- Be specific and make it as personal as possible.
- Make your offer of help, if appropriate, and suggest a time to meet.
- In the case of an employee, give any details that may be appropriate: work hours, lunch policy and times, parking arrangements, benefits, and so on.
- Close with an encouraging comment.
- Timeliness is very important. You lose the opportunity for the greatest impact if you don't send the letter immediately.
- Your offer of help will never be as valued as it is now, but be sure to set limits you can live with and be concrete in your offer.

ELIMINATE WRONG MESSAGES

- Don't mix messages. This is not the place for a sales message, for example.
- Don't include bad news or negative messages.

CONSIDER SPECIAL SITUATIONS

- A welcome to a new family member should ring with warmth and sincerity, expressing your pleasure at having the person join the family.
- Employee welcome letters are often considered the domain of the human resources or personnel department, and include a packet of information about insurance coverage, company policy, benefits, and other work-related matters. While this may be standard operating procedure, make sure employees are welcomed both verbally by other employees and also with welcome letters. This creates better relationships, allows the new employee to settle in more quickly, and promotes a greater sense of camaraderie and loyalty.
- Neighborhoods are often so insular that it is unusual to welcome a new neighbor with a letter. But we now have so many master-planned communities that the practice of sending a welcome from the homeowners' association should be routine. This can be done very nicely with a welcome basket and a helpful sheet on local shopping, professional services, a directory of families in the neighborhood, and other useful information.
- A personal welcome note to a new neighbor can be helpful in establishing a good relationship. "Welcome to the neighborhood. I look forward to having you over for coffee, so please give me a call when you get settled," says that you prefer to be called first rather than dropped in on. Such a note delivered with homemade cookies is especially welcome.
- Students, attendees, parents, and new faculty members of schools, colleges, and/or special academic programs will benefit from the information and be more at ease if they receive a welcome letter. The letter should include a list of the things they will need for the first class or session, and it should state some of the program benefits, and include an inspiring sentence or two about the session. Naming someone for the new person to contact before the first session is also very helpful.

- With the welcome letter to a potential business customer or client, include a reason for a well-timed follow-up call to help you establish a relationship. "I will call your office next week to arrange a time to stop by briefly and introduce myself, to give you a copy of the Glenwood Directory, and to answer any questions you may have."
- The Welcome Wagon or other new resident service may be a good source of new residents for you to contact if these are potential clients or customers for your business.
- The chamber of commerce, the new business section of the newspaper, and local business publications and websites may be good sources from which to glean the names of new businesses you may wish to contact with a welcome letter.

SELECT A FORMAT

- Business welcome letters, in which you are acting in an official capacity, should be typed on organization letterhead.
- For a welcome letter from you to a new coworker or employee, personal business letterhead may be used, and the letter should be typed.
- New-neighbor welcome messages and those to new members of an informal group or club are usually handwritten on personal stationery or a fold-over card.
- Student and attendee welcomes may best be handled by sending printed or handwritten postcards.

SELECT STRONG WORDS

belong	camaraderie	community	congratulations
conviviality	delighted	extend	fellowship
friendship	membership	mutual	reception
share	social	trust	welcome

BUILD EFFECTIVE PHRASES

among friends and colleagues	build solid relationships
common goals and purposes	convivial and helpful
cultivate friends here	enjoy the fellowship
extend a warm welcome	find real camaraderie
happy you're aboard	help get you involved
help you build your professional capital	introduce you to members
join our circle of comrades	mutually supportive and helpful
safe and secure place to spread your wings	supportive in so many ways
warm and close circle	wonderful atmosphere for learning

WRITE STRONG SENTENCES

Be focused and concise, then offer a sincere message.

A warm and sincere welcome to you.
I hope you will enjoy your membership as much as I have enjoyed mine over the past 15 years.

A hardy welcome to our project group from each and every one of us.
Welcome to the team! We're all rooting for you and ready to help in any way possible.
We are delighted to have you aboard. Welcome!
We look forward to a long and mutually rewarding relationship.
Welcome to this warm group, where I have found true fellowship and faithful friends.

BUILD EFFECTIVE PARAGRAPHS

Remember, keep it short and sweet.

With great pleasure, I welcome you to the Press Club of Mobile. Your application has been approved by the board and ratified by the members.

Welcome to Bentonville! It's been said that anyone who comes here never wants to leave. My family certainly agrees. We hope yours will too.

Welcome to the Baskerville team. I believe you will find that everyone has the spirit of working together to get the job done. We're very glad to have you, and I invite you to give me a call at any time to discuss questions you may have.

Welcome to West Concord Business Park. I have found this location convenient to all of the metro area, and an ideal location from which to get to the ski slopes on Friday afternoons. I'll call you next week to see if you would care to get together briefly to discuss Park procedures and policies. In the meantime, here's a directory of all the businesses in the area.

Welcome to our entrepreneurial family. I believe one of the greatest benefits of becoming a Small Business Chamber of Commerce member is the Members-of-the-Board sessions, where entrepreneurs help solve each others' problems. I know it's the best business decision I've ever made. Happy to have you aboard!

Welcome, again, to the Toronto Womens' Press Society. We are all delighted you have chosen to reactivate your membership after three years. Yes, we have changed our goals and are much more in tune with the needs of women working in the media today. We're so pleased to have you back.

A strong welcome to our little online authors' community. As you'll quickly see, we offer a brand of help and support here not otherwise available. It's probably the single most beneficial thing I do to help my freelance career. And the members of this group have become true friends. We have only a few rules written to promote online civility and avoid the problems that this medium has been known to spawn. I've attached a copy for you. Again, welcome. I look forward to your participation.

It was a pleasure serving you at The Regiment today, and I welcome you as a customer of the finest men's custom-made clothing store in the city. As we discussed, your final fitting for the suits will be Friday the 15th at 4:00 p.m. I look forward to serving you then. And again, welcome!

EDIT, EDIT, EDIT

Be sure your message is brief, warm, and personal.

To a New Family Member

Dear Jessie,

Welcome to the family!

David is so special to me. He stayed with his Uncle Jack and me during his mother's lengthy illness when he was four and five, and again when he was ten and his mother had surgery. I've loved him like a son since the moment he was born.

So, when I say I'm very pleased you two have decided to get married, it's the sincerest compliment to you, and the truest belief in the possibility of your extraordinary happiness.

I know you'll have a wonderful life together, and I'm thrilled for you both.

Your new aunt,
Bea

To a New Employee

Dear Stacey:

It's a pleasure to welcome you to Doodles and to the marketing department in particular. I believe you'll find this both an exciting company and a challenging department to work in.

I'm sure the human resources folks have given you all the necessary company information you'll need, but I'd like to extend an offer to meet with you for 10 to 15 minutes on the next four Thursdays at 4:00 p.m. to address any questions you may have as you get your footing.

I think you'll find everyone here eager to help you get up to speed. Welcome aboard, and let me know about getting together on Thursdays.

All the best,
Doug

To New In-Laws

Dear Bebe and Trek,

What could be happier news?

We've said it before, but now that it's official that the two people on the planet we love with all our hearts—Olivia and Ben—are going to get married, we'd like to make a formal declaration: welcome to our family! We adore Olivia, and also happen to believe she has wonderful parents.

We couldn't be more delighted that we'll be seeing a lot more of you two in the years to come. What joy!

Birdie and Edgar

To School Parent-Teachers' Association

Dear Ms. Alison:

The PTA at Logan wants to welcome you to our parents and teachers' working group. Our goal is to create a better educational experience for our children.

I feel sure your daughter, Jennifer, will enjoy Ms. Rudy's class. My daughter was one of her students last year, and I found Ms. Rudy to be an extremely skilled and concerned teacher.

Please plan to attend our Thursday social hour, September 18, at 7:30 p.m. in the gym for an informal welcome. I look forward to meeting you.

Sincerely,
June Addison

To a Student

Susan,

Let me introduce myself and say welcome to the fifth grade at Stanley Academy. My name is Mrs. Moore, and I'll be your homeroom teacher.

I believe you will enjoy our series on "The Birth of Democracy," the four field trips we have planned to the state capitol building and state representatives' offices, and our "Women in U.S. History" project.

It's going to be a wonderful year, and I look forward to meeting you next Thursday in room 43, opposite the administration office. Please bring the items listed in the margin, and wear a big smile!

Your teacher,
Mrs. Moore

As a Volunteer

Dear Gary:

Welcome to Big Friends Club.[1] In the next two weeks, you will be given three young friend candidates to review before you make your friend choice.

Last year in Cleveland, we were able to match 1,250 boys with Big Friends. On the back of this letter, we've listed some of the boys' comments about the differences their Big Friends have made in their lives. You'll also see some comments from Big Friends.

Being a Big Friend is inspiring, rewarding, and a lot of work. We're so pleased you have decided to help make a difference in a young boy's life.[2]

Remember, we are always here to help.[3]

Sincerely,

Rodney Baker

President

(1) State your welcome. (2) Offer something positive. (3) Offer help.

To a New Business Associate

Dear Gwen:

Welcome to Marmet, Missouri!

Since this is the "Show Me State," I'd like to suggest a breakfast meeting on the 15th, 8:00 a.m., at Robins Inn, with a group of new residents and a few of us old-timers. It will be an orientation for important things such as where to buy the best women's suits for the lowest prices, where to go when you need to have dinner for 10 in 40 minutes, and where to take your car for a purring tune-up.

We'd also like to give you the opportunity to ask us questions. We have been businesswomen in this town for two to thirty years. (There's a wealth of information here.)

Please call me at 616-555-0123 and tell me you'll attend.

Sincerely,

Joan Slosky

To a New Business

Dear Mr. Wilson:

Welcome to Wilkerson!

In the past two years we've added 18 businesses to those in town, and the owners all report that they have surpassed their own projections for this time period, some by as much as 40 percent.

Wilkerson has a great atmosphere for growing a service business like yours, and I encourage you to use the many resources of the Business Club, including the Owners' Roundtable, Retired Marketers, and Services for Trade.

Again, welcome. And please call me anytime if I may answer questions.

Yours truly,

Ralph Metor

(Also see DIRECT MAIL, page 361, and EMPLOYEE CORRESPONDENCE, page 161.)

10 INVITATION

Inviting guests to an occasion can be as informal as saying "Y'all come," or as formal as sending engraved invitations—pieces of art—created and then addressed by a calligrapher. Whether the event is an impromptu pizza party or the 125th Annual Governors' Ball, you'll want your invitee to feel you are expressing a special desire to have him or her attend. Social occasions often cross the lines between personal and business, making distinction between the two impossible. Certainly all such occasions present an opportunity to solidify connections, improve morale, create new relationships, or patch up old ones.

Everyone loves being invited. Create an invitation that makes the recipient eager to attend!

ETIQUETTE

An invitation is a compliment of sorts, and should be responded to in a timely manner (and according to any instructions it may include: "RSVP regrets only" means only if you aren't coming do you need to respond) as soon as possible. First, thank the host for the invitation. Most invitations carry the social obligation to reciprocate—not necessarily in kind. The exceptions are events like weddings, and the like.

DECIDE TO WRITE

You'll use invitations for many get-togethers:

- Informal parties
- Business events, including such things as trade shows, open houses, exhibitions, new product introductions, and premieres
- New business openings
- Fundraisers
- Celebrations of a family, religious, or educational nature including showers, rehearsal dinners, weddings, anniversaries, christenings, first communions, baptisms, bar or bat mitzvahs, confirmations, ordinations, graduations, and others
- Hospitality, such as an invitation to be a weekend houseguest
- Educational programs, such as workshops, seminars, conferences, or speeches
- Cultural events, such as concert or theater productions
- Social organization events
- Holiday or commemorative events

THINK ABOUT CONTENT

- Make the form and appearance of your invitation consistent with the formality of the occasion. Invitations to business events may take the form of a business communication, and strictly social events should follow the rules for a social invitation.
- Be sure to include all essential information: *what, when, why, where, who,* and *how much.*
- Begin with words of personal invitation or state the occasion or event: "You Are Cordially Invited to the Ninth Annual Preferred Customers' Pre-sale Event," "the Fifth Annual Goldminers' Ball," "the Grand Opening of Phinney's."
- List the date and time of the event, including month, day, year, and time, A.M. or P.M. (The day of the week may be listed before the month.)
- The address comes next. A cross street ("at Maple and Main") or brief directions ("turn south off Alameda onto Grant") may be given after the address, or a map may be included with the invitation.
- Supply helpful information for guests, for example, if food and beverages (and possibly which foods) will be served. Giving the time and sequence of events is also helpful. "A light luncheon for out-of-town guests will be served at four o'clock before the six o'clock ceremony."
- Charges and costs, if any, should be listed: "$125 per couple," "Open Bar," "Valet Parking." This information tells the invitees the arrangements and their anticipated expenses involved with attending.
- The RSVP tradition has become very blurred. Since every host needs to know how many, and possibly who, will attend, an *RSVP, Please respond, Please RSVP by (date),* or *Regrets only* should appear in the lower left-hand corner of the formal invitation with a telephone number and an address. Many formal invitations enclose a printed or engraved RSVP card and envelope, addressed and stamped for the invitee's reply.
- You may place information about attire in the lower right corner of a formal invitation. Designations most often used are *informal, semiformal, formal, black tie, white tie, casual, costume,* and *evening attire.* On informal invitations, the host may say something like "Come in slacks."
- When your invitation includes hospitality, multiple activities, or requires guests to make their own overnight or eating arrangements, provide as much information as possible. Making a statement like "Come prepared to enjoy swimming, tennis, and an evening hayride" gives guests an idea of the kind of clothing to bring. If your invitation is to a weekend rally of red 1965 Corvette owners, it will be helpful if you include hotel suggestions and reservation policies, and even information on restaurants in the area.
- You should not be shy about including the limits of the invitation. For example, "Please plan to arrive Saturday between 3:00 P.M. and 4:00 P.M., and depart Sunday between 2:00 P.M. and 3:00 P.M." "We're a nonsmoking home" will be helpful to you and your guests.

- Inform guests, too, about unusual arrangements: "Sleeping arrangements for the Gourmet Cowboy Weekend will be women in the west camp tents and men in the east camp tents. Bring your own sleeping bag, towels, and personal items. There is no electricity. Cots are provided."

- Miscellaneous information can be very important. If guests are to arrange their transportation from the airport, make that clear.

- Parking (and fees), inclement weather information, and notices about alternate plans should all be included. "In the event of rain, we will move inside the Grange Hall."

- Most important, make sure the invitation is warm in tone and leaves readers with the sense you look forward to having them attend: "Please RSVP with an acceptance." "We're so looking forward to seeing you. It's been such a long time. We have some serious catching up to do." "Please confirm by June 15 that you can make it." "It will be so good to see you." "We've arranged some events we think you will especially like."

- Corporate informal and general invitations for such things as an in-office party for a retirement, maternity leave, promotion, service celebration, and the like can be made in memo form, and by email. List the event, time, date, place, and refreshments. Information on contributions for a gift may be included, and if you need a response, a telephone extension number should be given with a time limit: "Call Susan at Ext. 3443 by Thursday at 4:00 P.M. and tell her how many from your department will attend."

- To help ensure a response to your invitation, place *RSVP* in the lower left-hand section of the invitation and enclose a reply card and envelope which is addressed and stamped. Or, list a telephone number or an address for the response:

    RSVP
    555-0123
  or
    RSVP
    110 Forest Lane
    Rockport, IL 60641

- If you have not heard from invitees by the time you need to make final preparations, telephone them.

- The response card should be a simple fill-in-the-blanks. The printer will have several options to select from, but it can simply say:

    M _____
    □ regrets □ accepts
    the invitation for
    Friday, January fifth
    at Willow Creek Country Club
  or
    M _____
    □ will □ will not attend
    Friday, January fifth

- When you enclose items in the invitation—the response card and envelope, raffle tickets for a benefit, a separate map, or seating tickets for a performance or graduation—place these items in front of the invitation with the writing side facing the mailing envelope flap so the invitee sees the writing when opening the envelope.

- Dress designations are not as strictly adhered to today, but "white tie" is the most formal, indicating a white tie, wing collar, and tailcoat for men. Women wear formal evening gowns. Today this kind of dress is reserved almost exclusively for official and diplomatic occasions. "Black tie" indicates men are to wear a tuxedo and bow tie. Jackets may be patterned and of almost any color. Women wear gowns or cocktail dresses. "Semiformal" has come to mean wear shoes, and don't wear T-shirts or jeans.

- The name game can be confusing. When in doubt, call and ask. Issue the invitation in the names of the hosts, for example, "David Greer and Sally Westmore invite you . . ." Address invitations to invitees by their preferred names. Many women now use a business name and another social name. Business invitations may list the titles of the hosts. It's also correct to issue an invitation in the name of a club, friends, a fraternity, or other organization.

- List the times of events in the invitation whenever possible: "Ceremony at six o'clock, reception at half past seven." "Cocktails at six o'clock, dinner at seven-thirty."

- The timetable for sending invitations depends upon the occasion, the distance guests must travel, and everyone's social calendar. Wedding invitations should be sent six to eight weeks ahead. For most formal events and dinner parties, invitations should be sent four to six weeks ahead. For informal get-togethers and casual dinners, two to four weeks is adequate. (Allow an extra ten days to two weeks for getting invitations printed.)

- Include a no-gift statement if appropriate: "Your love and friendship are cherished gifts. We respectfully request no other." "No gifts, please." "Please bring the gift of a favorite recipe." "Please bring the gift of a favorite photo or story to share."

- Fundraiser invitations will receive a better response rate if you enclose a postage-paid, addressed reply envelope.

- Invitations to guest speakers, panelists, and prospective conference attendees should contain complete information. Speakers need to know the composition of the audience, the goal of the conference or seminar, other presenters and their topics, time allotments, room size, accommodations, seating style, audiovisual equipment, and other special equipment and connections available for use. Be sure to include the name of a contact person (and contact information) who can answer specific questions. If you are using a hotel for the event, the hotel may offer a complete listing of this information.

THINK ABOUT RESPONDING

- Always respond to a personal invitation—whether it is business or social. Both "RSVP" and "Please reply" require a response. "Regrets only" requires a response only if you will not attend. Even if a dinner invitation is in conjunction with an annual sales meeting, board of directors meeting, or special convention, respond as indicated.

- Use the reply-in-kind rule. If the invitation is formal, reply in a like manner. Use the same language as the invitation. Write "Mr. and Mrs. Lewis Curtis accept with pleasure the kind invitation of Mr. and Mrs. Peter Graves for dinner on Monday the tenth of November at eight o'clock." Informal written responses may be made on personal fold-over note stationery. Emailed invitations may be accepted or declined by email.

- A response by either invitee of a married couple is correct. No longer is this considered the domain of women.

- If you must cancel at the last minute after accepting an invitation, both telephone or otherwise notify the host by using email or fax, and immediately write a personal note of regret with your explanation.

ELIMINATE WRONG MESSAGES

- Informal invitations may contain informal writing, like abbreviations; but formal invitations should avoid abbreviations except Mr., Mrs., Ms., Dr., Jr., Sr., Lt., Col., and other military designations. In formal invitations, do not abbreviate the states in the address. Numbers in the formal invitation should be spelled out, like "eight fifteen Sherman Street" and "seven o'clock." In conjunction with names, use Second and Third without a comma after the name, instead of II and III. Use a comma before Jr. and Sr.

- Don't be vague about whom you're inviting. List invited small children by their first name on the envelope under the parents' names. If you are inviting teenagers or older children, each should receive his or her own invitation. If the spouse of an employee is being invited, or if the invitee may bring a friend, make that clear. Use the individual's name whenever possible.

SELECT A FORMAT

- Formal invitations are usually on high-quality white or cream-colored cards with matching envelopes and are engraved. Other choices may be embossed or plain cards with a raised border (plate mark). There is a trend toward hand-crafted invitations for very special occasions. In either case, select cards with proportions of three units by four units. Good choices are 3 by 4 inches to 4½ by 6 inches. Ask the printer for samples.

- Select a typeface or lettering and ink color that are easy to read.

- Printing may be engraved, or, more economically, done in informal style by thermography, which produces raised letters.

- If you create your own invitations, use appropriate artwork or a nice quality card stock or notepaper and formal wording in the third person: "John and Judith Eisner request the pleasure of your company at a dinner party at their home at Ten Fox Dale Drive on September tenth. Cocktails will be served at seven, dinner at eight. RSVP 555-0123. Black tie requested."

SELECT THE RIGHT WORD

announce	attend	bring	celebrate
change	company	enjoy	greet
hope	hospitality	inform	join
joy	meet	new	open
please	pleasure	presence	receive
rejoice	reply	request	welcome

CONSTRUCT EFFECTIVE PHRASES

announce the coming	coming soon
event will be held	happy to announce
introduce the new	open house will
please join us	pleased to introduce
request the honor	request your presence at
starting at	wish to invite

BUILD STRONG SENTENCES

Start with a key word of invitation and build lean sentences with precise words of welcome. Here are some examples:

> We're really hoping Uncle Roy and you will be able to come and have Thanksgiving dinner with us this year.
>
> Will you join Joel Walton and me for lunch on Thursday? It would be so good to see you.
>
> During the Open House, First Bank's loan officers will be available to answer any questions you may have.
>
> This is your special invitation to our Ninth Annual Pre-Sale Celebration.
>
> Our party will be a success, if you'll be here.
>
> Please say you'll come.
>
> Your presence will make it a real celebration.
>
> Our special invitation to you for a very special evening.
>
> It will be wonderful to have a chance to catch up.

BUILD EFFECTIVE PARAGRAPHS

Put precise, complete information in its logical order.

> Please stop by our booth #566 at the Chicago Convention Center, Expo 104, September 10 to 12, and see the new Model 415. Register for a two-week vacation giveaway and a 25 percent discount on the new models.
>
> This is your invitation to a one-month free membership to Valley Racquet Club, 4300 Miners Road, Englewood. This entitles you to full use of the entire health club facilities (with the exception of the indoor tennis courts).
>
> Please bring in the enclosed 25 percent off certificate during our "Madman Special," Thursday, November 5, between 10:00 A.M. and 6:00 P.M. Free hot dogs and sodas for the kids.

The Marketing Department is hosting an after-hours reception to show-and-tell the fall campaign on Friday, August 30, 5:00 P.M. to 6:30 P.M. Please respond with a list of those from your department who will attend.

Monday Night Football happens at my house one hour before kick-off. Won't you and Sally join the rest of the softball team?

EDIT, EDIT, EDIT

The best invitations contain complete, concise information. Ask yourself if you have answered the *what, where, when, how, who,* and *why* of the event. Be sure, too, that you've included details guests will need to know, such as any costs involved, directions, special parking information, and so on.

To a Formal Dinner

[Printed]

Roosevelt and Suzanne Connors
request the pleasure of your company
at dinner
on Friday, the tenth of September,
at seven o'clock
at the Town Club
Heathertown, New York

RSVP
Ten Applewood Lane
Heathertown, New York 10045

To a Formal Ball

[Printed]

The Governors of Gateside Country Club
invite you to subscribe to
the Annual Springtime Ball
to be held at
The Gateside Country Club
on Saturday, the twenty-fifth of April
two thousand and six
at eight o'clock
Applewood, Connecticut

RSVP
Georgia Geiger
555-0123

To an Informal Business Open House

Dear Allyson:

I hope you will come by the hospitality suite, Room 430, at the Westmoreland Hotel on Thursday, April 27, between 7:00 and 9:30 p.m., and introduce yourself to our marketing team attending the Booksellers' Convention. I'd like you to meet Bill Ashton. I believe he will be a great contact for the Grizzly project.

This promises to be our best convention yet. There are already well over 125,000 registered attendees.

Best wishes,
Titus Teeter

To an Informal Social Open House

Willow Creek Country Club will hold
its thirty-fifth annual
open house for new members
one o'clock to five o'clock
Saturday the fifth of May
4500 South Willow Creek Drive

Refreshments   Informal Dress
Drawing

To an Informal Get-Together

Dear Rachel,

I would be so pleased if you would join us after baby Jennifer's christening on Sunday, the 12th, from 1:30 p.m. to 3:30 p.m. It will just be a small celebration with a few special relatives and friends.

We certainly hope you can make it. Please let us know by calling 555-0123.

Yours truly,
Celeste Castle

To a Graduation Reception

Jerald and Olivia Soderholm
request the honor of your company
at a reception to celebrate the college
graduation of their son
Christopher David Solderholm
Sunday afternoon, June twenty-fourth
at three o'clock
in the Crown Room of the Highmoor
420 Eastman Drive
Cleveland Springs, Ohio

Please reply to
744 Tamarac Drive
Cleveland Springs, Ohio

Acceptance of a Formal Dinner Invitation

Ted and Jane Turnett
accept with pleasure
the kind invitation of
Reginald and Jennifer Trumpet
to dinner
on Friday, the tenth of September
at seven o'clock

To a Working Business Dinner

Dear Jim:

I'm hosting an informal get-together on Thursday, May 12, at 7:00 p.m. for the key players in the Adams restructuring. We will have dinner and then review the proposed elements of the agreement, which I've enclosed. A map is also enclosed.

Please call my assistant at 555-0123 by Wednesday and let her know if you can make it. I'll also need your comments on the enclosed draft by Friday so I can have everyone's feedback distributed to all those coming on the 12th.

Sincerely,
Agatha Jeevers

Regrets to an Informal Invitation

Dear Electra and Warren,

Thank you for your kind invitation to dinner at the Metro Club on May 12 for your retirement celebration. Dede and I are so disappointed we will be unable to accept.

We are scheduled to be in France for the entire month.

Have a wonderful time. We'll look forward to getting together when we return. You must tell us all about the event. I'll call when we get back into town to arrange a time.

Best,
Warren

11 APPRECIATION

You will distinguish yourself if you express appreciation in personal and business relationships when another person has performed well. The letter of appreciation is distinctly its own breed, falling within the broad category of goodwill letters. While the distinctions between letters of appreciation, thanks, acknowledgment, and congratulations are often blurred, the right time to write a letter of appreciation is when someone was just doing his or her job, but in doing so made your life easier, or when you particularly admired the way he or she did the job. It is also appropriate to send a letter of appreciation when someone has performed in a manner that is notable or extraordinary.

ETIQUETTE

Expressing appreciation is a demonstration that you value others and their efforts, and wish to recognize and applaud them. Expressing appreciation promotes civility and a kinder and gentler society.

DECIDE TO WRITE

Send a note of appreciation in response to:

- Outstanding addresses, speeches, and instruction sessions
- Employees' extraordinary performance
- Pre-, early, or prompt payment by a customer
- Expressions of sympathy
- Letters or acts of congratulations
- An offer of assistance
- Complimentary remarks or acknowledgments in speeches, books, and the like
- Invitations to speak, chair a committee, sing, or sit on a panel
- Salary increase or bonus
- Outstanding or beneficial conduct or act of a teacher, family member, friend, associate, or supervisor
- Financial contributions
- Volunteer's efforts

THINK ABOUT CONTENT

- Begin with the point of appreciation and the rest will flow more easily.
- Make it brief and sincere.
- Express your feelings, naming what you appreciate in natural, sincere terms.
- Explain briefly why you are appreciative.
- If appropriate, offer to reciprocate.
- End with a reference to the future. If appropriate, encourage the recipient to contribute again or express your desire for a future meeting.

ELIMINATE WRONG MESSAGES

- Don't mix messages. Keep news items, meeting announcements, and similar notices for another communication.
- Examine your motives if you are having difficulty writing the letter. It may be that another type of letter is more suitable, or that a letter of appreciation isn't merited.

CONSIDER SPECIAL SITUATIONS

- Hybrid letters with a public relations or sales motive should be carefully thought out. Appreciation should be the primary message or the letter may sound insincere. (Also see Sales Follow-Up, page 368.)
- A letter in response to an offer of assistance should express appreciation, accept or reject the offer, and suggest the next step if the offer is being accepted.
- A letter to a team, committee, department, or group of people may address them as a whole. If appropriate, a copy may be sent to each member. Be sure to include everyone.
- Sometimes appreciation must be combined with refusal. If there is an offer to serve on a committee, or a gift is sent that you must refuse, emphasize your appreciation first. (Also see Refusal, page 274.)

SELECT A FORMAT

- Handwritten personal notes of appreciation should be your first choice. Use personal stationery or fold-over notes.
- Business letters of appreciation should be typed on letterhead if the recipient is associated with another organization.
- For internal business appreciation, it is usually best to use an interoffice memo or email.
- For routine, quick messages of appreciation for such things as product orders, a postcard may be used, or email. (Also see Acknowledgment & Confirmation, page 264.)

SELECT STRONG WORDS

admirable	admire	aplomb	appreciate
aspire	commend	commendable	entrust
esteem	excellent	exemplary	expertise
favorite	finesse	generous	grace
gracious	honor	impressive	inspire
inspiring	kindness	memorable	model
noteworthy	outstanding	pleased	praiseworthy
recommend	remarkable	respect	satisfying
sensational	superb	touched	treasure
triumph	unforgettable	unique	valuable

BUILD EFFECTIVE PHRASES

a job well done	accomplished with such aplomb
an exemplary performance	appreciated by so many
demonstrate such dedication	done with such expertise
held in high esteem by so many	hold you in high esteem
how delightful to see	I was so impressed by
must express my appreciation	offer my sincere appreciation
performed seamlessly	performed so outstandingly
set a high standard	set an outstanding example for
so grateful for your contribution	such an important contribution
unequaled in effort	your performance is noteworthy

WRITE STRONG SENTENCES

Your contribution to the new plant scheduling policy is one of the best I've seen in 20 years with the company.

I felt your insight helped the committee do a much better job than any of us expected.

Please call on me if I can return the favor.

BUILD EFFECTIVE PARAGRAPHS

It was extremely thoughtful of you to volunteer to be on hand for the courtroom drama. I really appreciate your vote of confidence.

Taking over for Karen Gross when she became ill was way beyond the call of duty. Your extra efforts and dedication to making the organization look good are greatly appreciated.

I really appreciated your demonstrated leadership in last night's meeting. You kept the whole issue from exploding.

EDIT, EDIT, EDIT

Be concise, brief, and sincere.

For a Prompt Payment

Dear Mr. Jepson:

We just received your letter and check for the landscaping of Green Acres. We appreciate your prompt payment.

It was a pleasure working on this lovely project, and we do hope you'll call us for further planning or maintaining the grounds.

We look forward to hearing from you.

Yours truly,
Annie Schmidt

For a Letter of Recommendation

Bob,

I have just received the copy of your letter of recommendation to Begones on my behalf. (Is this me you're talking about?)[1]

I greatly appreciate your kind words, and I will certainly keep you informed of the progress and outcome as the selection process goes forward.[2]

Kind regards,
Dave

(1) Name what you appreciate. (2) Refer to the future.

For Volunteering

Dear Janice:

It is very thoughtful of you to volunteer to take over three of my class sessions next semester while I attend the workshops. I thought I would have to reschedule the class sessions, and that presented some insurmountable problems. Your offer is a wonderful solution.

I will telephone you next week to set a time to go over the lesson plans. Please allow me to stand in for you next semester.

Best regards,
Nancy Letterer

For Help with Work

John,

It was a real sacrifice for you to change your plans, do double duty on the sales report, and also handle my trip to Atlanta while Anne was ill. I appreciate it more than I can say. There was a critical decision I had to make for her medical care on Thursday afternoon, and matters would have been seriously complicated if I had not been on hand. You're a prince.

Please allow me to do a good deed for you anytime.

Kind regards,
Bill

For an Extra Effort

Dear Mr. Richardson:

I have just received the reworked architectural plans for the addition to the children's wing of St. Joseph's. I know a lot of overtime went into this because of our tight timeframe, but your hard work will enable us to present the plans at the board meeting. We deeply appreciate your efforts. You did a great job.

The board meets in the morning, and I will be back in touch with you tomorrow afternoon to let you know how it went. I truly appreciate your fine work.

Sincerely,
Bill Babson

Writing a thank-you note or letter in response to an act of kindness or a gift received is both courteous and the civil thing to do. But if you start with that in mind, you'll undoubtedly produce one of those obligatory and lifeless messages that fail to connect with the person you're thanking. Go for a real expression of thanks—one that connects you to the gift and the giver. Make your message brief and write it in a pleasant, conversational tone. Write it promptly because timing sends a very strong message all on its own.

ETIQUETTE

Promptness and sincerity are the key words for expressing thanks.

DECIDE TO WRITE

Use a thank-you note or letter in response to:

- Gifts of all kinds for such occasions as weddings, showers, birthdays, holidays, anniversaries, and bar or bat mitzvahs, whether these are received personally or in the course of business (also see Wedding & Engagement Correspondence, page 82)
- Acts of kindness and gifts after a death in the family
- Business order or contract
- Job interview, or interview of any kind
- Referrals of clients, customers, or patients
- Reference for a position, whether business or personal
- Hospitality, either business or personal, or both
- Contributions to fundraising activities, events, and drives
- Membership in a club, association, or professional organization

THINK ABOUT CONTENT

- Focus first on the person who gave you the gift or performed the kindness.
- Think next about what you are thanking the person or company for.
- Reflect on what the gift or deed means to you: how you will use it or how it will help you.
- Connect the dots between the giver, the gift, and yourself.
- Name the gift early, and say thankyou early.
- Use a tone that is pleasant, even enthusiastic, and one that reflects the way you would talk to the giver.

- Mention the appropriateness of the gift or act.
- Add some detail about how the gift or act benefits you, what about it you especially enjoyed, or how you will use it.
- Be brief and sincere.
- Offer something in return if that is appropriate; or optionally, add a sentence or two of compliment to the giver.
- You cannot err in writing sincere thank-yous for acts of kindness or gifts. So, whenever the situation presents itself, use it to show your thankfulness and to make your relationship with the giver stronger.
- For personal thank-yous, don't mix messages. Don't tack on a thank-you in a letter with another purpose.
- For business and social thank-yous, use these guidelines:
  - ► When a dinner, evening, or weekend outing crosses from business to social at the home of a business associate, send both a written thank-you and a thank-you gift to the host.
  - ► When you are the guest of honor at an office or business luncheon or dinner, a thank-you note to the host—usually your immediate superior—is in order. If the company president attends, a personal, written thank-you should also be sent to him or her.
  - ► If you are one of many guests at an office party, or share a meal in the ordinary course of business, a verbal thanks is sufficient. You may also, in this case, want to add a note to your next business correspondence, such as "Thanks for hosting the Thursday luncheon. I look forward to working with you on the Sioux Falls project." This same rule is true for regular luncheons, but for first meetings and infrequent ones, a short thank-you note is called for. This may be either typed or handwritten.
- Send your thank-you note or letter promptly. Here are some general guidelines to follow:
  - ► Luncheon or dinner, write within one day.
  - ► Stay in someone's home or an act of hospitality, write within several days.
  - ► For wedding gifts, it's best to send thank-yous as gifts arrive, but all givers should receive thank-yous within three months of the wedding (also see Wedding & Engagement Correspondence, page 82).
  - ► For "get well" gifts and acts of kindness, there is some latitude, usually until after the receiver recovers. In the case of a serious or terminal illness, another person may certainly send an expression of thanks on the recipient's behalf. It is also generous to write periodic updates to keep friends, family, and colleagues informed. Ask if the giver would like to be included in weekly, monthly, or periodic updates, which you can write and distribute by email.
- Writing promptly makes the task much easier and ensures a much more genuine (and detailed) message.
- Be specific in naming the gift or act of kindness.

ELIMINATE WRONG MESSAGES

- Don't write a thank-you that is really a sales letter.
- Stay away from general statements; make your thank-you specific.
- Don't let your prose go beyond your true feelings. Flowery insincerity defeats your purpose. Instead, simply say "thank you very much."
- The mention of the amount of money received as a gift is sometimes considered tactless. If you know the recipient well, you may be certain that Uncle Joe won't be offended if you write "Thank you, Uncle Joe, for the check for $50." For others you don't know well, simply write "Thank you for the check."
- In the short thank-you, the use of "Thanks again" at the end of the note does not work well. Instead, conclude with a sincere compliment to the recipient. "You've proven again what a generous person you are."

CONSIDER SPECIAL SITUATIONS

- Don't procrastinate. A late thank-you may seem insincere, and your procrastination must be explained. However, don't belabor your tardiness; just get the note written: "I'm so sorry this note is late. The tornado hit just as we were arriving home." Or, "I'm sorry for not having written sooner to tell you how much I love the red sweater. It's a perfect match with my tartan plaid skirt." "The tardiness of my thank-you note reflects poorly on me, but certainly not on the wonderful wallet. Or on the very generous person, Aunt Jo, who sent it." "It's taken me a little while to digest the enormity of your generous act."
- Verbal thank-yous for gifts don't substitute for written ones. If you've verbally thanked the giver, still send a personal, written note.
- A written thank-you is required when a "thank-you" gift has been given.
- When a gift was sent collectively by a number of givers, each should be sent a personal, written thank-you. The exceptions here are when the gift is sent by a family, a company department, or a club or association. In these cases, address the family, department, or club, and request that your thank-you note or letter be circulated or posted.
- Thank-yous for flowers, contributions, and acts of kindness in the case of a death in the family must always be sent. Even written letters of sympathy should be acknowledged with a return note of thanks. These thank-yous may be written either by the person closest to the deceased, or by a close family member or friend. At such times, it is wise to have someone make a record to ease the task and make sure no one's kindness is overlooked. There is obviously much leeway in timing here, but generally thank yous should be sent within six weeks of the funeral.
- Business thank-yous should be sent by regular modes of transmission. To fax or email a thank-you would detract considerably from its personal quality. However, a routine thank-you for a regular business luncheon may be combined with a letter with another main message, or sent by email if this is acceptable within the organization culture.

SELECT A FORMAT

- The form of choice is most often a commercially purchased fold-over note card or personal stationery.
- Formal printed cards or stationery can be used to express thanks for very large events, like large political campaigns or major fundraisers. Still, a personal, handwritten note is in order for gifts.
- When the gift was personal or social, the thank-you should be handwritten.
- When hospitality was extended in a business associate's home, the thank-you is addressed to the home address.
- Business-related thank-yous are usually typewritten on company letterhead, personal business stationery, or a good-quality paper.
- When there are exceptionally large numbers of people to thank, or there is the possibility of oversight, as in the death of a community leader or when many people have contributed to a political campaign, it is important to write a public thank-you to local newspapers and other appropriate publications.
- A formal announcement of thanks does not substitute for personal notes to people whose efforts or gifts were exceptional.

POWER WORDS

cherish	delighted	elegant	enjoyed
excited	exquisite	generous	great
keepsake	kindness	lovely	noteworthy
overjoyed	perfect	remember	right
satisfied	stunning	surprise	thanks
thrilled	timely	touched	treasure
treat	unforgettable	useful	wonderful

POWER PHRASES

all-star gift	delightful choice
especially thankful	exquisite taste
extraordinary treat	frosting on the cake
generous gift	grace and style
great timing	how generous of you
I will always be thankful for	keepsake to treasure
lovely in the extreme	more than kind
no one else would have done this	offer my personal thanks
perfect choice	perfect in every way
perfect timing	perfect weekend
precious memento	precision and flair
selfless gift	something to always treasure
thrilled to receive	very special
unique gift	warm hospitality

we so benefited from

who else would have thought

wonderful selection

you are so thoughtful

your extreme thoughtfulness

what a kind thing to do

wonderful respite

you always add panache

you're an exceptional person

you've made my day

WRITE STRONG SENTENCES

Start with the gift and how it will be used. Then connect the giver with the act of giving, and with you.

Thank you for referring Alice Bannock to Adam, and more precisely, to me.

We are touched by your thoughtfulness.

Thanks to all of you at White and White for contributing the time and energy to the Women's Corner project.

Your crew did an outstanding job of answering the phones during the viewers' fundraiser; due to your efforts, we received $90,000 in pledged contributions.

All of the family was touched by your act of kindness in serving as head pallbearer at Dad's funeral.

I can't tell you how wonderful it was to see you come through that door in such a dark hour.

I can't remember attending a more relaxing and enjoyable dinner party.

It was extremely kind of you to call me about the opening at Formed Container.

Tickets to "Sherman's Forces" were unavailable, and we would have missed the event if it hadn't been for your generosity.

What an absolutely perfect dinner party.

I will always treasure this gift, but especially the fact that it came from you.

It's a perfect gift, and one that makes me feel even closer to you.

EDIT, EDIT, EDIT

Thank-you notes are generally not more than a paragraph or two, so make every word count.

For Dinner

Dear Millie,

Dinner was ambrosial! Just like every meal I've ever had at your house. Thank you for inviting Dick and me. We always enjoy getting together with you and Franz. It was a lovely, lovely evening, and we were especially "wild" about hearing the details of your African adventure.

Fondly,
Sherry and Dick

For a Gift

Dear Aunt Jennifer,

I've deposited your very generous check in my college fund. I'll use the money to purchase an alarm clock, so I expect I may experience mixed emotions when I hear it go off. But I'll always think fondly of you.

Thank you.

Your niece,
Lois

For a Job-Candidate Lead

Dear Dennis:

Thank you for referring Molly Swartz for the computer programmer position we discussed.[1] I have just interviewed Molly and I believe she is an outstanding candidate.

It has almost restored my sense of hope after being burned three times.

It was exceptionally thoughtful of you to follow up after our golf discussion. I'll let you know if this becomes a working relationship. We certainly need the skills and stability Molly possesses.[2]

Please let me know, as I said, if you want me to give you a couple of names for the drafting position.[3]

That was a great putt on the 18th, by the way; I'm determined to give you a greater challenge next week.[4]

Regards,

Lee Ann

(1) State what you're thankful for. (2) State why you are thankful. (3) Offer to reciprocate. (4) Embrace the future relationship.

For Serving as a Speaker

Dear Gabby:

Thank you for speaking to the Women's Press Club on Wednesday. The turnout was up 20 percent. I'm sure that was due to your popularity and your timely topic: "Blowing Your Own Horn."

Initial response after the meeting was that this was the best program we've had this year. I've also been asked if you would consider conducting a half-day seminar in the spring. We would, of course, pay you your regular fee.

Thank you, Gabby, for creating interest among our members.

Very truly,

Ruth

For Weekend Hospitality

Dear Daisy and Duff,

What an absolutely delightful weekend. Rox and I had just about burned out from four consecutive long, long weeks of back-to-back deadlines. Then this. What a breath of fresh country air![1]

It was a wonderful respite and change of pace. The card games were lots of fun, too, though I suspect I'd be even more enthusiastic if I'd have been on the winning team a few more times.[2]

A small token of our appreciation should arrive tomorrow. Do remember you've promised to allow us to reciprocate by accepting our brand of hospitality (city, not country) next month. There's a great new production at the community theater and a Broadway musical in town too. Are you game for one or both?[3]

All the best,
Rox and George

(1) State what you're thankful for. (2) State why. (3) Refer to the future.

For a Party

Caroline,

I've never been so totally surprised! How did you ever plan a 50-person party of office staff, organize it, and pull it off right under my nose, complete with those fantastic Caribbean decorations, without me getting wind of it? I never suspected. You are truly a wonder, and a very dear friend. Now when exactly is your birthday?

Affectionately,
Karen

For Conference Coordination

Dear Joel,

Thank you for doing such a perfect job in both orchestrating the entire three-day conference and working in all those thoughtful details so every single spouse and family member could have a custom-fit experience. I didn't initially think a dude ranch was a good choice, owning not a single set of spurs, but it was perfect. I've gotten a dozen enthusiastic calls requesting that we do it again next year.

Perhaps the bad news for you is that no one else will ever be able to fill your cowboy boots! You did an absolutely perfect job!

All the best,
Avery

For a Business Luncheon

Henry:

Thank you for orchestrating such a productive luncheon. The Back Room reservation was a stroke of genius. It allowed the privacy and quiet the Cooks team needed to listen to our proposal, discuss it in detail, and come to the decision to go with us as their project management team.

Well done, well done. And congratulations on this brand-new account. I'm looking forward to working with you and your whole group as we put in place this wonderful project.

Best,

Sam

(Also see ACCEPTANCE, page 269; APPRECIATION, page 71; ACKNOWLEDGMENT & CONFIRMATION, page 264; RESPONSE, page 257; and WEDDING & ENGAGEMENT CORRESPONDENCE, page 82.)

For an Interview

Dear Bea,

Thank you for the well-structured interview. Your planning, coordination, and interview techniques allowed me to both demonstrate my potential fit in terms of skills and expertise and also comprehensively assess what working with all the departments within Crackers is like.

I believe I would make a great fit on the marketing team, especially in contributing to long-range goals. Tom and I—it seemed in our interview segment—could work seamlessly together and challenge the best from each other.

Thank you for such a fine interview experience. I'll look forward to learning your list of finalists. I'm available for any follow-up questions you or other department heads may have.

Sincerely,
Jack

For a Funeral Bouquet

Dear Lynn and Lester,

Thank you for sending the beautiful arrangement of sweetheart roses to the mortuary for Mom's funeral. How thoughtful of you to select her favorite. I'm sure you remember her extensive trellis in the backyard from which she supplied the whole neighborhood with bouquets each season.

We'll all miss her and her rose garden, but what an appropriate and wonderful send-off. It meant a lot to David and me to have roses there.

Sincerely,
Susan and David

13 WEDDING & ENGAGEMENT CORRESPONDENCE

Engagement and wedding celebrations can be as varied as the people joining their lives. While many traditional rules have given way to expressions of individuality and creativity, it remains important that engagement and wedding communications reflect both the spirit of the occasion and your desire to have others join in the celebration. There will be many opportunities for both those being honored and those celebrating with them to express joy and good wishes in writing. Join in with a full heart.

DECIDE TO WRITE

- Decide how formal your wedding will be—casual, informal, semiformal, or formal. This will dictate the style, tone, choice of language, typeface, ink, printing method, paper stock, and color(s) that you will use for your correspondence.
- Determine the size of the wedding party and the number of guests to be invited.
- List the communications you'll be sending.
- Compute the total numbers of communications you'll send, then select a common paper stock, typeface(s), layout and design(s), and ink.
- Order some additional blank letter paper, note paper, and note cards for such things as inviting a friend to be in the wedding party and thanking the many and various people who will be helping you create your wedding.
- Consider the special situations of those on your list of friends, family, and associates. You may wish to send wedding announcements to some people you know won't attend, along with a personal note that indicates you wanted to include them in the celebration even though you know they won't be able to be at the celebration.

WEDDING COMMUNICATION TYPES

Thinking through your entire schedule of events very carefully—from announcing the engagement through sending out the thank-you notes for gifts and participation—will help you decide the types of communications you will need. Wedding consultants can help with many of your decisions, but first be sure to have your event and budget firmly in mind. Consider the following communications and select those you will use:

Sent by the Wedding Couple or Family
- ► Announcement to close family and friends of the upcoming wedding (informal, personal letters and notes)
- ► Notice to an ex-spouse, if appropriate (informal, personal letter or note)
- ► Announcements: newspaper and printed formal, or handwritten informal
- ► Introduction of bride and groom's families (personal letter by family members)
- ► Invitations to be wedding attendants and participants (personal letter or note)
- ► Save-the-date cards
- ► Wedding guest invitations
- ► Wedding announcements (printed and sent to those not attending)
- ► Reception or wedding dinner invitations (may be part of the wedding invitation)
- ► Confirmation of or request for items or services
- ► Wedding shower invitations
- ► Bachelor's party invitations
- ► Postponement or cancellation
- ► Wedding rehearsal invitations
- ► RSVP cards (included in the invitations, when used)
- ► Information on accommodations, maps, and activities
- ► Thank-you notes for gifts, assistance, special help, contributions
- ► Letter paper, note paper, and note cards for related wedding correspondence

Sent to the Wedding Couple and Family
- ► Congratulations notes
- ► Acceptance notes for wedding party participation
- ► Refusal notes, or notes declining invitation to participate in the wedding
- ► RSVPs to invitations (cards filled out, when included; or personal note RSVPing)

THINK ABOUT CONTENT

The busy days between an engagement announcement and a wedding include planning, printing or writing, and conveying much happy information. The following lists will help you with your pre- and post-wedding activities:

Engagement Communications
- **Informing the children.** When there are children involved, it's usually best for the marrying parent to first tell the children. The well-being of young children, of course, should be the first and foremost consideration. When the engaged couple has adult children, this may be done verbally, or with a written letter.
- **Informing close family and friends.** Even if you use the telephone to first make the announcement, it's still wonderful to send a written message. Order these letters so those who are dearest and nearest—parents, brothers and sisters, special aunts, grandmothers and grandfathers, close friends—are told first. You may want to include some brief information

about the couple: where each grew up; the college each attended; their degrees and career fields; when and where the couple met; where the couple plans to live; and when the wedding is to be (approximately, if the date has not been set).

- **Notifying an ex-spouse** can be done with a personal note or letter. (Legal restrictions may dictate how notification is carried out.) Where there's acrimony between divorced, childless people, the communication may best be made immediately after the ceremony.

- **Introduction of the bride and groom's families** may be done with a personal letter—traditionally the groom's family contacts the bride's family and the bride's family responds. The letters generally express delight and welcome the soon-to-be in-laws into the family. Today, when the parents live a great distance from each other, the introduction is sometimes first done in a telephone conversation or even a conference call where the couple introduces everyone. Sometimes further contact is made by email to arrange a meeting and carry out other arrangements.

- **Engagement announcements** can be made in many ways, from very informal to formal. A formal, printed engagement announcement is usually made by the parents, for example: "Mr. and Mrs. George Stomp of Maryville, Maryland, announce the engagement of their daughter, Diedre, to Bernard Dehm, son of Dr. and Mrs. Richard Dehm of Newcomb, Maine. A November wedding is planned." Older couples may make the announcement themselves, as may couples without close family members. Announcements, too, are often made public in newspapers and special publications.

- **A newspaper announcement of the engagement** will involve submitting information in the paper's prescribed form. This may be in writing (on any type of business stationery) or by email. Study the newspaper to determine the kind of information they will include, the preferred order, and whether they will use a photograph. Normally this will be (1) parents' names and place of residence(s) or hometowns; (2) complete names of the engaged couple; (3) colleges from which each graduated and/or current places of employment; and (4) date of wedding, or general plans.

- The **official engagement announcement**, which may include the formal introduction of the families, is often made at an engagement-announcement dinner or party hosted by the bride's parents, family, or friends. Sometimes the groom's family, when they live at a distance, will also host an engagement party or a party after the wedding to honor and introduce the bride to family and friends. The engagement announcement is traditionally made by the father of the bride, and a toast is made, whether or not the engagement is a surprise.

- Invitations to the **engagement-announcement dinner** or party may be informal or formal, handwritten or printed.

- **Invitations to wedding attendants and participants** are often made in person or by telephone, even by email; but it is also nice to write a personal letter or note expressing why the invitee is being asked to participate. (The same is true, of course, of the person sending a note of acceptance.)

- Be sure all basic information is included: what the total costs will be and who is paying for what. (Obviously, there may be a number of lengthy verbal discussions, but a handwritten note is a fine way to make this very clear.) It's very important to consider this carefully, of course, because such an invitation usually means a substantial expense for the invitee, and acknowledging this and allowing for a graceful way to decline are necessary.
- **Save-the-date cards** are used when a destination wedding is planned, or for a wedding planned for a particularly busy time of year. These will usually be sent 12 weeks or more before the wedding.

Wedding Communications

- **Bridal shower invitations** are usually sent to small, intimate groups of close friends and relatives who want to wish the bride well. Invitations are usually printed, or pre-printed fill-in-the-blanks note cards, with matching or coordinating envelopes. Sometimes inviting guests is done in person or by telephone, or, in the case of coworkers, by email. Be sure to inform guests if it's to be a surprise, if there's a theme (kitchen gifts, etc.), and/or if there will be gifts at all. Usually a close friend, bridal attendant, or relative sends the invitations and hosts the party.
- **Wedding guest invitations** reflect the style of wedding. For a small, informal wedding, you may choose to write a simple, informal invitation. Include complete information on a high-quality note card or fold-over note. This is best written in black or dark ink with a good pen. Be sure to include complete information, including to whom an RSVP should be directed. Begin writing your invitation with an informal phrase:

Theresa Trompe and Brendon Whittle invite you to celebrate their marriage. . . .

Joy Royce and James Beaver would be honored to have you share the joy of the marriage of their daughter . . .

Our joy will be more complete if you will share in the marriage of our daughter . . .

Sandra Spencer and Alex Bromm invite you to their wedding. . . .

Our daughter, Jennifer Rowe, will be married to Grunnar Hyatt, on Saturday. . . . They will speak their vows at . . . We invite you to join us to witness their vows, and be our guest at a reception that follows. . . .

- A **formal invitation** uses more formal language, is printed or engraved in a formal typeface, and uses high-quality card stock that is formal in both paper type and ink color. The invitation will have two envelopes, and the outer one should be hand-addressed—often lettered by a professional calligrapher. The inner envelope is not sealed and may be addressed to the invitees. Slipped into the inner envelope is the invitation, face up when the envelope is opened. A sheet of tissue or other decorative paper, traditionally to help preserve the engraving, may be placed in front of the invitation.
- There may be other enclosures as well: a pew card (for a large wedding), an invitation to a reception, admission cards for the service, maps, a listing of accommodations, and other

information about the area where the wedding is to be held. An RSVP card (required by the U.S. Postal Service to be at least 5 by 3½ inches) with its own addressed and stamped envelope will also be included. An at-home card that gives the couple's home address may also be included. The invitation text is written in the first person, and should include the formal names of parents, if they are extending the invitation; the formal names of each of the wedding couple; date, time, and place; and reception, if any. The invitation should include an expression of the couple's wish for the invitees' attendance. Formal or semiformal wording includes the phrase "request the honour [honor] of your presence."

> ▸ The full date, including the year, is always used in the wedding announcement.
> ▸ **Words spelled out.** On the wedding invitations, spell out the year: "two thousand and eleven." Also spell out the date—"Saturday, the eleventh of June" or "the twenty-fifth of July"—and the time—"at three o'clock" or "at half after two." Names should be spelled out in full. If someone prefers not to use his or her full middle name, omit it altogether.
> ▸ **Numerals.** Addresses with more than one number are expressed in numerals—"345 East Washington Street"—while single numbers are written out—"Number two Chester Lane."
> ▸ **Abbreviations.** Periods may be used after Mr., Mrs., and Ms. to abbreviate; but write out in full titles such as Doctor, and military ranks such as Colonel. (See Appendix, page 416, for a listing of titles.)
> ▸ **Punctuation.** Use commas only when phrases on a single line require them: "Saturday, the tenth of June."
> ▸ Include the proper phrasing for special religious wedding ceremonies; for example, when a Roman Catholic mass is part of the ceremony, include the phrase "and your participation in the offering of the Nuptial Mass" on a line below the groom's name.
> ▸ When you send an invitation to only the wedding service, do not include an RSVP.
> ▸ When a reception invitation is included, request an RSVP.

• **Reception or wedding dinner invitations** may be part of the wedding invitation, and may simply state, "and afterward at a reception at the College Club . . . ," or may be a separate invitation inserted in the wedding invitation. An invitation to a separate reception may be worded, "Mr. and Mrs. Donald Stikes request the pleasure of your company at the wedding reception for their daughter Georgia Rose and Mr. Elmer Quest . . ." When only a small group will be invited to the wedding, invitations may be given by telephone or in person, or with a ceremony card. It may be worded, "The honor of your presence is requested at the marriage ceremony . . ." It is mailed with the invitation to the reception. If the invitation is to the reception only, less formal wording may be used: "request the pleasure of your company . . ."

• **Wedding rehearsal party invitations** are the traditional territory of the groom's family, although many couples host this event themselves. Sometimes the rehearsal party is hosted by someone else. This event need not be a dinner, but may be a brunch after a morning rehearsal, or a light buffet after an afternoon rehearsal.

- The invitations should be sent by those hosting the event. Wedding participants and close family members, and their spouses or fiancés/fiancées, are usually invited. Others who should be invited are the officiant and spouse, and any children in the wedding party and their parents. Out-of-town friends and relatives who've arrived for the wedding are often invited to attend, but it is certainly not expected. The guest list may also include a few other select relatives and close friends, but too many guests may detract from this intimate and special occasion for the wedding party.

- The invitations may be handwritten, printed, or engraved, and should include time, place, and information about dress that is appropriate. Include a request for RSVPs, and give name, telephone number, and/or other contact information.

- **Bachelor's/bachelorette's party invitations** are usually informal, and may even be made by telephone and/or email. These events may be as simple as an evening get-together, or as elaborate as a long weekend of celebration for the wedding attendants and a few close friends. Sometimes the bachelor's party is arranged by the best man and the bachelorette party by the maid of honor.

- **Wedding announcements for the newspaper or other publications** have different requirements and rules for publication, so check early with the publications in which you want to publish your news. Often the information must be submitted several weeks before the wedding so it can appear immediately after the ceremony. Follow the newspaper's format, but check to be sure the following information is included: the full names of the bride and groom; date, time and place of the wedding; name of the clergy or officiant presiding over the ceremony; names of the members of the wedding party, including their relationship to the couple, if related; names, hometowns, and occupations or achievements of the parents of the couple (occasionally even grandparents and/or distinguished other relatives are included); and degrees and other titles or accomplishments of the couple. Descriptions of the wedding, including such items as flowers, the bride's dress, the attendants' attire, music, special ceremony notes, and the place of the reception, may be included. The general or specific address of the couple may also be included.

Other Communications

- **Thank-you notes for gifts and good wishes** are usually sent on note cards created from the same paper as your wedding invitations. Send your notes no later than three months after the wedding. Also send a personal note to each person who has sent special good wishes in lieu of a gift. Though once the responsibility of the bride, writing thank-yous is now shared by both the bride and groom. If gifts are received before the wedding, thank-you notes may be written then, though it is nicer to include information about how the gift is being used. However, a telephone call confirming the gift has been delivered or sending a printed acknowledgment that the gift arrived is appropriate.

In your thank-you note, name the gift, and make the connection between it and you, whenever possible. You may be able to tell the gift giver how you have used or will use it, and some nice detail about the gift and your appreciation for it.

- **Confirmation letters** are needed to document arrangements for engagement announcement dinners, rehearsal dinner, and other events (such as a bridal shower at a restaurant) as well as wedding arrangements: your reservation of a church, chapel, or temple; organist, instrumentalists, or soloist; restaurant; photographer and/or videographer; bakery; caterer; and any other arrangements specific to your wedding. In all correspondence, be specific and include all the details of the agreement. Always confirm all the conditions and the charges involved.
- **Congratulations cards** or notes may be sent to family members, as well as the couple, after the engagement announcement and/or after the wedding.
- **Broken engagement or wedding postponement announcements** aren't required if no formal announcement was made. If personal letters or notes were sent out in announcing the engagement, use the same means to briefly inform the same people of the change. No explanation is needed.

ELIMINATE WRONG MESSAGES

- While email responses are fine for emailed congratulations, they should not be used for responses to gifts or acts of kindness or service.
- Don't write collective thank-you notes to co-hosts of a shower or other special events. Each person deserves an individual note of thanks.
- Keep a detailed list of all those who helped in some way, including those who offered hospitality to out-of-town guests, the clergy who performed the ceremony, the organist, the soloist, and others. Your list will help eliminate the possibility that someone is overlooked when you write your thank-you notes.
- Money gifts are usually very welcome. Don't forget to include how you plan to use the money in your thank-you note.
- Don't ask where a gift may be returned if an unwanted or duplicate gift is received.
- Creating a web page for your wedding with a general welcome and note of general thanks is fine, but it's not a substitute for sending individual, handwritten notes of thanks.
- Avoid a one-size-fits-all approach when writing thank-you notes. Make each note personal and sincere.

SELECT A FORMAT

- Many options are now available for wedding stationery. Make your selections with the complete family of engagement and wedding communications in mind. Coordinating these pieces can go as far as being consistent with the colors and formality of the wedding itself.
- Be sure to select a typeface, paper stock, and ink color that can be easily read, and that will work well for all the pieces you will send. Remember that some colors (such as blue) don't copy well, if you will need to make copies of any piece.

SELECT STRONG WORDS

celebrate	ceremony	company	exchange
favour (or favor)	formal	happiness	honour (or honor)
informal	join	joy	keep
nuptials	observe	pleasure	presence
reception	rejoice	request	save
share	union	vows	wishes

EDIT, EDIT, EDIT

Be sure to proof and proof again each piece of your printed wedding correspondence before printing. (It's helpful to have more than one person proofread.) Errors result in costly reprinting and much lost time.

Semiformal Wedding Invitation

[Printed, though invitees' names may be handwritten in provided blanks]

Doctor and Mrs. George Foremost
request the honour of the presence of
Mr. and Mrs. Nigel Holmes
at the marriage of their daughter
Melody Renee
to
Mr. Cecil Strong
Saturday, the tenth of June
two thousand and eleven
at half after four o'clock
First Presbyterian Church
Indianapolis, Indiana

Reception Card

[Printed and enclosed in wedding invitation]

Reception
immediately following the ceremony
[or at four o'clock]
University Club
342 Central Avenue
Riverside, New York

The favor of a reply is requested [or RSVP].

Formal Engraved Invitation from the Bride's Parents

Mr. and Mrs. Worthington James
request the honour of your presence
at the marriage of their daughter
Judith Anne
to
Mr. Kirk Von Russell
Saturday, the ninth of February
two thousand and eleven
at half after the hour of three o'clock
Second Baptist Church
Summerfield, Ohio

Informal Invitation to a Small Wedding

[Printed or handwritten]

Dear Mr. and Mrs. James Royce,

Richard Cleft and I will be married on
June eleventh at three o'clock
at the University Club.
We do hope that you will join us for the
ceremony and for a reception immediately
afterward.

With love,
Jennifer Fox

Ceremony Card

[Printed and enclosed in the envelope with the reception invitation; used when the ceremony list of invitees is shorter than the list of invitees to the reception, but too long for handwritten invitations.]

The honour of your presence
is requested at the marriage ceremony
Saturday, the seventh of December
at seven o'clock
Redford Congregational Church

Informal Invitation from the Couple for a Home Wedding and Reception

[Printed or handwritten]

Esther Spoon and Victor Davidson
hope that you will join them in celebration
for their wedding and reception brunch
Saturday, June twenty-seventh
at half past twelve o'clock
220 East Walker Street
Spokane

RSVP

Acceptance to Be a Bridesmaid

Jasmine,

What joy! Yes, I'm delighted to accept your invitation. I shall be honored to serve as a bridesmaid at your wedding. I'll wait for your note with all the details, then I'll be in touch. What a happy day June 18 will be.

Best wishes,

Paula

Invitation to Be Matron of Honor

Ginny,

I know we agreed as kids that we would be in each other's weddings, and no one else can really fill your sisterly role as my matron of honor. But I also know that your college expenses have been extremely high, and that Rob's unemployment has caused a huge strain on your finances. I estimate that the dress and accessories will total about $400, and then there's transportation across the country, time away from your job, babysitting, etc. Airfare roundtrip will be about $1,500 if no special rates are available. Mom and Dad said they could underwrite $500 of the expenses, and I can come up with $250, but that still leaves a huge sum of well over $1,000.

I also realize May 15 is undoubtedly finals time for you, but we couldn't set any other date because of Jared's overseas assignment.

I won't hold you to your promise, Sis. I'll completely understand if you must decline. In fact, I propose a first anniversary dinner together instead. Jared and I will come to San Francisco, and we can make it a very special occasion. What do you think?

Sisters forever,
Laura

Confirmation of Matron of Honor Acceptance

Chelsea,

I'm so delighted you'll be my matron of honor. I really can't imagine walking down the aisle and not seeing you ahead of me as you have been all my life, Big Sister. You've made my joy complete with your acceptance!

Your little sis,
Melody

Letter to the Groom's Ex-Spouse

Tina:

I want you to hear this first directly from me: Ingrid and I have decided to marry. I know you may have concerns about how this will affect the children, shared custody arrangements, and schedules, so I'd like for the three of us to sit down and try to amicably work this out in the best possible manner for the kids. We suggest a Saturday meeting in two weeks at Friskies Cafe. Will 10:30 a.m. work for you?

We haven't made any public announcement, but we will tell the children just before the three of us meet, letting them know that we will all work very hard to be sure they will have all their needs met.

Although our differences are many at this point, and our relationship is long fractured, we share a huge interest in the welfare of three little people, and I believe for their sakes we can commit to put aside all our personal conflicts and structure the best future possible for them.

Please let Ingrid and me know if you will be able to meet as suggested. If not, please suggest a workable time and place.

Adam

Post-Wedding Letter to the Bride

Dallas,

Yours is only the second wedding I've ever attended where the bride and groom sang their wedding vows. It was truly angelic, and brought tears to my eyes. I now appreciate more fully what an absolutely perfect fit Egan is for your family. When your mother told me how you two are a match made in heaven, she didn't mention you were a heavenly duet; but now that I've heard it for myself I know that it's true.

What a bright and glorious future lies in store for your musical careers together. How happy I am for you, and how I look forward to embracing you as a couple.

With love always,

Aunt Erma

Note to the Bride's Ex-Spouse

Isaiah:

I wanted to let you know that on Saturday I married Jeremy Stone. I will now be legally Stephanie Stone, and will reside at 345 Adams, Berkeley, California. Please send any communications to this address.

Stephanie

Informal Note of a Broken Engagement

Pam,

I'm so sorry to have to tell you that Richard and I have broken our engagement. I am, therefore, returning the lovely linen tablecloth and napkins you were so thoughtful to send us.

Love,
Eleanor

Canceled Engagement

[Printed]

Mr. and Mrs. Justin Overton-Moore announce that the marriage of their daughter, Rachel, to Stephen Wells, will not take place.

Informal Wedding Rehearsal Invitation

Dear Janet and Jack,

David and I are hosting a rehearsal dinner for Jennifer and Rafe, Saturday, July 7, at 7:00 p.m. at Long Putts Country Club. We hope you will be able to join us.

We look forward to hearing that you will be able to make it.

Sincerely,
Deanna and David

Personal Note to a Special Relative

Dearest Aunt Susan,

I'm delighted to tell you that Booker and I will be getting married sometime in the spring. No date as yet, since he only asked me Saturday, on the second anniversary of our meeting, at a little gathering at Gotsford Park where our dogs were responsible for introducing us. Funny story: we finally introduced ourselves two years ago in this San Francisco dog park after our dogs, Molly (my Airedale) and Ace (his "kennel mix" happy dog), had become great romping friends. Well, our dogs, and those of all our friends were there to surprise me on Saturday morning at six! (Does this tell you something about the wonderful character Booker is?)

I'm ecstatic! Many, many more details over a lifetime of happy dog tales to come!

Your niece,
Madison

Save the Date to Close Family and Friends

To Our Dearest Family and Friends,

Yes, dear ones, we are finally getting married. Our happy day will be September eighth, and it is with full and hopeful hearts that we'd like to ask you to save the date to be present with us and help us make our public declaration of love and commitment complete by your presence.

A formal invitation and all the details will follow.

Sarah and Ben

(Also see ANNOUNCEMENT, page 18; ACKNOWLEDGMENT & CONFIRMATION, page 264; CONGRATULATIONS, page 28; INVITATION, page 63; REFUSAL, page 274; and THANK-YOU, page 75.)

Letter to Parents of the Bride

Alice and Bruce,

What a wonderful wedding service you orchestrated for your beautiful Kerry. I've never witnessed vows so rich in meaning as those exchanged by Kerry and Kendal.

Never has a bride looked more radiant, or gorgeous. Now I certainly appreciate what you have been going through all these months. Knowing you these twenty years, I appreciate that you are a perfectionist, but on the occasion of your daughter's wedding, you succeeded at the highest level. Not one tiny detail was overlooked. I couldn't believe that every table for the sit-down dinner for the entire 300 guests was festooned with scallops of tiny rose buds, and that each table had a pedestal of the loveliest arrangement of roses and ivy I've ever seen.

My, this wedding was a once-in-a-lifetime royal event, and one Newton and I will never forget.

We look forward to having you and the newlyweds over for a dinner party after they settle in. We'll be so happy to see the wedding photos, and hear all the behind-the-scenes stories.

Affectionately,

Newton and Adelle

Wedding Gift Thank-You Note

Janette and Derrick,

We love the waffle maker and have, in three mornings, had buttermilk, walnut, and golden waffles. How did you possibly know that the color is spectacular in our kitchen? Here's Rick on his morning operating the maker. See what a great match it is with the toaster, and even the wallpaper. Thank you both so much. We'll think of you with every waffle. Your thoughtfulness, gift, card, and all your best wishes touched our hearts. Stomachs too!

Sophie and Ricardo

14 PERSONAL LETTER

A personal letter is a wonderful way to spread your good news, offer comfort and solace, pass on information, create a special bond, and share a mutual sense of belonging. The time-honored method of sending messages—penned, addressed, stamped, and sent through the mail—has been a staple of our civilized society.

We cherish those penned personal letters, and marvel at those collections that have been kept over time, tied with a silk ribbon, and passed from generation to generation. Stored in lined and scented boxes, preserved in a climate-controlled atmosphere under glass, or even stuffed into a shoebox, these missives are very special. They seem infused with the essence of the person, him or herself. They offer the power to bind families and friendships together—perhaps in great part because they offer us a path to discovering who we are. They help define us.

There will always be a place for your personally penned, heartfelt message sent to a friend or family member. It will be treasured because it contains something of yourself in your own penned words.

DECIDE TO WRITE

When your message is very personal or you want to create a special connection to the person you are writing to, the best choice is a personal handwritten letter.

The following are examples of types of personal letters you may wish to write:

- Happy-news letters sent for birthdays, anniversaries, graduations, life achievements, and all sorts of occasions.
- Correspondence that keeps you in touch with friends and relatives.
- Letters of introduction, initiating a relationship, or observing the etiquette of introduction may have the character of a personal letter. An example of this is the traditional use of these letters between the parents of an engaged couple.
- Personal letters of appreciation following a death in the family or sent in response to acts of kindness, cards, and other deeds.

THINK ABOUT CONTENT

- Construct a light, humorous, and positive opening, or begin with a point of mutual interest.
- Get to the point of your letter, keeping the tone conversational.

- Think in terms of entertaining and storytelling.
- Include newsy bits and topics of interest to the reader, such as shared memories.
- Offer your opinions and ideas, but do it in an open, convivial manner.
- Keep the conversation going by asking your reader questions about topics of mutual interest. (But don't turn it into a questionnaire, and be sure not to include questions that could be interpreted as overstepping the bounds of privacy.)
- Include a definite invitation or statement that requests a response or further contact.
- Close with a warm greeting of affection and anticipation of hearing from or seeing the person to whom you're writing.

ELIMINATE WRONG MESSAGES

- Don't write in a time crunch or you're likely to produce a letter that sounds terse and incomplete.
- Starting with an apology or question for the reader sets the wrong tone.
- Don't just respond to questions asked in your reader's last letter; introduce news and stories of interest to the recipient. Eliminate negativity.
- Avoid conflicts, misunderstandings, and regrets by reflecting on your letter after you've written it and proofreading it thoroughly before you mail it.

TIPS THAT WILL HELP

- Develop a personal letter writing habit to create special connections with relatives and friends. Establish a place and time for writing personal letters so it becomes an enjoyable part of your schedule rather than a chore. Use a laptop letter-writing desk or a special, equipped desk, and choose a day and time that are just for writing letters. This will allow you to write in a comfortable, regular, and organized way.
- Keep a well-stocked inventory of personal stationery, note cards, postcards, and perhaps even something like the tools to create your own photo postcards from photographs you take yourself.
- Don't wait too long between writing letters. This can become a barrier to writing.
- Review the last letter from your friend or relative, and be sure to respond to the questions asked and comment on the ideas contained in it.
- Develop a "voice" or storytelling quality in your letter writing by including rich details that help draw verbal pictures.
- Make it a habit to collect things you know friends and relatives will enjoy. Keep them in your laptop desk or another assigned place. It's a wonderful surprise to open a personal letter and find something special—canceled stamps for a stamp collector, a special bookmark for a bibliophile, a newspaper clipping containing information of interest, art or school work from a child in the family to a grandparent or other relative, a photograph taken the last time you were together. Your reader will appreciate your thoughtfulness.

- The weather report can be obtained by anyone who tunes in to the media. If you include weather news, tell a story about it, how the weather affected you, or someone or something of mutual interest.
- If you include something of a sensitive or emotional nature in your letter, leave it on the desk for a day or at least a few hours. Reread it when you can do so objectively, and try to think like your intended reader. Even read it aloud to hear how it sounds. Giving your personal letter this test will help ensure that you don't send something you will later regret.

CONSIDER SPECIAL SITUATIONS

- Establishing a letter-writing habit with a small child can create a very special bond. Think of Beatrix Potter's wonderful stories and the sketches she drew and included with her notes to her little friends. You don't need to be an artist to include some drawings to illustrate your stories. Stories that include the child you're writing to are especially welcome. Ask questions the child will want to answer. Even enclose a self-addressed, stamped envelope to encourage a reply.
- Parents may teach children early to write letters, first by encouraging them to dictate very short ones while you record the words. A thank-you note is a wonderful place to start; and the child may write on the note or draw a picture. When a child is still small, establish a place and supplies for the child's own letter writing.
- The need for empathy can't be overstated. Write with your reader in mind. This will help you to avoid writing something offensive or something that can be misunderstood. Still, even though you take reasonable precautions, misunderstandings can occur. If you don't receive a reply to your letter after several weeks, send a short note or letter asking lightly or humorously, "Was it something I said?" or "Your letter has most certainly gone astray."
- Writing letters and even short notes to family members in your household can be very special: a letter explaining calmly how you feel about a conflict; a love note tucked into the suitcase as a spouse is leaving on a trip; or an "I love you" tucked under a pillow. For a child who's apprehensive about an afternoon test, a short note of "You'll do great" in his or her lunchbox will be very meaningful.
- When people are away from home—friends and relatives on extended business assignments, people serving in the armed services stationed overseas, or children attending summer camp—mail takes on added importance. Use your powers of empathy. Avoid emotionally charged statements or comments that may unduly create homesickness or sadness. Keep it thoughtful and cheerful.
- Sensitivity is needed, too, in writing a letter to someone who is suffering an extended illness, or who's received an unfavorable diagnosis and/or prognosis. If you can easily learn from someone very close to the patient how he or she is feeling emotionally as well as physically, this can guide you in writing. When you don't know, it's better to simply state you were sorry to hear the news, you care, and you want to offer help. (This should not be an empty offer. Mention something you've learned that may be helpful, and suggest a way you

would carry it out. Also, outline how you'll follow up to learn the patient's wishes.) When possible, include something positive about the person, perhaps his or her accomplishments, character, importance to others, contributions to a cause, or valued qualities. End on as positive a note as possible.

- Personal letters are legal documents when they contain items that would normally be included in a will or document concerning medical or end-of-life care. For example, stating that you want your niece to have your china may legally entitle her to it. The same is true in authorizing such things as medical care for yourself, or a dependent child or adult. Use a personal letter to make known your wishes about medical care of a dependent person. If a child is being cared for while you are out of town, for example, you may wish to write a personal letter stating, "I hereby authorize [caregiver's name] to act on my behalf in the case of a medical emergency for the welfare of my daughter/son [child's name] during my absence." Sign the letter, stating your relationship as parent. If you are the legal guardian for an elderly relative who would not want his or her life prolonged in the event of natural death (loss of heartbeat or breathing), a letter stating such and including the order "Do not resuscitate" should be written and signed by you, with the notation "legal guardian." Check with local legal counsel to ensure the proper procedure in your area.

SELECT A FORMAT

- Develop your own signature style of personal letters and notes.
- Select a family of coordinating stationery and note cards to create visual continuity.
- While you'll use a slightly more formal presentation and language in a personal letter of introduction to potential new in-laws, for example, use language that sounds conversational.

WRITE STRONG SENTENCES

It was wonderful getting to visit with you today, and learning all about the new puppy.

I've just read a wonderful book that I believe you'll enjoy.

I saw a fascinating special on the medical channel last night that gave information I believe you'll want to know about.

Here's the recipe I used for that soup you liked.

How wonderful to open the mailbox and find that ivory envelope with your handwriting on it.

It's a ritual here: we talk about you at breakfast, lunch, and dinner.

We're sure you must be totally moved in and unpacked at this point and ready to start your new East Coast life.

I'm sending special loving thoughts to you because I know that your procedure is day after tomorrow.

I know how tough it is to be recuperating from a loss of mobility, and I thought I'd send on a few ideas I'd love to have your input on.

Here's something I know you're dying to know.

BUILD EFFECTIVE PARAGRAPHS

It's a great day of rejoicing at this house! Daisy returned from her military tour of duty on Saturday. We spend every minute we can just looking at her and marveling that we have her back with us, safe and sound.

Let me tell you what I've learned about the workshop series and answer your question: is it worth the investment of time and money? If you are weak in the areas of real estate law you need to know, I'd say the course is definitely worthwhile.

This year's reunion is one you won't want to miss. As of today, I have yeses from all the original "Smarties." Here's the lineup so far . . .

I've started a list of items our homeless families need. Next to the list are the items we have collected so far. Please check your closets and storage areas, see what you have that you can spare, and give me a call.

I've been away from home now for sixteen days, five hours, and nine minutes, but who's counting? No one is calling "Mommie, where's my red sweater?" "Mom, he's hitting me," or "Who's got my baseball glove?" Why do I miss those questions so?

Here's my fish report, Dad, just in case you forgot you challenged me to surpass the family record set by you when you and Gramps went to Watchitaw: big-mouth bass, 13; walleyes, 17; and northern pike, 28. I'm thinking someone (that would be you) is going to owe someone (that would be me) a new fishing rod when someone (me) gets home. There are seven days left of fishing. Can you imagine what kind of totals someone (me) will have by then?

EDIT, EDIT, EDIT

Don't send your letter without rereading it to make sure you've eliminated all errors of spelling, grammar, clarity, or omission. To many of those you'll write, a penned and inserted correction here or there isn't critical, but you'll still want your letter to have a neat and polished look.

Sharing Ideas for a Fundraiser

Dear Lizzie,

Thank you for volunteering to help with this year's fundraiser. I find that I'm not bubbling with fresh ideas, as I'd hoped. The only things that come quickly to mind are using the old standbys of donated items to be auctioned off in a silent auction before the gourmet dinner, and asking a couple dozen celebs to donate a lottery "lunch with" to the highest bidder. Or, we could sell raffle tickets and select winners by drawing.

You are my secret winning-ideas weapon, so if you'd give these a spin in that marvelous ideas section of your super brain and let me know what you think, I'd greatly appreciate it. I know your ingenuity has no bounds, and I can hardly wait to hear what you come up with.

I'll need to have something together to present to the committee by the 15th. How about a lunch next week to brainstorm?

As always,
JoBeth

Resolving a Family Rift

Dear Jody,

I have a matter of fractured family relations I believe we may be able to resolve, and I've decided the best way to handle it is for me to write to you and ask for your input and cooperation. Here it is. As you know, my parents have recently been estranged from your parents, and I feel sure that this break in the wonderful relationship they enjoyed for 30 years may be as much a mystery to you and your parents as it was to me until last week.

Though this may be difficult to understand, my parents are also estranged from Uncle Arnie and Aunt Sue, and for the very same reason. It seems that during a series of family get-togethers last year, both your parents and Uncle Arnie and Aunt Sue asked numerous times about my brother, Sam. Jody, this is a very painful situation for my parents because Sam has separated himself from our family, and we hear nothing from him.

The last time this happened, Mom says, all four relatives asked repeatedly about Sam and pressed my parents for details about why we don't hear from him. This questioning, unfortunately, resulted in my dad feeling that your parents as well as Uncle Arnie and Aunt Sue had overstepped their bounds, or were deliberately trying to be hurtful and make him and my mother feel bad.

I've told my parents that I'm sure the questions were simply intended to demonstrate interest and concern. Their response is that I wasn't there, didn't hear them, and, therefore, don't know (which, of course, is true).

Here's my suggestion: If you're willing, would you please talk to your parents—I'm also writing to Aunt Sue and Uncle Arnie—and ask them to write to my parents. If they feel they can, I'd suggest that they simply explain they didn't intend to make my parents feel bad and they won't ever bring this painful subject up again.

Hopefully this will allow my parents to reestablish their treasured connection with yours, and with Aunt Sue and Uncle Arnie. I hope I'm not labeled a meddler here—I did tell Mom and Dad I was going to write—but I just don't want this family rift to continue.

Thank you, Jody. Please do contact me if you have any further suggestions or questions. I look forward to all of us getting together again in July for the Albert reunion—once again one big, happy family—with our fathers sharing fishing and hunting stories, and our moms reminiscing about their lives as sisters in the big city.

With love,
Susan

Response to Class Reunion Invitation

Dear Sue Ellen,

What a delightful surprise to see your announcement about a class reunion ten years after you were elected class reunion secretary by 249 rosy-cheeked, naive, 18-year-olds. Ten years ago on that day before high school graduation, I doubt I had any interest in a reunion in the "distant" future. But a reunion certainly appeals to me now, so here's my eager "yes" with my reservation and check.

I look forward to hearing all about your outstanding college career, and your soaring music career. I applaud your idea about sharing news before the reunion on the website, and I will do that. Maybe the old "In Tunes" could even perform that number we did for the spring concert of our senior year. What do you think? Count me in on that, too.

All the best,
Mary Dale

Welcome to the Minor League

Dear Randy,

Your mom is busting at the seams with pride at the announcement of your arrival to the minor league. We're all hopeful, of course, that you'll be the first in this family to wear the insignia of a major league team on your uniform. I know you've heard the stories (until you can recite them in your sleep), but I don't think anyone has shown you a picture of Uncle Will when he was in the minors back in 1933. In fact, I don't think anyone knew this picture existed. I just found it in the library with several stories about the team. I'm sending copies of them along too.

I need to point out that I was the first talent scout to realize your potential at first base. Remember you were always my first pick when we played those softball games at the family reunions!

We'll be glued to our TV and newspaper waiting for news that you're being sent up. Actually, I don't think we need worry about missing the announcement. Your mom just wouldn't let that happen.

Congratulations! We're all on your team, Kid.

Love,
Aunt Bea

Information You Requested

Dear Anna,

Here's my business card as you requested. It was a pleasure meeting you at the Bears' reception. Cary Regan is the senior editor to whom you would submit a query on the topic you mentioned. She's in charge of the lifestyle area, and querying her by email is fine. I've worked with her and find her to be a skilled and able editor.

If you'd like a better idea of what The Simpsons is looking for in new features, take a look at their editorial calendar at www.simpsons.com.

Best,
Ginger

Surgery Update

Dear Family and Friends:

Thank you all for your wonderful cards, emails, telephone calls, and other expressions of care and concern. I'll use this copied note until I get the opportunity to sit down and write each of you individually.

Jack did get through the surgery fine, and we will now wait for the post-surgery test results to learn if the cancer has all been removed.

Yesterday, as you can imagine, was not one of our better days. While Jack felt very ill, the biggest weight on us was the waiting to learn if and when the surgery would take place.

There isn't any more news at this minute, but I'll send it as soon as we receive it. I've created an email list, and I'll send out emails of update as news becomes available.

Do keep your messages coming. Jack is cheered and encouraged by your care and concern.

All the best,

Jenna (jenna@email.com)

(Also see APPRECIATION, page 71; SYMPATHY & CONDOLENCE, page 44; CONGRATULATIONS, page 28; INVITATION, page 63; and THANK-YOU, page 75.)

15 | LOVE LETTER

Is there any thought more delicious or closer to the heart than the one that anticipates receiving a love letter from that very special someone? It makes the heart skip a beat, the pulse quicken, and the sun shine just a little bit brighter in the sky. It has that extra special something a voice message, or even an email message, can't deliver—tangible evidence of love you can hold close, reread, examine again and again, and keep—all written in the telling penmanship of that very special person.

Handwritten love letters will never lose their magic.

Content is, of course, everything. And to make your letter express what's in your heart you'll want it to have a single focus—the person to whom you are writing. Either directly, or reflectively, you'll want your letter to feature him (or her)—his kindness, his bravery, his good looks, his eloquence. Secondarily, you'll want to express your feelings for him, and your hope for your future life together.

DECIDE TO WRITE

- Start by focusing on the person. The *who, what, why, when*, and *how* aspects of this person you love can get you launched: who is he; which of his attributes do you admire, and why? You may express some things reflectively—in terms of how your loved one makes you feel, what you particularly love about him, what attracted you to him.
- Jot down some words and phrases in a notebook. Keeping a love letter notebook is a great idea. You'll review it over and over again.
- Look for inspiration and beauty of expression in the poems of the great poets, or the words of great writers: Elizabeth Barrett Browning, Lord Byron, Henry Wadsworth Longfellow, William Shakespeare, or the Bible. Sources are everywhere. Even some of the world's great leaders have written some wonderful love letters. Check those written by John and Abigail Adams, Winston and Clementine Churchill. The list is long and the reading is inspiring. It's always appropriate to share a verse and credit the source. This could begin a beautiful practice between you and your love.
- Consider using both comparisons and contrasts—metaphors and similes—to express yourself. A simile uses two unlike words connected by *as* or *like* to make comparisons: "Your smile is like sunshine;" "Your voice is like a Harley Davidson purr;" "soft as goose down;" "subtle as a whisper;" "sweet as violets." A metaphor is a word or phrase that usually means one thing, but is used to mean something else: "You have brought a laser beam of light into

my coal mine soul;" "You are thermal heat to my iceberg heart." Dreaming up your own—
maybe from something the two of you have already shared—will make them all the more
delightful and special.

THINK ABOUT CONTENT

- Start with a term of endearment that sets the tone; probably something only you use for the
  person you love: "My Dearest Girl . . . ," "Sweetheart . . . ," "Baby Doll . . . ," "Bear . . ."
- Getting started may seem hard until you think that your love letter can begin just like any
  conversation the two of you have; or begin where your last conversation ended: "To continue what I was saying . . ." Or, take a stream of consciousness approach: "Arriving at the
  library, I am immediately swamped with the memory of our . . ."
- Shared memories are good; future plans are good, too. Including some of both helps to
  build the love bond between you.
- You may want to explore some of the traditional territory of love letters: How do you feel
  about being in love with him? When and where did you first realize that this person was
  your perfect soul mate? What little habits or foibles does your loved one have that you
  adore? What about your lover touches you deeply? When, how and why do you miss her?
  What do you imagine she is doing at the moment you are writing? What makes you think
  about him? Why and how do you admire her? This is the stuff of wonderful love letters. Be
  specific and detailed.
- Reflecting, expanding, and sharing ideas and opinions that have come up during your con-
  versations is a wonderful thing to include. This should be an exercise in discovery for both
  of you, a way to come to fully know and understand each other.
- In an interview, Joan Didion, in discussing her book, *The Year of Magical Thinking,* said
  that she needed to write something out to determine how she felt. You will find the practice of writing a love letter a wonderful process of self-discovery. For this reason alone, it is a
  wonderful art.
- Include repeated phrases and special words that belong to the exchanges between you—
  couple code. And use bits that you continue to build on in each letter you write: "How do I
  love you? Oh, yes, here's one more way . . . "
- Write in the flow. Consider what you write first as a rough draft, so do it in your love letter
  notebook. Once you start, continue until you feel you've come to the end of what you want
  to express. Don't stop to proofread or edit; just let the flow carry you along until you've
  expressed what's in your heart.
- Remember to make your letter conversational in tone. You'll want it to sound like you naturally speak—only better. Test this by reading aloud what you've written. Is that you?
- Go back over what you've written and edit, revise, maybe even rewrite. You'll want to make
  sure you've varied the sentence structure, the intensity, and even the tone to give your letter
  added life and interest. You may even want to add a little self-deprecating humor to enliven
  your prose.

- When you are satisfied, write what you've written in your final draft—the love letter.
- Give your letter a little bit of breathing time. What may seem brilliant tonight may not seem quite as wonderful in the morning. Reread your letter after a break just to make sure it says what you want it to say, how you want to say it.

ELIMINATE WRONG MESSAGES

- Humor is difficult, even between lovers. Make sure any attempts in your letter are consistent with humor you both enjoy; and stay away from anything that can be interpreted by your loved one as poking fun at him. Having it written down gives it more weight, and while it may be taken lightly in a verbal exchange it may not in written form.
- Maybe this shouldn't need to be said, but don't compare him (or her) to a former lover. This is poison to the tree of love. The same should be said of trying to promote jealousy. It can seem to bear the fruit of increasing your lover's interest, but it's not a fruit that nourishes a loving and long-lasting relationship.
- Love notes are very nice and may be as brief as three words—*I love you*—written on a post-it and stuck to the bathroom mirror; but love letters are best served long and full. This is one time when writing long is the best course.
- Never include something that would reflect poorly on you should it be read aloud in a public setting. Even love letters do find their way into unintended hands, and public places.
- Avoid those subjects that need negotiation. It's fine to start a discussion by introducing an idea in your letter, but be sure it gets discussed in a timely fashion to avoid misunderstandings or the development of cracks in your relationship fault lines.
- Do not commit your love messages to email. Not only does it seriously subtract from the art, charm, and beauty of this lovely missive called the love letter, it's important to remember that email is not a private forum, and many people have found themselves in emailed love-message difficulty.

CONSIDER SPECIAL SITUATIONS

- With the advent of matching and dating internet services, extra precautions need to be taken in the exchange of preliminary message writing, which usually takes place—at least for a while—through email. Proceed very slowly here. This is an exceptionally good time to cover broad areas of interest, and explore ideas, values, and views you may share—or not. Rushing from a "match," which means that you have been computer-selected as having similar interests and maybe some shared values, to writing love letters may rob you of all that adventure of getting to know each other. And writing love messages to someone you don't know very well (or know well enough) can have all sorts of undesirable consequences.

- The same precaution applies to writing that first declaration-of-love letter. This was traditionally the territory of men, but now women may be equal players in this game of risk. You will want to be quite certain that the one you love feels the same if you are going to avoid being tossed into the pit of rejection.
- There are many occasions when increasing the circle of love by writing special, loving letters is appropriate for others in your life: a very special letter filled with loving thoughts and shared memories to a small niece or granddaughter or grandson on Valentine's Day, or on special days of significance, will be something that is always treasured by her or him. Make it a tradition, and provide this wonderful gift to those in your life.

SELECT A FORMAT

- A style of writing that becomes one immediately identified as belonging to you is a nice way to establish a sort of "tradition" of your love letter writing. Even envelopes that are addressed the same way and bear a special commemorative stamp can be part of your signature style. It says this is from you.
- Using your own special stationery is another very nice touch. Since love letters will be kept and treasured, it is particularly nice when they have the appearance that care and thought went into the selection of the stationery. When they are all the same dimensions, paper, and color, it makes keeping them together much easier.

SELECT EVOCATIVE WORDS

ambrosia	awe	adorable, adoring	admire
beautiful	bliss	bold	boundless
bounty	delight	dearest	desire
dream	heart	happy	handsome
fulfill	joy	light	vision
wonderful	celebrate	memories	eternity
heights	perfect	trust	praise
mystery	sweet	marvelous	unforgettable
unique	passionate	pleasure	paradise
precious	pretty	love	lovely
forever	loveable	treasure	sweetest
immeasurable	prize	endear	stunning
exquisite	exceptional	enduring	matchless

BUILD LOVING PHRASES

a happy moment

am anticipating

beautiful eyes

completely lovable

fair as a spring morning

imagining us together

long awaited

miss you

my heart's desire

sweet as a promise

what a wonder

you are the best

a pure vision

amazed by you

can't wait

dream often

feelings of joy

in awe of you

long to hear

moments of wonder

surprised by joy

thoughts of you

you are my

WRITE EXPRESSIVE SENTENCES

You are exactly what I always knew love looks like.

How very precious you are to me.

I could never imagine happiness like this.

You know I love the gymnastics of your agile mind—right down to the last objection.

Of course I disagree with you; isn't that one of the beauties of our relationship?

I'm in complete awe of you, you know that.

You make my joy complete.

From the first moment we met, I knew we were destined to be "us."

We'll always have Saturday, won't we?

How very wonderful you are.

I don't believe there's another person on the planet who possesses your talent for anticipation—
for you it's an art form.

Do please write out your heart to me.

I will always cherish moments like we had on Tuesday when we held the stars.

You are not only a complete delight; you are also a wonderful wizard.

You know you've spoiled me for ever being happy without you.

You are the organization to my disorganization; the yin to my yang; the music to my soul.

BUILD ENGAGING PARAGRAPHS

Once there was a very dull boy named Jack. He didn't actually know he was dull. In fact, he rather thought of himself as a completely able, effervescent, and on-track person. He'd been places, important and interesting places; and he was going to new places, too. But you have ruined Jack's solo world with your lovely self.

To continue that thought: I love you because you are the most thoughtful person I know. Who else would have had a can of vegemite delivered to my office because she knew I'd left mine in the hotel in Australia? (Of course, My Love, you know I hate vegemite, but that's not the point.)

Let's agree never to leave a harsh word hanging between us when we part, okay? I love you too much. I love our spirited discussions, and totally appreciate your jaunty point of view. (I mean that in a good way.) Our life together will never be dull or routine. How wonderful!

How precious to me are your letters. Sure, I love getting your text messages and cockeyed emails, but it's the letters filled with love and caring—and those thoughtful little inclusions you manage to come up with—that are really dear to me. I have a very special place I keep each and every one.

I build my day around you—wonderful you. You are my first thought each morning, my pre-occupation all day long, and my last thought at night. Would it be accurate to say that in my world the sun rises and sets in you? I think it would be, My Love.

I'm so happy to hear that your meetings have all gone so well, and the project is ahead of schedule. Dare I hope that it all means that you will be returning to me sooner than we had thought? Oh, that is a delicious thought. I'm going to put it in my hope compartment.

EDIT, EDIT, EDIT

Even though your love is willing to forgive you many things, do make sure your letter expresses what is in your heart, clearly and completely.

Darling,

Yes, I will need to be here with Mother for a period of time until I can get her back on her feet. Of course I love her and want to be here with her, but it's very painful to think of being away from you for the next few weeks. Perhaps we can use this time to write out our hearts to each other in colorful, fat love letters. Me first.

I missed you so much yesterday, I walked the halls of the hospital and had an imaginary conversation with you. It was a great conversation, actually. Yes, I could hear you saying—as you did before I left—this is the time I need to spend with my mother, and make sure she gets the kind of care she needs. You are so caring and understanding, my Love. And very, very thoughtful.

I could use your very practical and ordered approach to dealing with the doctors here.

Did I mention that I really, really miss you? And, yes, I will call you to discuss the next steps to take after I've gathered all the information.

All My Love,
Chloe

Hey Baby,

I feel completely tongue-tied when we're together. Just being with you makes me fall all over my verbal feet. I love you so much. There, I said it here when I couldn't say it in person. You fill my dreams—day and night.

I've never known anyone quite so generous as you. Nor anyone as patient and kind and funny and gorgeous—all qualities I admire immensely. Here's to building a lifetime of dreams with you.

Kisses,
Me

Sweetheart,

It's too lonely without you. Hurry home. I love you.

Your red-eyed lover

III.

JOB SEARCH

A clear statement is the
strongest argument.

—*English proverb*

16 NETWORKING COMMUNICATIONS

Networking is the process of getting connected. Someone you know links you to someone you don't know so that both you and your new contact can exchange and gain information. In the case of job hunting, networking can give you a great advantage in receiving consideration for a particular position. Successful networking is reciprocal: you provide information and contacts for others, and they (or someone else will) do the same for you. For it to work best, regard it as the law that exists in the universe: paying it forward. Or, to borrow a Biblical concept: cast your bread upon the waters. Often it returns to you slathered with peanut butter and jelly! Give openly to someone, and someone will give generously to you.

You need to know several important points about networking: (1) it is best done as an ongoing exercise of friendship and professionalism; (2) it involves being positive and helpful; (3) it is best approached as an exercise of giving as much or more information than you receive; (4) often it is credited with being responsible for the majority of successful job acquisitions; and (5) it will be far easier to do if you create a system of sources and a method of follow-up that keeps you in touch with your contacts.

So, when you know that an effort to find new employment is in your future, your first step is to hone your networking skills—long before you begin your search for a specific job. Honing your networking skills is just as important as keeping up with information, technology, and skill changes in your career field. And wonderful news: networking has never been easier than in this time of instantaneous communication through social networks, special websites, and email.

Creating an effective networking letter (which may be sent by email) is one of your next steps. This serves both as a letter of introduction and as a personal sales letter when you use it to introduce yourself as a candidate for a job. It should contain your best persuasive writing. It is used to locate job openings or even to be the stimulus for creating them, and it must include enough crisp, powerful statements about your abilities to entice the reader to want to learn more. In our present job culture, where the dynamics of employee and employer are changing rapidly, this letter is becoming an increasingly important tool.

A networking letter should be sent out as an essential part of a job-search campaign to specifically identified individuals within carefully targeted organizations. It is the most positive, effective, and time-saving way to conduct a job search. In many cases it may be emailed.

Do not include your resume, but rather end your letter by requesting an exploratory or "informational" interview. If you're mailing your letter, enclose a self-addressed, stamped envelope and/ or include your email address for the reply to increase your response rate.

If you have gotten no response after four weeks, send a slightly different networking letter to the same executive or another carefully selected executive within the organization. The response rate for second mailings is as good as that for first mailings.

Networking letters are most successfully used by mature, established professionals. In addition to being used when you are searching for a job in your current field, they also are often used when you seek to use your skills in a new field.

DECIDE TO WRITE

Send this letter to:

- Request a personal interview in your present career field
- Investigate career-change possibilities
- Gather job or career information
- Get noticed by a number of people within a company
- Follow up after your first letter hasn't gotten a response
- Get the interest of recruiters (headhunters)

RESEARCH

Building your network must start with the people you know. Personal and professional associates can help identify organizations and key people to contact.

The most common starting places are school and college associates, and fellow members of professional associations. Researching these to locate people has never been easier. Now with extensive online resources, you can easily network without leaving your office. Be sure to check the following:

- Corporate listings
- University websites
- Professional and industry directories
- Online job boards
- Association websites
- Career and job listing websites
- Online search engines
- Newspaper ads and articles
- Yellow Pages (make a phone call and personal contact before sending a networking letter)
- Recruiters (headhunters)

THINK ABOUT CONTENT

Write so the reader will want to learn more about you. The reader needs to see something in your letter that identifies closely with a problem he or she is having at the moment that needs to be solved. All businesses, no matter how smoothly they run, experience one problem after another. Your letter must include actual deeds you have accomplished and problems you have solved. Here are some general rules to think about as you begin writing:

- Use action words, verbs instead of nouns, whenever possible.
- Be sure your statements convey a sense of power.
- Be specific, not general. Remember, you are asking about a specific kind of position.
- Address your letter to the person with the power to hire: the company president, chief operating officer, chief executive officer, or appropriate department head. Remember, in organizations things move much better from top to bottom than bottom to top.

More specifically, there are two types of openings in a networking letter: topical and accomplishment.

Topical Openings

Topical openings capitalize on current trends, current events, and identified industry needs. Timing and circumstances play a very important role here, making this opening difficult. A topical opening is, however, the most electrifying, if used properly.

If New Horizons Airlines is buying lots of TV time for their wild animal ads and you have extensive specialized experience in this, you might start your letter like this:

> I filmed charging rhinos in Nairobi last week as the ad director for the Sweetie account. I am responsible for all phases of the $36.2 million dollar campaign.

Here is another example:

> I believe there are still many practices of Japanese manufacturing we need to use in this country. I have just returned from Japan after five years of living and working there. I am now home to stay in Dallas.

Here are two examples written by an advertising account executive:

> Yes, Harry Smith is right. I did sell Californians orange juice from Florida.

> Bill Yeats is wrong; I didn't sell snow cones in Anchorage. But I did sell bathing suits and water skis.

Accomplishment Openings

Accomplishment openings are much more useful than topical openings simply because they are more adaptable. Where the topical opening depends on the right timing and particular circumstances, the accomplishment opening can be easily adapted from your resume. Use an example that fits the business situation or cycle at the moment, and, if possible, include the name of the contact from your network who is known to the person to whom you're writing. Here are examples:

> Sam Evert suggested that I contact you about your need for a new advertising manager. I developed the new-home ads that produced more than 455 visitors a day every Saturday and Sunday in Sam's new community, Lone Star Estates.

As Bobbi Boxer may have told you, as marketing manager for a consumer product, I helped increase sales 32 percent by creating and implementing a new marketing policy.

Janet Stearns was my assistant when I managed five multimedia continuing medical education programs that resulted in net profits of 24 percent over estimates.

As controller and treasurer of Teddie Greene's manufacturing company, I turned an operating loss into a net profit of 21 percent of sales before taxes.

Paragraph Two

Your second paragraph should tell the reader why you are writing:

Janet thought your marketing department may need a person with my skills and experience. If so, you may be interested in some of my other accomplishments.

Or, try some of these transitional second paragraphs:

Your company may need a marketing manager. My experience, therefore, may interest you.

I understand you're looking for a marketing manager with home-building training, experience, and expertise. I'd like to review some of my other accomplishments for you.

Teddie suggested I contact you and discuss your need for an advertising manager with my experience.

I understand you are expanding your marketing program and need someone with my experience and background.

Show Me

Then come the "for instances." Lift one, two, or three short and relevant examples from your resume and transplant them into your networking letter.

Don't overload your letter. Less is more. Let your examples stand out as if you'd thrown shocking red paint on a canvas.

Try to use no more than ten to twelve words per sentence, keeping paragraphs to a few lines each. This will take effort, but it will be well worth your editing time. You may want to throw in the name of your school, but not necessarily your specific degree. Name the school and degree if they say in an understated fashion: quality product. For example, if you earned an MBA from one of the country's top MBA programs, list it. Also, if you know the addressee graduated from your alma mater, list it. Many such items have been real door openers.

The Ending

In closing, ask or suggest action within the power of the reader. Don't be shy. Ask for the exploratory, or informational, interview. With as much zing as possible, say something like, "I'd like to discuss details of my experience with you in a personal interview."

Or, "I'll call you Thursday to learn when you might have time for a personal interview." You want to make sure that the ending will be the beginning.

Again, do not include a resume, and don't mention it in your closing paragraph.

ELIMINATE WRONG MESSAGES

- Don't write ". . . discuss any possible positions that you might have to offer." This statement weakens your letter.
- Don't mention your resume. If you do, the reader will ask you to send it, and you may have lost the interview opportunity.
- Never write "I would like to show you how I can help increase your profits." The reader may consider this presumptuous from an outsider.
- Don't mention any specific kind of training that could affect the intended direction of your letter. Do mention your educational background. This usually adds to the reader's receptivity.

Get the Word Out

- Develop your own contact list. Keep notes about your contacts and their responses to your letters.
- Always verify the correct spelling of your contact's name and his or her current title.
- Regard all your contacts as a community, and keep in touch with them.
- Send out new letters every week.
- Continue the campaign until you have accepted a position and have started work.

SELECT A FORMAT

- Letters should be typed on personal letterhead or stationery, or emailed if you have received an okay to do so.
- When emailing, carefully create your point of contact for your subject line—for example, "Bill Bly's friend" or "Fellow AGMA member."
- The visual appearance of the completed letter should be open and inviting. Indent points and create wide margins to produce a lot of white space. Use bullets often.

THINK ABOUT TIMING

- Four weeks after your first mailing, send a slightly different letter to those who haven't responded.
- After a personal or meeting introduction, follow up within a day.

SELECT ACTION VERBS

activated	built	changed	completed
created	cut	demonstrated	doubled
enabled	engineered	envisioned	increased
initiated	instituted	launched	obtained
organized	reduced	reorganized	restructured
revamped	saved	sold	solved (resolved)
stopped	succeeded	transformed	won

BUILD POWER PHRASES

completely revamped

created a new product

demonstrated the new

increased production by

increased sales by

instituted cost-cutting measures

reduced waste by

restructured the deal

saved the company

succeeded in building

created a new plan

cut costs by

developed a solution

increased profits by

initiated the cost-saving plan

reduced overhead

reorganized the department

restructured the debt

solved the overhead problem

won approval of

WRITE STRONG SENTENCES

Use action words. Replace nouns with power verbs whenever possible.

Reduced waste by 43 percent with a single, no-cost production change.

Doubled sales in 18 months.

I expanded the market for the Model X-123 while chief engineer by improving the product and designing four attachments.

BUILD EFFECTIVE PARAGRAPHS

I'd like to discuss further details of my experience in a personal interview. I will call you next Wednesday to arrange a time and place.

As marketing manager for Reholdt, Inc., I increased sales 18 percent in 12 months by instituting a new marketing policy. I believe you would find the details of this policy very interesting. The ads we developed launched the new product in great style. In the first year, it captured a 23 percent market share.

As a department manager in the largest department store in the state, I doubled the sales volume of the ready-to-wear merchandise in three years. Profits were 13 percent above the store's previous average.

EDIT, EDIT, EDIT

After finishing your letter, shelve it for a day or two so you can reread it with a fresh perspective. You may also want to ask people whose opinions you respect to read it and comment before you write the final letter.

First Contact—Offering Information to a Colleague

SUBJECT: Webmaster Info You Requested

Hello Jennifer,

Yes, I have an excellent webmaster (mistress?) I'd recommend. Her name is Josie Bails. She is swift in making changes to my website, listens carefully to my input, has a great eye for layout and innovation, and is very reasonable: $65/hour.

When I was in Europe without access to a printer, she even printed out a book proposal I emailed her and mailed it to my agent. All at a very nominal fee.

Josie's website is www.rightaway.com; her email address is josie@rightaway.com; and her phone number is 650-555-0123.

I've told Josie you may call. Please mention my name.

All the best,

Gertie

First Contact—Job Opening

SUBJECT: Your Next Job?

Hi Lizzie,

When I returned to the office last week after the conference, I learned from the university president that he's reorganizing the student loan department. He wants a take-charge professional like you to come in from the outside because of the politics involved.

I responded that I just happened to have been talking to a very qualified person at the conference, and I would ask you if you're interested.

He'd like to talk with you.

If you are interested, please email him at sml@phillips.edu, and put my name in the subject line. I, of course, didn't offer your name or any details, only said that you were, in my opinion, the sort of person who could do an excellent job with the reorganization he has in mind.

Please let me know if this works out. I'll be in this afternoon.

All the best,

Rose

First Contact—Offering a Job Lead

SUBJECT: A Manager Position Opening

Dear Rita:

My friend Dan Glover at Spikes needs a high-powered saleswoman like you. I know you'd like to make a change, and I believe this may be an ideal fit for you.

I've taken the liberty of mentioning your skills (not your name, or that you're looking), telling him I've been very impressed with your outstanding accomplishments. He'd really like to talk to you, I believe. Quote: "Now that's the kind of sales professional I'm looking for."

Please give him a call at 503-555-0123, if you're interested. And, of course, mention my name.

Best wishes,

Millie

Follow-Up Letter—after a Meeting

Dear Mr. Abbott:

Nice talking with you, if ever so briefly, at the MMA meeting yesterday. Here's a recap of what we discussed, concerning my four years at Critters Manufacturing:

- As marketing manager, I increased sales by 42 percent in 18 months.
- Launched three new products in one year that triggered first-year sales of $4.2 million.
- Recruited and trained 25 salespeople who became top producers within one year.

I graduated from the Wharton Business School, where I specialized in sales management and marketing.

I would be happy to discuss other details of my experience with you in a personal interview, including some of the ideas I've instituted that are working well here for a situation very similar to the one we discussed. I will call your office on Thursday morning to arrange a time.

Sincerely,

Daisy L. Sluggs

Seeking a Public Relations Opening

SUBJECT: Wonderful "Hot Rox" Piece in Creative

Dear Mr. Barker:

I just read the Hot Rox piece in *Creative* magazine, and I'm impressed by your organization's commitment to finding new creative talent. I believe some of my accomplishments fit your desired employee profile:

- Created and established a department that drew strong support from 85 percent of employees
- Recruited, trained, and motivated a highly diverse group of personnel from six departments into an effective team
- Developed and executed a community relations program that has won national recognition
- Administered a department program that reduced costs by 22% and increased production by 17%

Perhaps my search for a growth opportunity will fit with your search for an innovative, creative, and productive public relations leader. I would like to discuss the possibilities with you. I will call later this week to arrange for an appointment.

Sincerely yours,

Dumar Q. Tyler

Seeking a Sales Manager Opportunity

Mr. Ruben Sternberg, President

Dear Mr. Sternberg:

Mr. Len Lesser suggested I contact you about your need for a sales manager. As national sales manager of RemKo, I increased sales volume 32 percent in an industry that was growing at the rate of 4 percent a year. If your company faces growth challenges, you may be interested in how I accomplished this. I created a multifaceted plan which, when implemented:

- Combined five sales regions into two,
- Reduced manpower costs by 17 percent, and
- Increased profits by 22 percent.

Achieving this level of performance required recruiting and developing a top team of sales professionals, instituting a sales incentive program, and dramatically increasing—by 19 percent—the sales in two product lines. We were awarded the National Sales Association's "Top Performers" award four out of the past five years.

I'd like to share several of my ideas that might benefit your company. I'll call your office next Thursday to see about arranging a time.

Cordially,

Calvin R. Clements

Seeking an Entry Marketing Opening

Ms. Jeannine Trump, President

Dear Ms. Trump:

I just graduated from Duke University where I majored in marketing and graduated cum laude. I was the first African-American student to receive the coveted Student of the Year Award. Perhaps your marketing department would be interested in someone with my enthusiasm and capabilities. During the four years I worked before returning to college for my final year, I:

- Organized direct-mail campaigns of over 20 million letters and brochures that received an 11 percent response rate.
- Completed market research and sales forecasting that sold our services to four accounts over $500,000.
- Created a promotional package that established sales distribution in a 23-state area and gained a 67 percent label recognition for a start-up mineral water.

I would like to discuss my education and experience with you. I will call you next week to arrange a time and place.

Very truly yours,

Juliet S. Guest

Seeking an Accounting Opening

Mr. Todd Ryder, President

Dear Mr. Ryder:

Larry Grieves, my long-time prison friend, suggested I contact you. I have been in Dawes Prison 37 times. Each time I performed a professional audit as a public accountant examining accounts, costs, and the management records of the prison. I've also been in Blinder Mental Hospital a few dozen times—for the same reason.

Larry said Evergreen may need a diversified, well-seasoned professional to assume your accounting responsibilities. If so, you may be interested in my background and achievements.

I have completed general audit work for

- 24 government entities,
- 76 different business enterprises,
- 53 industrial manufacturers, and
- Over 135 other types of public and private institutions.

I also designed the accounting system, which became a model statewide, used for the townships of Marek County. I would welcome the opportunity to discuss with you how my skills can benefit Evergreen, and I will call you next week to arrange a time.

Yours truly,

Jamie S. Small

Seeking a Sales Manager Opening

Mr. Buck Rogers, President

Dear Mr. Rogers:

I just read about your plans to expand into manufacturing an upscale line of furniture, and I'd like the opportunity to discuss with you my experience in this area.

- As sales manager for a small Midwest manufacturer of fine furniture, I increased sales over 225 percent in two years.
- While managing a sales force of 22, I added two dealers and a manufacturer's representative to expand sales to 42 states.
- I developed and instituted inventory procedures that reduced inventory by 16 percent.

I will be in Columbus on April 10 for the National Furniture Convention, and I'm hoping we can get together for a discussion. I will contact you next week to arrange a time and place.

Sincerely,

Frederika R. Fink

Seeking an Engineer Position

Mr. Ivan Prather

Vice President, Engineering

Dear Mr. Prather:

As chief engineer I expanded the market for the Ryan Model 880 by improving the tolerances by 34 percent. This improved product has secured new sales in high-temperature and high-load applications not previously possible.

I believe Ramsburg's Model 4000 has similar product-application potential, and I would like the opportunity to discuss my engineering approach with you. I shall call your office next week to arrange a time and place.

Sincerely,

Lydia S. Squares

(Also see RESUME, page 126, and RESUME COVER LETTER, page 116.)

17 RESUME COVER LETTER

The resume cover letter is a sales letter—one of the most important sales letters you will ever write.

While the cover letter or transmittal letter (see Cover Letter, page 253) for reports and proposals is primarily a laundry list of the "covered," or enclosed, documents, the resume cover letter has three distinct functions: (1) get the reader's favorable attention, (2) clearly and quickly identify the job or position for which you are applying, and (3) compel the reader to read your resume.

The goal of the resume cover letter is to get the reader to delve into your enclosed resume and then call you to request an interview. Focus on one or two precise skills the employer needs. Highlight your achievements in those areas—with numbers whenever possible. Make your letter brief.

DECIDE TO WRITE

- Find out who is responsible for hiring for the position you want. Learn as much about the organization, position, and the hiring person as possible. Address your letter to that person. Personalize your letter, if possible, to demonstrate that you have done your homework. Beginning with "Dear Sir," "Gentlemen," or "Madam" does not convey the right message. There are many ways you can obtain the name of a particular person. Certainly calling the organization and asking for the person's name is one of the most direct.
- Organize your letter under three or four short paragraphs: (1) An opening paragraph that states the job, introduces you as a qualified candidate, and refers to your prior contact or network connection, if you have one; (2) a second paragraph with highlights of your experience and qualifications that make you uniquely right for the position; (3) an optional paragraph that offers a constructive idea about the solution(s) you can offer; and (4) a closing paragraph that is a call for action on the part of the reader. (If possible indicate when you will contact the reader to follow up on your letter.)
- Begin to draft your letter, and fill in details within the paragraphs.
- Identify the specific job immediately.
- Write something unique. It's important to convey your skills and even your personality, which eliminates the flavor of a form letter.
- Take a few risks. You must tell the reader why you are uniquely qualified for the position. Describe the value you can bring to the organization. Be sure to communicate your achievements and capabilities in a way that suggests assistance and support, but be careful that your tone doesn't smack of being boastful.

- Speak the language. Every specialty has a culture and its own particular vocabulary. Use it, but be sure not to overdue it. At the same time, keep your language conversational and friendly.
- Keep your sentences short.
- Demonstrate energy and enthusiasm.
- Lead the reader to examine your resume. Consider using two corresponding dots: one in the margin marking the statement in your letter, and the other marking the explanatory reference in your resume.
- Give full information on how, when, and where you can be contacted.
- Be innovative to get extra attention. A colored dot or a star adhered to one corner of your letter and resume (but not if you use the dot described above), a unique design approach, or even an audiovisual presentation (if acceptable within your business culture) can work to bring extra attention to your qualifications. But be sure not to sacrifice readability or clarity, or to otherwise cloud your message.
- Close with a friendly but proactive statement that promises or requests further contact. Ask for the next step: a meeting or conversation with the reader. Be as specific as you can. For example, "I will be in San Francisco next week, and would like to meet with you at that time. I will call your office on Thursday morning to see if you have time for a brief meeting late afternoon."
- Make your letter short. Rarely should it be more than a single page.
- Edit to give your letter punch.
- Reread and polish it until your letter sings.
- Consider handwriting a postscript statement, like a call to action, at the bottom of your letter.

ELIMINATING WRONG MESSAGES

- Avoid formal, dry, and vague words and terms.
- Use specialized technical terms unique to your field to show you are an insider, but don't overload it.
- Don't go on and on; be concise.
- Eliminate general statements. Be specific.
- Don't lift statements directly from your resume.
- Avoid addressing your letter to the human resources or personnel departments, unless absolutely necessary.
- Avoid an arrogant tone. Read aloud to check for flow and tone.
- Delete passive verbs; substitute active ones.
- Don't send a letter with typos or errors of any kind; double- and triple-check everything.

CONSIDER SPECIAL SITUATIONS

- Send a networking letter (see Networking, page 107) when it's more appropriate.
- Remember that each resume cover letter and resume should be tailored to the specific position. Think of your resume as a toolbox of skills, and each position as requiring a specific

tool from within that box. This will help you craft a better letter and resume and realize better results.

- When you request an exploratory interview or there is no present opening, a networking letter or a referral letter will offer a better first communication option. Use a resume and possibly a resume cover letter as a second step, preferably as a follow-up to a face-to-face meeting.
- Be sure to include all your marketable skills, especially if you're returning to the job market after a long absence, or if you are seeking your first job. Volunteer activities, achievements in scouts and other organizations, and experience in athletics and other endeavors are all things you may use in creating your resume and resume cover letter.
- If you are applying for a new position while still employed, be sure to state the fact in your resume cover letter to avoid any possible breach of confidentiality.
- If you know all the specifications of a job opening, you may want to use a comparative listing of your qualifications, sometimes called "executive summary," "briefing," or "skill summary." You can use two columns to create a visual comparison:

Job Specification	My Skill Summary

- When sending your letter to a third party, recruiter, or other employment service, you may be more informal. Concentrate on the kind of job you are seeking and your qualifications for it.
- When application forms are required, especially when you are using email, the employer usually won't accept a resume and resume cover letter as a substitute. In these cases, you will need to complete the application form, but you may also want to submit your resume cover letter and resume by either email or regular mail (or both) to the specific person(s) responsible for hiring.

SELECT A FORMAT

- White or open space creates the pleasing impression that your letter can be quickly and easily read. When your letter is emailed, keep the length to one screen, if possible. Check your word count: it should be no more than 250 words in 12-point type.
- Be creative. In the very competitive job market, make your letter distinctive but still within the realm of what is acceptable in your field. People in the arts, advertising, and public relations professions usually have more latitude than those in banking and publishing, for example.
- Sign your letter boldly and with confidence.
- A thoughtful and clear handwritten postscript statement on the letter will be read first. Make good use of this fact.

- Select a high-quality paper stock that matches your resume stock. A cream or ivory paper, or even a very light color may work well to distinguish your letter from others. Be sure to use something acceptable within the business culture.
- Use a typeface that's clear and easy to read, and is consistent with the business industry. Also, use one that copies well, in a case a reader wants to share it. Make sure your type is at least 10 picas in size for ease of reading.
- Leave at least a 1¼- to 1½–inch border all the way around your letter to create inviting white space.
- Consider placing a red dot or some distinguishing eye-catcher on your resume and cover letter, if this is acceptable within your industry.
- Hand-addressing the envelope to a specific person may increase the chance that the person will read it.

POWER WORDS

Start with a power verb. Use the first person and present tense whenever possible; use past tense—words ending in -ed—for action in the past. Avoid using adverbs—words ending in -y and -ly. They can dilute your message.

accept(ed)	accomplish(ed)	ace(d)	achieve(d)
act(ed)	actuate(d)	adapt(ed)	add(ed)
address(ed)	adjust(ed)	administer(ed)	adopt(ed)
advance(d)	advise(d)	allocate(d)	amend(ed)
analyze(d)	anticipate(d)	apply(ied)	appoint(ed)
appraise(d)	appropriate(d)	approve(d)	arbitrate(d)
arrange(d)	articulate(d)	assemble(d)	assess(ed)
assign(ed)	assist(ed)	attain(ed)	augment(ed)
author(ed)	authorize(d)	award(ed)	balance(d)
buy (bought)	build (built)	catalog(ed)	classify(ied)
compete(d)	complete(d)	conceive(d)	conduct(ed)
consolidate(d)	contract(ed)	control(led)	coordinate(d)
create(d)	decrease(d)	deliver(ed)	demonstrate(d)
designate(d)	design(ed)	develop(ed)	devise(d)
direct(ed)	dissolve(d)	distribute(d)	double(d)
eliminate(d)	energize(d)	enlarge(d)	establish(ed)
examine(d)	expand(ed)	facilitate(d)	govern(ed)
group(ed)	guide(d)	hire(d)	implement(ed)
improve(d)	increase(d)	index(ed)	interview(ed)
introduce(d)	invent(ed)	investigate(d)	launch(ed)
maintain(ed)	manage(d)	moderate(d)	monitor(ed)
negotiate(d)	orchestrate(d)	organize(d)	originate(d)
outperform(ed)	persist(ed)	persuade(d)	perform(ed)
pioneer(ed)	plan(ned)	prepare(d)	present(ed)
privatize(d)	problem-solve(d)	produce(d)	program(med)
progress(ed)	promote(d)	propose(d)	purchase(d)
realize(d)	recharge(d)	recommend(ed)	reconstitute(d)

recover(ed)	recruit(ed)	rectify(ied)	redesign(ed)
reduce(d)	regulate(d)	reinstitute(d)	render(ed)
renew(ed)	reorganize(d)	repair(ed)	replace(d)
replicate(d)	represent(ed)	reprogram(med)	research(ed)
reshape(d)	restart(ed)	restructure(d)	retool(ed)
revamp(ed)	reverse(d)	revise(d)	revitalize(d)
revive(d)	revolutionize(d)	rotate(d)	route(d)
schedule(d)	service(d)	simplify(ied)	slash(ed)
sort(ed)	specialize(d)	specify(ied)	start(ed)
streamline(d)	strengthen(ed)	structure(d)	succeed(ed)
summarize(d)	supervise(d)	systemize(d)	train(ed)
transact(ed)	translate(d)	trim(med)	triple(d)
trump(ed)	turn(ed) around	uncover(ed)	unify(ied)
unravel(ed)	widen(ed)	win (won)	write (wrote)

POWER PHRASES

Select precise action statements that convey your achievements and skills using results and solid examples.

Completed 8,000 flight hours without a safety infraction
Created employee benefit program with 94 percent satisfaction rate
Implemented 25 new standards in 14 months
Improved plant safety record by 23 percent
Increased production by 15 percent
Increased profits by 34 percent in 24 months
Outperformed competitors by 11 percent
Outsold a field of 55 salespeople for five consecutive quarters by at least 19 percent
Qualified the organization for accreditation in seven months
Reduced waste by 22 percent in six months
Wrote reports that received 89 percent positive reviews

WRITE STRONG SENTENCES

Start with a power verb to properly focus your sentences. Created, restructured, initiated, launched, conducted, controlled, administered, constructed, managed, interceded, established, enacted, and marketed are some examples. The sentences below include other examples:

Please review my journeyman skills demonstrated at Beck: I consistently—94 percent of the time—solved customer problems, on time, under budget, and with high rates of customer satisfaction.
I believe my skills, especially as demonstrated at Crystal's, could create the right solutions to your production crisis.
My award-winning writing at Golman was instrumental in increasing sales by 17 percent.
I haven't missed a deadline in seven years.
On my watch, production at Demming increased 18 percent and absenteeism fell 22 percent in five months.

My team revamped the inventory system in five months, reducing stock overhead costs by 23 percent.

I request 15 minutes of your time to show you my PowerPoint "New Goals" marketing approach that helped turn around Kramer Corporation.

Using my complete managerial skills, I've organized and supervised all inventory and shipping at Grace since 2008.

I will call your office on Thursday to inquire about arranging an appointment.

There are three things in my resume, I believe, you may want to review.

I look forward to discussing some specific ideas with you.

I'd like to explain in a personal interview details of my experience that I believe could benefit Arco Corporation.

I thrive on challenges such as the one you described in Sunday's Post ad.

I'm ready to step up to the position of director from associate director, and I'd like the opportunity to tell you why.

Theodore Sturgeon recommended I talk to you about your office manager opening.

I have a solid electrical engineering background and education, as well as award-winning design experience.

BUILD EFFECTIVE PARAGRAPHS

Be brief. Your letter should be no more than three or four paragraphs in length. Remember, shorter letters get read quickly and first. With this approach, you'll increase your chances of making a positive and lasting impression.

I believe my complete reorganization of Pester and Company's legal department—see the highlighted area on my resume—demonstrates the skills you seek in a person to head up your legal department. I'd like to discuss with you details of my experience.

I believe my marketing skills, as illustrated on my resume, can add value to the position of controller at Crinkles. I was able to increase Black's market position while controlling the budget.

I worked very hard to reduce overhead at Gator Corporation by 24 percent in five months. The expertise I gained in that position, I believe, uniquely prepared me to take on the challenge of your operations manager position. Please review the details of my responsibilities on my resume enclosed. I look forward to discussing with you how I implemented this change.

I was excited to learn you are looking for an account executive with award-winning experience in the home-building industry. I've won state, regional, and national awards (see marks on my resume) for creating the best marketing, ad, and public relations campaigns for my clients. I'd like to discuss with you how I believe these approaches could help create award-winning campaigns for Sanders, Inc.

Please note that although I'm a lightweight in copywriting experience—as you'll see on my resume—I'm a heavyweight in the areas of fresh ideas, enthusiasm, and real ability.

I've won four academic ad-writing awards, including one for cell phones. May I show you these ads from my portfolio in a 10-minute interview?

I've been preparing for the role of department head for 10 years. I'd like to discuss with you details of how I could be effective as your director of nurses.

EDIT, EDIT, EDIT

Give your letter some shelf time before you go back for final editing. This gives you the opportunity to see it objectively and allows you to remove excess words or phrases and weak statements. Place action words front and center, be concise, and check to ensure your tone is conversational. Most of all, be sure your enthusiasm shines through.

If possible, ask another professional whose advice you value to review your letter before sending it.

Make one final check to be sure your letter is visually pleasing and free of typos.

Comparison Letter—Response to a Job Posting

Celeste Vickers, Vice President

Dear Ms. Vickers:

I noted with interest your opening for an accounting manager in Sunday's *Tribune*. I am looking for just such a growth opportunity.

I believe my skills and experience closely align with the qualifications you are seeking:

Applegate Requirements
- Accounting degree and several years accounting experience.
- Demonstrated ability to manage and motivate staff.
- Strong analytical and administrative skills.
- Outstanding oral and written communication skills.

My Skills and Experience
- C.A. degree, 1999, from DePaul; and over five years of experience.
- Effectively managed staff of 14, including two senior accountants.
- Developed a base reference library for 350 clients.
- Initiated department staff meetings. Created skill training classes for four personnel levels with 95 percent participant "excellent" rating.

Some of my other achievements are outlined on the enclosed resume.

I would welcome the opportunity for an interview, and will call your office next week to inquire about arranging a convenient time.

Yours truly,

Jamie Baxter

Response to a Job Posting

Ms. Abigal Appleton, Deputy Editor

Dear Ms. Appleton:

Tom Uphill, your photographer at Baker and my friend, told me you are responsible for hiring the new senior editor, the spot advertised in Sunday's *Post*. He suggested I write directly to you.

Here's how I believe several of my skills match up with your advertised requirements:

Ad Requirements
- College journalism degree
- 3 to 5 yrs. editorial experience
- Works well under pressure

My Skills
- Graduated cum laude, University of Chicago, B.S. in journalism
- 3 yrs. assistant editor at Holbrook's
- Met all deadlines, under budget, in the past eighteen months.

Details of my experience are listed on the enclosed resume.

I'd like the opportunity to show you my portfolio, and will call your office on Thursday to arrange a convenient time.

Sincerely yours,

John Que

Follow-Up after a Chance Meeting

Mr. Frank Brown
Chief Executive Officer

Dear Mr. Brown:

It was a pleasure meeting you at the National Home Builders Association convention in Dallas last week. I especially enjoyed the opportunity to see the operation of your electronic skylights.

I'm following up our discussion, as you suggested, with this letter. Over the last six months with Wilson Windows, I have:

- Successfully introduced a new product line,
- Trained 45 sales representatives, and
- Realized substantial market penetration already, with profits for the year estimated to be in excess of $3.4 million (compared with $2.2 million last year).

You can see by my enclosed resume that I also have other skills that could benefit Atulac.

I'd like to discuss details of my experience with you. Wednesday morning I'll contact your office to see about arranging a meeting for the week of January 21.

Sincerely,

Germaine Q. Ruddick

Response to a Job Posting for Controller

Jeremy R. Levitts, CFO

Dear Mr. Levitts:

Your ad in the Sunday *Journal* for a controller especially interests me because I just sold my own business—Small Wonders, a children's toy company—for a profit, and I want to continue my career with a progressive company. I've enclosed my resume for your review.

I look forward to discussing with you how my qualifications, integrity, and seasoned experience might benefit Miracles.

Yours truly,

Jack Beams

Sending Resume after Telephone Contact

Philip Tinsdale
Vice President

Dear Mr. Tinsdale:

Thank you for the invitation to submit my resume for your international sales manager position. As I mentioned during our telephone discussion, Jack Belzer was enthusiastic about me contacting you. He did, in fact, cover many of the requirements of the position.

For the past five years, I have headed the international sales efforts at Manchester, a position that included:

- Creating sales offices in Belgium, France, Germany, and Great Britain;
- Recruiting and managing 34 independent sales representatives;
- Providing full training of all European representatives;
- Securing 43 percent, 34 percent, 28 percent, and 37 percent of the Belgian, French, German, and Great Britain markets, respectively; and
- Surpassing $45 million in annual sales with excellent margins.

I look forward to discussing details of my experience with you, including how I feel I can add value at Smith. I will call your office Monday morning about 10:00 a.m. to arrange a time and place for a meeting.

Sincerely,

Jacob Seles

Referral Follow-Up for Sales Manager Position

Ms. Audree Divers
Systems Manager

Dear Audree:

As we discussed on the telephone, Sarah Beele, your friend and mine, was insistent that my successes as sale manager are the perfect solution to your present sales force problems. I'm sure she has told you that here at Wickers I created a bonus program for our salespeople, which has produced a sales increase of 28 percent in eight months, and has improved sales staff satisfaction over 54 percent.

I'm intrigued by your opportunity, and would like to discuss details of my work here and at Beekins. As you requested, I've enclosed a resume describing my role at both companies. I believe my solutions may work well for you.

Please call me at 323-555-0123 to arrange an interview time. Or, if we haven't met, I'll introduce myself next week at the trade show in Las Vegas.

Sincerely,

Hazel Hubbard

Response to a Blind Job Posting with an Agency

Chairman of the Board

Dear Chairman of the Board:

I was dubbed the "turn-around king" by the North Chicago Chapter of the A.M.A. in the *C.M.A. Journal*, issue IV, June 15. Over the past ten years, I've taken three companies from the bankruptcy court to profits of $500,000, $2.1 million, and $1.8 million. One of these companies is Plastic Forms in Hollywood, Florida.

I would like the opportunity to discuss with you the details of what I've done and how my skills might work for your organization. I'm enclosing a resume for your review.

I will call your office next week to arrange a time convenient for a brief meeting.

Sincerely,

Cornelius M. Conover

Response to a Job Posting in Media Relations

SUBJECT: Director, Media Relations

Dear Kay:

I'd like the opportunity to discuss with you how my local, regional, and national media skills, in addition to my ability to serve as spokesperson and to create and direct a media relationship plan, may be the combination of skills you're looking for to fill your director of media relations position.

Please take a look at my website, iamsavvy.com, and click on "Media Projects" to see just a few of the media programs I've developed from inception through execution of the actual event. I'm also including below a complete resume and a client list for your review.

Please contact me to arrange an interview time. I am in the city this week, but not next, and I could meet with you either tomorrow at 2:00 p.m., or Thursday at 2:30 p.m.

Sincerely,

Melody Chimes

Applying for a Teaching Position after a Telephone Introduction

Dear Mrs. Grimm:

As we discussed on the telephone today, I'd like to teach at Buck Elementary on the third- or fourth-grade level. I will graduate from Anvil College this spring, and plan to move to your area immediately afterward.

I've had student teaching experience in the third- to sixth-grade levels in suburban, urban, and inner-city school districts.

During summer vacations I've taught "at risk" preschool children in the Head Start Program, and fifth-grade "at risk" inner-city children. I've learned to be creative, nurturing, and, most important, patient.

My goal is to continue to develop as a compassionate, enthusiastic, and intelligent teacher. I believe I can make a positive contribution to your school, and would like the opportunity for an introductory interview. I plan to be in Buck County next week, and would appreciate 15 minutes of your time, if you can spare them.

I'll call you on Friday to learn if you're able to arrange a time, or you may reach me until then at 503-555-0123.

Sincerely,

Pay D. Piper

Response to Association Website Job Posting

SUBJECT: Director of Marketing Communications Position

Dear Mr. Webster:

I'd like the opportunity to show you my portfolio, which illustrates exactly how I planned and executed a complete turnaround of the Adams Master-Planned Community, located just twenty-five miles from Harvey. In ten months, we took Adams from near foreclosure to profits estimated at more than $50 million. The community went from no sales in six months to 15 sales in a single weekend. (See my enclosed resume and list of clients.)

If you'd like, please review other examples of my creative approach and products on my website—marketingmasters.com—under projects.

Please contact me at 401-555-0123 to arrange an interview.

Sincerely,

Cecil Caster

Referral for a Summer Job

Jennifer Beales
Head Librarian

Dear Ms. Beales:

My friend on your staff, Mr. Rob Anderson, suggested I send you my resume and request an interview for the position of summer clerk. I am pursuing a library science degree at the University of Michigan and am a lifelong lover of books.

I have held several volunteer positions working with children and young adults, with the Girl Scouts, the Literacy League, and Children at Risk. I have also volunteered at Vulcan Library as a children's hour storyteller.

I will call you next week to request an interview time convenient to your schedule.

Sincerely,

Joan Diddly

18 RESUME

It's important to think of your resume as a toolbox. For every position you want to apply for, study the details of the opening, then select the best tools from your toolbox, and customize a resume that will demonstrate that you know what the employer is looking for, and that you have the demonstrated skills to do the job. Your resume must have the muscle of facts and figures, and it should have a certain flair and pizzazz. The proper balance of these elements equals the power and impact you'll need to sell yourself as a worthy candidate. When you are using your resume to promote yourself to a client, the same rules apply. Use the things from your education and experience that demonstrate your qualifications.

The secret to writing a great resume is knowing the audience—the person doing the hiring—and the organization. The second key, then, is writing your resume to show that you are the best person for that specific job.

DECIDE TO WRITE

Send your resume:
- In response to newspaper and other media ads
- In response to an invitation from an organization
- As part of your job-search campaign
- To accompany and support a proposal, report, or other document that is based on your qualifications and experience
- In connection with running for political, club, or association office
- To document your qualifications as a speaker, author, expert witness, or other type of authority

GUIDING RULES

- Think short. Unless you are a physician, academician, or attorney, keep your resume to a single page.
- Start off with a strong and clear statement that shows you understand what the employer wants, and how you fulfill the need.
- Use the experience from the last 10 to 15 years only, or that which showcases best your qualifications.
- Remove date references that could reduce your chances of being hired.
- Give your resume a cutting-edge modern look with great visual appeal.

- De-emphasize non-relevant experience.
- Always show your qualifications as results with solid numbers.

DECIDE ON RESUME TYPE

There are three basic styles of resumes: the *chronological*, the *functional*, and the *creative*. Select the style that showcases you the best and is best matched to your target audience. There is no "correct" or "incorrect" form. You may even want to use one style for one audience and another style for a different audience. And sometimes you may want to combine styles to best illustrate why you are the best person for the position.

Chronological Resume

The chronological resume is the most traditional. It uses a time sequence to list work experience and education, usually appearing in reverse order beginning with the present.

Use the chronological resume when:

- You are pursuing traditional fields (government, education, banking).
- Your work history shows a strong growth pattern or direction.
- Your title progression is impressive.
- You're continuing on the same career path.
- Your present or last employer is important.

The chronological resume is not the best form for everyone. If any of the list below applies to you, it is probably better to use one of the other styles.

Don't use a chronological resume when:

- You are just entering the job market (a recent graduate).
- You're changing career direction or goals.
- You have holes in your work experience (periods of unemployment).
- Your career has plateaued and remained there for some time.
- You are returning to the job market after a long absence.
- You do not wish to divulge your age.
- You've changed employers frequently.

Functional Resume

The functional resume focuses on capabilities and skills. Usually these are listed by areas, and may or may not include dates.

Use a functional resume when:

- You are changing careers.
- You are entering the job market.
- You are reentering the job market.
- Your experience lacks a demonstrated career path.
- You are a consultant, freelancer, or have completed temporary work.

- Your latest job appears to be a demotion over previous ones.
- Your work experience seems somewhat unconnected to the position for which you are applying.

Don't use a functional resume when:

- You have not targeted your resume toward a certain position.
- You do not have well-defined accomplishments and capabilities.
- You do not have enough experience to demonstrate functions performed.

Creative Resume

The creative resume is a free-form style and can be extremely effective in showcasing your skills and capabilities—particularly for artists, writers, actors, public relations personnel, and people in the media. An account executive looking for a new position in an advertising agency effectively used a resume with cartoons to land a high-powered position, for example. A CEO of a public relations agency was elected to an important association president post by preparing audio tapes of voice impersonations touting the various attributes that made him the best person for the job. He played it for association members at a campaign luncheon.

Executives of various disciplines, as well as actors, spokespersons, freelance photographers, and illustrators, have used audiovisual resumes of all types to land sales jobs, manager jobs, acting roles, and all sorts of other types of jobs.

And computer experts, graphic designers, actors, and photographers have created interactive resumes that they put on Internet systems or emailed to employers.

Use a creative resume when:

- The target of your resume is a creative or specialized audience who will appreciate it.
- You decide it is the only medium that can adequately express who you are.
- You especially want to showcase your creative talents.

Don't use a creative resume when:

- You are seeking a position in a traditional field, such as government.
- You are not well grounded in your own creativity.
- It won't be otherwise "acceptable" to your audience.

THINK ABOUT CONTENT

Learn as much as possible about the employer and target audience. Assess the position you are seeking—preferably a specific position within a specific organization—and the key ingredients needed to fill it.

Then work through the following steps of assessing and writing out your skills, personal characteristics, and experience, keeping in mind the guiding rules and resume style you have selected.

If you are changing careers, completing a resume for the first time, or are reentering the job market after an absence, you may want to complete the skills inventory that follows. Use the following steps as a working guide. Create separate categories of information in your computer file or on index cards—skills, characteristics, and results of your efforts at work or elsewhere—for ease in completing your final draft.

STEP 1

Make an inventory of your personal information, focusing on your skills, abilities, and strong points. There are really two types of skills: general and specific.

General skills, like analyzing, communicating, and writing, are often taken for granted because they seem like things everyone can do. List the general skills you use in your work, because every job requires them.

STEP 2

Select your twelve strongest general skills from the list, and translate them into specific technical skills that produce measurable results. These are job-related skills like inputting on a keyboard, which produces a piece of correspondence. Here are a couple of examples:

General skill	Organizing
Related activities	Making order out of chaos, establishing physical order, categorizing facts.
Specific skills	Setting up a filing system, creating a systematic way to categorize inventory in a warehouse, and rewriting and editing reports.
General skill	**Negotiating**
Related activities	Bartering, holding a position, convincing others, arranging terms, establishing standards.
Specific skills	Setting up conferences with hotels, establishing sales prices for products, developing contract terms, arranging details of sales, establishing salaries.

STEP 3

Factor into your skill statements those things that express your personal characteristics, and select those that best describe you. The following words may not appear in your completed resume, but they will help you in forming your final statements.

☐ Able	☐ Ambitious	☐ Assertive	☐ Careful
☐ Caring	☐ Communicative	☐ Creative	☐ Decisive
☐ Dedicated	☐ Determined	☐ Diligent	☐ Easygoing
☐ Energetic	☐ Flexible	☐ Forthright	☐ Friendly
☐ Hardworking	☐ Helpful	☐ Honest	☐ Humorous
☐ Imaginative	☐ Intellectual	☐ Intelligent	☐ Intense
☐ Intuitive	☐ Loyal	☐ Masterful	☐ Open-minded
☐ Organized	☐ Persistent	☐ Persuasive	☐ Political
☐ Precise	☐ Quick	☐ Responsible	☐ Results-oriented
☐ Sensitive	☐ Strong	☐ Supportive	☐ Tactful
☐ Thorough	☐ Trustworthy	☐ Warm	☐ Willing

STEP 4

List your accomplishments in the most powerful terms.

STEP 5

Include any pertinent special-interest areas and any results (accomplishments) from your experience in school, training, sports and hobbies, military and service, community activities, home, and, of course, work experience.

Education Examples

Achieved a 3.8 GPA while working 20 hours a week and participating in two extracurricular sports.

Established the Women's Republican Club and solicited membership from 1,320 undergraduates.

Served as editor of the class yearbook.

Initiated an Easter Seal spring frolic, which raised $5,240 for the Kids' Summer Camp program.

Special Interest Examples

Organized a tennis tournament for 520 participants.

Read the complete Great Books of the Western World.

Designed and created three new, complicated quilt patterns.

Improved my USTA tennis ability level from a 2.0 to a 4.5 in three months.

Training Examples

Graduated number two from the effective sales program.

Completed the AMA marketing-for-profit workshop.

Completed the Xerox sales training program.

Graduated from a women-in-business managing-your-time seminar.

Sport/Hobby Examples

Organized and initiated a fiction-writing group of 10 members.

Organized a tennis league and tournament for 54 participants.

Designed and built a seven-room vacation house in fourteen months.

Military Examples

Completed airborne training second in my group of 76.

Learned conversational German in five months.

Mastered an AS-11 guidance system in five months.

Community Activity Examples

Organized a group gubernatorial campaign for leading candidates in four months.

Implemented a Meal-on-Wheels program for the aged for 1,500 participants.

Initiated, organized, and conducted seven healthcare programs for 5,000 participants.

Successfully petitioned—obtaining 5,500 signatures—against irresponsible mining operations.

Family and Household Examples

Remodeled a seven-room house in my spare time in eight months.

Established a family trust fund for seven siblings.

Managed an annual family budget for nine on a $56,000 salary.

Rebuilt five small home appliances.

STEP 6

List your last four jobs, starting with the most recent, and work backward. Carefully sort through your experience, enumerating five distinct results for each position you held. Think in terms of results you can express in concrete terms of facts and figures. Make your results as action oriented as possible.

Here are a few examples:

- Organized a company library of 5,000 volumes.
- Prepared a career-advancement plan for five entry-level careers.
- Increased production by 20 percent by eliminating four clerical steps.
- Planned and administrated the orientation program for 35 employees.

Position:	
Dates:	
Employer:	
Five results:	

STEP 7

Focus on how the results you have listed relate to your career future. Go back over the items you have selected, and use a three-number rating system to indicate their relevance to your future career: a 1 represents very career-oriented results, a 2 represents somewhat career-oriented results, and a 3 represents results that are not relevant to your career.

Organization and Wording

- Think in terms of your career objective. Divide information into areas: objective, special skills, work history, education, training, and licenses.
- Arrange the elements within each area to showcase the best of what you bring to a particular position.
- Make your most powerful statements first. Place those less powerful in diminishing order.
- Keep it simple.
- List experience in a straightforward manner, with the employer's name, but not address, recorded.
- Emphasize action words and hard results.
- Keep statements to 15 words or less. Less is more.
- Use power phrases and bulleted statements.
- Be specific.

Experience

- Think in terms of value to the reader. Emphasize what you can do for him or her.
- State what you did, not what the reader should think about you. For example, "I am an excellent writer" is an evaluation. "I wrote four marketing analyses rated excellent by six department heads" exemplifies your expertise.
- Part-time jobs may be used by recent graduates looking for their first job.
- Personal references should not appear, but have them available in the event they are requested.
- Limit personal information to only that which is pertinent to the position or the demonstration of your character.
- Include personal awards or achievements if they are pertinent.

Education, Professional Training, and Affiliations

- Education, for anyone who has more than three years work experience, should appear at the bottom of the resume.
- Pertinent licenses, certificates, and other qualifications should be listed.
- Professional associations can be very important to your career, especially if you held a prominent office. List those that apply to the position you are targeting.

ELIMINATE WRONG MESSAGES

In a resume, it's crucial to communicate the message you want. It is just as crucial to avoid sending the wrong message. Keep these things in mind as you write:

Content

- Do not exaggerate, distort the facts, embellish, or lie.
- Do not use "I."
- Do not list an AOL email address for contact. Get a Gmail or Yahoo account.
- Don't be shy. State clearly and succinctly your best attributes without a braggart or flippant tone.
- Do not include statements that show you in a negative light.
- Get rid of statements that do not stress results.
- Check to be sure all errors have been removed. Proofread, proofread, proofread.
- Do not include an "Objective" that states your individual goals. Focus, instead, on your qualifications that make you right for the organization's position.
- Never state the salary you are seeking.
- Don't overload your resume. It should not include everything you have ever done.
- Unless it is relevant to the position, don't include personal information like age, weight, height, marital status, religion, or political affiliation; salary information; references or statements like "references will be furnished upon request"; or a picture of yourself.

Style

- Use sentences with fifteen or fewer words and paragraphs of three to four lines.
- Eliminate articles—*the, a, an*—whenever possible and select strong verbs to convey the meaning you want.
- Eliminate unnecessary descriptive words: creative, innovative, hard-working, futuristic, dedicated, bottom-line oriented. Dull resumes contain lots of descriptive statements that look like they were copied right out of corporate personnel manuals.
- Eliminate vagueness and jargon.
- Delete clichés and use strong words.
- Don't be wimpy. Use power verbs and precise, hard facts and figures.

WIMPY

Responsible for all sales activities for the year.

Wrote employee procedures manual.

Improved department efficiency.

Recruited and trained technical personnel.

Expanded laboratory operations.

Conducted in-college and university interviews.

Handled company's advertising.

Opened new sales offices.

Substantially lowered operating costs in division.

Handled all bookings for travel and accommodations.

Put on training sessions for department supervisors.

Managed personnel department.

Developed equipment that resulted in substantial company savings.

Initiated new employee programs.

Raised a family of six for the past 10 years.

Wrote a procedural manual for Museum of Natural History.

Reduced operating costs in my division.

POWERFUL

Increased sales 41 percent over the previous year.

Authored a 98-page employee procedures manual, which received rave reviews from 92 percent of department head reviewers.

Increased department efficiency by 35 percent (measured by time-and-quantity parameters).

Recruited and trained 75 technical personnel who performed at 94 percent efficiency after one year of employment.

Expanded laboratory staff from 85 to 425 technicians functioning at an overall efficiency rate of 94.5 percent.

Developed a new supply source of 195 top technical candidates by interviewing at 50 colleges and universities.

Increased inquiries from 65 to 97 a week by means of effective advertising.

Conducted feasibility research and established five new sales offices. Each operated at 24 percent above sales quotas in the first year and a half (seven months ahead of schedule).

Initiated cost-reducing plans in the division, which resulted in 45 percent ($47,000) cost reduction. There was no negative effect on production or future capabilities.

Negotiated travel accommodations for 35 executives that resulted in savings of $220,000 a year.

Conducted leadership training for 54 supervisors, 89 percent of whom expressed a "high level of satisfaction."

Headed personnel department of 46 professionals with annual budget accountability of $1.75 million.

Developed electrostatic production spray equipment that resulted in $3 million in company savings in 14 months.

Created and implemented two new employee relations programs that reduced employee turnover by 32 percent.

Managed and organized a six-member household on an annual budget of $42,000.

Conceptualized, organized, and authored an 80-page volunteer procedural manual for the Museum of Natural History.

CHECK FINAL DRAFT

- The employment section of your resume should include a maximum of four or five positions held. If you decide to use the chronological listing, do not leave periods of time unaccounted for.
- Document your pertinent education, association memberships, pertinent personal information, if any, and skills or training.
- Request that clients, colleagues, and associates write a recommendation for you on your pertinent website listings.
- Enlist the help of friends and professional associates whose judgment you trust. Ask them to critique your resume, using the following checklist:

	Yes	No
Are statements clear and concise?		
Are there any superfluous or unnecessary words?		
Is there anything that should be eliminated?		
Is it easy to follow?		
Are the accomplishments well showcased?		
Are there holes in the timeframes?		
Is there complete contact information: address, phone number, cell phone, email?		

SELECT A FORMAT

- Computers make it possible for you to target each resume. Select professional-looking typefaces (fonts).
- Use a high-quality printer to print your resume.
- Try to put all your information on a single sheet.
- Position your name, address, and contact numbers in the center, flush left, or in a manner so your resume looks balanced.
- When choosing a typeface, consider Helvetica, Times Roman, Schoolbook, or New Century. Don't combine styles unless you're an expert. Use boldface type, strong italics (many are too delicate), large type, and attention-getting spacing to make your point. You may want to use boldface type on your subheads and/or other items like name and telephone number, job titles, job objective (if used), education, and special skills and licenses. These are items you may want to stand out.
- Use 11 point or larger fonts for easy reading. You may want to use larger type for your most important information.
- Print in black ink for ease of reading and copying.
- Balance your material vertically and horizontally on the page so that it looks open and clean. Use the white space to get the reader's attention.
- Select a quality paper. If you're answering an ad, your resume may be one of hundreds. Isn't it worth the risk of color (buff or cream) to get extra attention? Using pastels and "shocking" colors is taking considerably more risk, however, so use these only if you know the target reader well and are sure your choice of paper won't be labeled "unprofessional." Test your paper selection to be sure it copies well. (Some heavy papers jam copiers.) Select envelopes that match your resume paper.
- Check to ensure you have no typos. Use the computer spell checker, but also go over the resume to catch correctly spelled words that are incorrectly used, like to for too.
- Give the resume a little breathing time before your final proofing. It's amazing how much difference just a little time can make in your ability to have a completely fresh, objective look.

Franklin Q. O'Day
13245 Osprey Drive
Wadsworth, Florida 33597
352-555-0123

EXPERIENCED COMPUTER MANAGER

QUALIFICATIONS
- Diagnose and repair at a 97 percent accuracy rate.
- Skilled in all major computer equipment types.
- Experienced both in working independently and supervising others.

EXPERIENCE
- Used diagnostic programs to locate defective components on all types of PET computers.
- Found and solved problems beyond the scope of diagnostic programs, such as thermal integrated circuit failure and unstripped wire in keyboard connector.
- Kept electronic equipment, including microcomputers, operating at 96 percent efficiency.

EMPLOYMENT
2000–Present | Senior Electronics Technician
University of California, Berkeley, CA
Radio Astronomy Laboratory
Test and install sensitive receivers and computer-control equipment for radio and optical telescopes, working from engineer sketches and diagrams.
1995–2000 | Electronics Technician
Beckman Instruments, Richmond, CA
Developed, tested, and repaired prototypes for high-speed electronic counters.

EDUCATION
- Santa Monica City College. Engineering major, three years.
- University of California, Berkeley. Electrical Engineering major, two years.

Chronological Resume—Public Relations

Myra Loomis
3444 Fuller Avenue, Phoenix, AZ 85283
Phone: 480-555-0123
Email: bigbird@willis.net

EXPERIENCED PUBLIC RELATIONS AND MEDIA RELATIONS EXECUTIVE

Areas of expertise: National, local, and trade media placement; and writing for clients in consumer products, energy, financial service, food, healthcare, restaurants, and travel fields.

EXPERIENCE

Principal
MDM Communications | Chicago, IL | 2001–Present
Provide media relations and writing service to 15 to 20 organizations nationwide. In one month, secured commitments for four feature placements among targeted media; placed feature stories in three local business magazines for national manufacturer seeking to improve national visibility; and secured positive news coverage for publicly traded companies among leading business media, including the *Wall Street Journal, Barron's,* Bloomberg Television, *Business Week, Financial Times, Forbes, Fortune, Investor's Business Daily,* CNBC, and CNN/fn.

Vice President
Scream Advertising | Dallas, TX | 1999–2001
Second in command for Client Services of public relations division at $50 million per year agency. Responsible for new business development, staff recruitment, and supervision. Spearheaded launch of Jolly Looney Tunes Meals for Kids that became Jolly's second largest brand within six months. Expanded Jolly account to include two additional product lines.

Senior Group Manager
Just Right Advertising | Austin, TX | 1996–1999
Supervised three of the full-service public relations agency's top five billing accounts. Consistent winner of monthly agency award for outstanding media placements. Promoted five times during tenure.

SKILLS

Consulting: business development, media relations, media training
Media relations: product introductions, targeted media placements, media tours
Project management: publications, special events, vendors, and freelance talent management
Research: product/category/competitor, soft soundings
Writing: advertorials, brochures, articles, collateral, case histories, marketing materials, newsletters, press kits, press releases, proposals, reports, scripts

AWARDS AND RECOGNITION

PRSA Award of Excellence (Silver Anvil finalist), 2010

EDUCATION

Bachelor of arts, journalism (with honors), University of Texas, Austin
Certificate of business administration, DePaul, Chicago
Graduate business courses, University of Texas, Austin

Chronological Resume—Financial Analyst

Conrad Cunningham Manchester
25 Outrigger Street
Marina Del Rey, CA 90292
310-555-0123

PROFESSIONAL EXPERIENCE

Senior Financial Analyst
Houlihan Lokey Howard and Zukin | Los Angeles, CA
1998–Present
- Manage all facets of securities analyses. Completed over 30 mid-sized corporation due diligence pro formas in 12 months, including quantitative financial analyses, debt restructuring, and offering memoranda for principal investment groups.
- Conducted over 20 separate real estate investment services, including in-depth debt restructuring, quantitative financial analyses, and due diligence on 30 deals.
- Completed merger and acquisition services on up to seven deals at a time, including 24 private placement and 23 exclusive sales of middle-market companies. Purchased and placed $125 million in corporate business debt. Executed 24 business valuations, including fairness and solvency opinions.
- Developed 35 new business opportunities with middle-market companies for purchase and corporate bond reissues.

Member, Board of Governors
University of San Francisco | San Francisco, CA
1998–Present
- Propose alternative fiscal plans to the Board of Directors. Establish student scholarship criteria. Represent Southern California alumni in fundraising activities and public relations.

Analyst, Restructuring/Litigation Group
Price Waterhouse | Los Angeles, CA
1994–98
- Provided restructuring and bankruptcy advice to 45 creditor corporations. Included due diligence and debt restructuring analyses.
- Prepared internal financial reports for 45 client corporations and evaluated alternative strategic plans for 37 restructured companies.
- Designed financial models for 36 distressed companies.

EDUCATION

Honor Student
University of San Francisco | San Francisco, CA
Bachelor of Arts, Economics/Philosophy

Chronological Resume—Middle Manager

Jennifer Maynard Boyles
1765 West Island Way
St. Charles, VA 29741
803-555-0123

PROFILE

Middle manager in healthcare setting with excellent communication skills and a keen eye for detail and accuracy. Self-starter with strong customer-service skills and the ability to work effectively in a high-pressure environment. Possess fine ability for accuracy in accounting, bookkeeping, and math.

EXPERIENCE

Resource Coordinator, MERCY HOSPITAL, Charleston, SC | 2003–Present
Work closely with physicians to identify and evaluate patients who need extended care. Attend all medical/surgery rounds to conduct patient psychosocial assessments. Consult with families to advise on extended care placement. Consult with physicians and social workers to implement patient-care programs. Organize and implement two healthcare teams that serve more than 200 patients per day. Coordinate all patient discharge, transfer, and referral records. Create statistical reports for extended care placement using spreadsheet software. Design and create database file system to update extended care and rehabilitation facility resources.

Patient Care Coordinator, ST. FRANCIS HOSPITAL, Charleston, SC | 2001–03
Coordinated and supervised all patient floor records and services. Received admissions and arranged discharges. Kept medical records current. Ordered and compiled lab work records. Inventoried, maintained, and ordered supplies as needed with 98 percent accuracy.

Program Coordinator, ST. FRANCIS HOSPICE, Charleston, SC | 1999–2001
Created and implemented new budget, which cut costs by 15 percent while increasing patient satisfaction by 17 percent. Prepared payroll for 65 employees and performed and/or oversaw accounting functions.

EDUCATION

Clemson University, Clemson, SC
B.S. in Human Services Management

Functional Resume—Assistant Restaurant Manager

Emma Cornell Worthington
1145 Evert Street
Cleveland, OH 44101
440-555-0123

OBJECTIVE: Restaurant Assistant Manager Trainee

RESTAURANT EXPERIENCE

Management
- Prepared payroll for staff of 25
- Completed light bookkeeping, made bank deposits, and maintained records for taxes
- Opened, balanced, and closed cash registers
- Ordered supplies and arranged for equipment maintenance
- Decorated restaurant
- Arranged special events for reservations of 15 or more

Personnel Supervision and Training
- Trained and supervised 20 waitresses and 12 hostesses
- Hired and terminated staff
- Successfully mediated dozens of employee disputes
- Completed work schedules for 25 employees

Menus, Food Preparation, and Presentation
- Ordered over $50,000 per month in food and liquor supplies
- Maintained inventory and organized stockroom, which resulted in savings of 15 percent
- Oversaw sanitation and preparation of food, which consistently received the highest health departing rating
- Planned menus and oversaw quality and accuracy of deliveries, which resulted in savings of 7 percent each month
- Supervised food presentation, which resulted in 22 percent higher customer satisfaction

EDUCATION

Associate of Culinary Arts, New York College of Culinary Arts

Functional Resume—Crisis Counselor

Jennifer M. Bateman, RN
3212 East Burlington Street
Wilmette, IL 60651
312-555-0123

QUALIFICATION HIGHLIGHTS

- Skilled in working with people in crisis.
- Work well independently or as a team member.
- Ten years successful research and collection of data as clinical nurse.

PROFESSIONAL EXPERIENCE

Counseling
- Crisis intervention and long-term counseling with individuals of diverse backgrounds and problems, including confinement, terminal illness, and institutional group living.
- Advised study group volunteers of positive test results including venereal disease, TB, high blood pressure, and other abnormal blood values.
- Directed and coordinated the medical follow-up for 300 individuals with problems.

Research
- Completed 40 human nutrition research studies.
- Established critical test procedures.
- Prepared samples for analysis and transport.

Management/Supervision
- Head nurse in charge of supervising support staff, research volunteers, and graduate students for a Northwestern University nutritional study.
- Authored two 80-page procedural manuals and delivered in-service training talks to 300 staff members.
- Taught data-collection and handling techniques to 75 research participants.
- Assembled data and wrote 42 reports of studies. (See bibliography.)

EMPLOYMENT

2001–Present | Research/Clinical Nurse II, Northwestern University/USDA
2002–Present | Health Consultant, Chicago School District

EDUCATION

BA, Journalism, DePaul
RN, Northwestern

Creative/Combination Resume—Health Education Administrator

Denise Leah Golightly
2345 West Highline Drive • Leadville, CO 80461
719-555-0123

OBJECTIVE
Community Health Education Administrator

QUALIFICATIONS
- Award-winning assessment and communication skills.
- Proficiency in program development, presentation, and group facilitation.
- Over 10 years experience in varied and complex human-relations responsibilities.
- MSW degree with fieldwork experience in medical and psychiatric settings.
- Proven ability to work independently and with multidisciplinary team.

PROFESSIONAL EXPERIENCE
Community Relations and Education
- Agency liaison to 24 secondary, high school, and college classes; lectured on health and education issues.
- Recruited 45 adoptive couples for hard-to-place children. Developed, organized, and coordinated 12 training sessions and 10 support groups.
- Developed and presented 32 special community education programs.
- Organized 18 community school workshop programs for parents.

Administration
- Established 10 in-house and interagency planning programs on extended medical care and adoptions.
- Prepared 15 comprehensive, expert reports, and recommendations for agency and court use.
- Contributed to establishing $2.5 million in budgets, and worked with financial officer to authorize monthly disbursements of $9,000 to $25,000 for monthly budgets.
- Supervised 17 caseworkers and technicians.

Counseling
- Achieved 87 percent improvement rate with individuals and families through use of crisis-intervention techniques and long-term counseling. Those counseled came from diverse backgrounds and statuses, and the presenting problems including life stress, illness and disability, and life transitions.
- Performed in-depth investigative interviewing and personal assessments.

EMPLOYMENT
1998–Present | Kaiser Hospitals, San Francisco, CA
Medical Social Worker

1996–98 | Marin Human Resources Agency, San Rafael, CA
Counselor for AdoptionChild Abuse

1995–96 | San Francisco Social Services
Caseworker—Low-Income Families

EDUCATION
BA, cum laude, Sociology—University of San Francisco
MSW University of San Francisco

(Also see BIOGRAPHY, page 394; NETWORKING COMMUNICATIONS, page 107; and RESUME COVER LETTER, page 116.)

19 ONLINE & EMAIL APPLICATIONS

Job searching has been revolutionized by the Internet. Certainly in the computer, computer software, and related industries, applying for jobs by posting a resume online or sending it by email is the rule and not the exception. In most other fields, as well, email is the vehicle most often used to introduce yourself as a position candidate.

But, because of its informality, anonymity, and immediacy, it's very important to use this medium carefully, and to be sure you've created the proper balance in your approach and tone. Email is often the casual Friday of the interoffice memo. However, when you are introducing yourself and your skills to a potential employer, your tone should be conversational, but not too casual. You want to be sure to communicate that you understand this is, after all, business.

With a press of the "Send" key, your application, resume cover letter, resume, and/or networking letter will instantly appear on the computer screen of the person who has the power to hire you. You'll want everything you send to promote you for the position.

DECIDE TO WRITE

Post your resume:

- On your website
- On job-search websites, such as Monster.com
- On association, alumni, or other organization websites and/or in directories

Email your resume:

- In response to an online ad
- When an email address is offered in a newspaper, magazine, or other publication ad
- To a person who has requested it

THINK ABOUT CONTENT

For your website resume and your resume to post:

- Study the principles of good web design, and examine lots of posted resumes before you decide how you want your resume to appear.

- Install a counter on your website (not visible to visitors) so you will know how many visits your website receives.
- Consider confidentiality. You may wish to use only an email address and/or cell phone number as contacts.
- Research employer ads and develop a list of "designator" nouns (interior designer, electrician, Lotus CLS) so your resume will be viewed when employers search for your qualifications. The more precise your designators, the more pre-qualified the search results.
- Study websites where you want to post your resume for any special requirements.

For your email resume:

- Format as a plain text file (.txt), or use ASCII-compatible characters so it will appear accurately across most systems and applications.
- Omit word-processing elements like boxes, bullets, underlining, graphic lines, italics, or boldface type.
- Use a simple font, like courier, of 11 points to 14 points.
- Use hyphens or asterisks (up to 60 characters per line including spaces) to create horizontal lines.
- Margins can't exceed 65 characters per line, including spaces.
- If special design features are included or required, scan your resume as a PDF file.

BEFORE YOU START

- Complete as much research as possible. Tailor your letter and resume to the specific position, and the specific person who has the power to hire you.
- Find out if the person receiving your email application prefers that you supply your resume as an attachment or inclusion in the body of the email.
- Review the rules in the appropriate chapter(s) of this book for the type of message you are sending.
- Focus on your reader; evaluate your message in terms of telling the reader what he or she needs or wants to know.
- Create your letter and/or resume first as a word processing document for ease of editing.

THINK ABOUT CONTENT

- Start with an informal greeting if you know the reader, slightly more formal if you don't.
- Communicate enthusiastically your motivation and skill strengths, and how they fit the position requirements.
- Present your skills as a solution to the reader's problem(s) whenever possible.
- Refer the reader to the details in your resume, if it's included or attached.
- In your letter, make a connection between the reader and yourself in the first paragraph, and immediately introduce the reason you are writing. Name any existing point of

reference: a referring person, an ad, or the like. If you've been referred to the reader, use the referring person's name only if you have permission to do so.

- Give details of what you have to offer—preferably a solution to the reader's problem—in the second paragraph.
- The third paragraph should be a strong close, and it should state how you'll follow up. Ask for the interview. Be sure to include your contact information.
- Use the inverted-pyramid structure in composing your message: most important information first, details later. Be concise.
- Use the subject line wisely. Think carefully about a concise, definitive, and attention-capturing line. For example, if you've been referred to the person, you may want to include the referring person's name in the subject line; or, if you are a member of an association to which the person belongs, you may want to include this in the subject line as an identifying point.
- Include a hyperlink to your website, if you have one, where you have more extensive resume information and appropriate visual and text work samples.

ELIMINATE WRONG MESSAGES

- Don't use ALL CAPS in the subject line. This is the equivalent of shouting. While this may get attention, it usually won't be positive.
- Wait to fill in the "To:" line until last, when you're completely confident you've input exactly what you want to say. That way you won't accidentally send a message you're not ready to send.
- Don't lift statements directly from your resume and put them in your letter. Duplication is boring and unoriginal. Your reader won't be impressed.
- Avoid the use of acronyms or emoticons in any of your business messages. They are too casual.

20 | LETTER OF RECOMMENDATION

The terms reference letter, letter of evaluation, letter of verification, and letter of recommendation are often used interchangeably. By strict definition, the verification letter is the most general of the four, and is used to document very general points of personal history: confirmation of employment (dates and position), credit status, and schooling.

The **reference letter** also includes general information such as dates of employment, position, credit status, place of schooling, and/or employment. This letter often includes a general recommendation about character, and was once used very routinely in the "To Whom It May Concern" format when an employee left an organization's employment.

This is not a general practice in today's business world, but there are often times when employers, prospective employers, or other organizations want verification of employment, scholarship, character, and/or credit status, so a letter of reference is requested. In response, send this letter specifically to the person requesting it and supply only the information requested that conforms with your organization's reference policy.

The **letter of evaluation** gives a more thorough accounting of both the negative and positive aspects of a person's history, although in our litigious society, negative points are often very limited or omitted entirely. This letter is often routinely completed as part of an employee's review process and is placed in his or her confidential personnel file.

The **letter of recommendation** promotes one person to another. It is generally written by a former supervisor in the workplace or a professor or teacher when requested by a former employee or student.

The organization and content of all these letters are very similar, but this chapter will concentrate on the letter of recommendation as it is the most commonly used. Most everything here applies to the other letters as well. (See samples at the end of the chapter for specific examples of the reference letter and the letter of recommendation.)

For your letter of recommendation to be effective, you must be familiar enough with the person's abilities, skills, and performance to offer specific information.

Before you start, review your organization's policy. It may prohibit you from answering a request for information on a former employee or associate. Many organizations have a policy that limits reporting to only certain broad, verifiable facts. If you do respond, stay away from information about the person's age, race, religion, sex, marital status, pregnancy, criminal record, citizenship, organization memberships, and mental and physical handicaps, unless—in an unusual case—the information is clearly related to the position. If you are not very familiar with the person, or you cannot recommend him or her, decline. (Remember, in most instances the person will be able to read your letter under the provisions of the Privacy Act.)

DECIDE TO WRITE

Compose this letter to:
- Respond to a request about a former employee or company you have been associated with
- Promote a candidate for a club, sorority, fraternity, association, or honor society membership
- Recommend a candidate for a job, grant, scholarship, or special award

THINK ABOUT CONTENT

- Identify and verify the request.
- Be sure you know the position for which the person is applying, and write the recommendation in light of that knowledge.
- Explain your relationship to the person, stating your position, title, and any other pertinent information.
- State the person or company's full name, position, or status. Include dates of employment or association, position titles, primary responsibilities, and professional or honorary associations.
- Respond directly to the inquiry, addressing the specific questions asked.
- Give a general recommendation that sets up the organization of the letter. Use a tone that is businesslike but friendly, warm, and informal. A cold or overly formal letter will not help the person being recommended.
- Organize the details in a decreasing order of importance.
- Be explicit and substantive. Vague and general statements distance you from the person you are recommending and are not persuasive.
- Be honest and truthful, and give every fact the emphasis it deserves. If you report a negative point, for instance, give only enough emphasis to convey an accurate picture. Because negative facts are usually given more weight in the reader's mind, it will be best to subordinate any given, or omit them.
- Detail two or three characteristics in their order of importance. Instead of "Julie has excellent skills," write "Julie consistently inputs 110 words a minute using WordPerfect, Paradox, or Harvard Graphics software." Listing more than three examples diffuses their impact.
- Verify the reason for the resignation or termination of an employee or relationship, as appropriate.
- Reaffirm and summarize your recommendation, and invite the reader to write or call for more information.
- End on a note of goodwill or best wishes.

ELIMINATE WRONG MESSAGES

- Don't go overboard or make statements you cannot prove.
- Avoid the "To Whom It May Concern" approach; address your letter to a specific person. If this isn't possible, use the memo format of DATE, TO, FROM, RE (with regard to): "Introducing Dana Ledbetter" or another suitable heading that indicates the memo topic.
- Don't advise the reader. Statements like "You should hire her fast" or "Don't let him get away" could work against the person being recommended.
- Don't give the information without checking your organization's policy about giving recommendations.

CONSIDER SPECIAL SITUATIONS

When Someone Asks You to Write a Recommendation

- Using a subject line, which identifies the request and the person, helps get your letter off to a direct start.
- When recommending a company or product, use only direct examples from your personal experience to state your case, citing, too, the exact application and method of use. It is wise to frame your recommendation in terms of your opinion based on this experience.
- Because we live in a litigious society, caution must be used in deciding the contents of your letter of recommendation, reference, or evaluation. Some organizations do not give this information either over the telephone or in writing. Many organizations will only confirm the person was employed, the dates of employment, and the person's title. Litigation charging negligence has ensued, too, where the former employer did not disclose the former employee had been charged with theft or other problems.
- Assume that anything you write may end up in a court of law, and if you do not want to defend it, don't write it. If there is any question about your statements being actionable, consult legal counsel before sending.
- Do not write a letter of reference if you can't honestly recommend the person.

When You Ask Someone to Write a Letter of Recommendation

- Be sure to give that person specific information that will help in tailoring the recommendation to your specific needs. For example: "Jim, I'm a candidate for the new-product manager position at the start-up company, Waddle's. In your recommendation letter for me, it would be most appropriate if you would review my position and work on the Model F-56 (development through getting it to market)."
- After the letter of reference has been sent, be sure to thank the person who wrote it. (Also see Thank-You, page 75.)

SELECT A FORMAT

- Type on letterhead. The appearance should be professional.
- Interoffice recommendations, references, and evaluations may be done in memo form.

SELECT STRONG WORDS

capable	character	commendable	competent
congenial	conscientious	considerate	cooperative
decorated	dedicated	distinguished	dynamic
effective	efficient	energetic	ethical
excellent	exemplary	honest	impeccable
integrity	invaluable	irreplaceable	irreproachable
loyal	meritorious	noteworthy	outstanding
productive	professional	reliable	remarkable
resourceful	respectable	trustworthy	valuable

BUILD STRONG PHRASES

can confidently recommend	constructs compelling arguments
could always be counted on	dedicated to doing an outstanding job
discharged his duties professionally	enthusiastic in taking on new responsibilities
entirely trustworthy	exceeded the job description
excelled in going beyond the required	exerted extraordinary efforts
extended himself to complete the work	first-class employee in every regard
I highly recommend	initiated new approaches to problems
organized and efficient	outstanding contributions
performed beyond the requirements	performed in an outstanding manner
recommend without reservation	set an outstanding example
solution oriented in facing problems	take-charge person
team player	took initiative
well respected by coworkers	wholeheartedly recommend

WRITE STRONG SENTENCES

Start with a powerful verb, and then construct strong, concise sentences like these:

Julia Barnes earned the respect of her coworkers.

Jennifer Bose had $11 million in unpaid royalties sorted out and deposited in the correct accounts in four months.

Carla Grieves increased production by 17 percent in seven months.

Employee satisfaction increased over 30 percent during Myron Fee's first year as director of personnel.

It was a sad day at Koelbel when Chico Martinez tendered his resignation.

BUILD EFFECTIVE PARAGRAPHS

I felt a great loss when Elsie Walkio resigned to move to Phoenix with her husband. For over 10 years she kept me prepared and on time. I don't expect I'll ever find another assistant as fine or as efficient as Elsie.

Here are just a couple of examples. Josie worked an entire weekend preparing separate project packets for a national sales meeting because our copy equipment had failed the week before, and no one else knew how to assemble the packets. She saved our company hundreds of thousands of dollars by revising the manual-review procedures; and she never missed an administrative employee's birthday.

Let me know if you need any additional information, and please give Robert my best regards.

EDIT, EDIT, EDIT

Make your recommendation clear, concise, and detailed enough to be credible.

Letter of Verification	Recommendation for a General Contractor
Dear Ms. Griswald:	Dear Mr. and Mrs. Beem:

Letter of Verification

Dear Ms. Griswald:

I hereby confirm that Roscoe Wallace was employed by Ditty's in the shipping department as a processor on April 5, 2001. Mr. Wallace's employment continued for five years until he tendered his resignation on June 10, 2006, at which time he was a process supervisor.

Mr. Wallace's record indicates no disciplinary action during his employment, and he left Ditty's voluntarily.

Sincerely,

Mildred Owens

Human Resources

Recommendation for a General Contractor

Dear Mr. and Mrs. Beem:

I'm pleased to recommend Conceptions General Contracting for your custom home remodel. I hired Ted and Alice Reilly, Conceptions' owners and principals, eight months ago to complete three bathrooms, kitchen, den, and foyer—a complete redesign through reconstruction. The Reillys scheduled subcontractors so we could continue to inhabit our home while the remodel took place, and they orchestrated every detail exactly as they had promised.

The entire remodel was completed on time and on budget, and we are delighted with the workmanship and quality of every detail. I also found the Reillys' suggestions and recommendations to be invaluable, and they saved us both many dollars and undue frustration.

If there are any other details you'd like to discuss, or if you would like to see the work they completed in our home, please contact us to arrange a time (775-555-0123).

Sincerely,

Dee Yates

Letter of Reference for a College Student

Mr. Bradley Turnnet
Director of Human Resources
Prommet Enterprises
43 Spring
Springfield, OH 45502

Re: Kelly Vassel Reference

Dear Mr. Turnnet:

As Kelly Vassel's former professor and employer, I am pleased to recommend her for your position of controller. I've known Kelly Vassel for four years, first as a student in two of my economics classes, and then as an intern and research assistant on my Fuller Project.

Kelly was an excellent student, with far-above-average grades. She consistently maintained a GPA of over 3.8 (A = 4.0). It was on the basis of her applied scholarship as well as her initiative and participation in class that I offered her the position of intern and research assistant. In this role, Kelly performed independently (after my approval), and was a very worthy employee, demonstrating maturity, creative thought, and the ability to take responsibility. Her work succeeded in helping to secure two grants for the Fuller Project. Her reports and grant applications were well written and comprehensive.

I enthusiastically recommend Kelly to you. She has demonstrated that she is very capable of doing an outstanding job as controller.

Please let me know if I can offer any additional information.

Sincerely,

James Broyles

Professor of Economics

Personal Reference for a Friend

Dear Mr. Archibald:

I'm writing in response to your May 18 letter requesting a personal reference for Saul Bellweather. I have known Saul for 11 years. His father and I are partners in the same law firm, and his mother has been my wife's CPA since 1998. Our families have gotten together socially over the years of our affiliation, and Saul and my son, Teddy, are best friends.

Saul possesses fine character traits. He has always pursued his own path, excelled in what he set out to do, and carried through on assigned tasks.

If you need further information, please call me. Obviously, I give Saul the highest recommendation.

Sincerely,

Barclay Withers

Recommendation for Promotion within the Company

MEMO

DATE: September 5, 2005

TO: Derek Woodward

FROM: Maria Whitmore, VP of Sales

SUBJECT: Leah Harvey Promotion

Leah Harvey has completed her tour here in the fast-track program. Although the youngest in the sales department, Leah has performed well in decision making, problem solving, and negotiating. In fact, she is our top performer. She closes at the highest rate (76 percent) and in the shortest time (31.5 minutes) of anyone in the department.

Leah desires to be a district sales manager, and I believe she possesses the skills to be one of the best. I recommend we place her in the opening for Region 13.

Recommendation for a New Law School Graduate

Reference: Your Letter of May 12 Requesting a Recommendation for a First-Year Lawyer

Dear George:

Yes, I have an exceptional recommendation for the position at Krause and Krause. I was fortunate enough to have Neil R. Reynolds in three of my classes at Stanford Law School. He is a breath of fresh air. Not only did he finish in the top of his class, he demonstrated rare leadership skills on special team projects. Neil has an intuitive sense of justice—real justice—and came up with completely innovative ways to carry it out to the advantage of all involved on three occasions I recall in detail. I've never seen another student with this ability. I could go on and on.

I tried to get Neil in at Stanton and Gregg, but we took three new graduates last year, and our practice is presently undergoing some changes in scope and direction.

Neil comes with my highest recommendation. If I can offer any additional information, please call.

Sincerely,

Bernardo Blackburn

Recommendation for a Long-Time Customer

Reference: Your Request of April 15 to Supply a Reference for Sidney Wales

Mr. Ray Karnes:

We have done business with Mr. Sidney Wales for 12 years. We are pleased to refer him as an outstanding customer who conducts his business in a conscientious and satisfactory manner.

There has never been an unresolved dispute or an overdue notice in all these years. Oh, that all our customers were so prompt and honest!

If you have any further questions, please call.

Cordially,

Samuel Wise

Recommendation for a Former Employee

Dear Mr. Bellows:

I highly recommend Robert Levine. He worked as my assistant in the office of the president, and as statistical clerk for five years. He had a confident, take-charge manner, which was, at the same time, cordial. His statistical work was accurate and thorough.

In five years, Robert missed three work days. He was always eager to see a project through to completion, even if it meant staying after hours. I don't believe Robert ever angered a customer calling over the telephone (even though there were a few who angered me). In fact, Robert's skills in dealing with clients and callers in this office were outstanding.

Obviously, I recommend Robert. If you'd like any additional information, please call.

Sincerely,

Nathan Neustetter

Employment Letter of Reference

Ellen Dorms

Dear Ms. Dorms:

I'm responding to your request for an employment reference letter for Alex Tributes. Our policy is to provide the following information: Mr. Tributes was employed by Shakers from June 5, 1999, through March 10, 2003, as a machinist. His employment was entirely satisfactory, and he left Shakers to move out of the area.

We do not provide salary information or other details of employment.

If I can be of further assistance, please contact me by telephone: 574-555-0123.

Sincerely,

Hazel Nutt

Human Resources

Recommendation for a Former Graduate Student

Dear Dean Callan:

Edward A. Meyer, PhD, is an outstanding scholar, a capable teacher, and a diligent and tireless worker.

Dr. Meyer's scholarship is demonstrated by his 3.8 GPA (out of 4.0) here at Marquette, as well as his undergraduate performance at MOO U. He was in two of my human resources classes and did excellent work, making A's in both. He demonstrated a keen, scholarly inquisitiveness, and worked diligently to excel. I expect that these traits will help him make a great contribution in the field.

I believe he has already begun on that course with the publication of portions of his dissertation in *HR Magazine* and *Administrators' Digest*.

I have heard three of Edward Meyer's speeches, and he did an excellent job in all of them. I have also observed many of his classroom sessions while he served as my graduate assistant for two years. He entered the classroom well prepared, maintained a thoughtful learning atmosphere, and challenged the students to stretch a bit.

In summary, I recommend Dr. Edward Meyer as a teacher of behavioral management. I'll be pleased to discuss any of this information in greater detail if you care to call me.

Sincerely,

Herbert K. Kline, PhD

Offering a Neutral Recommendation

Dear Otto:

Star Reising held the position of customer service representative with Stitches from May 10, 2005, to March 15, 2006. During this period of time she was promoted twice within the department with appropriate salary increases.

Star left Stitches to return to college.

Sincerely,

Melvin Whales

Declining to Give a Recommendation

Dear Jackson:

My assistant relayed the message that you called and asked for a recommendation to Breakers for the position of manager you have applied for.

Reflecting on the years we worked together, I do not feel I worked closely enough with you to offer a meaningful evaluation and recommendation on the factors that Breakers will want. I certainly will confirm your employment and salary history if you would like to have someone contact me for that information.

Best wishes in your job future.

Sincerely,

Stanley Blacker

(Also see REFUSING AN APPLICANT, page 154; REPRIMAND, page 184; REQUEST & INQUIRY, page 246; CREDIT DENIAL, page 340; and THANK-YOU, page 75.)

21 REFUSING AN APPLICANT

Since this is a bad news letter given to a recipient who may already be under stress, the utmost tact is needed in constructing it. The objective is to maintain a spirit of goodwill, if possible, and to avoid antagonizing the recipient of the letter.

At the same time, it's necessary to state your decision conclusively. You need not justify it; doing so may invite the recipient to try to get you to change your mind. (Also see Declining a Position, page 157, and Refusal, page 274.)

THINK ABOUT CONTENT

- Start with a positive, neutral statement.
- Thank the applicant for applying, using a positive statement about his or her skills or qualifications, if possible.
- Set up the explanation for refusal, stating only the organization requirements.
- Make a clear statement of refusal.
- Tell the applicant what will happen to his or her application and future prospects with the organization.
- Close with a goodwill statement, offer suggestions or alternatives, or compliment the reader. Any good suggestions, referrals, or compliments will enhance your goodwill efforts.

ELIMINATE WRONG MESSAGES

- Do not make negative statements.
- Make no comparisons with the winning candidate.
- Offer no excuses, and leave no question about the finality of your decision.
- Never blame others for the refusal.

CONSIDER SPECIAL SITUATIONS

- Respond quickly to minimize disappointment.
- Cast your response in terms of your company's needs, and don't reflect on the applicant's lack of qualifications. For example, don't write "You don't meet the requirements" but rather "The position requires at least 10 years experience."
- Applications and resumes received by email may also be refused by email.

SELECT A FORMAT

- Business refusals should be typed on letterhead when your response is by mail.
- Email responses may be sent to those who applied by email.

USE STRONG WORDS

consider	consistent	decline	demonstrated
experience	future	match	qualifications
respond	review	skills	seasoned

BUILD EFFECTIVE PHRASES

after the committee's review

appreciate your time and effort

cannot offer you

do not have other openings at this time

final candidate has been selected

many excellent candidates

please contact us again

reviewed your excellent qualifications

the selection process was difficult

appreciate your application for

can assure you careful consideration was given

carefully considered

evaluations were exacting and thorough

have selected a finalist

our decision was made difficult by

require extensive experience

thank you for applying

will keep your resume on file

WRITE STRONG SENTENCES

Thank you for applying for the office manager position.

The selection committee has selected a candidate with extensive experience in this exact research.

It was a pleasure meeting you.

We will keep your resume on file for six months in case an opening suitable for your qualifications should present itself.

BUILD EFFECTIVE PARAGRAPHS

It was apparent to our selection committee that you have a very bright future in genetics engineering. They were especially impressed with your ideas on cell division.

Thank you for your resume in response to our opening for a marketing director (April Marketing News). Your experience is impressive, but this senior position requires at least 15 years in the field.

I would like to suggest you contact Mr. Ray Miller of IN-PLANT Placement. He provides an extraordinary service in connecting candidates with positions in this field.

With your permission, we will keep your resume on file so we may consider you for future openings. Our procedure is to review resumes on file first when a position opens up or is created. If an appropriate position becomes available at Carlisle, we will be pleased to consider you for it.

EDIT, EDIT, EDIT

Make your message as positive, brief, and concise as possible.

Refusing an Applicant

Dear Jack:

Thank you for applying for the production management position at Castle. Mr. Kane and I were very impressed with your accomplishments over the past five years. The production management position, however, requires extensive experience with the Roberts equipment.

Your inquiry will, of course, be kept confidential, and we will keep your resume in the engineering file should something else open up in the next six months. I wish you continued success in your career.

Yours truly,

Jack Buboinis

Refusing an Underqualified Candidate

Dear Ms. Curtis:

Thank you for considering Mason and Mason Engineering as a place of employment. You made a very positive impression here with your outstanding work history and interview skills. As we discussed, however, the present status of our design department and the projects we have in-house demand that we hire a candidate with skills and experience in these specialized areas.

We would like to keep your resume and copies of your work samples on file. We anticipate that six to eight months down the road we may be expanding the design department. At that time, we'll reevaluate our needs. Should you meet them, we will contact you to arrange an interview.

Best wishes for what we know will be a brilliant career.

Sincerely,

Kim Sanders

Refusing a Candidate Due to Internal Delay

Dear Ms. Schneider:

I was pleased to meet you and discuss the position at General Television for an administrative assistant to the executive director.

I was very favorably impressed with your skills and poise.

Since your interview, we have had other changes in the organization, which have required that we delay hiring an administrative assistant for at least five months.

I would like to keep your resume on file to reconsider at that time, and I invite you to contact us in four months about the position. Again, thank you for coming in. Perhaps we will have the opportunity to discuss this position or another one at a future time.

Sincerely,

Sally Weinstein

Declining a Freelance Submission

SUBJECT: Picnics Query Response

Dear Jody:

Thank you for submitting "Picnics" for our consideration. It has been read here by several editors, and it is our determination that it doesn't meet our current editorial needs.

"Picnics" shows great promise, and we do hope you'll submit another piece to us in the near future.

All the best,

Ed Getty
Senior Editor

(Also see REFUSAL, page 274.)

22 DECLINING A POSITION

The letter used to decline a job offer is a refusal letter with the central theme of goodwill. While you'll want to leave no uncertainty about your decision, your refusal should be stated tactfully. (See Refusal, page 274.)

THINK ABOUT CONTENT

- Open with a friendly or neutral "buffer" statement.
- Thank the employer for the job offer.
- Review the facts and give an explanation, if applicable, for declining the offer.
- State in definite, clear, and positive terms that you must decline the offer based on the explanation you presented.
- End the letter on a cordial note, one that establishes or reestablishes a positive relationship.

CONSIDER SPECIAL SITUATIONS

- Make sure you understand the timeframe and respond within it.
- Always leave a situation on good terms.
- Keep the lines of communication open even after you have declined the job offer.

ELIMINATE WRONG MESSAGES

- Do not leave your decision open to debate.
- Don't belabor the bad news.
- Don't leave the impression that you will reconsider a modified offer.

SELECT A FORMAT

- The letter should be typewritten on personal stationery.
- Email a response if the application process was conducted through emailing.

SELECT POWER WORDS

appreciate	choice	consider	consideration
decision	decline	description	difficult
enjoyed	fit	flattered	generous
goals	offer	opportunity	options
pleasure	recognize	reply	respond

BUILD EFFECTIVE PHRASES

a difficult decision

after weighing all the factors

I cannot accept the position

I do sincerely regret

I have, of course, considered it carefully

I must say no

my decision must be

after careful consideration and deliberation

I am flattered, of course, but

I do appreciate the offer

I have concluded that it isn't a proper fit

I must decline

my final answer is

thank you for offering

WRITE STRONG SENTENCES

It was a pleasure meeting your fine staff of engineers yesterday.

I was very impressed with the efficiency of the quality-control operation.

Thank you for orchestrating the interview process, and for the offer of the marketing manager position.

BUILD EFFECTIVE PARAGRAPHS

I have enjoyed the past month of interviews and screening for the position of plant manager at Wickliff.

I believe you, Brad Williams, and Dennis Bradley make an outstanding team.

I am flattered by the offer of vice president of client affairs at Metcalf and Metcalf. It's an exceptional opportunity; but after careful consideration, I must decline.

Your generous offer of a partnership at Lockhart and Wendell is everything I've worked for these past 12 years. I'm honored that you, David, Lance, and Jacob feel confident in my abilities to fill the position. Ironically, after two days of soul searching and lengthy discussions with Carol and the boys, I must decline.

Meeting you and the other people at Cruthers was a pleasure. I was very impressed with the attention to detail the entire department exhibited in doing their work. And I was, of course, pleased to receive the generous job offer that followed the interviews.

EDIT, EDIT, EDIT

Your ultimate job is to say a concise "no" with a written smile.

Declining Employment Due to Accepting a More Suitable Position

Dear Mr. Harrison:

I was pleased to receive your offer of employment as a systems analyst for Smathers. I was very impressed with the teamwork that characterizes your staff, and the pride in workmanship that is demonstrated in the products you produce.

However, since the interviews with Smathers, I have been offered another position, which is more closely aligned with my career goals, and I have accepted it.

Thank you for your time and the vote of confidence in selecting me. Please give my thanks to Paul Westbrook and David Winters. I enjoyed meeting all of you and the rest of the Smathers team. I sincerely hope our paths connect again in the future.

Yours truly,

Rick Watters

Declining an Inadequate Offer

Dear Ben:

Thank you for the offer to head up the public relations operation at Skaggs. I've reviewed all the aspects of the position, and have tried to make the numbers work, but there's simply not a common ground here. I must decline.

I wish you well, and hope you will find someone with the skills you're looking for to fill the post.

Sincerely,

Gerri Grover

Declining Employment Due to Accepting a Job That Fits Family Goals

Dear Mr. Broward:

Yes, I did receive your second offer. It was very generous of you to increase the benefit package.

I appreciated the courtesies extended to me during the interview process, and certainly the after-hours interview arrangements.

I enjoyed meeting the therapy team, too, and feel your program is a very important one. I'm sure it will do very well over the next several years with the goals you have set.

All this made it extremely difficult for me to come to the decision to accept another position in Los Angeles that fits not only my career goals but also allows complete coordination with my wife's career.

Thank you for all your efforts on my behalf. I greatly appreciate your thoughtfulness, and hope we will be able to serve together on one of the various professional committees in the future.

Sincerely,

Reginald McDonald, MD

IV.

EMPLOYMENT & EMPLOYEE COMMUNICATIONS

A powerful agent is the right word.

—*Mark Twain*

23 EMPLOYEE CORRESPONDENCE

Employment correspondence is a category rather than a specific type of letter. Many of the letters and memos in this category are actually types covered elsewhere in this book, but it's important to think of these as a group of communications that details the history of the relationship between the employer and the employee.

Both the employee's and the employer's perspectives are reflected here because all this correspondence should become part of the employee's personnel file reflecting his or her relationship with the organization.

Starting when an applicant tries to secure a position, there may be a number of letters written between the potential employee and employer. Obviously, it's in the applicant's best interest to make as many appropriate contacts with a potential employer as possible.

During each telephone conversation and each face-to-face meeting, for example, the applicant may create the opportunity to follow up with a note, memo, or letter. These communications can be pivotal in demonstrating his or her writing skills. If this applicant is hired, it is likely that copies of these communications will make their way into the employee's personnel file. During the course of employment, written communications between the employer and the employee become even more important in documenting the history of the relationship.

Because of our litigious society, some of the most important communications to have as part of the file are negative messages, such as a reprimand, termination, or resignation. Because they are so important, they need special consideration. (See Reprimand, page 184, Employee Termination, page 192, and Letter of Resignation, page 188.)

DECIDE TO WRITE

This group of letters, memos, and other documents may be used to:

- Respond to a job applicant or candidate
- Apply for a job
- Communicate with an employee
- Communicate with an employer
- Become part of the record of that tells the story of the relationship between employee and employer, including performance reviews, salaries, raises, vacations, healthcare insurance coverage, promotions, reprimands, and so on.

THINK ABOUT CONTENT

- Keep job applicants informed in order to create a positive impression of the organization.
- Make it a practice to tell people when they are doing a good job. It does wonders for goodwill and usually improves work quality.
- It is important to maintain a written record of letters of employment; any and all agreements between the organization and the employee; changes of status with titles and financial agreements; and other decisions made between employer and employee. Make sure you commit these to writing, and keep copies in the appropriate personnel records.
- In addition to following the instructions for the type of letter being written, make sure your letter is clear and to the point.
- Introduce the subject of the letter; state it clearly and concisely.
- Offer the explanation, backing it up with facts.
- Close with a statement of goodwill, or end on an upbeat note, if possible.
- In our litigious society, it's important to document all corrective actions that are taken and make these a part of the employee record. (See Reprimand, page 184.)
- Keep current on legal requirements in relationships with employees, and keep all related records.

ELIMINATE WRONG MESSAGES

- Review pertinent laws, regulations, and policies before writing to avoid any statements that could result in a legal battle.
- Don't write negative messages if you can avoid it. Almost anything you have to say can be said in a positive statement. If you are angry, process your anger privately, not in a letter that will become part of your employee record.
- Don't use a written message to avoid a verbal exchange. The written employee message, for example, should usually be used to document what has been said in a face-to-face meeting.
- Don't communicate personnel matters through email exchange unless you have an established organizational policy to do so, and a secure computer system.

SELECT A FORMAT

- The interoffice memo is the most commonly used vehicle for employer and employee communications. The exceptions are the letters of employment, termination, and resignation. In these instances a formal typewritten letter on personal or organization letterhead is appropriate.

WRITE STRONG SENTENCES

There was no safety officer on duty from midnight to 8:00 a.m. on February 17 through 25.

Your scheduled date for the complete physical examination is July 5.

You are being promoted to Corbett Vice President of Finances, effective July 1, 2011.

You used all of your allocated sick days for the employment year of April 1, 2011, to March 31, 2012.

Thank you for your request to go on a flextime work schedule.

BUILD EFFECTIVE PARAGRAPHS

As I discussed with you, the vacation schedule you designed for your department for July and August of this year, 2011, impaired business operations and resulted in extra expenditures, and possibly the loss of two accounts. We had 23 customer complaints of double billing, for example, because payments had not been entered in the computer, and there were about two dozen complaints from our personnel that there was no one in your department to answer questions.

I've reviewed your request for a leave of absence from March 1 through July 31, 2012.

Please be in my office in the morning at 10:00 a.m. to discuss this. Bring with you a copy of your physician's recommendation for this leave.

I'm sorry to learn of the interpersonal conflict within the marketing department. I have reviewed possible transfers for you, as you requested. There are three options open. Please be in my office at 10:00 a.m. on Friday to discuss them.

EDIT, EDIT, EDIT

Cut out unnecessary words, and arrange paragraphs so the reader may easily understand the message. Even with difficult communications, end on as positive a note as possible.

Sexual Harassment Claim

[Date]

Dear Lisa:

I have reviewed your complaint of sexual harassment by your supervisor, Allan Reek. Again, as we discussed in my office, Dimensions wants to provide a positive work environment for all employees, and that means we will not tolerate sexual harassment.

I have initiated a full investigation by Mort Jansen, plant manager, and Jennifer Swan, vice president, Human Relations. One or both of them will contact you in the manner you requested within the next couple of days.

We will make every effort to resolve this situation swiftly and justly. Please contact Jennifer Swan or me if you have any other questions or comments.

Sincerely,

Marla Drapples

Warning about Intoxication

[Date]

Dear Lars:

Following up on our discussion of this morning, this is your second and final warning that McGraw Tools & Trucks does not tolerate intoxication on the job. Your first warning was issued on May 15, 2011, for the incident that occured on May 12, 2011, when you were found to be intoxicated. (Report copies are attached.)

Please be in my office at 9:30 a.m. tomorrow to tell the employee committee why you should not be terminated effective June 15, 2011. The committee will give you their decision on Thursday. As you know, there is a required treatment plan to follow to remain employed here.

Lars, we all want to see you turn this around. We don't want to lose you.

Sincerely,

Joseph Dutton

Resolving Favoritism Complaint

TO: Nicole Lazar, Manager
FROM: Sandra Lewis, Director of Personnel
DATE: May 10, 2011
SUBJECT: Employee Complaints

As I discussed with you this morning, we have had four complaints alleging favoritism in your treatment of subordinates.

I believe you can resolve this problem by holding a department meeting and explaining the criteria and the selection process that resulted in the promotion of JoAnn Beales to assistant manager.

Please let me know by October 12 whether you feel this is satisfactorily resolved without intervention from Personnel.

I will get back to you on October 17 to discuss the resolution of this complaint.

Promotion Denied

Dear Alex:

Thank you for your bid for the job opening number 99821. It was an extremely difficult decision, and you were well in the running. But after final evaluation of all of the 21 final applicants, Mel Berger was awarded the position.

I was sorry to deliver this disappointing news in our meeting this morning, but I'm sure that your skills and outstanding record will allow you to obtain an equal position in one of the openings coming up in the next few months.

Sincerely,

Martina McPhee

(See also ACCEPTANCE, page 269; ACKNOWLEDGMENT & CONFIRMATION, page 264; CONGRATULATIONS, page 28; EMPLOYEE TERMINATION, page 192; LETTER OF RESIGNATION, page 188; REFUSAL, page 274; REFUSING AN APPLICANT, page 154; REPRIMAND, page 184; REQUEST & INQUIRY, page 246; RESUME, page 126; RESUME COVER LETTER, page 116; THANK-YOU, page 75; and WELCOME, page 57.)

Recommendation for Employee Promotion

TO: Jackson Davis
FROM: Vivian Long
DATE: January 10, 2011
SUBJECT: Daniel Vider's Promotion

I recommend Daniel Vider for the Region Four sales manager position, effective July 1, 2011. His performance over the past 18 months meets the criteria, and even surpasses it in some areas:

- His sales are the highest in Region Four. Dan sold 11 percent over his own projected goals.
- His management skills, as demonstrated in his customer correspondence, rank at a 98 percent "very satisfied." He is also held in high esteem by all the other salespeople.
- Dan's planning I must rate very high also. He set a goal of 45 new customers this year and he has 57. He planned the mail out of four new direct-mail pieces, and met that goal with a 12 percent response rate. His follow-up converted all these respondents to customers, and he brought in another 10 percent from his original mailing list. He has also demonstrated the ability to adjust his planning to company changes.

I conclude that Dan rates very high in our criteria for both can-do and will-do, and even though he is junior in seniority, we should reward him with this promotion.

Report of Unsatisfactory Performance

MEMO

TO: Richard Parks
FROM: Jim Fuchs
DATE: October 5, 2011
SUBJECT: Rick Hanson's Unsatisfactory Performance

I have just received the fourth customer call this month that Rick Hanson has made a substantial error in analyzing a customer account. Dick, these errors occurred on four of our top accounts. (See attached reports.)

All of these customers have requested a change of analysts. Would you please handle this and let me know by Friday who the new analyst will be?

24 INTRODUCTION

The letter of introduction was created for a much different society, to introduce one person to another for social or business purposes. Today, we live in a very mobile society, equipped with many forms of instant communication, and in a business and social climate of assertiveness. Therefore, the written letter of introduction is seldom used as it once was. When it is used for business introduction, it carries little obligation; the social introduction carries more.

The letter of introduction is more often used today to introduce yourself, in situations like that of a professor teaching a class online. It is also used to introduce a new employee or organization representative, such as a product manager or sales representative. And it is used to introduce new products or services.

Today the purpose of the letter of introduction is a combination of reference, recommendation, and explanation. For example, the professor teaching an online course will introduce him- or herself with a short personal biography, a listing of course materials (and/or a reference as to where these will be posted on the course website), an introduction to the course, what the class will cover, and what will be expected of students.

DECIDE TO WRITE

Use this letter when you want to introduce:

- One person to another
- A new employee
- A new product or service
- One service or organization to another
- Yourself to subordinates, clients, students, or others with whom you are initiating a business or social relationship

THINK ABOUT CONTENT

- Since the letter of introduction implies the approval of the person being introduced, agree to write it only if you can do so wholeheartedly.
- Give the full name of the person you're introducing and some of his or her background. For a new employee, state the person's position, effective date of employment, and, if appropriate, the person to whom he or she has reporting responsibility. List the pertinent information: new employee's experience, education, expertise, past employers, major clients, special projects, and awards. Ask other employees to welcome the new employee.

- State why you want to introduce the two people. Give any characteristics, points of interest the person and the reader may have in common, and any other helpful information.
- Make your letter cordial and brief.
- Offer more than one or two points of commonality, if possible.
- Suggest a meeting time, place, and an arrangement that does not obligate the recipient to entertain the person you are introducing.
- Tell the reader the possible benefits of meeting the person, using the service, or joining the organization.
- Give the reader an opportunity to decline.
- Thank the reader.

ELIMINATE WRONG MESSAGES

- Don't write the introduction casually. Don't, for example, agree to write for a person you do not believe merits it.
- Do not presume the reader will be anxious to meet the person, and don't make statements like "I know you'll be glad to meet him" in your letter.
- Don't just plunge in. Give full consideration to the reader, even though you may be making the introduction as a favor to the person you are introducing.
- The letter of introduction should not obligate the reader to socially entertain the person you are introducing. Be sure not to imply or suggest this.

CONSIDER SPECIAL SITUATIONS

- When you use a letter of introduction to introduce a new sales employee to customers or clients, all the same rules apply. In addition, it's important to affirm your support to both parties.

SELECT A FORMAT

- Unless the recipient is a personal friend to whom you send handwritten letters, the letter of introduction should be typewritten on letterhead or on business, personal, or plain stationery.
- A form letter may be used when the message is being conveyed to a number of recipients, such as the introduction of a new sales representative or a salesperson to customers or clients.
- Introductions to clubs, groups, or associations are best typewritten on personal stationery or the appropriate letterhead, but certainly may be handwritten.

USE WORDS OF CORDIALITY

admire	advocate	associate	benefit
character	colleague	endorse	enjoy
favor	interesting	introduce	meet
mutual	pleasure	recommend	suggest

USE EFFECTIVE PHRASES

a great fit	benefit from discussing with her
don't feel obligated	greatly appreciate
I admire her very much	if you have time
introduce to you	I respect very much
may I suggest	much in common
my dear friend and colleague	my pleasure to introduce
recommend you meet	you may enjoy meeting

WRITE STRONG SENTENCES

I think your time will be well spent if you can spare 30 minutes to meet her.

I've heard you mention you would like to meet Dr. Allan Beard.

I'm sure both you and Jennifer will benefit from a brief meeting.

One of my dearest friends, Alex Rivers, will be in Los Angeles next week.

You have heard me mention Joan Brookstone in reference to the new theory on disease control.

BUILD EFFECTIVE PARAGRAPHS

One of my dearest friends, Jenny Creighton, will be in Los Angeles the week of the 21st for the National Advertising Convention. I believe her graphic designs are just what you are looking for to use in the Cooler campaign.

As I said on the telephone, Alice Bradford will be staying at the downtown Empire Hotel, and a message may be left for her anytime after the evening of the 20th. She said she has no plans for lunch on the 22nd or 23rd, and, as we discussed, I told her you may call her.

In addition to her great campaign work, Tink is a fine person with interests in several areas similar to your own: quarter horses and hang gliding. And I believe you could use her skills on future projects. I hope—if you can manage a meeting—that this works out.

EDIT, EDIT, EDIT

Your job is only to create an opportunity. Make sure your information is direct, clear, concise, and bears the tone of cordiality.

Introducing Friends

Dear Claire:

As I mentioned to you on the telephone, Adeline McDougell is a designer for Limone's. She will be in Baltimore next week for the Women's Forum, and will be staying at the downtown Fairmount Hotel. I believe the two of you have much in common. Since you will both be attending the Forum, what better time to meet?

Well, I'll leave the rest up to you. Adeline and I will understand if prior commitments—producing the Forum must be a huge task—make it impossible for you to schedule a time to get together.

My best wishes for the success of this important event.

Sincerely,
Stella Dare

Introducing Friends to a Club

Dear Delmar:

It is a pleasure for Sandra and me to introduce Winn and Gloria Stickler to the Greenwood Country Club. The Sticklers have been distinguished members of the Shaker Heights Country Club in Omaha for over 15 years, and have just moved to Denver in the past three months.

It has been our privilege to have been both business associates and personal friends of the Sticklers for over 17 years. They are truly two of the finest people we know, and people who have contributed greatly to the community in terms of fundraising for lung disease.

If the Sticklers desire to join Greenwood, Sandra and I would be honored to sponsor them. (They could help us win that elusive mixed doubles tennis championship.)

Sincerely,

Dexter Dowd

Introducing a Sales Representative to a Customer

Dear Bernie:

This will introduce Ned Remick, Smith and French's new Region IV representative. He will be calling on Rx Inc. on Wednesday, next week.

After graduating from Victoria College, Ned spent seven years with Johns and Johns sterile products' division in New Jersey. He distinguished himself for five years as sales representative of the year for their medical instrumentation division.

I think you will find him extremely knowledgeable about our entire product line. He has a well-earned reputation as one of the finest and most conscientious salespersons around.

I think you'll be delighted to know, too, that Ned's a stockcar driver and huge Buff's fan.

Please take a few extra minutes to talk to Ned. I hope you will think as highly of him as I do.

Cordially,

George Cordiss

Introducing a Graduate Student

Dear Dr. Rodham:

This will introduce Kevin B. Doerr, PhD candidate in our department here at the University of Iowa. As we discussed, I greatly appreciate your willingness to show Kevin your work on the absorption experiments. I'm sure you will find him a brilliant student. He is also prepared to discuss with you our related work here.

Please let me know if I may return the favor for one of your associates. I'd be happy to consider a candidate you would recommend for our program here.

Kevin will call your office on Wednesday morning to set an appointment time.

With regards,

Giles Newbuck

Introducing a Business Associate

Dear Conchita:

It's my pleasure to introduce Margaret Merritt, who served as vice president in charge of book buying for Bookworms for over 15 years. Since a family move takes her from us to Bakersville, our considerable loss may be your gain.

Margaret is fully capable of stepping directly into the management of your store, so you may start that carefree retirement you so deserve.

Margaret and her husband, Jim, are in Bend until the 25th, and I'm sure she would be happy to arrange an appointment. You can reach her at 555-0123.

So nice to hear from you. Give my best to Ralph, and I look forward to receiving those postcards from remote and exotic places. You've earned it!

Best,

Jo Roberts

Introducing a Business Service

Dear Maggie:

We talked a number of months ago about finding an accounting firm for auditing and other financial services we both needed. I'd like to introduce you to Arthur Q. Small and Associates, a full-service, small-business accounting services firm, located in the southeast part of town near my business.

Maggie, this man is excellent. He comes to my office, picks up my records (or examines them on the spot), and gets back to me with the results and completed audits, or whatever else I need, the next day. I couldn't be happier with the quality of his service, his charges (well, maybe if they were free!), or the ease of having him complete the work. I must also say he has already saved me a considerable amount of money by creating a new billing process, which he also administers on my behalf. Take a look at his website, www.small.com, for a complete listing of services and charges.

If you are still looking for this service, you may want to contact him at 555-0123.

Best wishes,

Elena Boots

Introducing Yourself as Professor

Dear Students:

I'd like to introduce myself. My name is Daniel Q. Rogett, PhD, and I'll be your professor for the online creative writing class 402.A: "Writing for the Big Screen."

I graduated from the University of Iowa's MFA program in 1988, and then attended the University of Colorado's law school, graduating with a JD in 1991. After seven years in the fantasy world of law practice at Herbert, Jacobs, and Hazelnutt, I returned to the reality of my true passion, writing lifelike characters for film. I also continue to practice part-time as an attorney in the area of literary law. Over the past seven years, I've written seven screenplays, four of which sold to Dreamfield Productions. These were produced, and have appeared on the big screen as the films *Just Desserts*, *April Fools*, *Warlords*, and *Celebration*. (If you have any criticisms of these films, you'll get an opportunity to state them in class.)

All the details for the class are listed on the website I've set up: www.isu.edu/screenwriting. The class text, assignments, and schedule are also listed there. Online chat room discussions, which you are required to attend, will be held on Tuesday evenings from 7:00 p.m. to 9:30 p.m. Forum questions and comments may be posted on cwlists@isu.edu.

You may reach me, or my assistant, Dana Smith, with any additional questions at 805-555-0123 or by email at drogett@isu.edu.

Welcome to "Writing for the Big Screen." You will work very hard in this class, but by the end of the semester, you will have finished your first complete draft of an actual screenplay.

Sincerely,

Daniel Q. Rogett, PhD

(Also see LETTER OF RECOMMENDATION, page 146.)

The memo, or memorandum, is the lifeblood of any organization. It is the informal, written communication used within the organization among its members. A memo may be a short note, a report, or a much longer document such as a plan, analysis, or proposal. The memo is also used to communicate with outside organizations and individuals with whom you have an ongoing relationship. Today memos are often, if not always, sent by email.

While memos vary in formality and length, the quality of writing should be conversational in tone and tailored to the reader. A few organizations still call these memos internal letters, interoffice letters, or intraorganizational reports, though more often, when they are sent electronically, they are simply referred to as "emails."

Effective memos are essential to the success of any organization because they provide a clear record of decisions made and actions taken. They also inform, delegate, instruct, announce, request, and transmit documents. It's important to know that careers are made and broken on memo writing power or the lack of it. Remember, each good memo you write will help your reputation and promotability.

DECIDE TO WRITE

Use the memo wisely to:

- Distribute information across organizational lines
- Communicate policy and procedures up and down organizational ranks
- Create a permanent, organizational record of plans, decisions, instructions, and actions
- Confirm verbal discussions and decisions

THINK ABOUT CONTENT

Before You Write

- Understand your organization's memo policies and protocol, particularly reporting responsibilities, etiquette, and the filing system for storing memos. Follow protocol when you decide whom to address and whom to copy. Here's an example: in many organizations, if a middle manager addresses the memo to his supervisor and a vice president, this indicates the manager has a direct reporting relationship to both. Sending a copy to the vice president, in this example, may indicate a direct reporting responsibility to the supervisor and a reporting access to the vice president. In some organizations, sending the memo directly to the vice president would be considered circumventing the proper chain of command.

- Determine the need for your memo. (Creating a blizzard of paper or electronic messages should not be your objective.)
- Be sure you have all the information you need. Do more research if in doubt.
- Consider consulting the people affected to get their input before writing a memo.
- Do the necessary research to make sure you have all the background facts and information.
- Apply the principles in chapter 1, "Getting Started," to ensure your best writing.
- Remember, one message equals one memo. Two messages equal two memos.
- If you find yourself unable to take a clear position, reexamine the need to write the memo.

As You Write
- Begin by distilling the subject matter into a concise, core statement.
- Have your reader firmly in mind, and select the most appropriate language. Keep it conversational yet businesslike and easy to understand.
- Outline the memo points, dividing your information into introduction, body, conclusion, summary, and recommendations. You may select the time sequence pattern or the cause-and-effect pattern, whichever is more logical. For clarity and ease of reading, use subheadings, lists, and numbers when appropriate.
- Use the subject line to tell the reader the specific topic of your memo. For example: "Subject: New Newton Copier (Model 150) will be installed Friday." Remember, the subject line will also be used to file the memo. Here are several examples:

Change This	To This
Subject: Performance Evaluation	Subject: Robert Kurtz, Performance Evaluation
Reference: Vacation Schedule for July and August	Reference: Shipping Department Vacation Schedule for July and August
Subject: Sales Training Seminars	Subject: Sales Assistant Sales Training Seminar May 10-25

- Write concisely, using positive statements and action words whenever possible.

Editing What You've Written
- Reread, delete, rearrange more logically, and edit out the non-essential.
- Ask yourself:
  - Have I included all the facts the reader needs to know?
  - Have I answered *who, what, why, where, when*, and *how*?
  - Do the points in my memo progress logically?
  - Have I used section headings and numbers where they could add clarity?
  - Does it flow?
  - Have I used transitions to carry the reader from one paragraph to the next?
  - Does my memo have a conclusion, and/or a call to action?

ELIMINATE WRONG MESSAGES

- Don't transmit legal, accounting, or private personnel information through email without insuring there's a secure system in place, and fully understanding Sarbanes-Oxley Act compliance and your organization's email policy.
- Don't copy and/or paste someone's material into a memo without first getting permission and properly crediting the person.
- Don't be ambiguous or vague; be direct, specific, and concrete.
- Don't use an autocratic tone (for example, "I demand," "You must," "It has been decided," and so on). It is unacceptable in most organizations today.
- Don't assign blame or whine.
- Don't pad. Keep your memo to the point.
- Don't deliver a "me-too" message just to have input unless you have been asked for an opinion or vote. Then only "I agree" or "I disagree" is appropriate if you don't have new material to add.
- Don't use officious, stuffy, or formal words when simpler words will work better. Do use the correct technical word when that's the most precise and acceptable.
- Avoid negative, accusatory, demanding, or harsh words and phrases. Negative emotions should not be expressed in your memo. Here are some examples of words and phrases you may want to replace:
    - you have failed to
    - compelled
    - remit promptly
    - you made an inexcusable error
    - no excuse will be accepted
    - tardy for work
    - I insist
    - you ignored
    - failure on your part
    - delinquent
    - a wrong action has been taken
    - unsatisfactory performance
- Avoid superlatives. Facts, numbers, and statistics are much better.

CONSIDER SPECIAL SITUATIONS

- In our litigious society, it's important to avoid memo content that could be actionable. One way to avoid problems is to keep your memo free of race and gender references. If you have any questions about the content of your memo, consult an attorney.
- Know that anything you write can come back to haunt you in a very public way, even if you've labeled it "confidential." Your so-called private memo could one day be published right after your name.
- Always give yourself "think time." Tomorrow you may not want to send that negative memo. In fact, try to put every memo in positive form.
- Give the reader visual clues. An appealing layout of your memo helps your message.
- Measure the words you've used; don't go to extremes. "Never" and "always" aren't good choices, nor are accusatory names or characterizations. (Incidentally, make sure you destroy

what you've thought better of. The contents of wastebaskets and harddrives can show up in embarrassing places.)

- Don't generalize. Be sure to document what you've written.
- Use the proper organizational channels. Don't circumvent the lines of authority.
- Memos not only cover tails; they also document sources. Your good ideas should be put into memo form and copies kept in your files. If your organization allows it, copy up the organizational line to superiors.
- If you state a problem, offer a solution, or at least alternatives and/or a plan for further action.
- For memos about upcoming *meetings*, do the following:
  - ▸ State your objective.
  - ▸ Outline the plan of action.
  - ▸ Assign tasks to people to ensure they are involved and come prepared to participate.
  - ▸ Ask yourself *who, what, when*, and *where* to check for complete content.
  - ▸ Give reasons and credit. For example, if the meeting is in response to staff requests, point that out.

- For meeting *agendas*:
  - ▸ Give your agenda an action bias.
  - ▸ List the *who, what, when*, and *where*. (The *how* and *why* may be the goals of the meeting.)

- For *progress reports*:
  - ▸ Use significant action headings.
  - ▸ Use action words.
  - ▸ Make the report succinct but complete.
  - ▸ Summarize the action.

- For *announcements*:
  - ▸ Get organization members involved. Major changes should be discussed, comments and feedback considered, and alternatives weighed before decisions are made. This eliminates the possibility of people feeling insulted and/or left out of the process.
  - ▸ Promotions, resignations, and transfers should be given verbally and followed up with a written announcement.
  - ▸ For personnel appointments, it is helpful to include a statement or two about the person's interests and hobbies.

- For *bad news memos*:
  - ▸ Make sure members of your organization hear it from you first, not from an outside source.
  - ▸ Start out with a positive statement, whenever possible.
  - ▸ State specifically what the problem or bad news is, and what the organization is doing about it.

- ▶ Take responsibility for any errors or misjudgments you've made: state them clearly, but don't grovel.
- ▶ Relate the impact on the organization and its members.
- ▶ Ask for specific cooperation and/or action.
- ▶ Promise to keep members informed and keep that promise.

- For *policies and procedures memos*:
  - ▶ Be specific about why changes are being implemented, and be sure to give the *who, what, where, when*, and *how*.
  - ▶ Explain the nature of the changes in terms of what exists now.
  - ▶ Make a response as easy as possible.
  - ▶ Use bullets, numbers, and headings to help readers absorb points more easily.

- For *recommendations*:
  - ▶ Put recommendations up front. Let your readers know why they are important.
  - ▶ Give the reasons for the recommendations.
  - ▶ State the benefits briefly.
  - ▶ End by restating your recommendation and telling the reader the next action step to be taken.

NOTE SOME EXCEPTIONS

- Some organizations use memos to communicate with other organizations. One example is public relations or advertising agencies, which often use memos to communicate with client organizations. A "Client Memo" or "Contact Report" from the agency to the client organization records decisions and supplies information for accounting purposes. (See other appropriate chapters in this section.)
- A few organizations still use form memos so handwritten messages to customers are quick and easy. The forms have several sheets and a copy of the original message stays with copies of responses.
- Subsidiary organizations under one corporate umbrella may use inter-organizational memos.

USE POWER WORDS

action	analysis	announce	assign
attached	conclude	confirm	deadlines
guidelines	information	initiate	input
instructions	list	meet	notice
order	outlines	policy	procedure
progress	proposal	propose	reminder
renew	report	reverse	review
revise	start	status	summary

BUILD EFFECTIVE PHRASES

all our in-depth research and discussion indicate

all the facts aren't in, but here's what we

all the facts indicate that

I believe this will clear up the confusion

I'd appreciate your input by

our preliminary conclusion is

plan to start using this procedure

please confirm you will be able to attend

please distribute this information

the effective change date will be

this plan of action is proposed

this summarizes yesterday's meeting

we're all pleased to announce

you will be pleased to learn that

you'll see why these conclusions were reached

WRITE STRONG SENTENCES

Use simple, strong words and eliminate unnecessary ones.

Thank you for recommending Jim Baker for the assistant director position.

I'm impressed with your recommendation to start a flextime policy.

Unfortunately, I can't approve your July 1 to 15 vacation request.

April production figures slipped 4 percent below present levels.

I just want you to know you are a candidate for the position; the selection process will start December 7.

For the first time, production figures surpassed estimates.

A special sexual harassment seminar will be held for all manufacturing supervisors,

Level II or above, May 16–17, 9:30 a.m. to 4:00 p.m. (lunch will be served) at the Regency Hotel.

At the suggestion of Dick Power, I'm requesting a copy of your memo dated February 7 on the Model P-14 performance.

BUILD EFFECTIVE PARAGRAPHS

Subject: New Flextime Increases Production and Reduces Absenteeism at Drexel

Drexel Systems reports a 16 percent increase in production and a 15 percent reduction in absenteeism over six months after converting Level II personnel to flextime. I believe we can adapt Drexel's flextime changeover plan to work well at Lexington. Here's the background information, a discussion of the advantages and disadvantages (including impact on other divisions), a fiscal impact statement, and recommendations for implementation.

Subject: Final Fisher Contract Attached

Attached is the final Fisher contract as amended during our conference call today. Please review it. If you find items not in compliance with the necessary safety requirements, contact me by 4:00 p.m. today. Here's a list of the changes:

Page 7

Line 4 changed from "to all those involved" to "assembly-line personnel."

Page 9
Line 12 changed from "The contract shall be in effect for 7 months" to "The contract shall be in effect for 9 months."

Subject: Graystone Hotel Collateral Pieces Status Report
I met with Joe Adams to complete the review of the insert sheets for the new sales brochure. Everything was approved. I am waiting for his final figures so we can finish the typesetting and complete the printing. The folders are now being printed.

EDIT, EDIT, EDIT

Use simple, clear, powerful words. In addition to the list below, see the list on page 9.

Instead of	Use	Instead of	Use
pertaining to	about	along the lines of	like
with regard to, with reference to	about	in the nature of	like
inasmuch as	because	may, or may not	may
prior to	before	under no circumstances	never
on the basis of	by	at this point in time	now
on the part of	by	on the few occasions	occasionally
take under advisement	consider	on the grounds that, owing to the fact that	since
in the course of	during	in the near future	soon
in the amount of	for	with a view to	to
on behalf of	for	as of this date	today
in a satisfactory manner	has	be desirous of	want
in the event that	if	whether or not	whether
provided that	if		

Board of Directors Meeting Assignments

SUBJECT: Assignments for the Board of Directors Meeting

The meeting will be held on October 10 at 2:00 p.m. in the Main Boardroom.

Presenter	Agenda Item	Purpose	Time Allotted	Background Reading
K. C.	Production	Information	10 mins.	Mfg. Report
E. E.	Cost analysis	Information	10 mins.	Financial Reports
A. M.	Market report	Discussion	45 mins.	Market Research Report
S. B.	Facilities	Information	15 mins.	Operations Report
M. M.	Long-term plan	Decision	45 mins.	Annual and Planning Reports

Appointment Announcement

Subject: Aimee Spicer Named Vice President
            of Marketing

I'm pleased to announce that Aimee Spicer will become our Vice President of Marketing on April 1. Aimee has been with Adams Electronic Systems as Assistant Marketing Director for the past five years, and has helped Adams grow from $21 million in gross annual sales to over $35 million. She knows our business extremely well and has already begun to formulate plans for the expansion of the Circuit Board Division.

A graduate of MIT, Aimee spent the first three years of her career on the West Coast with Pacific Systems, where she served as regional chairperson for the United Way.

Let's all make Aimee feel welcome.

New Procedure

Subject: New Computer Backup Procedure

Friday's fire in the reception area resulted in our insurance carrier, Stateside Inc., insisting on a procedural change in computer files backup. While McGaw didn't lose any files in the fire, we could have because we have not been consistent in requiring that every department back up their computer files, and that there be an additional set of backup files stored off-site.

After much discussion and input from all of you, here is the new policy, which begins today:

- Those working on computers will be responsible to make and update backups every hour. Specific assignments will be made in each department.
- If you are working off-site, be sure you back up on corporate systems.
- Every week, Margaret Willis will check on all the essential data backup off-site storage. Coordinate this information from your department with her.

Please reply to me, indicating you have made all the assignments in your department, by 4:00 p.m. today. If you have any questions or comments, please call me.

Request for Recommendations

Subject: Personnel Manual Recommendations
            Due Feb. 10

February 10 is the deadline for recommended changes to our personnel manual. Here's how we will handle the revision process:

1. Please review the present manual, discuss recommended changes with your department personnel, and make notations on policies your people feel need to be changed.

2. Submit these recommendations to me in writing by February 10.

3. I will prepare and return to you a complete set of all recommendations, "Employee Manual Recommendations," by April 25.

4. Please discuss these recommendations in your department and return any further comments to me by May 1.

5. Department heads will meet May 10 at 9:30 a.m. in the boardroom to make final revision decisions.

Recommendation

Subject: Mary Turney Recommended for
            Media Relations Spokesperson

I recommend we appoint Mary Turney to act as media representative for Action Toys. This will eliminate the media problems that have arisen since the introduction of our new Buffalo Bill miniature. The media has been interviewing anyone leaving the plant, and this has resulted in inaccurate information being disseminated to the public. It has also portrayed an inconsistent and sometimes negative image of Action Toys.

Mary's experience in media relations and newscasting qualifies her for this job. I believe her appointment will correct our image problem and help get our Buffalo Bill promotion back on track.

I recommend we vote on the appointment Friday, January 15, 2:30 p.m., at the board of directors' meeting. Please put it on the agenda.

Client Memo

Subject: Chateaux Advertising/Sponsorship in the Steve Watson Golf Classic

I talked with the producers of the Steve Watson Golf Classic Program this morning and reserved the ¼-page black-and-white ad in the *Classic Program* magazine. This makes us a "Hole Sponsor," which includes two tickets to play the golf tournament and two tickets each to the banquet, breakfast, and luncheon. We may now elect one (or none) of three options:

1. Upgrade the Hole Sponsorship to a full page, four-color ad (instead of the ¼-page black-and-white ad) for $1,600.

2. Add one golf player to the Hole Sponsorship for an additional $250.

3. Select a "Corporate Sponsorship"—we could enter three golf players—for $2,250. For this price, we would not get the bells and whistles—the banquet, the breakfast, and the luncheon—but we could host a table in the hospitality tent.

I recommend we select option #1. This is the best value because it allows us to narrowcast our advertising in this publication (10,000 are being printed), which will be kept as a memento.

Please let me know your decision by May 26.

Establishing a New Program

Subject: Establishing a Residential and Commercial Real Estate Education/ Internship Program

I would like to discuss with you the possibility of establishing a residential and commercial real estate education/internship program here at Woods, using NACREE members as guest lecturers. Can you meet Friday, April 23 at 2:00 p.m. in the board-room for a 30-minute discussion of program topics, specific people, and dates?

Please respond by 4:00 p.m. tomorrow.

Loss of an Account

Subject: Loss of U.S. Army Telephone Services Account

I am sorry to announce that the new U.S. Army Telephone Services contract, which represented 35 percent of our business this year, was awarded to Action Systems, beginning November 1. This will slice our gross income at TTI by approximately 42 percent.

This, of course, will impact all departments. I will have complete information on the details of that impact after Jim Harrison, CFO, finishes his computations on November 4.

It is important to say that TTI personnel performed well on the U.S. Army account and the change in services contractor is routine. It does not reflect any customer dissatisfaction.

It is important to tell you, too, that our Sales and Marketing Department is in final negotiations on $24 M in bids to three potential customers for contracts that will begin January 1. The department has another $45 M in bids in process with contract dates to begin between February and May. (The Sales and Marketing Department has secured nearly 65 percent of the accounts bid over the past two years.)

Immediately, the loss of the Army account has made it necessary to furlough eight service technicians, four home office accounting personnel, and eight part-time clerks. These people have all been notified. Also, the position of Assistant Marketing Director held by Henry Madison has been eliminated and Henry will leave TTI on Friday. I do not believe any additional staff reductions will be necessary.

I will keep you informed of new developments, and I request your best efforts to help TTI pull together in these transitional weeks ahead.

(Also see ANNOUNCEMENT, page 18; INFORMAL REPORT, page 220; INTRODUCTION, page 165; LETTER OF RECOMMENDATION, page 146; and TECHNICAL REPORT & TECHNICAL WRITING, page 225.)

26 MEETING NOTICES, AGENDAS & MINUTES

Organizations are powered by meetings. And meetings operate best if there are a stated purpose and a plan known to those who will participate. It's important to create a permanent record and to let those who don't attend know what happened at a meeting. For these reasons, meeting notices, agendas, and minutes were created.

The meeting notice gives the place, date, time, and purpose of the meeting. It usually asks for a response concerning attendance, and sometimes a vote.

The agenda also includes the place, date, and time of the meeting, but its primary function is to list topics that will be covered.

Meeting minutes provide a chronological, written, and accurate record of what happened at the meeting. Minutes may be a brief outline or a very detailed and prescribed form, depending on the audience. Besides providing a record, the process of taking minutes helps direct the group to take action. Minutes also inform absent members and a larger audience (if circulated) about what went on.

The meeting report, unlike the minutes, is not comprehensive. The report (see Informal Report, page 220) presents conclusions, recommendations, and sometimes a summary of the points and discussion.

THINK ABOUT CONTENT

Meeting Notice

- Meeting notices are sometimes given long in advance and sometimes on the spur of the moment. In either case, it is necessary to inform enough participants to make sure there will be the attendance needed to conduct business. (The number of qualified participants needed to vote on issues and whether absentee or proxy voting can be used must be checked with the organization bylaws and/or local laws.)
- The written notice must include date, place, time, and the business to be conducted. Remember to cover the *who*, *where*, *when*, *what*, and *why*.
- Ask for confirmation of attendance. If possible, include the meeting agenda, and make any pre-meeting assignments or requests.
- Include all materials necessary so that participants will understand the issues to be discussed.

- Enclose an absentee ballot or a proxy voting form if provided for in the organization bylaws.
- Ask those who won't attend for their input before the meeting.

Attendance Response

- To confirm attendance, state you will attend; confirm the place, date, time, and any travel arrangements; confirm you will complete any pre-meeting assignments; and give input on any agenda items.
- To decline attendance, identify the meeting; state why you can't attend; mention how you plan to follow up (reading minutes, sending someone in your place, telephoning an attendee, etc.); and give any input, approvals, voting power, comments, suggestions, etc. that will be helpful or necessary to the success of the meeting.

Agenda

- Identify the date, place, and time of the meeting. When a speaker, meal, or other item is included, the agenda may be called a program. (*Robert's Rules of Order* covers procedures for the agenda.)
- Arrange items of business in a logical order. Times may be listed for each of the items. The order is usually a call to order, reading of approved minutes from the last meeting, reports from the officers and committees, old business, new business, announcements, and adjournment.

Minutes

- Minutes are difficult to write. The recorder must thoroughly understand the dynamics of the group as well as the history of the subject. The recorder, usually the secretary, must summarize the reasoning of the group without being subjective. Select the recording person carefully.
- List the date, time, place, and kind of meeting; the name of the group; those in attendance; and those absent.
- Produce minutes in abbreviated or full form, depending upon the organization bylaws. But do include the following information:
  - List members and any substitutes or guests present.
  - Note whether the minutes of the last meeting were approved and any corrections made.
  - Include a mention or summaries of any reports. Copies may be attached.
  - All main motions in their final form with the names of the sponsor and seconds must be listed. Give the decision made concerning each motion.
  - Record all the action in the order it happened.
  - List the date the minutes were written and the name and signature of the writer under "Respectfully submitted."
- Complete the writing and approval of the minutes effectively:
  - Tape-record meetings if formal minutes are required.

> ► Write minutes as soon as possible after the meeting.
> ► Make sure dates, days, names, and actions are accurate.
> ► Have others review minutes and make any corrections before they are finally edited, if possible.
> ► Proofread and incorporate any reviewer changes.
> ► Distribute copies.
> ► Approve and accept minutes of previous meeting.
> ► Keep a copy of the minutes in a permanent file.

ELIMINATE WRONG MESSAGES

- Omit summarizing discussions and routine announcements.
- Never include personal comments or opinions. Make sure the minutes are completely objective.

SELECT A FORMAT

- Format is dictated by the organization. If minutes, notices, and agendas are printed out and not just submitted by email, they should be done on organization letterhead, typed, single-spaced, and arranged with a minimum of one inch of white space on all sides.
- Use headings, subheads, numbers, and indentation to make the minutes visually appealing and easier to read.

Announcing a Meeting

Dear Dylan:

I have scheduled a producers' meeting for 2:00 to 4:00 p.m., July 7, in conference room 4B on the lot. Can you make it?

We need to decide on final details, cost factors, and the final supporting cast members for the Last Knight production. We also need to fill the remaining production openings. (See my list of issues and candidates attached.)

Let me know immediately if you have a conflict, and to confirm your attendance. Come with your choices and recommendations. We need your input to get this wrapped up.

Sincerely,

Jeff Spellbinder

Confirmation of Attendance

Dear Dexter:

Of course I'll be at the September 15 meeting at the Broadmoor in Colorado Springs. I agree, the four mornings will be very heavy.

Yes, I'd be pleased to make my "Marketing Blunders" presentation. Given the schedule, I'll make it interactive. I'll need a blackboard, an overhead projector, and a portable microphone. Will you please have your department coordinator arrange these items?

Please confirm my hotel late arrival on the 14th. I can't get in until 10:45 p.m.

I look forward to the meeting. It sounds like an outstanding lineup.

Sincerely,

Sidney Bartles

Meeting Notice and Agenda Letter

Dear Ellen:

The Regional Sales Representative Quarterly Meeting is set for March 12 at the Executive Inn (I-25 and Belleview) in the Orchids Room from 9 a.m. to 5 p.m. (Please print out the following agenda for your reference.) Unless I get an email telling me differently, I will expect you to attend.

We will have full details on the new product lines with complete training sessions.

9:00–10:30 a.m.	Customer Profile	Darlene Darling
10:30 a.m.–12:30 p.m.	You, the Salesperson	Logan Greene
12:30–2:30 p.m.	Luncheon	
2:30–6:30 p.m.	Big Sales Country Seminar Breakout Sessions	Cleo Pengass, Frank Dickens, Alex Saunders, Jennifer Fenders, Marilyn Dougherty

See you there.

Sincerely,

Robertson Givens

New Organization Meeting Announcement

Dear Audrey:

I finally have some news about the meeting of the ARRF alumni in the Savanna area. We will meet on August 6 from 6 to 8 p.m. in the Brown Palace Regency Room.

The purpose of the meeting is to get acquainted with other alumni and to decide if we will form a local chapter. Mr. Edward Keivers, executive director of the alumni organization in Los Angeles, will give a 30-minute presentation on what their chapter is doing. He'll also answer any questions about local activities.

There are over 30 local ARRF alumni organizations across the country, and Ralph Weiner will take about 15 minutes to give us an overview of what those organizations have accomplished for members and their communities.

Please respond, letting me know if you will attend and indicating your level of interest in this organization. If you have any questions, call Myron Meeker at 818-555-0123.

I look forward to seeing you on the 6th. Please come early and get acquainted.

Sincerely,

Byron Bennett

Meeting Agenda

GREEN ACRES HOMEOWNERS' ASSOCIATION BOARD OF DIRECTORS' MEETING

January 11, 2011

7 p.m.–9 p.m., Clubhouse

Residents Welcome

Agenda
Call to Order
Minutes of the Last Meeting
Management Report, Harry Stropp
   and David Piper
Financial Report, Jeff Swindler
Old Business
   Surveys, Bill Waverly
   Recycling, Bill Waverly
New Business
   Landscaping/Gardening Recommendation,
   Kathy Klein
Financial Committee Proposal, Jeff Drummer
   Audit
   Cash Management Policies
   Reserves/Dues Increase
Management Contract Bids Review
Misc.

Adjournment

Meeting Minutes (Abbreviated Form)

AARD Meeting Minutes

Meeting was September 14, 2011

Commission Members Present: Jerry Holder, Janice Johnson, Bill Wesson, David Wrestler

Staff Members Present: David Weaver, Daphne Justice, Warner Stiles

Staff Members Absent: June Cummings

A regular meeting of the AARD Commission was called to order at 7:05 p.m. on Wednesday, September 14, 2011, at the headquarters conference room, 3400 Riverfront Drive, Phoenix. The president was in the chair, and the secretary was present.

The minutes of the August meeting were read and approved upon a motion by Jerry Holder, seconded by Bill Wesson.

The treasurer's report was a financial statement with a balance on hand, as of September 1, of $455,655.76.

New business included a proposed motion by David Weaver "that we appoint a subcommittee to review the possibility of investing Commission funds for greater financial return."

A motion was made by Daphne Justice "to hold the annual picnic as we did last year." The commission voted to hold a picnic, and Janice Johnson was appointed to head a picnic committee.

After a review of the new approval procedure, the meeting adjourned at 9:35 p.m.

Respectfully submitted:

Janice Johnson
Secretary

27 REPRIMAND

The letter of reprimand is used by a person in a supervisory role when an employee or associate has committed an error or a willful breach of policy, procedure, or practice. The effective reprimand separates the act from the person, and deals only with the action to correct the problem. The objective is to produce compliance and/or a positive result.

An indirect or direct approach may be used. (See Refusal, page 274.) You must decide, based on your knowledge of the person involved. In the case of a direct subordinate in the workplace, a direct approach is usually best.

DECIDE TO WRITE

You may be required to write this when:

- An employee has committed an error or has willfully broken company rules
- A member, associate, or student has committed an offense or breach of contract
- An organization with which you have a relationship or contract has breached the agreement

THINK ABOUT CONTENT

- Know the laws, regulations, and organization policies that impact the specific issue.
- Remember, your objective is to effect a positive change in behavior.
- To be effective, your anger must first be dealt with so you can be objective.
- Learn all the facts. Conduct any investigation necessary, and record precise details on a timeline. This should be done in an objective way without implicating anyone. And, of course, all the information should be kept confidential.
- Write the reprimand as soon after the offense as possible. The letter should not, however, substitute for a face-to-face meeting. It should be a follow-up record and a notice of corrective action.
- Introduce the reprimand. Set it up with a positive statement about overall or past performance, if this is a first offense.
- Make the letter short. Introduce the problem; state it; give any succinct, constructive criticism; and list any possible action to be taken.
- State the reprimand—be specific—and focus on the act, not the person.
- List any ramifications or any corrective action that will be taken.
- Set realistic, attainable, and measurable goals for improvement or corrective action, and give a time frame.

- Make a positive statement about the person and his or her positive performance, if possible, and list specific goals for improvement.
- Give the person an opportunity to respond.
- Offer encouragement or end on a note of goodwill.
- Have another person well-versed in company policy and the appropriate regulations read your reprimand before you send it to ensure objectivity and compliance with regulations and policy. (Don't violate any confidentiality issues, however.)
- Have legal counsel review the letter, if appropriate.

ELIMINATE WRONG MESSAGES

- Do not make a personal attack; deal with the offense only.
- Omit lengthy explanations, which diminish the impact of your letter.
- Don't belabor the corrective action.
- Don't criticize or use derogatory comments.
- Never send this letter by email.

CONSIDER SPECIAL SITUATIONS

- When the offense is against another employee, such as sexual harassment, consult specialized legal counsel. Both punishment and education may be indicated. Organizations are also advised that legal action against the offender may be indicated. A record should be kept in the organization's central headquarters. The organization must have stepped procedures for corrective action in place and properly documented, and if the behavior isn't corrected, the employee should be terminated. These procedures should be reviewed by an attorney specializing in gender, sexual harassment, and diversity issues.

SELECT A FORMAT

- Most reprimands are typed on organization letterhead, though some organizations use a special form.

USE POWERFUL WORDS

action	admonish	cease	censure
correct	demand	eliminate	immediately
infraction	reform	rules	stop

USE EFFECTIVE PHRASES

cease and desist	demonstrate a change in behavior
eliminate such infractions	recommended steps of correction
regret that intervention will be necessary	reverse a negative trend
seek necessary help	violation of company policy

WRITE STRONG SENTENCES

I look forward to a new attitude in your work performance.

Punctuality is vital to the operation of the reception area.

The disregard for safety regulations will not be tolerated.

Your behavior was out of character, and I am concerned.

Your tardiness is an exception to your otherwise fine performance.

EDIT, EDIT, EDIT

Always allow yourself time to take an objective final look at your letter before sending it. Make any changes needed to produce a letter that will completely resolve an offense, and, hopefully, restore an employee to productivity.

For Rules Violation

Dear Jack:

As you know, company policy states that repeated infractions of the sleeping-on-the-job rule receive (1) a verbal reprimand; then (2) a written reprimand; then (3) suspension without pay for three days; then (4) dismissal. (See page 43 of your employee manual.) On July 10 you were found sleeping at 2:10 a.m. in the employee lounge. The 1:00 a.m. safety checks for your shift had not been made, and the boiler pressures had risen into the caution zone.

On July 21 you were found sleeping at 3:21 a.m. in the cafeteria. The 1:00 a.m. safety checks had not been made, and the boiler pressures were in the caution zone.

This is your written warning before suspension. You know the seriousness of failing to do your job; it creates a safety hazard for other employees, as well as for the surrounding residential area.

Be in my office at 2:00 a.m. Thursday, July 23 to explain your plan of action to correct this problem.

Sincerely,

J. K. Lund

For Inappropriate Behavior

Dear Sassy:

I have received a complaint from Mr. Dennis Simons of ReCoil stating that you, while placing an order on July 11, used abusive language when he told you our shipment scheduled for a July 12 delivery would be delayed. We all share your frustration when commitments aren't kept, but it is not acceptable here to exacerbate a delay by creating a delivery cancellation. This is what Dennis threatened when he called me.

I have resolved the dispute with Dennis, but you must find a way to deal with him if you are going to perform your job. We have a contract with ReCoil for eight more months.

As you know, our relationship with ReCoil is vital to our operation and profitability. Please be in my office tomorrow morning at 8:30 a.m., and give me your proposed solution to the existing friction between you and Dennis Simons.

Sincerely,

Jacob Boiler

For Tardiness

Dear Marie:

On five occasions in the past three weeks you have been from 30 minutes to one hour late in arriving at the office. Marie, the work of your department depends on your being on time, and company policy clearly states that administrative personnel will start work at 8:00 a.m.

If there is something I should know about the facts that created this tardiness, please make an appointment with Alice to discuss it with me before Friday. Otherwise I will expect to see you in your office by 8:00 a.m. each morning.

I will appreciate your cooperation in getting this problem resolved.

Sincerely,

Julie Adams

For Error

Dear Arnie:

Mrs. Anna Gable, age 72, widow for 10 years, was in the laboratory last week for a PB3 test. She just called me saying she received the laboratory test results report, which explain that her "toxicity levels during the third trimester of pregnancy are slightly elevated." Really?

This is the third time within the past five weeks that a patient has received the wrong report. These errors must stop.

Tomorrow at 3:30 p.m., I want a full report that details how these errors in mailing out reports occurred, and the action you are taking to ensure the problem is completely corrected.

Sincerely,

Mike McPhee

For Personal Activities on Company Time

Dear Darla:

Your work record until August of this year was outstanding, but since that time I have received three complaints that (1) coworkers have not been getting routine reports from you, (2) there have been six or seven occasions when you were away from the office for several hours without Mr. Jenkins knowing your whereabouts, and (3) there have been several meetings in your office during working hours for political campaign committees. Darla, as you know, these are all infractions of company policy. (See 4.15–4.32 in your employee manual.)

I expect you will make the necessary changes in your volunteer work to resume your past fine performance here. Please be in my office on Wednesday, 3:00 p.m. to explain to me your plan of action.

Sincerely,

Sandra Layton

For Late Expense Reports

Dear Jeraldo:

The accounting department has notified me that your expense reports have been as much as three months late. This is a problem because they cannot finish department expense and overhead reports, and we all need this information to operate efficiently.

If there is an explanation I should know, please get it to me by Friday.

From Friday forward you must submit each month's expenses by the first of the following month, complete with required supporting documentation.

Thank you for complying.

Yours truly,

Sidney Ryder

28 LETTER OF RESIGNATION

The letter of resignation is essentially a refusal letter (see Refusal, page 274). This bad news may be given either indirectly or directly, depending on the situation. In either case, make your letter as positive as possible, using tactful, supportive statements. Assume full responsibility for your resignation and include an acceptable reason for resigning, if possible.

DECIDE TO WRITE

- After you have accepted a position with another organization
- If you are asked to resign by the organization
- When you have decided to retire
- After you have reviewed the organization policy to check timing, procedural, and policy issues
- After you have given your resignation orally

THINK ABOUT CONTENT

- Start with an expression of goodwill to set up your resignation statement.
- Follow your set-up statement with a logical, clear, and positive statement of resignation.
- State that you are resigning your position (use your title) and give an effective date.
- State why you are leaving in an objective, factual tone.
- End with a goodwill statement of appreciation for the experience, training, and/or relationship. You may want to state positive aspects of the company, and/or the people with whom you worked.

ELIMINATE WRONG MESSAGES

- Don't make angry statements. Your letter will remain on file, and this could come back to bite you.
- Don't forget to include some positive points of your relationship with the organization.

CONSIDER SPECIAL SITUATIONS

- Be sure to check the organization policy concerning resignations carefully, especially in respect to the person to whom you should tender your resignation.

- Consider all the ramifications of your resignation. In an effort to leave under the best of circumstances, you may wish to give your organization more than the standard notice policy requires and offer to train your replacement.
- Most often resignations are given in a face-to-face meeting, and the written resignation is simply a follow-up.
- It is often organizational policy that resignations are made in the form of a memo. Comply with any such requirements.
- Though it may not seem ethical, an organization may wish for an employee tendering his resignation to leave immediately. Be prepared for this possibility.

USE STRONG WORDS

appreciate	benefited	built	developed
effective	enjoyed	grown	growth
new	opportunity	resign	strong
tender	thank you (thanks)	trained	valuable (invaluable)

BUILD EFFECTIVE PHRASES

benefited from my time here	change career directions
continue to be challenged in new ways	enjoyed working on the team
excellent learning experience	expand horizons
gained valuable skills	move in a new direction
new growth opportunity	provided a growth opportunity
seek a new challenge	special camaraderie

CONSTRUCT STRONG SENTENCES

I gained irreplaceable experience here at Gault.

I shall never forget the great learning opportunity my years at Diddles afforded me.

Shores offered me, a new graduate, an outstanding career-development opportunity.

I'm most thankful for the opportunity you gave me to serve on the Blisters team.

I learned more in my 18 months at Riggers than I did in six years in undergraduate and graduate school.

I shall always cherish my years here, and will always be proud to be a Jitters alumni.

I've experienced three invaluable years of career development in my role here.

BUILD STRONG PARAGRAPHS

I realize I've been fortunate to have been an employee here for three years. This experience has afforded me real career collateral, and I shall always regard my time here fondly.

No more 5:30 A.M. meetings with Jim Greely. No more 5:30 P.M. meetings with Jim Greely. No more 10:30 P.M. meetings with Jim Greely. I must say I will miss each and every one of them, and I'll miss all five engineers in this department who've been such an important part of my cherished memories of working here.

I am very sad to have to end this wonderful working relationship. But I now need to stretch beyond my comfort zone of the great learning experience I enjoyed with the accounting department here.

Thank you for the opportunity to be a Monster employee. There isn't another place I'd have preferred to start my career.

How green I was when I entered the Ortho offices on that bright May morning five years ago. How patient you all were. Thank you for the gentle and terrific seasoning-of-a-rookie experience.

Though I'll be changing organizations, I won't be leaving the many friends I made in this place. I'll be in touch with all of you in shipping.

Though we had marked differences, I appreciate the fact that at Expound each and every employee is given the opportunity to express his ideas. Thank you for the great learning experience.

SELECT A FORMAT

- Usually a resignation is first given verbally, and the written form is a formality that follows.
- Use the standard organizational format. This may be a memo on letterhead, or a letter on letterhead.

EDIT, EDIT, EDIT

Since this provides a final and lasting impression—and is a part of your permanent employee record—make sure every sentence is just right.

Memo—Resigning Due to Loss of Position

TO: R. R. Beams
FROM: Ted West
DATE: March 6, 2011
SUBJECT: Resignation from Choice Matters, Effective April 1

The fact that my position here is ending doesn't diminish the great professional experience I have enjoyed. It has been outstanding.

Thank you for the opportunity given me at Choice Matters. I wish the organization great success in the future, and wish the best for each any every one remaining on staff.

Resignation after Reorganization

Dean Synder

Dear Dean:

It's a bit like musical chairs, isn't it? And now that I find myself without a chair, I must say it has been both a great experience and a wonderful opportunity to learn.

Thank you for your help in everything, especially your efforts at connecting me with other opportunities. My best wishes to you. I am confident that Quest Corporation will survive and grow.

Sincerely,

Ralph Boggs

Memo—Resigning to Take a New Position

TO: Casey Walters
CC: Doreen Rigors
FROM: Jake Straight
DATE: May 5, 2011
SUBJECT: Resignation from Cool Effective
              June 1, 2011

My four years at Cool Inc. have been the most intense learning experience of my life, and I have undergone a tremendous professional development growth spurt. I arrived here a complete novice, and both you and Doreen Rigors took me under your expert wings. Thanks to both of you for fine-tuning those academic skills, and tutoring me in real business practice done the Cool way.

I'm sad today to announce I am leaving, but I know you appreciate that it's time for me to move into a new area, and develop another set of professional skills.

I will miss each and every one of you, and will always be thankful for the great opportunity offered me to be a Cool employee. My best wishes to each of you, and best wishes for a bright future for Cool.

Resignation after Accepting a New Position

Alex Chang, Department Head

Dear Alex:

I am tendering my resignation, as I stated. I've accepted a position in Sacramento at Meade. As you know, this was a family decision made to coordinate both Beth's and my professions, and to create the best school environment for our children, Madison and Ben.

Thank you for your understanding. I will certainly miss all of my teammates in this department (and our champion softball team as well). My best wishes to everyone. Best wishes, too, for the continued success of Nerf.

Sincerely,

Dan Withers

29 EMPLOYEE TERMINATION

A letter of termination should never come as a bolt out of the blue. This news should first be given verbally in a face-to-face meeting, if at all possible. This letter is then simply the written documentation. If an employee is being terminated because of his actions or failures, other opportunities to correct his performance should first have been given.

Before writing this letter, be sure the criteria of pertinent laws, regulations, and organization policies and procedures have been met. This letter must be direct, stating the reason for the termination; and it should end on as upbeat a note as possible.

THINK ABOUT CONTENT

- Set the stage by stating your regrets.
- Make a clear statement of termination.
- Give the date termination is effective.
- Give an honest explanation concerning why the decision was made.
- Include any conditions that may apply.
- State any help, such as career counseling, or outsourcing that is being offered.
- Make a statement of goodwill, if possible.
- End with a cordial note or one of encouragement without being false.
- Include the name of someone who will answer any remaining questions, if applicable.

ELIMINATE WRONG MESSAGES

- Avoid being negative or hostile.
- Do not leave any doubt in the reader's mind that he is being terminated.
- Don't lay the blame elsewhere.
- Never use email to transmit your letter of termination.

CONSIDER ALL THE FACTS

- Know the pertinent laws and regulations.
- Have a supervisor you trust review the letter before you send it, if appropriate.
- Request legal counsel review, if appropriate.
- Assure the recipient you will not be giving a negative reference, if that is the organization's policy.

USE STRONG WORDS

action	cancel	conclude	decision
effective	employment	end	final
immediately	regret	sever	terminate

USE EFFECTIVE PHRASES

bring to an end	effective immediately
employment will be terminated as of	sever our relationship
terminate your employment	with full consideration

WRITE STRONG SENTENCES

I am sorry to deliver this message, but we must terminate your employment effective immediately.

I'm extremely saddened to have to deliver this news, but due to noncompliance with company policies outlined in letters to you dated March 15 and May 7, we must terminate your employment effective June 1.

Unfortunately, many of the positions at Richmond Instruments will have to be eliminated because of duplication of personnel after the merger.

BUILD EFFECTIVE PARAGRAPHS

There is no good way to say you are being terminated. As of June 15, we must eliminate your position due to the company's present financial crisis.

We must terminate your employment with General Evidence effective July 1. Your hearing with the human resources manager indicated that you were apprehended on June 15, 2011, 7:07 p.m. stealing three computers from the production area.

Copies of all the facts and violations of company policy are attached for your review. These are the same documents that were reviewed during your employee hearing on June 6.

EDIT, EDIT, EDIT

You will, of course, want to remove any ambiguity that might remain; and you'll want to end on as positive a note as possible.

Termination for Poor Performance

Cassidy Lindsay
433 Birch Lane
Rockville, MD 20852

Dear Cassidy:

Regrettably, it is necessary to terminate your employment at Bikers. After several discussions with you (see enclosed memo copies), and three reviews of your work, you have not improved your performance to match the duties of the job description.

Although separation from a company is never easy, it is often the best solution for everyone involved. After a careful review of all the facts, I believe this is true here.

I assure you we will strictly observe Bikers' policy regarding any future references concerning your employment here: we will release only the dates of your employment and your job title, and we will verify your salary with us only if the caller has obtained that salary information from you.

We do wish you every success in your future work.

Sincerely,

Donna Laurent

Position Terminated Due to Downsizing

Dear Rachel:

As we discussed, the economic slowdown in the Cleveland market for HighFlyers demands we close the regional office. Sadly, this eliminates your position.

We will terminate your employment with us on July 1, 2011, as agreed, and you will receive severance pay equal to three months' salary. The company will pay your medical insurance for the remainder of the year. In lieu of our bonus program, you have agreed to accept a one-time payment of $26,000. Your retirement benefits will be retained by the company until we receive instructions from you. The personnel department will send you a letter containing all the actual figures.

Rachel, we will all miss you here, but we are confident that your skills will land you an excellent position very soon. Please have any future employer contact me for a reference.

Sincerely,

Marika Lovelace

Termination Due to Downsizing

Dear Jennifer:

This is the day we all hoped would not arrive, but due to continuing loss of market share, we must terminate your employment with Cloudy Skies, effective June 15, 2011.

You will have the complete support of our job-locating services, and I've taken the liberty to schedule an interview with Rick Himes in HR to start that process. Rick will also discuss with you the severance package details.

Thank you for your service to Cloudy Skies over these past five years. We wish you well in your future career.

Sincerely,

Alice Bonkers

Termination for Intoxication

Martin May
3223 Race Street
Denver, CO 80223

Dear Martin:

Because your intoxication on the job impaired the safety of employees at Jinx, we must terminate your employment effective April 4, 2011. Attached is a copy of the incident report filed on March 28, 2011, as well as two other earlier reports.

As you know, when this problem was initially reported you agreed to complete the program outlined in the disciplinary action, but did not. We have no choice, therefore, since your continuing this behavior threatens the safety of other employees.

Your final check will be sent to your home address.

Sincerely,

Kenneth Bacon

Termination for Absenteeism

Melvin McReynolds
433 Archer Drive
Atlanta, GA 30345

Dear Melvin:

Your absenteeism has prevented you from performing the requirements of the position of assistant plant manager. I had hoped after our last meeting—the third such meeting—on September 15, when you indicated that you would correct this problem, that this action would not be necessary. But as you know, we have reviewed this matter in detail three times.

You employment with Vickers will be terminated effective November 1. Your final check will be mailed to your home, along with other personnel details.

I truly wish you success in the future.

Sincerely,

Marian Leeburg

V.

PROPOSALS & REPORTS

Make everything as simple as
possible, but not simpler.
—*Albert Einstein*

30 PROPOSAL

A proposal is basically a plan to do something. Its purpose is to persuade. It's a sales communication and is usually written in response to an invitation to supply a solution to a need or desire, but not always. Sometimes a proposal is submitted unsolicited or on speculation.

Your proposal may be as short as a sentence, or as long as a number of volumes. It may be as informal as an interoffice memo or verbal presentation, or as formal and complex as a lengthy government document.

A proposal is direct. It must be well organized and complete, whether it is unsolicited or requested, informal or formal, short or long. It should start with the reader's needs converted into the writer's purpose. A proposal should include background elements, a full description of the proposed plan, details (time requirements, schedule, costs, alternative factors, performance standards, etc.), ability to deliver, qualifications, benefits, and a summary or conclusion.

All this information should point to the writer's recommendations—the focus of the proposal.

UNDERSTAND THE TERMS

- An internal proposal usually recommends change within your organization.
- An external proposal is made to an outside organization.
- A sales proposal, technical proposal, or budget proposal usually recommends products or services to a customer.
- An unsolicited or speculative proposal is one you submit without an invitation ("submitted on spec"). Inquire first to see if it will be considered.
- A solicited or requested proposal is one you submit after receiving a request for proposal (RFP) or a request for a bid.
- Bid specifications (specs) or guidelines are the rules and requirements proposal writers or bidders receive from the customer and must follow.
- *Nonresponsive* means the bidder didn't comply with the specifications.

THINK ABOUT CONTENT

Preliminary Actions

- Qualify for the proposal process. Many government, private, and for-profit proposal processes are conducted on an invitation-to-bid basis, or a request for proposal (RFP). You must go through a preliminary qualifying process in order to obtain the opportunity to submit a proposal.

- Research. Complete knowledge of the problem, need, and/or desire of the recipient is essential. If past proposals are available (especially winning ones), review them as part of your research.
- Study and know your reader. To persuade the reader you must know his or her level of knowledge of the subject, bias, examples he or she will respect, and how he or she can best be persuaded.

Content Order
- Open with a clear and concise preview that will get the attention of the reader.
- Next, craft an **introduction**. Begin with a statement of the reader's need or problem, and a statement of the proposal's purpose. When the proposal is being submitted in response to an invitation, this should be stated here. When the proposal is unsolicited, you must get the reader's attention and overcome any resistance in this section.
- Insert a statement of **background information**, a detailed description of the need or problem. In the case of a proposal to reorganize a corporation, for example, this section would give a historical description of the beginning of the corporation and its development, then explain the need to reorganize.
- Include a **need** or **problem statement**. The background will naturally flow into a statement of the need or problem. In a very brief proposal, the need statement may appear without a background statement.
- Develop a **plan of action**. This is the core of the proposal. It must be well organized, clear, and complete. This must be stated as an effective solution that will appeal to the reader.
- Include enough **details** to anticipate the reader's questions and objections. In a long proposal, this section will contain timetables, materials, costs, requirements, performance standards, quality controls, etc.
- List your **qualifications**. Give sound reasons why you (or the organization) is uniquely qualified to perform the proposed plan. This may include giving personal qualifications like resumes, job references, operating procedures, and financial statements.
- List the **benefits**. Cover the positive effects that will accrue if your proposal is completed.
- Give a **recommendation**. If it hasn't already been stated, this is where your most persuasive statement belongs. It's best to close the circle. Refer back to the beginning: "This plan will meet your needs of realizing a 15 percent return by . . ."
- Include a **summary** and **conclusion**. In a long proposal, it is necessary to briefly summarize the proposal points. Any additional information needed will also appear here, and the conclusion must call for action.

Other Considerations
- If the reader's interest is low, put your strongest points first. If the reader's interest is high, put your strongest points last.
- Choose your "testimonials" from people and examples the reader knows, or can relate to.
- Tailor your proposal to the reader's attitudes and beliefs, if you can.

- Use well-organized headings, subheadings, and divisions.
- Develop an effective solution that will appeal to the reader.

ELIMINATE WRONG MESSAGES

- Do not use sensational claims. Stick to examples within the reader's scope of experience.
- Do not propose elements you cannot back up or deliver, but remember that you will not change the reader's attitude by presenting information alone.
- Eliminate everything that isn't carefully focused.
- Eliminate stilted prose and jargon.
- Never mention people or examples without considering the effect on your reader.

CONSIDER SPECIAL SITUATIONS

- Getting on the qualified list of bidders for government work or some for-profit accounts can be a long and difficult process. Start early.
- Study every related, successful proposal you can get your hands on.

SELECT A FORMAT

- Informal proposals often use the memo form. These are usually simple, routine proposals, and are transmitted by email.
- Formal proposals will be much more complex. Organize your material carefully to make your proposal easy to follow, interesting, and convincing.
- Use enumerations and subheads for impact, understanding, visual interest, and clarity.
  A formal proposal format:
  I. TABLE OF CONTENTS
  II. INTRODUCTION
  III. NEED/PROBLEM
      A. Scope
          1. *Objectives.* The overall objectives and specific accomplishments. Give the rationale.
          2. *Approach.* Clearly outline the plan of work and the phases.
          3. *Materials, Labor, and Methods.* Details and methodology you will use. Cover your expertise and any difficulties.
          4. *Timetable, Schedule, or Level of Accomplishment.* Break this into relative parts.
      B. Qualifications
          1. *Experience.* General background, specific, and similar experience.
          2. *Personnel.* Qualifications/resumes. Name the responsible person and subcontract sources.

Proposal Features

A proposal may include some or all of these features:

COVER MATERIALS
- Cover Letter or Letter of Transmittal
- Title Page
- Table of Contents
- Table of Illustrations or Figures
- Abstract or Summary
- Introductory Materials
- Introduction (Grabber)
- Statement of Purpose
- Reference of any association with the organization or any association with the problem.
- Problem or Need
- Background (of Problem)
- Needs Analysis
- Solution Statement
- Benefits to Be Gained from Solution
- Methodology
- Feasibility of Solution
- Personnel or Staffing Plan
- Design and Organization of Personnel Team
- Personnel Qualifications
- Task Breakdown or Specific Responsibilities
- Time and Work Schedule
- Testing
- Evaluation Procedures
- Progress Reports or Checks

MANAGEMENT
- Project Organization and Management
- Administrative Structure
- Management Policies
- Cost-Accounting Methods
- Payroll and Timekeeping Methods and Procedures
- Credit References and Ratings
- Facilities
- Quality Control and Assurance Guidelines
- Personnel Qualifications and Subcontractors
- Experience
- Financial Qualifications and Resources
- Organizational Support

BUDGET
- Direct Costs
- Indirect Costs
- Subcontracts
- Contract Definition and Terms
- Method and Timetable of Payments
- Late Penalties

CLOSE
- Summary
- Conclusion
- Call to Action/Recommendations

APPENDICES
- Letters of Reference
- Recommendation, Letters of Support, and "Testimonials"
- Resumes of Key Personnel
- Applicable Policy Statements, etc.

EDIT, EDIT, EDIT

Before your proposal is finished, it will undoubtedly go through a number of rewriting and editing procedures. Use all your writing skills to make it as clear and persuasive as possible. Get as much input as possible from professionals you admire, and from people qualified to proof the proposal. You may want to hire a professional editor. Check facts, critique content, and check for grammatical errors and typos.

(Also see COVER LETTER, page 253; REQUEST & INQUIRY, page 246; and RESUME, page 126.)

Work Proposal

Rose Design Group
200 West Petunia
Oakland, Missouri 64101

(660) 890-7600

Proposal

(Date)

Crystal Lake Homeowners' Association
5200 East Walker Drive
Oakland, Missouri 64101

Attention: Sayer Applewood, President

Reference: <u>Landscaping Renovation</u>

This proposal includes completing the following work by (date).
To accept, sign the attached sheet, General Conditions.

	Cost
1. Prepare the site thoroughly, including, but not limited to the following:	$935
a) remove and dispose of existing junipers	
b) grind out pear tree stumps	
c) remove lowest branches on existing trees	
2. Furnish and install 5 yards of compost.	440
3. Furnish and install 110 feet of edging.	145
4. Furnish and install flagstone step stones.	290
5. Rebuild existing rock wall at west side of garage.	430
6. Remove and dispose of existing exposed aggregate.	460
	$2,700

In its simplest form, the proposal communicates to the reader all the information he or she needs to know to make an informed decision. When agreed to, the proposal can become the contract between the writer and the reader. This requires that the proposal be crystal clear, down to the last detail.

Proposal/Crystal Lake Homeowners' Association/(Date)/page 2 of 2

<u>GENERAL CONDITIONS</u>
UNFORESEEN SITE CONDITIONS

The contractor has made a reasonable effort to accurately estimate the costs for Material and Labor required to complete the project as specified. However, the Contractor may be required to revise this Contract based on "unforeseen" and/or "undetectable" circumstances, which may arise during the completion of the project. Should any "unforeseen" and/or "undetectable" circumstances arise, the Contractor shall notify the Owner of estimated additional costs required to rectify the situation and obtain written authorization to proceed through the use of a Change Order.

MATERIAL QUANTITIES

The Material quantities specified in the Contract are considered to be appropriate quantities, plus or minus 10%. If any additional Materials are necessary to complete the job, the Contractor shall notify the Owner of the additional costs required to rectify the situation and obtain written authorization to proceed through the use of a Change Order. If less Material is needed to complete the job, the cost shall be credited back to the Owner.

CHANGE ORDERS

All additional Work to the conditions of the Contract shall be subject to additional charges and the Contract price adjusted accordingly. No additional Work shall be performed by the Contractor unless written authorization (Change Order) to proceed with such Work, including the price of such Work, shall be issued by the Owner.

UNDERGROUND UTILITIES

The Contractor shall be responsible to have all underground utilities located.

PERMITS, TAXES, REGULATIONS, CODES

The Contractor is obligated to obtain and pay the cost of all permits, licenses, certificates, inspection and other legal fees that are necessary to do the Work, as applicable.

INSURANCES

The Contractor shall be required to carry and keep in force throughout the duration of the Work General Liability and Workers' Compensation Insurances.

CLEAN UP

The Contractor shall leave the site free of debris and surplus material at all times and, at the completion of Work, remove all waste, rubbish, excess materials and equipment generated by the Contractor and leave the site in a clean, completed condition ready for Owner's full use and enjoyment.

DISPUTES/ARBITRATION

Any controversy or claim arising out of or relating to this Contract, or the breach thereof, shall be settled by arbitration in accordance with the Construction Industry Arbitration Rules of the American Arbitration Association or the procedures of the Arbitration Committee of the Associated Landscape Contractors of Colorado. Arbitration shall be binding and the decision to enter into such Arbitration shall be initiated by either party of this agreement.

PLANT WARRANTY

All plant material (excluding annuals, bulbs, and transplanted materials) shall be guaranteed to be alive and in satisfactory growing condition one year following the date of installation. Any material that is considered dead shall be replaced, one time only, by the Contractor at no charge to the Owner. The Owner shall notify the Contractor immediately as soon as any plant material begins to show signs of stress (e.g., yellowing, wilting). The Contractor shall not be responsible for plants that have been adversely affected by factors or circumstances beyond the Contractor's control, including, but not limited to, severe winter or unusual temperature fluctuations during any given time of the year, tornado, vandalism, animal damage, improper application of fertilizers or pesticides, and lack or excess of moisture.

IRRIGATION SYSTEM WARRANTY

All components of the irrigation system shall be guaranteed to be free of defects and in good working order for one year following the date on installation. This warranty does not cover the system if it has been damaged due to freezing conditions. It is the Owner's responsibility to insure that the system is protected from temperatures below 32 degrees F.

OWNER _____   DATE _____

CONTRACTOR _____   DATE _____

This second page of the proposal, when signed, becomes the legal contract between the writer and the reader.

31 CONTRACT (LETTER OF AGREEMENT)

A letter that outlines the limits and details of an agreement between two people, or parties, can be very useful in avoiding conflicts and disputes. When both people, or parties, sign the letter it becomes the legal bond between them. For those contracts that involve complex details and/or sizable amounts of money, it is wise to have your contract letter (or letter of agreement) reviewed by an attorney specializing in the particular field. This letter is only as effective as your ability to anticipate what might come up during the task or matter about which you've written, so think it through carefully. (Also see Proposal, page 197; Order, page 326; Complaint & Protest, page 282; Negotiation, page 298; and Settlement, page 303.)

WHEN TO USE IT

- Employment agreement
- Work to be performed on your home, or for your business
- Family agreement
- Private loan
- Changes in existing contract (change order)
- Change to a will (codicil)
- Rental or lease
- Granting access, or permission for use
- Barter agreement, or exchange of services

THINK ABOUT CONTENT

- Research the matter thoroughly, and know your rights and legal obligations.
- Think through the entire matter carefully, and outline the duties of each party. (Look at relevant contracts; have your contract reviewed by experts, whenever possible.)
- Approach the contract thinking of the parties as partners—each having a vital role. Fair play, reasonable expectations, and appropriate alternatives will ensure that both parties are satisfied.
- Anticipate what could interfere with successfully completing the contract.

- List all the points that need to be included: completion of stages, e.g., "all old paint will be removed by June 10"; "materials and supplies will be purchased [from, by, who pays, etc.]"; "construction permits will be obtained from county . . ."; "inspections will be completed by . . ."
- Provide alternate measures for satisfactorily completing your agreement—possible resources for both parties.

HOW TO WRITE IT

- Use simple, concise language.
- State the purpose early and precisely, e.g., "REFERENCE: Painting Exterior of the House at 1200 East Young Street."
- Open by defining your agreement: "This contract defines the agreement between [Party One] and [Party Two] . . ."
- Follow with the complete names of the parties, their addresses, and their roles in the agreement, e.g., "[Party One, address], house owner, and [Party Two, address], painter . . ."
- State completely what each party will do, give, provide, receive, be paid, etc.
- Include the terms of performance, such as specifications, start date, payments and due dates, completion date, etc.
- Provide for negotiations and/or terms under which the contract may be canceled by either party, e.g., "Failure to complete the work by July 1, 2011, will result in the contract being canceled . . ."
- Specify the deadline for executing the contract, e.g., "This contract must be signed and received by [Party One] by [date] to be in effect."
- Provide signature and date lines or space for both parties at the end of the contract. (You may also want to include a fax number or email address for the return of the contract.)

ELIMINATE WRONG MESSAGES

- Don't think of the other party as an adversary; think, instead of the parties as partners working to accomplish a single goal.
- Avoid cluttered construction with terms hidden in long paragraphs. A list of the function of each party clearly set out in exact terms will avoid problems later.
- Imprecise language or terms can result in conflicts. Specify everything in measurable absolutes, if possible. Example: "The new paint will be applied in two coats to measure a thickness of . . ."

CONSIDER SPECIAL SITUATIONS

- In our litigious society it is far better to have an agreement executed and in place than to try to reconstruct one from the impressions of the two warring parties after a conflict has arisen.

- Use a contract letter instead of a verbal understanding even when dealing with close friends and family members. This will insure that everyone agrees to the terms, and may avoid fracturing a relationship.
- Don't be afraid to ask the other party to indicate his/her knowledge and agreement even when he/she may think it unnecessary. An example could be an agreement with school administrators that your child be excused from physical education class for the semester because of an injury or allergy. "Please sign the end of this letter indicating your agreement and return it to me" will afford you a record, which could be very valuable later.
- In writing a contract for a loan and its repayment, be sure to specify repayment dates, amounts, and any other details important to the deal.

SELECT A FORMAT

- A proposal may contain signature and date lines. When both parties have signed and dated it, and agreed (by initialing) to any changes either has made, it becomes the contract. No additional contract letter is required.
- A memo may become a contract when it is used in the same way.
- Use enumerations and subheads for impact, understanding, ease of reading, and clarity.
- Contract forms are available for many small business uses. Use these for expedience if they express what you need.
- Use a letter form for a contract, typed on business letterhead or personal letterhead stationery.

CHOOSE STRONG WORDS

agree, agreement	affirm	arrangement
assure	attest	attain
bind, binding	breach	cancel
certify	claim	clause
collect	conditions	confirm
conform	consent	consider, consideration
defective	delay	endorse
estimate	evidence	indemnify
groundless	guarantee	grievance
negotiate, negotiation	negligence	malpractice
mediation	obligations	partner
propose	provision	perform, performance
procedures	reasonable	recompense
reimbursement	remedy, remedies	responsibility
settlement	stipulate, stipulation	terms
transaction	understand, understanding	underwrite
unsatisfactory	verify, verification	warrant

BUILD STRONG PHRASES

agrees to

as outlined here

compensatory damages

gross negligence

mutual satisfaction

in return, you agree to

written record

completion by

in compliance with, comply with

contingent fees

expert opinion

bad faith

improperly installed

faulty work

in full consideration

made whole

small claims court

legal action

legal violations

in compliance with

up to code

second opinion

please sign and date

terms of this agreement

effective as of

articles of agreement

best efforts

delineated below

in complete settlement

mutual benefit

workmanlike fashion

effective date

no later than

consequences of delay

defective work

good faith

substantial performance

hazardous condition

full extent of our agreement

complete extent of our agreement

reimbursement for

techniques used

legal costs

on condition that

unannounced changes

acceptable standard of care

deviation from approved, deviation from agreed

return the signed and dated letter by

specified terms

obtain such approvals and licenses as are required

WRITE STRONG SENTENCES

I'm outlining all the terms of our agreement here.

This reflects the complete extent of our agreement.

This contract is good if signed, dated, and received by me by May 15, 2011.

This will serve as the contract for the painting of the exterior of the house.

Please read the complete extent of this contract outlined in the points after each of our names.

Please note that I have made a change to point #15 of the contract, and I've initialed it in the margin.

This serves as the contract between Mary Green, artist, and Joan Roach, homeowner, for the execution of a decorative, handpainted mural on the dining room wall, as specified below.

This agreement outlines the responsibilities and remuneration for Alice Green, 2040 Grand Blvd., Detroit, housekeeper and personal caregiver, in the care of Mildred Moore, 1010 Redford Rd., Detroit, client.

BUILD EFFECTIVE PARAGRAPHS

Often a paragraph or two will contain the entire contract.

The terms of the loan and the repayment are quite simple: I, Bill Bigbucks, will loan you, Jack Sponger, $15,000 on June 1, 2011; and you will repay the loan in installments of $1,000 each starting on December 1, 2011, and on the first of each month that follows for a total of 15 consecutive months until the total loan amount $15,000 is repaid. An additional payment of a $1,500 loan fee is due on March 1, 2012, which, when paid, will complete the contract between us.

The completion of the revision of the text will be done in the style and tone of the present edition of *Perfect Words*, with the new content consisting of approximately 30% new material, including new chapters on contracts, wills, websites, and blogs. In consideration of this work, you will receive a $50,000 advance to be paid in two equal installments of $25,000: one upon execution of this contract, and the second upon submission of a satisfactory revised manuscript on May 1, 2012.

As we discussed and agreed on the telephone, we have just documented (see Aaron Fine, M.D.'s statement attached) that our daughter, Grace Oberstein, in Mrs. Adams' fifth grade class, has an allergic condition, which will prevent her from participating in physical education this semester. This substantiates our agreement that she will be allowed to develop with the help of her physical therapist a plan for physical activity, which she will be putting into practice starting at the beginning of next semester. Please sign and date this agreement and return a copy to me for our files.

EDIT, EDIT, EDIT

Be ruthless and exacting in editing your contract down to its essential clearest and best. More good intentions are lost in excess verbiage than by blatant error.

Contract for Snow Removal Services

This is the contract between the residents of Downing Circle (Beth and Jerry Affleck, Judy and George Wily, Mary and Steve Smiley) and Ben Wright, 2022 Glendale Ave., Denver, for the snow removal from the Downing Circle—houses #35 through #37—for the period November 1, 2011 through April 15, 2012. When the snowfall accumulation exceeds 1.5 inches the snow will be plowed into piles—and moved into the designated areas only—-by Ben Wright. Ben agrees to use his truck and snowplow, and work as an independent contractor, carrying the necessary liability insurance required by the state of Colorado. Downing Circle residents will be billed each month at the rate of $65 per hour for Ben's snowplowing services.

This contract is dependent upon showing the required liability insurance coverage. Please submit proof of this insurance coverage, attach it to the dated and signed contract agreement, and return it to us by October 1, 2011.

This contract may be canceled by either party without cause with thirty days written notice.

We look forward to working with you again this season.

Signature:_____(Date)_____

Signature:_____(Date)_____

Signature:_____(Date)_____

Signature:_____(Date)_____

Agreement for Exchange of Services

Dear Gabby,

This contract defines how we will exchange services: I, Cynthia Kraft, President of PR Pros, will exchange 25 hours per month of public relations services (writing press releases, placement of feature stories, organization of special events, and interview opportunities with media and blog sources) for GreenBay Designs, in exchange for the web services of Jodi Cruise, President, of GreenBay Designs, who will provide 25 hours per month (creation, design update, and web hosting services) for the website and blog posting on MyWay.com.

Contract Term: This contract shall be in effect for an initial period of three months, or a total of 75 hours of services by Cynthia Kraft for GreenBay Designs, in exchange for 75 hours of services from Jodi Cruise for MyWay.com.

Procedure: Jodi and Cynthia will each submit to the other an overall plan for work to be done during the three-month contract period. Each week each party will conduct a "client" consult with the other, during which each will describe the project goals for the month, and the work and progress to date. At the end of each week, Jodi and Cynthia will each report to the other the work done and the results to date, and discuss any change of strategy desired by the "client."

Neither Cynthia Kraft nor Jodi Cruise will pay the other for these services, and each will be responsible (with prior approval only) for any expenses incurred on behalf of her organization. These fees may include such things as securing a website name, brochure printing, special event expenses, postage, etc.

This contract will run from June 1, 2011 through August 31, 2011, and may be terminated by either party during that period without cause with thirty days written notice.

Signed:

Cynthia Kraft _____(Date)_____

Jodi Cruise_____(Date)_____

32 BUSINESS PLAN

The business plan is like a road map: write it to think through your goals and create a way to go forward. It should be constantly revised and updated to keep your business vital, current, and healthy.

Write a business plan to gain support for your idea—to persuade. Your audience may be potential investors, bankers, or executives within your organization. You may need to convince a bank or investors to offer financing, or your organization's executives to offer cooperation, resources, or even enthusiasm. You may also want others to offer an evaluation, additional ideas, and counsel. Business plans are generally of limited distribution, and are kept confidential.

THINK ABOUT CONTENT

- The business plan will include a simple overall vision for the organization: its mission, objectives, strategies, and goals. Distill each of these into a few simple statements. The end plan may be only a single page in length.
- For an outside audience, focus your plan on a precise recipient, e.g., your bank.
- Research your audience to determine the elements it wants to see. The banker, for example, will have very prescribed requirements, like a balance sheet, profit-and-loss statement, cash-flow projections, projected expenditures, break-even points, and so on.
- Develop the plan sections:
  - ▶ The **general business description** will state the business type, products and/or services to be produced, and the market positioning. Start with the legal name of the organization, its location, and status (for example, "X Company is a California Corporation, located at 324 Locust Street, Los Angeles, licensed to do business as . . ."); describe what the organization will do; include a statement about the customer or client base; describe the growth opportunity; explain where the product(s) or service(s) will fit in the competitive field, and what makes the plan viable. Make a brief statement about future growth. This section may be only a sentence to a few paragraphs in length.
  - ▶ A **mission statement** briefly defines the purpose and reason for existing. Distill this to a simple statement. For example, "X Company will offer an affordable alternative to Y Company's . . ."
  - ▶ **Goals** may be segmented into short, mid, and long term, and should be projected precisely. Be realistic, offer specific and measurable terms, and be conservative.

> ▸ **Management team members** should be identified and their expertise described. Include key support team members, too, like outside consultants, accountants, lawyers, insurance agents, and marketing experts who have committed to work with the organization. Describe their expertise and list some of their references. (You may include their resumes in the appendices.) This section may also include a listing of organization positions that will be added in the future, and projections about staging and expansion.

> ▸ **Market analysis** is the heart of your plan. Demonstrate that you understand the market. Analyze competitive organizations and products or services, and then show how your product or service can compete and become successful.

> ▸ The **marketing plan** must lay out, in concrete terms, how you will use various promotional, advertising, and public relations techniques to launch the organization. Include this information for each particular service and product, and for each market segment.

> ▸ The **financial analysis** must show how finances will be used to achieve success. Include all investments and starting capital, as well as debt. Projections for financial growth must include a discussion of strengths and weaknesses, cost-control measures, and potential problem areas. Show how you are prepared to deal with them. Include here a balance sheet, profit-and-loss statements, and cash-flow projections for the short, mid, and long term. Usually projections will go to six months, and one, two, and three years—at least for banks.

> ▸ Use **appendices** or **supporting documents** to bolster your case; resumes of key team members; customer or client contracts or orders; letters of support by experts in the field; marketing studies or focus-group responses; positive reviews of the product or service; patents or licenses; incorporation documentation, name rights, patents, and other unique legal documents; statements about demand for the product or service. Include anything that helps to make your case, carefully tabbed and correctly referenced in the appropriate business plan section.

CONSIDER SPECIAL SITUATIONS

- Think of your business plan as a work in progress. It will need to be rewritten.
- Check your progress and update your internal business plan at least once each quarter.

SELECT A FORMAT

- Create a visually appealing printed document by using double-spaced text on 8½ by 11–inch quality, white or off-white bond.
- For the printed and bound hard copy (paper) plan, prepare a title page; a table of contents, if needed; and a table of graphs, illustrations, and charts, if appropriate.
- Prepare and print graphs, charts, and illustrations in professional-looking color to illustrate the main points of your plan.

- Make your presentation in person, whenever possible. Use an audiovisual format that allows you to "show and tell" whenever possible; as well as actual products and/or service samples. Practice your presentation until you can make it flawlessly. Anticipate and prepare answers to key questions.

Business Plan

New-to-You Business Plan
(2012 and 2013)

Vision	New-to-You is a consignment business with top designer retail shop appeal; based on the belief that recycling is a beautiful, chic way to live. It will provide: • the latest in shoes, purses, belts, jewelry, and scarves • custom alterations • wardrobe consulting
Mission	Provide upwardly mobile women with designer accessories at budget prices; and alterations and wardrobe consulting to fit them for the boardroom.
Objectives	$1.5M in accessories sales in 2012. • $1.75M in alterations and wardrobe consulting sales. • Achieve profit margin of 45% in 2012. • Increase total sales by 20% in 1st quarter of 2013. • 20% in 2nd quarter of 2013; 25% in 3rd quarter of 2013; and 28% in 4th quarter of 2013. • Start "Vintage Chic" fashion shows in 2013.
Strategies	Use Twitter, FaceBook, and other social media to locate designer accessories for resale. • Build networks with women's social clubs, spas, salons, gyms, and dry cleaners. • Advertise Asa and Wally customized alteration to high-end designer and department stores. • Capture theater alterations and costume-fitting business.
Plans	Establish 40/60% split with consignees. • Hire Asa, Wally, and four sales personnel. • Issue invitations to in-store fashion shows for spring, 2013. • Invite clothing sales personnel from area designer and department stores to fashion shows. • Propose in-spa, gym, and social club fashion shows. • Hire two interns to learn alterations techniques.

33 FORMAL REPORT

The formal report collects and interprets data and reports information. Reports are used to inform, analyze, recommend, and persuade. They are usually written in indirect order—presenting information, analyzing it, making conclusions, and making recommendations. The formal report is often very complex and may be bound like a book. (An example is The 9-11 Commission Report. See samples at the end of this chapter.) In the business setting, the informal report is usually used for internal distribution, and the formal report is prepared for external distribution to stockholders, customers, and the general public. The formal report is often a written account of a major project. Examples of subject matter include new technologies, the results of a study or experiment, analysis of locations for corporate relocation, an annual report, or a year-end review of developments in the field. Careful planning and meticulous organization are necessary to guide readers through the material. Good writing and excellent editing are required to keep their interest.

Three main sections—preliminary, or front, material; body; and back material—help give the report form. Within these sections, there may be a number of subsections as needed:

PRELIMINARY (FRONT) MATERIAL
- Title Page
- Letter of Authorization
- Letter of Transmittal
- Abstract
- Table of Contents
- List of Figures
- List of Tables
- List of Symbols and/or Abbreviations
- Statement of Problem, Abstract, Synopsis, or Summary
- Foreword
- Preface

BODY
- Executive Summary
- Introduction
- Text (with Appropriate Headings, Subheadings)
- Conclusions or Summary
- Recommendations

SUPPLEMENTAL (BACK) MATERIAL
- References
- Appendices
- Bibliography
- Glossary
- Index

Preliminary or Front Material

Front material describes the purpose of the report. It provides an overview and lists specific content.

- The **title page** lists the topic or subject, scope, and purpose; lists the writer with title and/or role and affiliate organization; date of issuance (and period, such as quarterly, annual); and the name of the commissioning organization. This page isn't numbered, but is page i; the blank back of the page, also unnumbered, is page ii.

- **Letter of authorization** lists the sponsoring organization (or person) commissioning the work and the report.
- **Letter of transmittal** is a cover letter identifying who the report is sent by, and to whom it is being sent. It may point out special sections or points of interest.
- The **abstract** gives the major points of the report.
- **Table of contents** lists the major sections or headings, in order of appearance, and the page numbers on which they begin.
- **List of figures** (when there are five or more) shows the pages on which they appear.
- **List of tables** is used when five or more of these are used. It gives the page numbers where they appear.
- A **foreword**, when included, contains an introductory statement by someone other than the author(s), giving background and perhaps comparisons to other reports in the field. The writer's name appears at the end, along with the date.
- The **preface** is the author's statement about the *what, why, when*, and so on of the report.

Body

Here's where the methods, procedures, tests, and comparisons used are covered. It also includes the results, analyses, conclusions, and recommendations, if any.

- The **executive summary** is an overview, more detailed than the abstract.
- The **introduction** indicates the report's purpose, scope, and other information.
- The **text** details how the study, investigation, and research were pursued or explored, and the initial findings.
- **Conclusions** or a summary distills the findings, results, and outcome, and offers deductive conclusions.
- **Recommendations** may be combined with conclusions. This usually states a course of action or results that indicate the need for the next step.

Supplemental (Back) Material

The back material lists sources, documentation, and supplemental materials.

- The **appendices** contain supporting information that is either too detailed or would disrupt the flow of the report if inserted in the text.
- The **bibliography** is an alphabetical listing of sources used by the author of the report.
- The **glossary** is an alphabetical listing of terms and definitions.
- The **index** is an alphabetical list of the terms, subjects, or names used in the report, and the pages on which they appear.

THINK ABOUT ORGANIZATION

After determining what sections you'll need to write, start to organize your material in outline form. (Also see chapter 1, "Getting Started," and chapter 2, "Design & Layout.") To organize the report in a conventional outline manner use:

    I. Major or First Level Heading
        A. Minor or Second Level Heading
            1. Subhead or Third Level Heading
                a. Fourth Level
                    (1) Fifth Level
                        (a) Sixth Level

To arrange the report by the decimal system use:

1.0 First Level Heading
    1.1 Second Level Heading
        1.2.1 Third Level
            1.2.2.1 Fourth Level

In typing the report, the outline form may be presented in the outline methods mentioned, or in one of the following:

    I. MAJOR OR FIRST LEVEL HEADING
        A. Minor or Second Level Heading
            1. Subhead or Third Level Heading
                a. Fourth Level Heading or Paragraph Heading

Headings may be typed without numbers or letters:

MAJOR OR FIRST LEVEL HEADING
<u>Minor or Second Level Heading</u>
Subtopic or Third Level Heading
    Fourth Level Heading or Paragraph Heading

THINK ABOUT CONTENT

- Remember that most **formal reports** use an indirect approach. (This is a pattern where the information order is: a "buffer" statement of neutral information or an explanation, followed by a statement of the bad news or the problem, followed by a conclusion statement offering good news or a solution.) This approach introduces the problem, then gives the facts with analyses (when needed), and summarizes the information given.
- The **informal report** often uses the more direct approach, offering the conclusion or recommendation, followed by the facts, but often given much more briefly. (See Informal Report, page 220.)

- Begin by answering why this report is needed, and make your statement of problem specific. It may be to convey information, to analyze, and/or to recommend a course of action.
- The statement of problem should include the reader. For example: "Our sales representatives need to know why competitive products X, Y, and Z are outselling our product A." Focus your statement of problem on a specific goal or purpose statement. It can be expressed as a question, a declarative statement, or an infinitive phrase:

  Question: "What do our sales representatives need to know about competitive products X, Y, and Z in order to effectively sell product A?"

  Declarative Statement: "Our sales representatives need to know the features of competitive products X, Y, and Z in order to effectively sell product A."

  Infinitive Phrase: "To sell product A effectively, our sales representatives need to know the features of competitive products X, Y, and Z."

- Divide the task into its component parts. You will want to look at subtopics within the purpose statements.
- If you are reporting information, such as the results of an experiment or a list of books on a topic, the structure will be a straightforward, logical narrative. Make sure your report is objective; base it on facts. This helps free it of opinion and bias.
- If you are making analyses, drawing conclusions, or making recommendations, you probably need to carefully organize some additional elements. Take the case of our product, for example. After defining the broad subtopics—product X, product Y, product Z—you may want to complete some initial observations or surveys of competitive products. You may give these responses to the question "Why are products X, Y, and Z outselling product A?":

  1. Products X and Z are cheaper than product A.
  2. Products Y and Z are available in designer colors; product A isn't.
  3. Products X, Y, and Z are packaged in carrying cases, which buyers seem to prefer over product A's packaging.

You will want to research some facts that can be used as sales points for product A. You may find that:

1. Although product A costs more, it outperforms and outlasts products X and Z.
2. Product A is not a fashion accessory. Designer colors aren't related to performance.
3. Product A is self-contained and has no detachable parts, so it is handsome and more convenient without a carrying case.

At the same time, your observations and surveys may lead you to develop some theories or hypotheses about your product:

1. We should reduce product A's price to be more competitive with products X and Z.
2. We should make product A available in designer colors to compete with products Y and Z.

    3. We should develop a useful carrying case for product A to compete favorably with products X, Y, and Z.

- Evaluate your hypotheses by assigning point values to each or by using another test method. They may all be partially true or false. If your hypotheses prove false, you may have to advance some additional hypotheses to evaluate. In the case of product A, research may indicate that price, a wide range of colors, and a carrying case are the three top buyer criteria.
- Break down the subtopics into sub-subtopics, if this is helpful to get at the real solutions to the problem.
- Gather all the information. This can require personal research, data collection, surveys, or experiments. Business problems usually rely on surveys, scientific problems on experiments. Information problems may be solved using library research. Employ objective, proper, and thorough methods here to avoid invalidating your solution.
- Test your gathered data:
  - ▹ Is it objective? Keep an open mind and consider all aspects to determine if sources are reported fairly and completely. Guard against bias.
  - ▹ Do others agree? Use the input of others to question and challenge your interpretation.
  - ▹ Is it reasonable? Check conclusions with logical thinking and make the surrounding facts support them.
  - ▹ Does it hold up? Play devil's advocate, taking the opposing viewpoint, and see if your conclusions hold up. Represent them fairly in your report, showing supporting evidence.

  Statistical data and interpretation are key in many reports. But scientific accuracy and integrity must be used in reporting this information. Check this out thoroughly before including it in your report.
- Organize the information into a report format, keeping precise records of sources.
- Write the rough draft.
- Be consistent in tense. Either present or past works well, but use the same tense throughout.
- Be consistent, too, in personal or impersonal (third person) viewpoint. The personal "I" or "we" can be as effective as the impersonal tests and facts, but different organizations and disciplines prefer one over the other. Often the informal report will use the personal and the formal report will use impersonal. Check your organization's style preference.
- Use effective transition words to begin new paragraphs. This helps keep the reader's attention.
- Make effective use of graphs, illustrations, and charts to make points.
- Enliven your writing by using effective, vigorous action words, but don't overdo it.
- Revise. Cut nonessential parts, and check for stilted words, jargon, inconsistencies, redundancies, and errors in logic. Eliminate any general, abstract, or vague statements. During this process, ask these questions:

- ▸ Does the introduction establish the scope and methods to be used?
- ▸ Are all the points in the introduction fully developed in the body?
- ▸ Is the development of points logical and complete?
- ▸ Are there ideas or sections that should be combined or relocated?
- ▸ Is there a clear solution to, or a complete discussion of, the stated problem?
- ▸ Is there a clear relationship between ideas and facts?
- ▸ Does the report flow logically?
- ▸ Is information complete for reader understanding?
- ▸ Is opinion correctly identified from fact?
- ▸ Have all the facts been double-checked?
- ▸ Do headings and subheadings properly reflect content?
- ▸ Are all grammar and spelling errors eliminated?

- Review and proofread with as many other people as practical.
- Shelve your report a few days; then give it a fresh look.

ELIMINATE WRONG MESSAGES

- Don't embellish facts, use them out of context, or misinterpret them to support a point.
- Don't use material without giving proper credit.
- Do not make faulty or illogical cause-and-effect conclusions. And remember, conclusions are not always necessary. Some things are inconclusive. Say so.
- Don't assume a lack of evidence proves the opposite is true. Maybe it isn't.
- Do not compare apples to oranges. Data must be similar in nature for comparisons to be authentic.
- Eliminate erroneous digressions or unfocused material. These can easily derail the report.

SELECT A FORMAT

- Establish a consistent format for all your organization's reports.
- Use an approved and consistent reference system, such as is shown in the *Chicago Manual of Style*, to record footnotes and bibliography listings.
- Create all the necessary graphics in visually appealing forms to promote understanding.
- Print and bind the report in a professional manner.

EDIT, EDIT, EDIT

- Employ key content experts to review the report and check all facts included.
- Use a professional proofreader to check for proper grammar, consistent tense, redundancies, and other problems or errors.
- Use a proofreader and the spell-checker to eliminate any typos.

Formal Report—Contents

The 9-11 Commission Report (Listing of Contents):

Front Matter

Table of Contents

List of Illustrations and Tables

Member List

Staff List

Preface

34 INFORMAL REPORT

The informal report functions to inform, analyze, and recommend. It usually takes the form of a memo, letter, or a very short internal document like a monthly financial report, monthly activities report, research and development report, and the like. This report differs from the formal report in length and formality. It's written according to organization style rules and usually includes an introduction, body, conclusion, and recommendations sections—but usually doesn't contain the preliminary (front) and supplemental (back) material (see pages 212 and 213). The informal report is usually more conversational in tone and typically deals with everyday problems and issues addressed to a narrow readership inside the organization.

Participatory management diminished the role of the informal report, but computers revived it, especially since management team members are frequently in different locations. An informal report is usually completed quickly and transmitted electronically.

DECIDE TO WRITE

There are many forms of the informal report:

- Progress report
- Financial report
- Literature review
- Acceptance or rejection of proposals
- Sales activity report
- Feasibility report
- Recommendations and suggestions

THINK ABOUT CONTENT

- **Informal reports** usually do not include introductory material, but include it if necessary.
- Start by asking yourself, "What does my reader need to know, precisely, about the subject?" Put this into a purpose statement in a single, explicit sentence. In a memo format, this can be your subject line.
- Use direct order organization. Begin with the most important information, usually the conclusion and a recommendation, for most routine problems. This approach saves your reader time. It offers the important information right up front. Write this down in outline form. For example, if you believe your copy machine should be replaced, you would start with this subject line: "Recommend replacing copy machine." In this, you would back up your recommendations with the reasons:
  - ▸ Required 12 repairs in the past month.
  - ▸ Requires clerk for operation.

> ► Produces too few copies per minute.
> ► Is out of warranty.

- Or, use an indirect approach. Start with general information, review the facts, and end with your recommendation. In the indirect approach, you might start with this subject line: "New copy machine offers superior performance."
- Follow this rule for selecting the direct or indirect approach: When your audience favors your conclusion or recommendation, state it directly, then back it up with facts. When your audience resists your conclusion or recommendation, or knows little or nothing about it, give the facts first and state your conclusion and recommendation at the end.
- Organize your information under the subtopics of your report.
- Use a personal writing style—using I, you, he, they, and we—if your organization allows it.
- Write and rewrite until your report is interesting, concise, and flows well.
- Make a conclusion, summary, or recommendation statement at the end, even if it repeats your subject line.
- Be sure you have completely answered or solved your subject problem or statement.

ELIMINATE WRONG MESSAGES

- Do not assume a level of knowledge your reader doesn't have.
- Using a direct approach does not relieve you of listing all the facts. Be sure all your backup facts are logically listed.
- Don't fire off a report without giving it an objective, second look.
- Don't make your report too long. This is usually a sign that it lacks organization. Keep it to under one page for simple subjects.
- Don't automatically begin every report in a direct approach. In our example, for instance, if the facts or evidence is not so clear-cut, you may be considered biased, capricious, or arbitrary. In cases where the subject is not on the top of everyone's mind, an indirect approach may work better.

SELECT A FORMAT

Use memo, letter, or report form. Informal reports are usually sent by email.

EDIT, EDIT, EDIT

- Check and recheck your information to be sure it is accurate and complete.
- Have others review and critique your report in draft form, if possible.
- Give your report (and yourself) some reflection time. If time permits, go back and read it when you are fresh to make sure you are satisfied with it before sending.

Informal Report—Internal Memo

TO: Employees and physicians
FROM: John Allen, president and CEO
RE: "Give Health a Hand" Campaign
DATE: Nov. 22, 2011

With flu season upon us, Good Samaritan Hospital is working to keep central Nebraska healthy through a new campaign called "Give Health a Hand."

Good Samaritan developed Give Health a Hand to remind children and adults that frequent hand washing is the best way to prevent the spread of germs. We have retained Omaha-based Redstone Communications and Hanser & Associates for regional advertising and public relations services surrounding the campaign.

In recognition of National Hand Washing Awareness Week, Dec. 5–11, Good Samaritan will be visiting schools, businesses, and restaurants to demonstrate proper hand washing techniques and distribute hand washing kits and posters. The campaign, which has been endorsed by the Nebraska Health and Human Services System, will continue through February.

Highlights of the campaign, to begin Monday, Dec. 6, include:
* TV and radio spots with hand washing theme song
* Hand washing posters and kits (containing hand washing instructions, a bar of soap, and a coloring book)
* Announcement of campaign to area news media
* Guest column in the Kearney Hub
* Ongoing hand washing events in the community (December through February)

I thank all employees and physicians at Good Samaritan for your ongoing commitment to rigorous hand washing at work, home, and in the community. Our community is trusting you, me, and all of us at Good Samaritan to Give Health a Hand.

Help us spread the word about Give Health a Hand by sharing information about the campaign with your family, friends, neighbors and others in your community. Key points include:

* Frequent hand washing is the best way to prevent the spread of germs that cause illness.
* It takes vigorous scrubbing with soap and warm water for at least 20 seconds to wash germs away.
* It is especially important to wash your hands before, during, and after handling food, as well as before you eat.
* Washing up after using the restroom is imperative. After you've washed your hands, use a paper towel to turn off the faucet and to open the door of a public restroom. Properly dispose of your paper towel.
* Alcohol-based disposable hand wipes or gel sanitizers are good alternatives if soap and water are not available.
* In addition to frequent hand washing, these four good health habits will help ward of flu and other viral infections:
  - Cover your mouth and nose when you sneeze or cough.
  - Avoid touching your eyes, nose, or mouth.
  - Stay home when you are sick.
  - Avoid close contact with people who are sick.

Contact the Corporate Communications Department at 555-0123 for more information about the campaign, or if you would like to help conduct hand washing demonstrations or have suggestions on possible venues.

(Also see FORMAL REPORT, page 212, and MEMO, page 170.)

35 FEASIBILITY REPORT

The feasibility report defines a need or proposed idea, then analyzes, compares, and recommends a course of action. When your organization is considering a new location, expansion, or the purchase of new equipment, for example, it's imperative that you look closely to see which course of action is best and if that course of action is likely to succeed. A list of questions should start the process:

- What is the cost?
- Will it be profitable?
- What are the advantages and disadvantages?
- What will the impact be?
- What legal considerations exist?
- Is it practical?
- What are the personnel, training, and skill considerations?

THINK ABOUT ORGANIZATION

This report should contain an introduction, body, summary or conclusion, and recommendation sections. (Review Business Plan, page 209; Formal Report, page 212; and Informal Report, page 220.)

- The **introduction** sets out the proposal, the purpose of the report, the background, scope, any limitations, and the methods and procedures used in coming to a recommendation.
- The **body** gives detailed evaluation and analysis. It will set out the possible alternative solutions or products, for example, and common criteria used to evaluate them.
- The **conclusion** gives a summary of the results, which will help in making the best decision.
- The **recommendation** is a statement of the writer's opinion of the course of action to take.

THINK ABOUT CONTENT

- Develop a purpose statement. Make this statement as specific as possible. It should include a problem statement if this is part of the reason for the study and report. It must state both the objective and the scope of the report. For example:

Our present installation technique is too labor intensive and its service life is too short. This report compares four new installation techniques and recommends one for use by our installers.

- Make a list of all the questions that must be answered. Get the input of all the people involved to develop a complete list. For the example just given, here are some questions you might include:
  - ▶ What are the materials costs of each new procedure?
  - ▶ What are the training and skills requirements of each new procedure?
  - ▶ What are the time and labor requirements of each new procedure?
  - ▶ What improvement in serviceability and service life does each new procedure offer?
  - ▶ What is the sales impact of each new procedure?
  - ▶ What are the equipment costs to complete each of the new procedures?
  - ▶ What are the projected savings in service calls for the new procedures?

- Turn these questions into criteria statements by which to measure each alternative, such as:
  - ▶ The materials cost comparison for Procedures A, B, C, and D.
  - ▶ The training and skills requirements comparison for Procedures A, B, C, and D.
  - ▶ The time and labor requirements for Procedures A, B, C, and D.
  - ▶ The service life comparisons for Procedures A, B, C, and D.
  - ▶ The sales impact comparisons for Procedures A, B, C, and D.
  - ▶ The equipment cost comparisons for Procedures A, B, C, and D.
  - ▶ The comparative savings in service calls for Procedures A, B, C, and D.

- Develop a preliminary study and report outline.
- Complete the information gathering, tests, investigation, and fact-finding and collection.
- Develop the final report outline.
- Write the report, using visually effective graphs and comparison charts to make the information interesting and easy to comprehend. The report should include a precise introduction of the problem, purpose, and scope; a body of detailed evaluation of the alternatives; a conclusion, which summarizes the evaluation of each alternative; and a final recommendation.
- Rewrite, edit, and review. Use other people to review, too, making sure the report is complete, polished, and easy to understand.

SELECT A FORMAT

- Use headings, subheadings, and sub-subheadings to clearly guide the reader.
- Use white space to make the report visually inviting to read.

(Also see FORMAL REPORT, page 212, and INFORMAL REPORT, page 220.)

36 TECHNICAL REPORT & TECHNICAL WRITING

Good principles of writing—whether the content is technical or not—remain the same for all disciplines. When the subject matter is highly specialized and the report (or other material) is being written for a group of "insiders" who use and understand a special vocabulary of technical terms, the process may be considered "technical writing."

A special language is needed by many disciplines and industries. As in all kinds of writing, the contents should be dictated by the audience, the precise purpose, and the particular discipline or industry. Many organizations have very strict rules and procedures for these reports. Often there are legal requirements for writing them as well.

For example, the research and development department of an equipment manufacturer needs to write troubleshooting reports that list possible causes of precise symptoms or problems. These reports name a symptom or problem, set forth test methods, and then offer possible solutions. They may be written for field-service personnel or technically trained customers who use the equipment. The audience and purpose dictate the content and format.

What technical reports and technical writing have in common are an emphasis on the audience, a well-defined purpose, and a consistent format that reflects the needs and conventions of the discipline or industry the report serves. It is important to know both the "report culture" and organization protocol. Check present and past reports of your organization, industry, and discipline. Also see Feasibility Report, page 223; Formal Report, page 212; and Informal Report, page 220.

DECIDE TO WRITE

Use this communication to report:
- Investigative findings
- New facts
- Evaluations
- Progress
- Accidents or incidents
- Solutions to problems
- Statement on problems
- Status

THINK ABOUT CONTENT

- Review reports used by your organization, industry, and discipline to determine the acceptable form.

- Be sure you understand the audience before you start. Make sure you are writing for a technical audience.
- Obtain or create a glossary of audience-tested technical terms and learn them thoroughly.
- Ask detailed questions until you have focused the problem, purpose, and scope of your report.
- Write a preliminary outline, then review it with others involved in the process, if possible.
- Complete the information gathering, investigation, testing, and research, making detailed notes and recording figures and sources.
- Write a final outline.
- Write your report, focusing the content on completely answering, solving, or fulfilling the promise contained in your beginning problem, purpose, or scope statement.
- Rewrite, edit, and review. Get others to help to ensure objectivity and comprehensiveness.

CONSIDER SPECIAL SITUATIONS

- **Progress or contact reports** emphasize what has happened or changed over time since the last report. One of the most common examples of this is the sales report. But it is also used extensively—in a very different format—for government projects, political campaigns, advertising campaigns, construction, and many other industries. This report creates a record and keeps others informed. Straight reporting of information with a minimum of comparison is used for this report, which is usually written for a limited audience.

  Use action headings, and make statements concise. Structure the report with an introduction that identifies the project, director, and the project goals. Include a brief summary of the last progress report; a body listing progress, problems, comments, notable features, and budget considerations; a section that previews expected progress for the next reporting period; and a closing section that gives a conclusion about overall progress.

- **Status reports** emphasize the current condition of a project, detailing what exists (rather than what has changed). They are divided into the necessary component parts, and the writer includes detailed observations and some evaluation for a limited audience.

- **Trip reports** and event reports are required by organizations to keep other employees informed and establish a permanent record. These reports should be brief, with the emphasis on new information. They are usually done in memo format, addressed to the writer's supervisor, and copied to others. The subject line lists the destination and date. The body gives the purpose of the trip, persons visited, and accomplishments. Include only important events, and use subheads to identify them. End with conclusions and recommendations.

- **Trouble, incident, or accident reports** are usually internal memos dealing with accidents, equipment failure, unplanned work stoppage, or other problems. They create an official record and inform a limited audience. Management uses these reports to determine causes and the need for changes to avoid a recurrence. Often these reports are used for insurance or legal purposes, so it is vital that information be factual, accurate, as precise as possible, and complete—without unsolicited opinion statements.

The subject line should list the precise problem. The body describes the problem. Be sure to answer these questions:

- Was anyone injured?
- Where exactly did the problem occur?
- What happened?
- What was the exact time?
- Was there any property damage? What?
- Was there work stoppage?
- Who witnessed the problem? (Record complete contact information.)

Record accurately the time, date, location, treatment for any injuries, damage to property, names and addresses of witnesses, statements of witnesses, equipment damage, and any other important information. Take a photograph record and drawing and/or diagrams of the event whenever possible. Make the tone objective, and place no blame. Conclude with the action taken, and future action that will be taken to ensure that the problem does not occur again.

- **Investigative reports** may give the results of a survey, marketing study, product evaluation, literature search, or procedure investigation. The purpose of this report is to give precise analysis of the subject and offer recommendations.

   Open with a purpose statement. In the body, first completely define the scope of the investigation. If it is a survey, for example, define the number and composition of those surveyed by age, education, geographical location, occupation, income, interest, opinions, and any other information that impacts your information. Define the limits of the survey technique, then report the findings and their significance. Conclude with recommendations. (See Questionnaire and Survey, page 242.)

- **Literature reviews** and **annotated bibliographies** are literature or printed-material summaries on specific topics, published in a specific time period. These reviews offer a complete listing with an evaluation, and serve as sources for further research. For example, a literature review may list all the information published on email over the past five years. A literature review or annotated bibliography may also be part of a larger report.

   Literature reviews help professionals—industrial, medical, academic, and others—keep abreast of new things in their fields.

   Sources may be listed chronologically from the earliest source, or they may be arranged by subtopics covered.

   In the heading or brief introduction, give the scope of the subject to be covered, the sources (books, magazine and journal articles, online sources, etc.), and dates of publication or origination. In the body, give each listing accurately and completely so readers may easily locate listed sources. (Follow a stylebook like the *Chicago Manual of Style*.) For each listing, give the scope of the work and its value to the reader. Be concise.

- An **abstract** gives a very brief synopsis of a longer report or book. A descriptive abstract defines the purpose, scope, and methods used; and an informative abstract includes this information and the results, conclusions, and recommendations. The abstract should focus on what is important to readers.

- **Staff reports** are written to document and analyze problems, and to recommend solutions. Because this report is usually standardized by the organization, it is easy to develop a macro or merge document on computer software. The report can then be set up in memo format with sections for problem or summary, related factors, facts, discussion, conclusions, and recommendations. Standard responses can be part of the software program so that only particular details must be filled in. Because these reports may play a part in some legal action or employee issue, they must be completed in precise, concise detail. Employees involved are usually asked to review and sign these reports if they will become part of the employee's file. Such reports have serious confidentiality considerations. Therefore, transmission online must be handled by secure systems only.

- The **executive summary** may be a separate, brief document or part of a much longer report. It is similar in structure to the abstract but usually longer. The objective is to briefly cover all the points of a formal report: purpose, scope, methods, results, summary, conclusions, and recommendations. It gives enough concise detail to inform readers of the entire report contents so they will not have to read the full-length version.

  Write this summary to stand alone. Cover the essential information proportionate to the coverage in the full report. Do not refer to tables, charts, or other illustrations not included in the executive summary. Use technical terms understood by the audience. Visuals aren't included unless they are integral to the summary.

(Also see FEASIBILITY REPORT, page 223; FORMAL REPORT, page 212; and INFORMAL REPORT, page 220.)

The book proposal is a sales tool written to persuade an editor at a publishing house to buy your nonfiction book. (Fiction is almost always bought by a publisher after the author has completely finished the book—certainly for the author of a first work of fiction.) Because each book a publishing company takes on represents a substantial financial risk, and because there is so much competition to get a publisher's interest, you need to convince the publisher why your idea is unique, why you are the perfect person to write the book, who will buy the book, and how the book can be successfully marketed to realize the number of sales that will make it a financial success.

All these factors define why your book proposal must be very well researched and exceptionally well written.

DECIDE TO WRITE

Use a book proposal to persuade:

- Subject experts to contribute or coauthor a book
- Subject experts to agree to review and "blurb" (a short critique of praise) your book
- A literary agent to represent the book project to a publisher
- An editor to present the book project to his or her publisher's editorial committee
- A book packager to take on the project
- A special sales outlet to carry the book
- An organization to offer a grant or sponsorship for the book project
- A book representative to sell your book to bookstore buyers

THINK ABOUT CONTENT

Your book proposal will need to demonstrate and include the following elements to be successful:

- A unique idea, uniquely presented
- A distinctive voice that works well with the subject matter
- Writing that is impeccable, clear, and accessible
- Development of the idea that is well organized
- Your outstanding credentials to write on the subject
- A clear and precise definition of your audience and how you will reach them. (Your "platform" and unique qualifications are included here.)
- A sample chapter that demonstrates your writing skills

To make your book proposal stand out, you will need to:

- Create a **title page** (see model at end of chapter) that lists the working title of your book; your name, address, and contact information; and/or possibly the name, address, and contact information of your literary agent.
- Develop a **table of contents** for the book proposal, which lists the sections of your proposal and the page number where each section starts.
- Write a brief and compelling **overview**, introductory, or concept statement that encapsulates your book idea and names the market for it. This must be your strongest sales statement—usually in 150 words or less. You must convince the editor to read on.
- Draft an **About the Book** section that you can continue to refine as you research and write your proposal. This section expands upon your first, brief overview. It answers the *what, why, where, when*, and *how much* questions about your book. Be sure to include any and all of the following to make your proposal complete.
  - ▸ Identify the problem or need your book will answer or fill.
  - ▸ List the book's additional benefits.
  - ▸ Supply supporting statistics or quotes.
  - ▸ Give the unique approach that your book will take.
  - ▸ List any special features your book will include, like photos or illustrations.
  - ▸ List the end result for readers, or the greatest benefit readers of your book will enjoy.

- Write an **About the Author** section that details your unique qualifications to author the book. Make a solid case for yourself as the best author choice based upon your education, vocation, profession, experience, research, special connections, knowledge, and/or exclusive information.
- The strongest sales point today in many publishers' decisions to buy a book is the demonstration of the **author's "platform,"** which simply means those people to whom the author already has established a relationship, who are likely to buy the book. This is usually expressed in terms of the author having an active website, blogging (and the numbers of those who read the blog, or view the website each day, week, or month—expressed in "hits"), and how effectively the author uses the tools of social media marketing—how many Facebook "friends" he or she has, how often he posts online and/or uses other popular social media, and how many contacts or followers he or she has on each. It's often necessary to have first developed this kind of interest in your book subject and your authorship to demonstrate that there is a market for the book, and there are buyers ready to purchase it.
- Develop an **About the Market** section that clearly identifies who will buy your book and how you plan to reach these targeted book buyers. If you've carefully set out the need for your book, then defining your targeted readers and how you'll reach them is that much easier. In this section, include any direct-sales avenues you plan to use, like speaking engagements at which you will sell books (with number projections based on a proven track record, if possible); special sales ideas you may have, like selling your book on the Civil War at Civil War museum gift shops; institutional sales you have investigated or arranged;

subsidiary sales ideas you have; sales partnerships you have arranged or plan to arrange; and so on. This section is also crucial in today's book-selling process. Use concrete numbers, names, and connections, if you can. This helps the publisher estimate the number of sales your book can immediately command.

- Research the **About the Competition** section thoroughly. It must be complete and current. Gather as many hard facts as possible, reviewing all the competitive (or partially competitive) books and upcoming books. Make accurate comparisons, and provide the numbers of these competitive books that have sold. Your objective here is to illustrate that there is a market for your book. Further, you want to point out why and how your book will outsell competitive titles. Be careful here to include the strong points of other books as well as their shortcomings, pointing out how and why your book, comparatively, will sell.

- Consider including an (optional) **About Book Production** section if you have concrete reasons for wanting the book produced in a certain size, color, or format. The appearance of a book often positions it properly with its competition. Or, you may elect to cover this in the competition section, where you advocate having the book printed in the size and for the price of a competitive gift book, for example.

- Include an **About Publicity and Promotion** section that includes your plans to hire a publicist or public relations agency to help create awareness of the book. Name the publicist, your precise plans, and the amount of money you will invest, if possible. Beyond this, you should list your media connections, and how you plan to publicize and promote the book.

- Create a **Table of Contents** section that lists the chapter titles in your book.

- Plan a section entitled **Chapter Summaries** that includes a carefully written synopsis of each chapter. When you have a particularly strong passage, an anecdote, or some other very impressive material written for a chapter, include snippets of text in the synopses to demonstrate your writing skills, voice, tone, and approach.

- Include, if possible, a **sample chapter** or chapters, which are usually, but not always, required or requested by the publisher. Make yours as near to a finished chapter as you can write. This should usually be the first chapter, unless there is a very strong reason to include another chapter.

- Include an (optional) **Appendix, Bibliography,** or **About Sources** section if you have a strong list of authorities and/or sources, permissions, endorsements, or other exclusive agreements. This is more important in scholarly works where your exhaustive approach to researching the subject may be key to a book's success.

CONSIDER SPECIAL SITUATIONS

- Your book title—though subject to change by the publisher—can be instrumental in selling your proposal. Be sure to study all aspects of titles thoroughly before deciding on one. Study best-seller list titles, the publisher's list of lead titles, and the competitive book titles in the category for which you are writing. Ask yourself: what makes these titles work (or not)? Try brainstorming with other writers, and test your title on a number of writers, book readers, and bookstore personnel to get their feedback. The best titles often come from unlikely sources.

- The average book proposal length is about 25 to 40 pages, though this varies widely.

- Book proposals are often submitted electronically and read online by opening an attachment file.

- Because editors must often read book proposals in their "spare time," make sure yours is inviting and easy to read. For example, the use of bulleted, concise (short) statements that appear in boldface type, followed by short explanatory paragraphs, in the About the Book section can hook the editor into reading more. That, of course, is your objective.

- DVDs of television interviews; links to online interviews, blogs, postings, etc.; copies of related magazine and newspaper articles you've written or been quoted in; and/or examples of unique sales or promotional items you'll use to market your book may be included in your book proposal. The proposal may be packaged in a double-pocketed folder with a die-cut for the insertion of a business card. If you are using an agent, this folder (and your proposal in bound form) is usually supplied by the literary agency.

ELIMINATE WRONG MESSAGES

- Don't be too eager to send off your proposal. An unpolished proposal will be quickly rejected, and you will have lost the opportunity to send an improved version to the same editor or agent. Have a trustworthy expert, or several, review your proposal. But even before you submit it to an expert, set it aside for a while, then reread it with fresh objectivity. Edit it again to make it your very best effort. Good book proposals may take months, sometimes years, to write.

- Sending your proposal to the wrong agent or editor will result in both time wasted and rejection. Carefully research the kinds of books an agent and/or editor handles. Then send a simple query letter or call the agent or editor to briefly present your idea and ask if he or she would like to see your proposal.

- Don't overlook or discount small publishers. They often put more promotional effort into the books they publish, and they often keep books in print longer.

- Talk to authors who've published books similar to yours with a publisher you'd like to publish with so you learn what the publisher is likely to do, and what you need to do to make sure your book sells well.

- Unless you or your agent has a very good reason to exclusively submit to a single publisher, don't limit the submission of your proposal to one publisher at a time. Do simultaneous submissions to a number of carefully chosen publishers. Often it works well to initially submit to three or four publishers (perhaps your second-ranked choices), and examine their responses to determine if there's a common theme that indicates some area where you can improve your proposal. Make any changes indicated, then submit it to your top choice(s).

CHOOSE STRONG WORDS

appeal	capture	current	demand
discovery	drama	examines	exclusive
facts	first	fresh	idea
immediacy	market	must-read	need
never	new	nonfiction	popular
purpose	readership	research	resource
revolutionary	story	style	success
trend	untold	value	voice

CREATE EFFECTIVE PHRASES

best resource	competitive titles
creative plan	dramatic story
draws on life experiences	examines in-depth
find an audience	first-hand experience
first-time release	fresh idea
hidden until now	narrative story
new method	new research findings
newly discovered	offers competitive edge
popular beliefs	powerful examples
proven, yet unknown, facts	revolutionary idea
riveting tale	unique experience
unknown facts	untold story

WRITE STRONG SENTENCES

This book will prove the author's premise.
No competitive title covers this important topic.
Contrary to common belief, this book will prove the opposite is true.
This is an amazing story.
There is an urgent need in the marketplace for this book.

BUILD EFFECTIVE PARAGRAPHS

Carefully build effective paragraphs, using positive statements. State the idea in the first sentence, and follow it with sentences that explain, expand upon, and/or examine the idea.

Keep your paragraphs short: an average of five or six sentences. And always bear in mind your target reader: the harried editor who wants to know immediately and exactly what your book idea is, how you will present it, why you are the perfect person to write the book, and how you believe it can be marketed and effectively sold for a profit. Editors, too, will immediately turn to your sample chapter to determine if you have the skills to write the book.

EDIT, EDIT, EDIT

The strength of your proposal may well depend upon the editing. So, don't short-cut this part of your work. It can mean the difference between a sale and a rejection.

It's often beneficial to have one or more subject experts and editors go through your book proposal draft to check for everything from structure, to facts presented, to superfluous words, to typos. Effort and time spent here can pay big dividends.

Book Proposal Sample Pages

Sandra E. Lamb
4567 Street Address
City, State 98701
Telephone: 510-555-0123
Fax: 510-555-0124
Email: sandy123@email.com
Website: www.SandraLamb.com

Nonfiction/Gift Book
Approximately 250 Pages

Personal Notes: How to Write from the Heart for Any Occasion
Sandra E. Lamb
A Book Proposal

[Note: Usually book proposals are not written in the first person, but because of the nature of this proposal, I did use it.]

OVERVIEW

There's a new reality in the whacked-out, frenetic pace of our lives: we're becoming disconnected and isolated. Why?

The biggest response to my book, *How to Write It: A Complete Guide to Everything You'll Ever Write* (Ten Speed Press), has been by people who say, "I love the section on personal notes, but I wanted more. Lots more." This sentiment has come from general users of the book, book reviewers, and "off the book page" reporters. Even radio and television interviewers most often direct their questions at those "sticky problem areas" requiring an outpouring of more than just words. (See attachments: the *Denver Post* interview; my piece for *Family Circle* on apologies; my piece, "When Bad Things Happen to Good Friends," which appeared in *Working Mother;* and my short piece on personal notes in the November issue of the *Woman's Day.*)

Typically the comments I receive about the personal notes sections of *How to Write It* range from "This is wonderful," to those like I just received from a *Family Circle* editor when I proposed a new piece on the subject: "This is just what's needed out there, because we never know what to say; what to write, especially in situations of grief. . . . What do you say? What do you write?"

Personal Notes will help you experience and process your own feelings. Then it will help you connect with the people in your life through writing what's in your heart.

The bonus this book will give you is the opportunity to peek into the personal emotions and notes of historical personalities and contemporary, internationally known figures, because a variety of notes from these people will be included, too. This will also reinforce the message that there's great value in writing personal notes, as you see how our heroes have valued them throughout history.

ABOUT THE BOOK

WHY THIS BOOK IS TIMELY

- **We write 75 to 80 percent fewer thank-you notes, appreciation notes, congratulations notes, thinking-about-you notes, and just-a-note notes than our grandmothers did.**

  For the past 20 years, my friend Jenny has created hand-crafted Christmas gifts for her nieces and nephews, and then for them and their children. The number of gifts has escalated from seven to 52. She has yet to receive the first thank-you note from even one of these people, aged four months to 42 years old. We need to recapture the art of thanking each other through written, personal notes!

- **The latest scholastic achievement reports indicate our children are falling far, far behind at reading and writing. They are performing as much as two grade levels below standard. Why?**

  Because our society isn't writing personal notes like our grandparents did. Even like our parents did. Kids certainly aren't writing them. They don't see us, their parents, doing it, and no one is teaching them to do it. Writing—especially writing personal notes—is becoming a lost art. And this isn't good news. It means our society is losing some of the vital civility and social nuances it has taken us centuries to develop. We are because we write.

  We need to reinstitute the value and art of writing. We parents need to start writing, and we need to teach our children why they need to write, and how to express themselves to others on paper.

- **Lines between our business and personal lives are disappearing as businesses move into our homes, and more of our business associates become social and personal friends.**

  Those "social graces"—and personal notes—we once reserved for a separate category of people, family and personal friends, must now be used equally for business associates.

  These new, multifaceted relationships are more complicated to maintain, and personal note writing is even more important in this new emerging society. (See "When Bad Things Happen to Good Friends," from *Working Mother;* enclosed.)

- **Electronic advances are dehumanizing. The subtle combination of intimate, immediate, anonymous, and very often truncated communications we now have online is taking the humanity out of our communications.**

  There is something very emotional, and very human, that happens to us in the act of taking a pen in hand and writing down our thoughts on paper. This act can't be electronically duplicated. The weight and import of a message are far greater when it comes in handwritten form. Handwritten messages are vital to keeping us connected to each other.

- **We've all become too busy to write. In our frenetically paced society, we no longer take the time to really express our emotions.**

  Writing by hand is a type of therapy. It can keep us sane and keep us connected to our own inner feelings.

- **Ironically, our mobile, electronic society has left us feeling isolated. We are suffering from a universal and growing failure to connect with other humans and to create those "human moments."**

  No woman—no matter how she tries—is an island. In fact, most of us do very poorly in isolation. Words like lonely, disconnected, desolate, and depressed come to mind. We need to connect to others, and this book will show you how.

- **The new "spiritual awareness" has awakened in us a desire to relate to others.**

  Now is exactly the time to provide this wonderful guide to really communicating—connecting, communing—with the people in our lives through writing personal notes.

TABLE OF CONTENTS

38 RESEARCH

How to write it often depends on knowing how to research it. This can be the most exciting and interesting part of writing. The process of in-depth learning about the subject takes some special skills, and it must not be shortchanged; investigation, or research, is the key to giving what you write the ring of authenticity and authority. Where and how you begin your research will depend upon the subject matter and where you enter the process. Sometimes you'll work from the general to the specific; other times, from the specific to the general.

There are two basic ways to get the information you need: primary, or firsthand research; and secondary, or indirect research. Primary sources include both unpublished and original sources, such as organization records and your own observations, experiments, and surveys. Secondary sources are published works such as encyclopedias, almanacs, directories, various other kinds of publications, periodicals, books, and statistical sources.

START WITH PRIMARY SOURCES

Every writing project will start with primary sources that include your firsthand experience. You'll need to take some or all of the following steps to get this part of your job done:

- Ask yourself what you want your reader to learn. Be precise.
- Brainstorm with and interview people to determine the need for what you're writing, and to develop your scope and purpose statement.
- Conduct an experiment, take a survey, and gather other firsthand information.
- Set up and conduct your own systematic observations and research online by using discussion groups, newsgroups, and/or email queries or requests.
- Test what you've written—information or instructions—on a sampling of your readers before completing your final draft.

CAREFULLY SELECT AND USE SECONDARY SOURCES

Secondary sources are generally more accessible, less costly, and more complete than primary sources. These include published books, articles, reports, online discussions, correspondence, memos, brochures, operating manuals, etc. You'll be able to find sources both on the Internet, and directly through libraries.

In today's fast-paced world, making sure your information is "up to the minute" is vital. Often your secondary research will start with limiting sources to the most current and focusing subject matter to precisely what you need.

RESEARCH THE INTERNET

- Use the tools on the search engine to conduct your search. (See the help page.) Enter the term for which you want to search.
- Use qualifiers (Boolean operators)—*and, or, not*—to restrict your search. Also use quotation marks around phrases you want to research (for example "mechanical engineering") to limit results to the phrase as a unit.
- Use the advanced search whenever you need it.
- Try a number and variety of search engines to ensure you've gotten the best results.

Internet Research Sources

While public and university libraries now have catalogs and databases available through the Internet, you may first want to use a search engine to locate sources. Here are some basic ones, though the list changes frequently:

- Machine-generated databases that use "spiders" or "bots" to travel the web searching for information include:
    www.google.com
    www.altavista.com
    www.excite.com
    www.webcrawler.com

- Human-generated search engines index fewer pages but offer directory trees that help organize content:
    search.yahoo.com
    lycos.com
    search.msn.com
    www.bing.com

- Hybrid search engines search the Web and also their own databases of articles to provide indexes not available elsewhere. These include:
    www.hotbot.com (Lycos powered)

- For selective, scholarly web research, try one of the following directories:
    infomine.ucr.edu (Infomine)
    www.vlib.org (World Wide Web Virtual Library)
    scholar.google.com

- For metasearch engines that search the web using a number of search engines, try these, but be sure to carefully define and limit your search:
    www.metacrawler.com
    dogpile.com

- To locate web businesses and government sources, start here:
    dir.yahoo.com/Business_and_Economy (Yahoo's Business Resources)
    www.fedstats.gov (FedStats)
    www.lib.isu.edu/gov/index.html (Federal Government Agencies Directory)

- Evaluate your sources for authority, accuracy, authorship, bias, and currency. Following are the domain name suffixes:
    - aero–aerospace industry
    - biz–business
    - com–company or individual
    - coop–business cooperative
    - edu–university, college, or educational source
    - gov–government
    - int–international organization
    - mil–U.S. military
    - name–individual
    - net–network provider
    - org–nonprofit organization
    - pro–professional, such as a lawyer or doctor

RESEARCH THE LIBRARY

- Develop a research strategy and outline of the sources you may need to find.
- You may want to contact a reference librarian in a particular area and discuss your goals. This can usually be done by telephone and can help you search more efficiently by directing you to precise sources.
- Go to an online library homepage and access its catalog, databases of articles, and other sources. Libraries license databases, and you will need to be a library cardholder to access these.
- Start your search by subject, author, or title.
- Use the library's online databases to search other sources:
    - InfoTrac is a collection of databases containing full text and abstracts of articles in business, health, and general areas.
    - ProQuest is a database provider (aggregator), which sells databases to libraries. These include databases specializing in biology, nursing, psychology, historic newspapers, specialized academic indexing, professional indexing, etc.
    - EBSCOhost is a family database with articles in a wide range of subjects.
    - FirstSearch is a collection of specialized databases showing some full text and some abstracts from many library collections (WorldCat and ArticleFirst included).
    - Lexis/Nexis is a collection of databases featuring business, legal, congressional, and other articles in both full text and abstracts.

Library Resources

You may want to start with standard references—online, texts, or microfilm in the library—in your quest to find the best sources. Typically you'll divide these into the following categories and sources:

GENERAL GUIDES
* *Guide to Reference Books*

ENCYCLOPEDIAS
* *The Encyclopedia Americana*
* *Encyclopaedia Britannica*
* *The Encyclopedia of Careers and Vocational Guidance*
* *Grolier's Academic American Encyclopedia*
* *McGraw-Hill Encyclopedia of Science and Technology*

MAGAZINES AND SPECIAL PUBLICATIONS
* *Business Periodicals Index*
* *Index to the Times* (London)
* *Magazine Index*
* *The New York Times Index*
* *Psychological Abstracts*
* *Reader's Guide to Periodical Literature*
* *Social Science Index*
* *Wall Street Journal Index*
* *Women's Studies Abstracts*

MORE INFORMATION
* *American History Sourcebook*
* *American Statistics Index*
* *Directory of Special Libraries and Information Centers*
* *Encyclopedia of Associations*
* *The Official Museum Directory*
* Telephone books

BIOGRAPHICAL DIRECTORIES
* *Dictionary of American Biography*
* *Who's Who in America*
* *Who's Who in the East*
* *Who's Who in the Midwest*
* *Who's Who in the World*

ALMANACS AND ATLASES
* *The World Almanac and Book of Facts*
* *Microsoft® Encarta® World Atlas*

TRADE DIRECTORIES
* *America's Corporate Families*
* *Directory of Corporate Affiliations*
* *The Million Dollar Directory*
* *Thomas Register of American Manufacturers* (thomasnet.com)

GOVERNMENT PUBLICATIONS
* *Government Reports Announcements and Index*
* *Monthly Catalog of US Government Publications*

STATISTICAL SOURCES
* *American Statistics Index*
* *Statistical Abstract of the United States*

CONSIDER OTHER INDIRECT SOURCES

- Use interlibrary loan services though your library.
- Use association, newspaper, and corporation library sources.
- Use public relations people in corporations, hospitals, and associations.
- Search public records in the courts, prisons, and other public entities.
- Research people connections online through www.peoplefinders.ws.
- Buy the research services of a reference librarian, private investigator, or search organization.

THINK ABOUT CONTENT

Research is the first step of the writing process:

- Focus on the reader to determine the need for writing.
- Prepare a purpose statement that defines the scope of what you'll write.
- Perform the needed extra research.
- Organize and draft the written document.
- Revise, edit, and polish what you've written.

39 QUESTIONNAIRE & SURVEY

Sometimes the best way to get information is to ask questions. But which, and of whom? You will need to establish a survey method and develop a questionnaire, especially if you need information like personal attitudes, opinions, or evaluations.

First, you must identify the information you need to acquire and then determine if you need direct research sources for that information. If you do, you must decide how to select a representative sample of the people you need information from, and decide on the format and delivery of your questions. Will you use personal interviews, telephone interviews, or a printed and distributed questionnaire to get the answers you need? Will you interview by email or on the Web? Choose the best format and delivery for your questions to elicit the highest numbers of responses.

The terms *questionnaire* and *survey* are often used interchangeably, though surveys are often brief opinion polls, whereas questionnaires often request detailed responses. Either may be an interview on paper, by email, or on the Web. These methods for getting information have the advantage of asking for and getting uniform answers from a large number of people at the same time, thus saving both time and money. They can also allow anonymity, which can be an advantage in getting more candid responses. Other advantages can be that those responding to questionnaires are allowed reflective time in which to give more complete answers; and those questioned aren't being influenced by voice inflection or facial expressions.

Possible disadvantages? More opinionated people may respond, whereas others may not; it eliminates nuance in answers; doesn't allow for impromptu follow-up questions; and this method of getting answers can take longer.

Determine the information you need; then eliminate, as better alternatives, direct and secondary research sources for that information (see Research, page 237).

You will need to establish audience selection and distribution methods, and develop an effective survey instrument or questionnaire.

Be sure the format and delivery of your questions will get the best response. (For some surveys, you may want to use personal interviews or telephone interviews to get the answers you need.)

DECIDE TO WRITE

Use a survey or questionnaire when you need special information not available through any of the sources you've investigated.

THINK ABOUT CONTENT

- Select a representative sample of the entire audience. You may need to study and employ scientific selection techniques to ensure a sample that will produce valid results. Check marketing resources with a reference librarian.
- Write a questionnaire based on what you need to learn.
- Make sure the questions are easy to understand.
- Gear the questions toward facts, and request quantitative responses whenever possible.
- Create a layout that is visually appealing to readers and allows adequate space for responses.
- Test your questionnaire on a pilot or test group first, get feedback, and incorporate any changes.
- Establish a method for evaluating the results. Remember, you must be able to present the findings clearly and completely, which will require you to objectively interpret answers to questions.

AVOID WRONG MESSAGES

- Avoid leading questions.
- Avoid questions that touch on areas of personal prejudice or bias (unless this is the information you need).

Homeowners' Association Questionnaire

SUNSET HOMEOWNERS

The Sunset board of directors would like to create more ways for residents to participate in the functions and activities of our community. Please let the board know your preferences by completing one questionnaire per household. It will be helpful if you read the entire survey before answering.

Name (Optional): _____

House # (Optional): _____

1. *Concerning the process of decision making at Sunset, we:*
   - ☐ are pleased with the elective process we have now with the Board interpreting the Covenants and Codes for Community Living.
   - ☐ would like to see a more direct democratic process, and we pledge to actively participate by voting on decisions.

   Other: _____
   _____

2. *Concerning the interpretation of the Codes for Community Living, 2.3 Unsightly Articles, we believe the following should apply (Y—yes; N—no):*
   - ___ Portable basketball hoops should be allowed in front of homes if they are taken in at night.
   - ___ Permanent basketball hoops should be allowed to be attached over garage doors if kept in good condition.
   - ___ Basketball hoops of any kind should not be allowed in front of homes because they are dangerous so close to the street, as well as unsightly.
   - ___ Basketball play should be restricted to the neighborhood hoop at the clubhouse.

Other concerns: _____
_____

3. *Concerning the quality of life at Sunset our family enjoys these amenities (please use O—often, more than once a week; I—infrequently, about once or twice a month; or S—seldom, less than once a month; N—never):*

___ Swimming pool	___ Tennis courts
___ Jacuzzi	___ Clubhouse
___ Exercise equipment (in clubhouse)	___ Park area

___ Enclosed and gated community that eliminates outside traffic during night hours

Other qualities and services we enjoy and want to preserve: _____
_____

Additionally, we would like to see these changes or additions in these items: _____
_____

4. *We would like to see Sunset expenditures focus on the following areas (numbered in importance; 1—top priority, through 5—least important):*

___ Extended summer swimming pool hours:
    ___ to ___ Monday through Friday
    ___ to ___ Weekends (Saturday and Sunday)
___ Beautifying the park area
___ Creation of a baseball area in the park
___ Purchase of additional exercise equipment in the clubhouse to include: _____
___ Signage and landscape lighting on Drury Lane at entry

Other: _____

5. *Concerning holiday lighting:*
☐ What we have is fine.
☐ We would like small white lights on the trees at the entry.

Other: _____

6. *We would like to see these activities (Y—yes; N—no):*
___ holiday community get-together (☐ November; ☐ December)
___ an active Sunset garden club
___ book club meetings in the clubhouse
___ exercise classes at the clubhouse
___ swimming instruction at the pool
___ summer family picnic (☐ June; ☐ July; ☐ August)

Other: _____

7. *We are willing to organize/volunteer to serve on the following:* _____
_____

We have these additional comments and suggestions for the Board: _____
_____
_____
_____

Fold your completed survey and place it in the HOA slot to the left of the mailboxes, or mail to Sara E. Faust, 2400 E. Drury Lane, Unit #45, Phoenix, AZ 85001.

VI

INQUIRIES, REQUESTS & RESPONSE COMMUNICATIONS

Inside you there's an artist
you don't know.

—*Jalai Ud-Din Rumi*

40 REQUEST & INQUIRY

At the heart of the request letter is the need to effectively communicate what you want. You must ask that the information you're seeking be sent in response, or that further direction be sent to help in your quest. Your letter should be brief, functional, and, above all, gracious in tone. Your goal is to make the reader *want* to help you.

A letter of request or inquiry may be as simple as asking for a price or a free brochure. It may be as complex as requesting the specifications for a product you are including in a bid. The word *inquiry* often has a legal connotation meaning an investigation, and is sometimes used in a more formal letter: "I wish to inquire . . ." or "Referring to your inquiry . . ." (Erroneously, too, a query letter may be referred to as a request letter. When a writer corresponds with a publisher proposing his composition be published, it is much more a sales than a request letter.)

If you are requesting routine information, make it as precise and brief as possible. But always make it clear and courteous. This type of letter is, of course, one of the mainstays of business life. And in this, as in all letters, you will leave the reader with an impression about yourself and/or the organization with which you are associated. Business requests are usually made through email, but when a request is made through the mail, use business letterhead.

DECIDE TO WRITE

When you are seeking one of the following, you'll use a request letter:

- Advice
- Appointments, interviews, meetings
- Business or personal assistance
- Bids, consultations, proposals, estimates
- Change of status: variance or zoning changes, name changes, changes in marital status, etc.
- Contributions, donations
- Information: copies of credit reports, documents, medical records, instructions
- Interviews
- Loan (see Offering an Adjustment, page 350; Credit Inquiry & Providing Credit Information, page 331; and Request for Payment Adjustment, page 345)
- Information about job openings

THINK ABOUT CONTENT

- Think through your request before you start writing so that you can clearly state what you want.
- Be sure you understand the protocol of making your request. If you are, for example, requesting a copy of your credit report, you must conform to the particular requirements of the credit company, which usually involve properly identifying yourself, enclosing a statement or copy of credit denial, and enclosing a check for the report. The processes of requesting your military records, medical records, or similar information will have their own special requirements. Find out what these are, and comply in your request to get the results you want and quickly.
- When addressing an organization that receives large volumes of requests on a variety of topics, use a subject line to immediately aid the reader in identifying yours: "Subject: Report 2011-B Request."
- If you have several related queries or requests, list them from the most important through the least, so the reader can easily check the items off. Numbering your request items is also helpful to the reader.
- Be sure your request is so detailed that you get precisely the response you want. This is essential when you're requesting bids, for example, because unless your request contains the complete specifications for the work, the reader will be unable to respond. Also include all sources for further information and all deadlines.
- Make responding as easy as possible for the reader. For example, enclose a permission form to use copyrighted materials; a sample of the product you need help with; your email address; your telephone number; a self-addressed, stamped envelope; a postcard; a fax number, etc. Put yourself in the reader's place here, and try to make his or her work as easy as possible. This will also benefit you.
- For long, difficult requests that require much of the reader, and requests that have a response deadline or time frame, telephone and give the recipient advance notice before sending your request.
- Introduce yourself, if yours is anything other than a routine request for prepared information.

MAKE YOUR REQUEST

- Begin with a clear, concise, and courteous statement of your request.
- Be as specific as possible.
- State, if appropriate, the reason for your request and the use you will make of what you are requesting.
- Include a reason why the reader may be interested in responding.
- Let the reader know where (and how) to send the information, or how to contact you with questions.

- Include the invitation to call you collect with questions, if this is appropriate.
- Conclude things in the last sentence or two, restating your request briefly if it is complex and making a statement of appreciation for the reader's cooperation. For example, "All the specifications and references are listed on pages 11 through 18. We appreciate your company's interest in this project, and we look forward to receiving your bid by the end of business on April 7. We will share with you our decision by April 15, along with any reasons for our decision. Thank you."
- Express your appreciation for the expected cooperation of your reader.

ELIMINATE WRONG MESSAGES

- Do not use a commanding tone. "Send me your report A-510 by return mail" may make the reader bristle.
- Eliminate, too, an apologetic tone, or any tone that does not expect an answer to your letter. "I'm sorry to bother you with this, but I need a copy of the report on early therapy for diabetes," and "If you are unable to send me a copy of the report, I will certainly understand" are too weak.
- Don't bury the items of your request in long paragraphs. Don't write: "Please send me your brochures for Model 75-74; Model 610-66; Model 774-23; Pipettes 566-43; and the Analyzer 511-10." Instead, indent so the reader can easily see what your want. "Please send me your brochures for:

  ☐ Model 75-74
  ☐ Model 610-66
  ☐ Model 774-23
  ☐ Pipettes 566-43
  ☐ Analyzer 511-10"

- Avoid vague requests that may go unanswered or simply be discarded. Do more research in advance so you can make your request specific. If possible, get the name of the person who will be able to help you.
- Don't fail to conclude your letter with a statement of appreciation, which may further energize the reader to help you: "Thank you for handling this request." "I appreciate your help in this matter." "May I receive this information by March 15? Thank you for your help." "I look forward to receiving this material, and thank you." "I thank you in advance for your help in this matter."

CONSIDER SPECIAL SITUATIONS

- Make it a policy to put all requests in writing, and always be explicit. A simple "This confirms my request for reservations for the Elks meeting at the Boulderado, May 13" won't do. In that example, your request should include the number of guests for whom you are requesting rooms; the number and time of meeting rooms you'll need, and how each will be arranged; the times your guests will arrive; and the number of people, time, menus, and service expected for meals. If possible, use a request form from the hotel. You could also ask the hotel or conference center for an example of a request for a similar meeting if you don't do this regularly.

- A request to quote should include a form with all the pertinent information and a place for the reader's signature. Include in your request a completed form with the exact quote defined—"I request permission to quote the following: . . ."—and list the exact source including book title, author, page number, and the complete information about where you want to use the quotation. Include the publisher/publication date, price, and the relationship of the quoted material to the whole piece.

- A request to quote should be responded to with a signed permission letter.

- When requesting a change of address, indicate both the old and the new:

Please change my address in your records
FROM: 315 South Cherry Detroit, MI 49334
TO: 776 East Alameda Denver, CO 80220

- When requesting that copies of your medical records be sent to another physician, you will be required to sign a special consent form. Check on this first to save yourself time. If you're emailing, faxing, or writing your request, it should be stated in the affirmative: "I hereby authorize the transfer [or copies] of my medical records to be sent to . . ."

- If requesting a speaker to make a presentation to your group, use both special tact and precision. You will undoubtedly want to check on the potential speaker's performance record before requesting his or her services. Include complete information about the date, time, location, setting, audience size and composition, focus and subject matter of the meeting, allotted time for the speech, and a list of suggested topics, if appropriate. There's nothing quite as inappropriate as having a "famous" writer as the guest speaker at a writers' banquet, for example, and witness him then use the occasion to vent his unrelated political views, especially if you are promoting the speech as "how you can sell your book."

- In making any request of a government agency, check first to learn the required form and protocol for your request. This will save you considerable effort and help ensure the response you want. If, for example, you are requesting a reevaluation of your property taxes, you will undoubtedly have to include the legal lot number or other location and description information, and detailed information on values of comparative homes in your immediate area. This is usually done by price per square foot.

- In writing to any governmental agency or bureaucracy, use identifying name and numbers: "Please send me a copy of proposed Bill Number 555-543: City Crime, May 21, by Senator Q. K. Jackson." It's also important in requesting government information to state the legal provision under which you are making your request, if applicable. For example: "Under the Federal Freedom of Information Act . . ."

- In requesting changes in governmental policy, designated zones, usage, etc., do your research first. You must understand the history of a particular zoning requirement, for example, because your request must be made in terms of the inappropriateness of that designation and the reasonableness of your request. There may be any number of requirements in getting your request into the right form and obtaining agreement among those concerned. Researching all related matters and complying with form and content requirements will increase the chances of your request being granted.

SELECT A FORMAT

- Simple personal requests for such things as sales literature or a free sample may be requested by email, or handwritten on a postcard, fold-over note, or personal letterhead. For longer, more complex requests, email may be used, or type the request on letterhead.
- Routine business requests to another company may be made through email, by telephone, or on preprinted postcards, preprinted forms, or letterhead. Longer or complex requests should be typed on letterhead. If time is a factor, check with the recipient to see if you can email, telephone, or fax your request.

SELECT STRONG WORDS

aid	answer	appreciate	ask
assistance	help	information	inquire
prompt	request	respond	response
return	submit	thank you	time frame

BUILD STRONG PHRASES

as soon as possible	ask for your assistance
by return mail	could you offer your assistance
I need this information by	I need your help in locating
I request the following	I request your information by
I would appreciate your cooperation	I'm writing to inquire
if I may supply any additional information	if there are additional questions
inquire about information	it would be a great help
may I inquire	please call me collect
please respond to this request	request your help
would you be willing to supply	you may email me at

WRITE STRONG SENTENCES

As directed by Mr. R. Roberts, I am requesting a copy of *Patient Care 145: Healthcare Reform*.

I request a double, nonsmoking room (a king-size bed), on the fourth floor, if possible, for Thursday, April 2. I am arriving at 3:10 p.m.

I think we need to have further discussion about our strategy on the Pepper account, and I request that you let me know if you have an hour available on the afternoon of either the 14th or 15th, so I can set it up.

Jack Adams has done some outstanding work on the job descriptions, and I would like to receive a copy of his report at your earliest convenience.

EDIT, EDIT, EDIT

Give your request or inquiry a little time to sit after you're finished writing. Then review it again and ask yourself if you've answered the *what*, *why*, *when*, *where*, and *how much* of your request in precise and concise terms.

Information Request

Dear Ms. Jackson:

I enjoyed your presentation at the Gates Tennis Club and request specific information on rates at Tennis, Inc.'s camp on the following dates:

April 12 through April 22
June 17 through June 27
August 15 through August 25[1]

Please also give me a listing of the advantages (if any) of being a guest at one time over another.[2] I am a level 5.0 USTA evaluated player, and my objective in attending is to raise my tennis skill level to a 5.5 level. Thank you for your assistance. I look forward to your response.[3]

Sincerely,

Walter Gill

(1) Be specific. (2) Be cordial. (3) Make reader want to help.

Request for Samples

Dear Robby,

Please send me eight samples of the AA-345 Gaskets from the production run made on August 8. I also request that you include a copy of the tensile strength tests performed on these.

We plan to run our tests next Wednesday. I will give you a copy of our results the following Friday, so you may incorporate our data into your month-end report.

Thank you.

Cordially,

Ed Beattle

Report Request

Dear Mr. Williams:

Ms. Jobs asked me to request a copy of the report passed out at the last meeting of the Atlanta Water Board of Directors. The subject of the report is projections of water usage in the year 2006.

She will appreciate receiving a copy by the 15th. Thank you.

Sincerely yours,

Janet Reems

Request for Job Leads

Dear Jack:

It was nice seeing you at the National Product Managers' Association meeting in New York. I'm happy to hear that the Simmons lead from our meeting resulted in a long-term project.

Jack, confidentially, I am casting about for product manager positions in medical instrumentation corporations with a proactive, employee fast-track philosophy. Since you are in the know with your consulting work, I wonder if you have any recommendations. Obviously, I will treat any information as completely confidential.

I would appreciate any direction you may be able to give here, and will certainly continue to recommend to you any organizations looking for your particular type of consulting services. You may send any such leads to my personal email address: tbottoms@bigbottoms.com.

Regards,

Tim Bottoms

Request for City Information

Dear Mr. Taggs:

I have spoken to several residents of Prescott who sing the praises of your city and highly recommend it as a location for retiring. Please send me information on new, low-maintenance housing available, demographics of the city, and information of special interest to newly retired people.

My wife and I will be retiring in 18 months, and we desire to find a suburban location with golf and community resources within walking distance. We are both 55 years old and desire neighbors of all ages. We will be prepared to buy a home in the price range of $250,000 to $300,000, in a one-story, ranch style. We also wish to purchase a new home.[1]

Thank you. Enclosed is a SASE for your reply.[2]

Sincerely yours,

Liam Buyers

(1) Be concise and precise about what you want. (2) Make it easy for your reader to respond.

Request for Processing of Employee Records

Dear Mr. Snipple:

As we discussed today, please process the permanent employee paperwork for Jack Jumper, and issue the following:

- Status 2A clearance
- a telephone credit card
- family medical insurance coverage
- an office key to the production department

Mr. Jumper's permanent employment date is August 14, but he will leave on an out-of-town assignment on August 13. I request all his required signatures, etc. be obtained this week, and he be issued his permanent employee packet no later than August 12.

Please contact me immediately if you are unable to comply. Thank you for your efforts in this matter.

Sincerely,

Denise Diver

Request for Order Status

[Date]

REFERENCE: ORDER # 3234[1]

Dear Bob:

There's some confusion here about the status of our order for retainers submitted on April 29.[2] Margie Stich of your office indicated to our Louise Cole that you are out of several of the sizes we need: #4, #6, and #7. Please give me a status report on our order, in writing, by tomorrow. Please fax it to my office: 440-555-0123.[3]

We must have all these sizes in here by next Wednesday to keep production going.[4]

Yours truly,

Jim Riser

(1) Be specific. (2) State a time frame if needed. (3) Give full response information. (4) State urgency, if appropriate.

Request for Credit Report

Dear Mr. Allen:

As I stated on the telephone, I was denied credit at Crooners Bank on April 10. Enclosed is a copy of that report. Mr. Jesus Garcia, Customer Service Representative, noted that this credit report from your organization indicates a number of late payments and other credit problems. However, none of these are factual.

I've enclosed a self-addressed, stamped envelope. Please send me a new copy of my current credit record with the corrections we discussed properly indicated. I need this immediately in order to refute and correct this error.

Yours truly,

Lea Grimes

(Also see CREDIT APPROVAL, page 337; CREDIT DENIAL, page 340; CREDIT INQUIRY & PROVIDING CREDIT INFORMATION, page 331; COLLECTION LETTER, page 354; and RESPONSE, page 257.)

41 COVER LETTER

The cover or transmittal letter has a simple and direct job: to quickly and persuasively direct the reader to the material it covers. It takes the place of what you would say if you were face to face, offering only the pertinent information about the contents and composition of what it is attached to.

If your cover letter accompanies a report, first tell the reader so, then include the goal of the report, and refer to its authorization.

The resume cover letter is slightly different. It introduces the contents it "covers," or what is enclosed, and more actively tries to persuade the reader to read the resume. (See Resume Cover Letter, page 116.) The fax cover sheet lists the person to whom the fax is directed; the person sending it; the date; the fax number of the sender; the subject of the material sent; and the number of pages sent.

DECIDE TO WRITE

Use a cover letter when you send:

- Reports, proposals, contracts, agreements, and other documents
- Applications
- Manuscripts
- Instruction manuals/booklets/sheets
- Contributions
- Samples, prototypes
- Checks unaccompanied by a copy of an invoice or a statement
- Complimentary tickets
- A fax

THINK ABOUT CONTENT

- Address an individual person.
- State what is enclosed, attached, or has been sent under separate cover. If you are responding to a request, name the requesting person.
- If appropriate, give the number of enclosures, or briefly list the content items.
- State the purpose or goal of the contents and who authorized them.
- If needed, explain how to use the contents.

- Include your complete contact information.
- End on a strong note of goodwill, appreciation, or statement of the next action to be taken.

ELIMINATE WRONG MESSAGES

- Don't be verbose or repeat passages from the document. The cover letter should never exceed one-eighth the length of the report. Much shorter is better.
- Do not write a cover letter that is inconsistent with the voice and tone of the report. This applies to the form and format, too.

CONSIDER SPECIAL SITUATIONS

- Report cover letters should name the report, tell why it was written, who authorized it, its contributors, and then briefly summarize it.
- Cover letters for manuscripts sent to a publisher or agent are challenging. Publishers often require authors to describe their manuscripts in one short paragraph that compels editors to read it. A single sentence is even better.
- Routine items are usually self-explanatory and do not require a cover letter. These items include invoices, payments, shipments, or other specialized letters.
- Sample or sales literature cover letters need to be unique and also explanatory. (See Direct Mail, page 361, and Sales Follow-Up, page 368.)
- Resume cover letters need to snag the interest of the reader so he will read the resume. (See Resume Cover Letter, page 116.)

SELECT A FORMAT

- The standard format is the typewritten letter on business letterhead.
- An informal email may be used when this is the standard way you communicate with the reader and you are electronically transmitting what is "covered," usually an attachment.
- For interoffice use, an email or a company memo is the proper vehicle. Both are used, too, for clients and colleagues in organizations with which you have an ongoing working relationship.
- The form of the cover letter should be consistent with the contents of the mailing. When its function is sales and there is an enclosed sample or gift, an attention-getting note is usually the best choice.

USE STRONG WORDS

attached	details	documents	enclosed
examine	included	instructions	look

BUILD EFFECTIVE PHRASES

As promised	Call your attention to
Details of the experiments	Examine the charts
Here's a listing of what's attached	I'd be happy to answer any additional questions
I'm enclosing a check for	I've attached the report
Please contact me at 555-0123	Thank you for your interest in
The amazing results	This sample is sent
To aid your review	You will want to examine
You'll note that	You'll see immediately

WRITE STRONG SENTENCES

Focus on the contents you're sending and your objective. Concisely describe both.

I've enclosed copies of checks numbered 346, 754, 332, and 987 as you requested.

Your feedback to this initial report will be greatly appreciated.

You may also want copies of our Report #443 on changes in the habitat.

This is your free copy.

The details of the experiment are on page 15.

BUILD EFFECTIVE PARAGRAPHS

I'm returning the spacer prototypes you sent. We tested these on our neoprene Elastomeric roof installation, and found the spacers would not withstand the wind uplift. Our installation details, test conditions, and phased results are included in the final report enclosed.

Here are the amazing results of our laboratory tests, which you requested. I believe you'll find this reading fascinating.

Here's my proposal, including the chapter outline and sample chapter you requested for *The Owner's Manual for Retirement*, the humor gift book we discussed. I'll be eager to learn your take on it.

This new Employee Manual A-40 was designed to deal with our current issues of diversity at Cobal. Carefully review each section, especially the summaries, and give me your feedback by April 10.

For everything that goes "squeak," now there's Quiet. Try this sample on your biggest noisemakers and you'll never go back to wimpy lubricants.

Did you think you'd never find a bandage that would stick? Try this new Bonzo on your next boo-boo.

Thank you for your interest in the Gus Grant Program. Complete the enclosed form and return it to us by September 1 to be eligible for grant funds.

As you requested yesterday on the telephone, I've enclosed the broken desk handle. I've also enclosed a photograph of the desk with the broken handle in place.

EDIT, EDIT, EDIT

Be concise. The most effective cover letters are often only a sentence or two.

For a Report

Dear Mr. Able:

Here is the Salespeople Report on the survey you asked us to conduct on August 15. As you'll see, our observations pointed to some specific needs for new and extensive sales training.

Following the procedures we outlined and you approved in September, we have included these needs in a revised curriculum plan that we will submit to your training director, Jim Bacon, on November 10. We are confident this curriculum will help correct the skill-level deficits of your sales force.

We appreciate the opportunity to serve you. I look forward to reviewing the details here on Tuesday, but please call me in the meantime if you want to discuss anything immediately.

Sincerely yours,

Robert Berk

For an Annual Report

Dear Ms. Miller:

Here's our latest annual report. I hope this contains the kind of information you want on the goals and success of the company, especially in the past two years. You will find those explicit figures and comparisons on pages 5 through 12. But the entire report gives the complete picture of Canto's expansion and growth.

Thank you for your interest in our company, and please call me if you need any further information.

Yours truly,

Victor Weise

(Also see RESUME COVER LETTER, page 116.)

For a Franchise Application

Dear Mr. Beemer:

Enclosed is the franchise application, which I have amended according to our discussion. Please carefully review the amendments III, VI, and VIII, as well as the insertions on pages 4, 5, 9, and 11.[1]

I believe this now represents a fair and equitable agreement with the parent company, Pets, and it is my belief this will be an extremely profitable endeavor for Dog Kisses, Inc.

Please call me if you have any further concerns or questions. If not, please sign all four copies and return them to me. I've enclosed an extra copy for your files.[2]

Thank you.

Yours truly,

Michael Beers

(1) Identify contents. (2) Give precise information.

For a Shipment

Dear Ms. Betts:

Here's the new brochure. Under separate cover, I'm sending the 450 brochures you requested. The four-color printing is beautiful. It was the right decision to use the fall cover photo; it'll be a very effective promotional tool for you, I'm sure.

All the brochures will be delivered to the central office Tuesday morning. Don't hesitate to call me if you want some taken to the branch offices. We can easily do that.

We look forward to working with you again.

Sincerely,

Stanley Barker

42 RESPONSE

A letter of response, whether business or personal, is most effective and usually takes less time if done immediately. The other key ingredient is that it needs to be focused on giving the information that has been requested.

Successful businesses have been built upon the simple principle of a prompt, thorough response. It says to the customer, "I value you, I understand what you want, and your business is important to me." Make sure your response is timely. When your response is personal, it sends the same valuable message.

DECIDE TO WRITE

Common sense and company protocol are the bywords here. Many companies state that outside correspondence always requires a written response; internal correspondence often requires only a verbal one. Consider writing a response when you receive any of the following:

- An invitation (see Invitation, page 63, and Refusal, page 274)
- An announcement
- A gift (see Thank-You, page 75)
- An inquiry
- A complaint (see Complaint & Protest, page 282)
- A request
- A contribution (see Thank-You, page 75)
- A payment
- Information
- A note of condolence or sympathy (see Sympathy & Condolence, page 44)
- An apology (see Apology, page 306)

THINK ABOUT CONTENT

- Start with the reason for your response. Mention the communication you received: "Thank you for your letter of July 12, requesting the shipping date of the Wickets."
- Make your letter both as complete and as brief as possible.
- Be sure you have responded to all the points of the recipient's correspondence. Sometimes it is best to organize your response in the order of the communication you received. For example: "In paragraph one of your letter . . ."

- Use indenting, bullets, dashes, and the wise use of white space in long or complicated communications to help make your response clearer.
- Repeat vital information like the date, time, and location of a meeting.
- Offer other sources of assistance, when appropriate. Make it easier for an inquirer to follow up by offering additional contact names, numbers, and addresses. For example: "No, we don't carry the Thingys you requested, but Every Product, located at 322 Grace St. in Houston, or at everyproduct.com, has them in all sizes."
- Immediate acknowledgment is the first and best line of action in your response. Often letters of inquiry, requests for information, or complaints require some work before an intelligent and comprehensive response can be given. So, send an initial response that acknowledges the communication you have received, and tells the reader you are working on a more complete response.
- A response letter to customers should offer value added whenever possible. Many companies have built a strong and loyal customer base by expending that extra effort to include a pertinent research report or send valuable samples of the product. This does not mean stuffing a huge envelope with unrelated sales information, which is never appreciated. It also doesn't mean dodging the point of inquiry.
- A written response to invitations should match the invitation. If the invitation is in third person, for example, respond in third person: "Alex and Mable Wilborough accept with pleasure Frank and Edna Edmond's kind invitation for dinner on Thursday, the twelfth of June at eight o'clock." If there is an RSVP request, you are obliged to respond as promptly as possible; write or call, whichever the invitation indicates. "Regrets only" on an invitation means you are not required to respond if you *will* attend. However, if two people are invited and one will not attend, if other commitments require you to be late, or if other special circumstances exist, convey this to the host by calling in a timely manner, or by writing a response note (see Invitation, page 63).
- Invite further correspondence, if appropriate.

ELIMINATE WRONG MESSAGES

- As a rule, do not go beyond the scope of the correspondence you received. (This is a rule sometimes wisely broken when you have valuable information to offer.)
- Do not let correspondence go unanswered. A polite response is always in order, even in cases where a rude or unmerited complaint has been received, the wrong company has been contacted, or the request seems ridiculous.
- Rude or insensitive responses are never in order. Don't ever send a harsh response or one that contains a moral judgment to someone who has had bad news or has suffered a loss.
- Don't let your response start with "Sorry I didn't respond sooner, but . . ." The proper way to handle this is to respond immediately with something like "I am looking into a solution to your problem . . . and I will be in touch as soon as I . . ."

CONSIDER SPECIAL SITUATIONS

- Complaints require immediate responses. Agree on some point with the writer or thank him or her for writing. Relate the action that has been (or is being) taken, and conclude with a goodwill statement.

- A threatening or abusive letter must be handled very carefully. If litigation is mentioned or implied, it is best to refer the matter to an attorney. If there is a particularly threatening tone, refer the matter to the proper authorities. If it is simply an angry letter, respond as respectfully and objectively as possible, expressing you are sorry the writer is upset.

- Responses to personal requests for contributions should include an opening statement of why you are, or aren't, donating. Enclose the provided form, if any, and request a receipt if you need it for tax purposes. If you do not wish to be on the computerized mailing list for an organization, a note, email, or telephone call stating simply "Please remove me from your mailing list" (or solicitation list) is sufficient.

- Respond to invitations to celebrations like birthday parties, anniversaries, bar or bat mitzvahs, and other events in like manner. A commercial greeting card with a personal message is appropriate, even if you won't attend, and a gift depends upon your relationship to the guest of honor.

- Messages and expressions of condolence and sympathy require a written response. This can take a number of forms: (1) written notes; (2) printed thank-yous with a handwritten note to those who were close to the deceased, ill, or injured person; and/or (3) a thank-you message placed in the local newspaper for someone who is/was a public figure. Responses certainly may be brief, and may be handled by a designated person outside the immediate family. Responses should be sent within six weeks of the event or, in the case of an injured or ill person, as soon as the person is able (see Sympathy & Condolence, page 44).

- Responses to an invitation for an interview are usually handled verbally, but there may be the opportunity to send a confirmation. If so, do it. This is an opportunity to impress a potential employer that you are skilled in business etiquette. It can also help you set the stage for a very productive interview. Include a last sentence like "looking forward to discussing my Cropper experience."

- Respond to an apology by acknowledging you received it, accepting the apology (if appropriate), and thanking the sender. If it's appropriate, you may wish to add that you look forward to a future relationship with the sender.

- A response to a note of congratulations should start with "Thank you." A statement about your appreciation for his/her thoughtfulness can be followed by a sentence or two of follow-up news.

SELECT A FORMAT

- Business responses should be typed on company stationery.
- Responses to formal invitations should be done in like manner. If you do not use personal printed note cards or stationery, type your response, with the information requested, in the same layout.
- Responding in kind by email is simple. Send a personal, sincere response—although it may be almost entirely boilerplate.

USE APPROPRIATE WORDS

acknowledge	appreciate	check	confirm
follow up	follow through	inform	investigate
notify	received	responding	thanks

WRITE EFFECTIVE PHRASES

appreciate your consideration	as we continue to research this
as you noted	delighted to hear the news
expect another response from us on	expect to hear from me
have carefully evaluated	here are the responses in the order of your complaint
here's the current status of the follow-up	I'll be watching this closely
I've enclosed	investigate this immediately
please let us know	responding to your
so pleased to hear from you	thank you for your letter
the next step	value your business
we have received	what great news
will be handling the next step	will follow up on
will keep you informed	your thoughtful note

BUILD STRONG SENTENCES

If I can answer any other questions, please don't hesitate to call or email.

We were sorry to learn that the fishing rod you purchased on October 5 isn't satisfactory, and we are happy to offer you full credit, a refund, or a replacement.

If you have any remaining questions, please call me.

Please accept my apology for the error in your January billing.

Your account has been credited with the amount of $45.87.

You are a valued customer, and we will do everything possible to resolve this problem.

As you requested, here is the brochure that describes the greening process.

BUILD EFFECTIVE PARAGRAPHS

Here is the research report on the milk contamination in New York. We will put you on our notification list to receive further reports as they become available.

Your letter concerning a customer-service problem in our Englewood store was given to me for handling. I am presently investigating this incident, and will be in contact with you within the next two weeks to report what I've learned. I am sorry you had an unpleasant experience in our store, and I will do everything I can to try to resolve it to your satisfaction.

I was very surprised to learn you received two Model C-120 Monitors instead of one. Thank you for returning one. Enclosed is reimbursement for the postage and a certificate for you to use in your next purchase of a BillyClub product.

Thank you for detailing your frustration in trying to return the Wacket Thumper. I will investigate the event in the next two weeks, and then I will be in touch with you again. In the meantime, on behalf of Wacket, please accept our most sincere apologies for an unpleasant experience.

We are shipping you two dinner plates today to replace the two you reported arrived broken. I'm sorry this happened. You should have the replacement plates in three days.

Yes, we certainly will honor our guarantee, and I'm glad you brought it to our attention that salespeople in our stores are not aware of the details of this policy. Please return your battery to Steve Watson at Store #31, Yosemite and Arapahoe, and he will take care of it.

Here is the proposal you requested. To meet your Requirements A through K, see the responses below.

I appreciate your apology, and accept it. It does, in fact, restore my confidence in your customer-service statement.

Thank you for submitting your resume for the manager position. I've forwarded it to the hiring committee, and someone will be in contact with you in the next two weeks.

We're always delighted to hear good news, and yours is especially welcome. How terrific that your book has come out, and you'll be signing at Stutters. We'll be there at the front of the line.

Just wanted you to know that we received your invitation to the graduation ceremony. We're juggling our schedule in the hope that we will be able to attend. I'll get an answer to you in a couple of days.

We have received your novel, and look forward to reviewing it. Presently, this process is taking eight weeks to complete. Please plan to hear from us by July 1. And thank you for your demonstration of confidence in our literary agency.

Your order has been processed and will ship today. Expect the products to arrive on Tuesday. Thank you for doing business with Slammers, Inc. We look forward to serving you.

EDIT, EDIT, EDIT

Be sure your message is clear and your communication ends on a positive note.

To Congratulations

Dear Bobbi,

Thank you for your kind note of congratulations.[1] Your interest, care, concern, and involvement in my education over the years have helped me get to where I am today: from the distinguished ranks of the PU graduating class of 2005 to the unemployment line! (Certainly not your fault.)

I'm sending out a zillion resumes a day and have listed on 10 online employment job-search websites.[2] And I'm happy to report that I've actually had two interviews: one in Chicago and one in San Francisco. (The jury's still out on both.) I'll let you know when I move into the ranks of the gainfully employed. Your interest and thoughts of concern are greatly appreciated.[3]

Robbie

---

(1) Thank the reader. (2) Offer information. (3) Close cordially.

To a Job Refusal

Dear Bob:

I don't envy you the difficult decision of selecting the person to head up the Phoenix operation. Of course I'm disappointed that I wasn't selected for the job, but at the same time I realize the position presents the new manager with some very large challenges that can't be solved without some other key factors being in place.

I appreciate your time and our exchange of ideas during the interview process, and I want to thank you for keeping my resume in your active file. If another managerial position opens up with Mizer, I'd like to be considered as a candidate.

I will call you about that golf game, too. I think you will enjoy our little course here at Sand Trap.

All the best,

Sam Simmer

To Customer Dissatisfaction

Dear Mrs. Lincoln:

I'm sorry the draperies for the yellow room aren't what you envisioned. Of course we'll work with you to come to a satisfactory solution.[1] Our interior decorator did survey the room, and he has three suggestions:

1. We can repaint the walls, adding white pigment to the original paint you selected;[2]
2. We can add a valance in a Schumacher designer fabric to the draperies that will majestically blend wall and drapery colors and pull the entire room together;[3] or
3. We can refit these draperies for use in another room and start over with another fabric.

I will call you on Thursday to arrange a time to bring over a number of samples that will make these alternatives visually clear.[4] Mr. Roberts feels you will be extremely satisfied with any of these solutions.[5]

Sincerely,

Gloria Van der Bloom

---

(1) Empathize with the reader. (2) Respond precisely. (3) Offer value-added solutions, if possible. (4) Clarify next step. (5) Close on a cordial note.

To a Fundraising Request

Sam:

Regrettably, I'm not able to make a contribution this year, but I am able to serve on HealthCare Day, and would be delighted to do so.

Please forward this email to the correct person. I can serve from 9:00 a.m. to noon.

Thank you for your valuable contribution to this great service.

Sincerely,

Rob Diner

To a Customer for an Error

Dear Mrs. Wiley:

I'm sorry your request for a change in your payment plan was mishandled. I'm still looking into how you could have received a form letter for a delinquent account, and I will explain it when I learn the details.

I have resolved the other matter, and the terms of your extension and the amount of future payments are detailed in the faxed contract. Please review it, and call me if you have any questions.

We value your business, and thank you for working with us to resolve this unfortunate misunderstanding.

Sincerely,

Michael Clinton

To a Bid Received

Jack:

Your bid just arrived, and it looks spot on to me after a very quick review. We have five qualified bids coming in, and yours is the first.

Jennie Crumm will be the project engineer on this project, and she'll be in touch with you within the week with additional questions for follow-up.

Thank you for bidding this. It was great seeing you at your presentation on Friday.

Best,

Giddy

To a Request to Alter a Price

Jimmie and Ruddy:

Thank you for your letter listing the items that need to be repaired on the house at 1010 Statesman Street before you make an offer. This may be handled in one of two ways: (1) you may request the present owner make these repairs, or (2) you may estimate the cost of these repairs, list them, and total them. The total may then be used to negotiate a deduction from your formal offer price.

Thank you again for being so alert, and I will be happy to work with you in any way possible—I have sources for bids on repairing these items—so you may complete your computations.

I shall call you tomorrow to learn your decision.

Best,

Ron Moe

To a Request for a Replacement Product

Dear Mr. Brokett:

Your request for a replacement motor for the Decker Docker saw has been forwarded to our service department at the store where you purchased it. Mr. Fred Mamet, service department manager, will need to see the saw to make a final determination. He asks that you call him between 9 a.m. and 5 p.m., Monday through Friday, to arrange a time to take it in.

I'm sorry you had this problem, and we will work with you to get it resolved.

Regards,

Mike Bolster

(Also see COMPLAINT & PROTEST, page 282.)

43 ACKNOWLEDGMENT & CONFIRMATION

The letter of *acknowledgment* is a tool of business record keeping (often for legal purposes). Its job is simply to record receipt and say "Yes, I received what you sent."

The letter of *confirmation* is also tool of business record keeping. Its primary purpose is to retell the reader what action was taken, and to reaffirm the decisions made and terms agreed to. It may have a number of secondary purposes as well. These may include acknowledgment, building goodwill, thanks, appreciation, acceptance, and documentation for legal purposes.

DECIDE TO WRITE

Use one of these letters to:

- Acknowledge materials, documents, or items received, or to confirm discussions held
- Reiterate decisions made
- Confirm upcoming meeting information or attendance
- Confirm reservations
- Create a record

THINK ABOUT CONTENT

- To confirm verbal discussions that change details of an agreement or contract, refer to the original agreement, and define what is changed.
- The confirmation letter may easily become a hybrid. When it confirms the decisions of a meeting between the sender and a client, it may go into explanations of the positions, discussion, and changes involved in reaching a decision.
- Form letters are often used for routine acknowledgments and/or confirmations, and with email this is easily and quickly done. These may be as simple as a boilerplate statement, or prepared list of items that can be checked off and sent with a brief note.
- It is entirely acceptable to include with a letter your own acknowledgment or confirmation form upon which the reader checks an item or pens a brief response. An author may send a self-addressed, stamped postcard, for example, to receive an immediate confirmation from a publisher that his or her manuscript has been received. Grant applications, legal

documents, and many other types of notices may be treated in the same manner. The postal service offers a similar kind of receipt: confirmation of delivery.

- State the points to be confirmed in the context of action taken, discussions, information received, and date, time, place, etc. Brief, complete information is best. Most acknowledgment letters are only a sentence or two; confirmations may be as short, or only slightly longer.
- Give any and all pertinent identifying information, including how to contact you, if necessary.
- Close with a friendly comment, and thank the reader for his or her efforts.
- Include a signature line for the recipient if the letter is to become a legal agreement or contract.

ELIMINATE WRONG MESSAGES

- Avoid talking down to the reader: "Be sure to make a note to bring your calendar. . . ." Keep the message brief and objective.
- Don't let a simplistic tone creep in.
- Do not go beyond the bounds of confirming information.
- Don't list future, unrelated action items, or try to persuade.

CONSIDER SPECIAL SITUATIONS

- Confirmations for reservations at hotels, motels, the theater, fundraisers, etc., may mean that you are agreeing to pay for the reserved item, whether you use it or not. Always check, and make sure you understand the terms for actual charges. This confirmation is often made by telephone and involves giving a credit card number. When payment is involved, or reservations include special preparation or accommodations, a written confirmation may also be required. In this case, be very specific about date, time of arrival, length of stay, price, accommodations, special arrangements and provisions, specific facilities, and inclusions.
- It is always good to confirm that you have received a customer/client order, agreement, change, and/or special request. Keep the acknowledgment letter brief and close in a friendly manner. Acknowledgment letters are required when the intended recipient is not available to respond. In this case, the designated person should send a brief letter acknowledging receipt, and stating that the intended recipient will respond as soon as possible.
- A confirmation should be sent in response to an invitation, if the host requests it. This is often done on an informal fold-over note card. (See Invitation, page 63.)

SELECT A FORMAT

- Email, postcards, form notes, or letters can be used to acknowledge receipt of manuscripts, documents, requests, packages, etc. When you send a manuscript or documents that you want to know arrived safely, you may ask the recipient to send you an email indicating receipt. Or, you may include a self-addressed, stamped postcard with the materials that the recipient can easily return to you. For example:

> Please let me know by completing the following:
> ☐ We have received your proposal.
> ☐ We will get back to you with a response in approximately _____ weeks.

- Business acknowledgments and confirmations can be made by email or typed on letterhead. Check organization protocol.
- Interoffice acknowledgments and confirmations may be done by email or on simple, printed memo forms that allow the recipient to check the appropriate response.

SELECT THE RIGHT WORDS

accept	acknowledge	affirm	agree
approve	assure	comply	confirm
deliver	indicate	notify	receipt
received	respond	return	verify

BUILD STRONG PHRASES

as agreed	the agreement will now read
the changes indicated include	these changes reflect our discussion
this updates the contract	we hereby confirm

WRITE STRONG SENTENCES

Start with the action, and write a concise statement.

> Thanks for your call.
> I'm looking forward to our meeting next week.
> The five cartons of computer parts were just delivered by air express.
> This confirms our agreement that your company will start the renovation on Monday, April 1.
> The Jackson Report arrived in our office this morning; we will be meeting to review it on Wednesday.
> Got it.

BUILD EFFECTIVE PARAGRAPHS

> As we agreed on the telephone, Rounder and Long will be pleased to represent you in the Webster matter. I have set up a meeting for Thursday, October 7 at 2:00 p.m. with Bill Webster here in my office. I shall be in contact with you immediately after that meeting.

> We have received your application to be part of the Aging Study. We have been overwhelmed with applications, and it will require another two weeks for us to process them and select the participants. Please be patient, and we will contact you in approximately three weeks.

Thank you for your grant application, which we have now received. The winners will be announced on July 15, and all applicants supplying the requested postcard will be immediately notified.

EDIT, EDIT, EDIT

Make sure your communication is simple, clear, and complete.

Confirmation of Bid Changes

Jan,

Yes, we'll spring for the 3¼-inch-wide flooring in Victorian clear maple, an increase of 33 percent over the bid we have.

Best,

Raymond

Acknowledging Receipt of Manuscript

[Self-addressed, stamped postcard mailed by sender for recipient's signature and return]

Yes, Bender and Scrooge has received your manuscript, and will add it to the stack of potential best sellers in waiting.

(Signature) _____

Please expect a response from us in _____ weeks.

Confirms and Documents Agreement

Dear Mr. Beevis:

This confirms our agreement of this morning's telephone conversation. Yes, you may have access to your pastureland by using my private road, as long as your conduct causes no stress or threat to my livestock grazing in the adjoining pasture.

Your truly,

Bea Holden

Confirmation of Receipt of Information

Dear Mr. Logan:

We have received your mortgage loan application. Because of the number of credit references, employers, and previous lenders on your application, please allow two weeks for loan processing.

If you have any questions, please contact Bonnie McGregor at 555-0123.

Sincerely,

Thirsty Blocker

Confirms Verbal Changes in Employment Agreement

Dear Ms. Gupta:

This confirms the changes we made this morning on the telephone to your employment agreement. We will (1) increase your salary to $165,000 per year, (2) increase your vacation after one year of employment to fourteen days, and (3) raise your bonus percentage to seven percent.

Please make these changes in the contract, initial them, and send them back to me for my signature.

We are so pleased to have you coming aboard. Welcome! I feel sure your relationship with Cunning will be an extremely rewarding one.

Sincerely,

Bebe Gunliffe

Confirmation and Agreement for Speaker

Dear Lee:

We at Business Women are so pleased you have agreed to be our premier speaker at this year's convention banquet at the Peachtree Hotel on June 5.

The setting for our meetings will be informal, starting with a cocktail hour at 6:30 p.m. in the Blossom Room. Dinner will be served at 7:30 p.m. You will be introduced by Janet Rewfrow at 8:30 p.m., and we have allowed 30 minutes for your presentation with another 15 minutes for a question and answer period to follow immediately.

Business Women will pay you an honorarium of $2,500 for your participation, plus we will cover the cost of your flight (coach class), a hotel room for two nights, and meals on June 5.

The audience, an expected 400, will be composed of member professionals who will be well versed in sexual harassment issues. Their questions, I expect, will center on cases and verdicts, outcomes in terms of financial settlements to plaintiffs, and future legal trends. We will have an overhead projector and lapel microphone ready for you. Please plan to bring any handouts because getting copies made was a problem last year. As agreed, you may bring copies of your book for participants to purchase. We can furnish a volunteer to handle book sales, if you like.

Rudy Wilkes, who will be carrying a sign with your name on it, will meet your flight: United #221, arriving in Atlanta at 7:30 p.m. on June 4. If there is any change in your plans, please call Rudy at 555-0123.

I will arrive at the Peachtree on June 4 at about 4:00 p.m. I have reserved Room 433. Please leave me a message after you arrive.

If there is any additional equipment you want for your presentation, please contact Sally Dithers at our offices, extension 256, as soon as possible.

We are delighted you will be joining us this year. Please sign below, confirming you agree to these terms, and fax a copy to me at 555-0124.

Yours truly,

Sadie Hawker

Lee Radwitz _____

Date _____

Confirmation of Nomination

Dear Alice:

I will accept the nomination to serve as next year's president, as long as you agree to be vice president. (Some might call it blackmail.)

It should be a great opportunity to work together. I look forward to it.

Sincerely,

Valerie Sower

44 ACCEPTANCE

A note or letter accepting a dinner invitation is easy. Just express your gratitude for the invitation, say "yes" you are coming, and express anticipation of the future enjoyment. The general rule for invitations, at least, is to reply in kind. For formal invitations it may be even simpler because there may be a RSVP card that only has to be filled in and returned.

Accepting a job offer or an invitation to be seminar speaker is more difficult. Your letter may be the only documentation of the agreed-upon terms. Be sure of your decision to accept, then write in a timely and enthusiastic manner.

DECIDE TO WRITE

Send an acceptance in response to:

- An invitation to a wedding, dinner, party, meeting, seminar, conference, or hospitality
- A job offer
- A proposal, bid, contract, or a change to these
- A special contribution or donation
- An offer of a favor, help, or recommendation
- A membership approval or invitation to join a club, association, organization, committee, or commission
- A speaking invitation

THINK ABOUT CONTENT

- Consider the person issuing the invitation, especially in the case of a dinner or party, and express your delight and enthusiasm.
- Address your acceptance to the person from whom the invitation, document, etc., came.
- Thank the reader for the invitation.
- State your acceptance, expressing your pleasure at being able to accept.
- Confirm the time, place, and details, if appropriate.
- End with a statement of anticipation or your expectations for the event. (If you find this is something you cannot generate, it may be better to decline the invitation.)

ELIMINATE WRONG MESSAGES

- Don't digress into unrelated business.

- Avoid placing conditions and/or qualifications on your acceptance. Your acceptance should not place conditions or additional demands on a host, for example.

CONSIDER SPECIAL SITUATIONS

- Timing is always important. Send your acceptance within a day of receiving it, or as soon after as possible.
- If you have questions, call the host or designated person for clarification.
- When the acceptance is for one of an invited couple, check with the host, if appropriate, to make sure this does not present a problem.
- In accepting a television interview or seminar speaking invitation, be sure you understand all the requirements and details. The first paragraph of your letter—after you state your acceptance—should confirm the details: the time, date, and place, etc., and it should include any questions to be addressed before the event. Be sure the topic is mutually agreed upon in writing. There is no such thing as an "open-ended" interview.
- Teach children early to write acceptances.
- If something comes up after you have accepted, call the host immediately and explain, but remember that your acceptance is a contract—your good word.

SELECT A FORMAT

Reply in the same format as the invitation. If you were invited by email, respond by email. A typed invitation on a business letterhead requires a typed acceptance on a business letterhead; an informal handwritten invitation requires an informal acceptance, usually a telephone call. The exception is if you receive an engraved invitation, and there is no enclosed, engraved reply card. Send a handwritten reply on a card or fold-over note using the same wording and layout as the invitation:

Mr. Horacio and Ms. Katherine Phinney
accept with pleasure
the kind invitation of
Mr. Peter and Ms. Nancy Kowaleski
for dinner
on Saturday, the tenth of December
at eight o'clock

USE EFFECTIVE WORDS

accept	affirm	answer	attend
believe	delighted	glad	pleased
pleasure	regard	welcome	will

BUILD STRONG PHRASES

accept with pleasure

agree to the terms

delighted to be invited

I shall look forward to the opportunity

I'm very enthusiastic

pleased to accept

we can satisfy every requirement

will comply with your request

yes, indeed, I will

accept your gracious invitation

completely satisfied with your proposal

I feel honored

I will be able

it really pleases me to

we are willing and able

what a splendid idea

yes, I'd be pleased to

you will be delighted with our

WRITE STRONG SENTENCES

Yes, I'd be happy to accept your invitation.

I believe the conditions you set forth are fine, and I accept your offer.

I'm so pleased to be honored in this way, and I'd be delighted to be your speaker.

I am pleased to accept your offer to be manager of Dusty's Tavern.

We respectfully accept the invitation to attend the State dinner.

Yes, I would be pleased to present the "Stock Watch" portion of the Investors' Program on March 12, 2:30 p.m. at the Bellview.

Please count on me for the Board of Directors Meeting, January 12, at 7:00 p.m. at the Clubhouse.

We certainly wouldn't miss the opening game of the Tigers, and we accept your kind invitation for the tailgate party at 2:00 p.m.

We are looking forward to working with you.

Yes, these changes to the agreement are fine with us.

Yes, we're on board with this all the way.

I do accept your apology for the error in charges.

BUILD EFFECTIVE PARAGRAPHS

I am extremely pleased to be voted into the Businesswoman's Hall of Fame. It is truly an honor. I shall look forward to the banquet on February 15, 7:00 p.m. at the Turner Center.

We are pleased to inform you that your bid for the reroofing of the Sports Center has been accepted. The board of directors just met this afternoon. Please call me to arrange a time to sit down and discuss the start date and other details.

Jenny and I will be delighted to come to your costume Halloween party. I bet you won't guess who we are.

EDIT, EDIT, EDIT

Use clear and concise language. Short, enthusiastic, and to the point is the best acceptance.

Accepting a Pickup Game

Jim:

Count me in. I'll be happy to sub for Jack on Thursday. See you at the park at 4:30 p.m.

Cleats on.

Bob

Acceptance to Appear as a TV Interviewee

Dear Anne:

Thank you for your invitation to be a guest on *Business Talks*. I am very pleased to be invited and I enthusiastically accept.

I will, as you suggest, arrive at the 4News studios at 1:00 p.m. on Thursday, June 5, for the preparation before taping the segment. I understand the topic is "Starting a New Business," and I will be prepared to go through the basic steps. I shall bring five four-color charts with bulleted items. I will be prepared to answer your questions about accounting, legal counsel, banking, and consultant resources for new entrepreneurs in our community. I would also like to know the names and organizations of the other two guests who will appear on the program, and their exact topic areas.

I have been instructed by my wardrobe people not to wear white or large prints. If there are any other cautions or directions in this area or tips on preparing for the makeup session, please contact my secretary, Biddie Brindle.

Sincerely,

Denise Copperfield

Acceptance of a Proposal

Dear Mr. Hill:

Congratulations. Your proposal to provide public relations counsel for the Celebrity Tennis Tournament has been accepted.

We will want to amend our contract, as discussed, to include our brochures, press releases, the annual report, and other written communications.

The telephone surveys and letters will be handled by our public affairs department. Mr. Corey Kettle will be in charge of these activities, and he will also be the person to whom you will report.

Please make the above changes in the contract, and call me to arrange a time for all of us to get together. We all look forward to working with you.

Sincerely,

Donahue Bugle

College Acceptance

Dear Byron:

Congratulations! We are happy to announce that you have been accepted to Smuthers for the fall semester. A complete schedule of orientation activities and events is enclosed.

Most of your classmates will arrive here the morning of August 28. We request that all new students go directly to Haver Hall to check in, and there you can set a time to meet with your advisor.

We look forward to having you at Smuthers.

Sincerely,

Jimmie Dithers

Accepting a Wedding Anniversary Invitation

Dear Satchel:

Rachel and I accept with pleasure your kind invitation to attend the 25th wedding celebration for your parents, James and Demi Whittman, on July 7, at the Grange Hall, 4:00 p.m.

Sincerely,

Darrel Demming

Formal Acceptance for One for Dinner

[Date]

Catherine Bauer
accepts with pleasure
Robert Q. Pompus and Lila Simpson's
kind invitation to a dinner
on Friday, the tenth of August, at seven o'clock
but regrets that
Howard Stern
will be unable to attend.

Accepting a Request to Write a Recommendation

Dear Darin:

I am delighted to accept the invitation to write a letter of recommendation for you to the Dean at Bowens. I shall sit down and do it right now.

I'll be eager to hear how it turns out, and I'll keep my fingers crossed. I could never tell you before, of course, but you were always one of my favorite students.

Cordially,

Bernie Hill

Acceptance of Informal Business Meeting Invitation

Dear Melvin:

I was pleased to receive your telephone call and invitation to serve on the Germ Inhalant Committee, and attend the initial luncheon meeting on September 16 at noon at the Regency in Denver. I will fly in the evening before and stay at the Regency overnight. (My secretary will make all those arrangements.)

I will bring 12 copies of the Sneezer's Report and information on conference facilities in Tahoe.

Thank you for arranging this first meeting. I'm pleased and eager to work on this worthwhile project.

Sincerely,

Conrad Greeves

Accepting an Informal Invitation with Substitution

Dear Nina:

Thank you for extending the invitation for me to represent Nickors at the annual Fireman's Banquet in New York on October 10. However, as I discussed with you, I will need to modify the topic area you requested, "Trends in Inhalation Techniques," to "Equipment for the New Century." I've attached a copy of the presentation I made last week in Los Angeles.

I will be pleased to make the presentation in the 40-minute format, and all the equipment you have listed in your letter of August 12 will be needed. The accommodations you have described are fine.

Please call me with any additional details as they become available. I'm looking forward to attending the banquet and believe the audience will be especially pleased with the new developments I will describe.

Sincerely,

Ezra Newton

(Also see INVITATION, page 63, and REFUSAL, page 274.)

The refusal letter has two main goals: to say no and, at the same time, to promote good-will. This bad news may be preceded by a positive statement, or, if you know the reader prefers directness or will receive the bad news routinely, use a direct approach. In either case, end with a goodwill statement.

DECIDE TO WRITE

Use this letter to respond to:

- An offer of admission to college
- An offer of membership
- Credit applications (see Credit Inquiry & Providing Credit Information, page 331, and Credit Denial, page 340)
- Requests for volunteer participation, financial contributions and donations, letters of reference, loans, bids, raises, appointments, meetings, and interviews
- Adjustments (see Request for Payment Adjustment, page 345)
- Proposals or bids
- A job offer
- Contractual invitations
- Returns
- Gifts
- Sales
- Invitations to social events, dinner parties, fundraisers, weddings, etc. (see Invitation, page 63)

THINK ABOUT CONTENT

- First be sure you understand the request or problem.
- Respond as promptly as possible.
- Start by thanking the reader for the offer, invitation, or effort in preparing a proposal, applying, or giving a gift, if that is appropriate. For example: "Thank you for your invitation to participate in creating a scholarship for young authors."
- Determine the logical explanation or reason for your refusal, making an effort to empathize with the reader during this process.

- Open with a sentence that sets up the explanation. It may be a thank you, it may agree with the reader on some point, or it may combine an agreement and an apology. This helps set a positive tone for the letter and helps to gain the reader's cooperation. Or, begin with a neutral response to the request to help set up your next statement: "Your efforts to establish the Young Authors' Scholarship Fund are very commendable. I wish you success in this worthy endeavor." This is preferable to opening with "We cannot contribute to the Young Authors' Scholarship Fund."

- If you use an indirect approach, the reader is ushered through the logic or reason for your refusal before he or she reads the refusal itself. This allows him or her to gain more understanding of why you are saying no or are responding with bad news: "We at Great Water value promoting young literary talent. That's why we budget five percent of profits each fiscal year to support such causes."

- Stating your case in positive terms can make all the difference: "We have committed this year's funds, but we will place your request in our file for consideration for next year. Please contact me again in December with updated information about your needs for 2012."

- State your refusal in a clear, unequivocal, and positive statement.

- Always be tactful, even in the face of an outrageous request, and make your refusal devoid of personalities and comparisons.

- Include a counterproposal, compromise, or a suggestion, if possible: "Ms. Susan Sloan is a very qualified speaker who has won several awards for her presentation skills. She would do an excellent job."

- Close with a goodwill statement such as best wishes, or a related compliment: "Best wishes for the success of this year's Young Authors' Fund project. I look forward to hearing from you in December."

- If you have any concerns about possible legal action, consult with an attorney before sending your letter.

ELIMINATE WRONG MESSAGES

- Don't make negative statements.
- Don't offer excuses.
- Avoid unconvincing arguments or opening opportunities for the reader to debate the matter further.
- Don't be harsh.
- Don't leave a question in the reader's mind about your refusal so he thinks he may still persuade you if he tries hard enough.
- Lying is not a good approach.
- Never blame others for your refusal.

CONSIDER SPECIAL SITUATIONS

- In the case of an invitation, the refusal letter may also carry the job of making an apology. (See Invitation, page 63, and Apology, page 306.)

- In refusing an invitation, send your letter or note to the person listed under RSVP, or the first host, and mention any others.

- Explanations for refusing an invitation will depend upon the type of event, the number of attendees, your relationship to the host, and your function at the event. If you are invited to be an attendee at a large convention, seminar, or conference, you may not be obliged to respond, or you may make only a cursory refusal: "I will be unable to attend . . ." If you are scheduled as the keynote speaker at an international banquet of 2,000 clients, your refusal—especially if you initially accepted and are now refusing—should include a detailed explanation. It should, of course, be made only in the event of a very serious and unexpected situation, not because you got a better offer. You should also make suggestions and/or arrangements for a replacement.

- When you decline to do a favor, such as a letter of reference, an introduction, or set up a meeting, you are not obliged to explain yourself.

- The credit adjustment refusal letter should begin with a neutral statement, which sets up your next statement of strategy but does not give away your decision. The next statement should be positive and factual, and explain your position or reason. You must then refuse clearly and positively, and, if you can, offer a counterproposal. Remember to make your statements in positive terms. Conclude with a complimentary, encouraging, or upbeat message.

- When you use a direct refusal, be sure to start with a warm greeting or neutral opening: "Thank you for your letter of May 20 asking me to volunteer as scoutmaster." In the case of a personal friend, the refusal can open casually: "It was great to hear from you." State your refusal in positive terms: "My commitment to the Safe Neighborhoods Project this year demands all my spare time."

- Be sure to completely identify the request you're refusing by naming the essential information of project, date, and time.

- Direct your letter to the proper person.

- Remember, your objective in refusing a line (or extended line) of business credit request is to keep the customer or client. Offer an alternative solution or counterproposal whenever possible. It is especially important here to set up the logic of your explanation, and lead the reader through it in an effort to appeal to his or her sense of fair play. It is also important to be firm and positive in tone: "We extend a line of credit to businesses that have operated in this location for over one year. We invite you to reapply to Mr. Albert Green in November with the references listed on the enclosed sheet, and we sincerely hope to do business with Sun Screens at that time. In the meantime, please consider the advantages of setting up all your company checking on First Bank's 'System One Plan' as a preliminary step."

- Refusing inducements and gifts can be done by thanking the reader, and then stating a firm policy of turning down all such offers or items.
- In refusing a bid for a job or project, be as helpful and informative as applicable regulations will allow. The bidder probably expended a considerable amount of time, energy, and funds in an effort to get your business. He or she deserves as much courtesy and support as you can offer. Also remember, the reader may be a future supplier. List areas or items where the bid did not meet specifications or guidelines, and, if possible, list why the winning bidder was awarded the work. Close on an upbeat note.
- Keep blame out of your refusal letters. When terminating business or personal relationships, objective information and taking participant responsibility are the best approaches. Honesty, tact, and kindness are the principles here, and it is wise to avoid detailed explanations. Your decision should be briefly stated, firm, and clear.

SELECT A FORMAT

- In refusing a job offer, respond first with a verbal answer and then follow it with a formal written refusal.
- Personal refusals are often handwritten.
- Business refusals should be typed on the proper letterhead.
- To make form refusals as individual as possible, create a template (boilerplate) you individualize in the writing process.
- When refusing an invitation, respond in the same form as the invitation was issued. (See Invitation, page 63.)

SELECT APPROPRIATE WORDS

apply	conclusion	considered	decision
decline	deny	determination	encourage
evaluated	extend	final	invite
opportunity	reapply	refuse	regret
revisit	unable	unfortunately	welcome

CONSTRUCT EFFECTIVE PHRASES

after careful consideration	are not now accepting
cannot participate	determined after study and comparison
doesn't qualify	due to other commitments
I am sorry to be the bearer of bad news	I must tell you we cannot
I recommend you contact	I'm sorry to have to say no
I'm sure you will find support	if you care to resubmit next year
may we invite you to apply again	must conclude that
not able at this time	our application period is closed
our final decision	thank you for applying
there is no way	there's no easy way to say no
unable to help	unfortunately, our final decision must be

unquestionably, I must decline

we are unable to invite you

we have no other choice but to refuse

we must decline your kind invitation

we must say no

we regret we are unable

we wish you great success

your idea is a good one

we are so disappointed we cannot

we have evaluated your

we look forward to another opportunity

we must deny

we regret to report

we will be unable to attend

will reconsider next year

yours is a worthy cause

WRITE STRONG SENTENCES

Start with a strong, positive verb and build your sentences carefully.

I must cancel my conference reservation.

My volunteer calendar is completely full at this time.

I appreciate you asking me to join the Jumpers' Club.

We have selected a bid that more closely meets our specifications for the number of workers to be on site during the contract period.

Please call me next year.

We appreciate all the outstanding work that went into your preparation of the Crichton proposal.

We look forward to receiving your bid on a future project that is closer in scope to your resources.

BUILD EFFECTIVE PARAGRAPHS

Thank you for submitting your proposal for the Wayland Project. We felt your graphics were especially strong.

I enjoyed talking with you on May 10 about the product manager position at Harper. Our selection task was made very difficult by having 25 extremely qualified applicants.

I am honored at your invitation to speak to the Farmers' Association. I am aware of all the good work the organization is doing.

Thank you for your letter of March 19 describing the problem with the golf clubs. You are correct in assuming that we want to hear about any sales problems.

I have carefully reviewed your letter of June 7 describing the problem with the evening gown. I know that as a 12-year Marks customer, you know we make every effort to satisfy our customers.

We have received your notification that you will be unable to attend day two of the Martinville Conference. Our policy is that we must charge attendees the total conference fee, since our costs for the accommodations remain the same.

EDIT, EDIT, EDIT

Be sure your message is clear, firm, and ends on a good note.

Decline to Be a Club Officer

Bob,

I'm flattered at the suggestion that I would make an excellent president of the Futures Club, but I have committed all my free time for next year to Jamie's Scouts and Jennie's Little League.

I would certainly consider it next year, and I appreciate your vote of confidence.

Sincerely,

Douglas Viders

Refusing an Employment Candidate

Dear Martin:

It was a pleasure meeting you and discussing how your qualifications might fit the position of sales manager at Basco. You have especially strong leadership skills. However, I believe you'll agree the position requirements aren't the right match for you. All of us here—Jack Mason, June Lockham, Alice Kardon, and I—wish you the best in finding the right situation.

Thank you for your interest and time, and our best wishes for your future success.

Sincerely,

Joe Wagner

Decline to Volunteer

Dear Robin:

It's indeed a compliment to be asked to serve on the Program Committee for the Authors' Club, but I have filled my volunteer capacity for this year with several other commitments.

I believe the programs are a very important Authors' Club function, and I shall be happy to consider serving next year, if you need me.

Sincerely,

Eleanor Quinn

Deny Customer's Request to Accept Return of Damaged Goods

Dear Mrs. Whitmore:

Thank you for your letter of April describing the problem with the red ball gown. As you know, we at Bates try very hard to satisfy our customers.[1]

Three of us in customer service reviewed the problem after you brought the gown back to the store on April 10. I have also discussed the situation in detail with the manufacturer's representative to try to come up with a solution.[2]

Since the gown was worn and stained, we cannot, of course, sell it as new merchandise. And, as the manufacturer explains in the enclosed letter, the staining problem is a characteristic of the silk fabric, and not a defect in design or construction.[3]

I am returning your gown to you. Both the manufacturer and I suggest you may want to contact Lace's Dye in Evanston to see if they can dye the garment.[4]

On behalf of Bates, I would like to offer you, as a long-time, valued customer, the enclosed gift certificate for $25, which can be used at any of our stores within the next year.

We look forward to serving you in the future.[5]

Sincerely,

Judi Wolf

(1) Start on a positive note. (2) Show due consideration. (3) Explain.
(4) Offer a solution, if possible. (5) End on a positive note.

Decline a Social Invitation

Dear Jack and Joan,

How very nice of you to invite us to the reception for Susan on June 10.[1] We have, unfortunately, committed to be adult sponsors at Gary's Young Republicans' party that night.[2] We're very sorry to have to miss such a special occasion. Susan is dear to us.

Please do give her our best. We look forward to toasting the new graduate soon.[3]

Sincerely,
Mary and Jack Burrus

(1) Start with thanks. (2) Offer an explanation. (3) End on a positive note.

Investment Opportunity Refusal

Shurabh:

Thank you for thinking of me in conjunction with the slot machine investment. Yes, I have heard this is a very hot area, and your plan sounds like a sound one. Potentially a very profitable one.

Unfortunately other commitments have my capital tied up for the next two years. I'm sorry to have to pass, but there it is.

Do contact me again in 20 months, if you have a group you're putting together.

All the best,

Bambi

College Application Refusal

Dear Rubin:

Thank you for applying to Hudson College for your undergraduate studies. The admissions committee has now finished their evaluation of applications for the 2012 fall semester at Hudson, and we regret that your application has been denied.

We'd like to encourage you to consider applying for entrance to Abbott Community College in your city for the fall semester and reapplying to Hudson in the spring. Successful completion as a full-time freshman at Abbott with a 3.4 GPA will give you an excellent chance of qualifying as a sophomore transfer student here.

We wish you every success in your academic endeavors.

Sincerely,

Jennifer Stiffle

Director of Admissions

Refusal to Fill an Order Due to Past Credit Problems

Dear Mr. Vilas:

Thank you for your Order #3423 of March 10 for Marker Tools.

You may recall that your last purchase in 2010 resulted in our taking collection action for payment through Action Collection.

To establish a new working relationship, you need to send payment for this present order in the amount of $1,582. We will immediately respond by rushing you the tools within 48 hours.

Thank you for considering us again, and we hope to hear from you soon.

Sincerely,

Holly Parker

VII

PROBLEMS, SENSITIVE MATTERS & RESOLUTIONS

It is not the hand but the understanding
of the man that may be said to write.

—*Miguel de Cervantes*

46 COMPLAINT & PROTEST

The letter of complaint or protest has a single objective: to get a problem solved in a positive way. To accomplish this, try to take the place of the recipient so you can make a simple list of what he or she needs to know in order to take corrective action or understand your point. This letter demands careful organization of the facts, a direct approach, persuasive writing, suggestion of a resolution or statement of further action, and, whenever possible, a statement of goodwill. In the case of a complaint, it's often helpful to think in terms of what will reasonably make you whole again.

Simple complaints or protests may be quickly handed with a telephone call, or by email to the customer service online address. Detailed or complicated matters, or those that could involve legal action, should be handled with an emailed or mailed letter to create a written record.

DECIDE TO WRITE

You may need to write this letter for one of the following situations:
- A purchase that is wrong, damaged, defective, delivered too late, spoiled, broken, has missing parts, no instructions, or lacks the warranty
- Neighborhood problems
- School problems
- Pet problems
- Social, club, and community problems
- Errors in billing, order, financial statement, minutes, or a collection procedure has been initiated against you
- Employee problems of payment, productivity, attitude, incompetence, or sexual harassment
- Whenever legal problems are suspected
- Illegal activities such as fraud or false advertising
- Misrepresentation
- Legislative problems or disagreements
- Human rights violations
- Business policies and practice disagreements

THINK ABOUT CONTENT

- A written complaint shouldn't usually be your first course of action. If, for example, the neighbor's dog barked all night, a telephone call is a better response than a two-page letter.

As a matter of fact, a timely telephone call should be the first line of complaint for most problems.

- Gather and review all the facts, so you have them firmly in mind and logically and chronologically in order. Make notes so you can cover them quickly and accurately on the telephone, and in a letter.

- In social, personal, pet, children, and school complaints, it is usually best to try to resolve these disputes with a calm and tactful face-to-face conversation with those involved. First review the rules and policies, then state your complaint in terms of infractions, and suggest corrective action or resolution.

- Emphasize the solution or corrective action in objective terms. Stay away from "I" statements like "I want," "I feel," "I need." Use statements like "To correct this problem . . ."

- Make a written record of all the facts, persons, contact addresses, and telephone numbers involved in your complaint each time something new happens. This will allow you to be accurate, precise, and complete. Include in your information the date, time, and any person spoken to, and the content and outcome of each conversation.

- Keep all original documents, and make copies to send with your letter. Also keep all subsequent correspondence and documents in a file.

- Offer additional documentation, like photographs of broken merchandise, whenever possible.

- Write your letter in a timely manner. Although you may need time to get over the initial anger before writing, it is important to write as soon as you have documented all the facts of the problem. Not only will your letter be stronger, but your chances of getting the corrective action you desire will be better.

- Begin by using a positive statement such as the fact that you chose the product because of its reputation, have been a long-time customer, etc., and write in the full expectation that you desire to take corrective action.

- Unless you are stating a number of items that point to a central problem, use the one-complaint-per-letter rule. If, for example, you are complaining about the lack of service of a department store, and you state three examples that took place during your last visit to the store, you should list them very briefly. If you want to complain about three separate policies your senator endorses, write three separate letters.

- Cover the problem completely, even if you discussed it with the reader on the telephone and he or she has some knowledge of the facts. You might start, "As we discussed, I received . . ." Remember, your letter may be referred to someone else within the organization.

- Address your letter to a real person. This may require calling to determine the proper person's name.

- Whenever possible, complain to the person with the authority to take corrective action. Otherwise, you can waste a lot of time and effort, and/or the problem may be exacerbated by dealing with the wrong person. Always ask for the name and position of the person with whom you are speaking, and keep a complete record of date, time, and person, and what was said.

- Use a "Reference" or "Subject" line, if appropriate, to focus and direct the reader's attention to the problem. State the problem here and/or in the opening sentence of your letter.
- Be direct and state specifically what is wrong.
- Present the facts briefly and clearly, using any reference dates, persons, invoice numbers, inventory numbers, order numbers, prices, and specifications that are applicable. State these in logical or chronological order.
- Use bullets, numbers, and indentation to emphasize your points, and to make it easier for the reader to note and respond to them. This works especially well if you have points to list or chronological events to note.
- Tell the reader why your complaint needs to be resolved.
- State the specific adjustments, corrections, or action you seek. If possible, include a couple of choices for the reader.
- Be polite. The person to whom you are writing is often—if not usually—not the person who created the problem.
- Use a third-party expert if an objective opinion or evaluation is needed, and mention this person in your letter. If the person offered a written opinion, refer to it, and enclose a copy. (Indicate the enclosure on the copy line of your letter.)
- Give the reader a timeframe for taking corrective action.
- Close on a positive but firm note. State your confidence that the matter will be taken care of as you suggest.
- Include your complete contact information: name, home and email addresses, and work, home, and/or cell telephone numbers.
- Attach copies of any pertinent documents that support your letter.
- Close with a statement of when you will make your next contact if you doubt the recipient will resolve the matter in a timely manner without urging.

ELIMINATE WRONG MESSAGES

- Do not use harsh, accusatory, sarcastic, abusive, blaming language or terms that could be interpreted as a personal attack.
- Never let your letter wander into side issues or nonissues.
- Don't be vague.
- Do not leave the course of corrective action or the response date up to the reader.
- Do not threaten to sue. It is far better to send a positive letter and indicate a CC: to your attorney with the title of "attorney at law" listed after her or his name. You certainly may state—if applicable and if you are prepared to do so—that if you do not receive a satisfactory reply by a specific date, you will take the matter to small claims court. But be sure you have exhausted every possibility of negotiating first.
- Do not use unreasonable or out-of-line suggestions for corrective action.

CONSIDER SPECIAL SITUATIONS

- Many complaints must take a certain form. First call the organization and talk to customer service to get any required complaint form or number. Get the correct name and title of the person to send it to, the information to be included, the name of the person to whom you are speaking, etc. A primary example of this is a complaint about a problem with your credit statement.

- In disputes about purchased merchandise that you have charged on your credit card, you must immediately let the credit card company know there's a problem. Call the appropriate telephone number first (on your credit card) to make sure you follow their complaint procedure.

- For airline problems, state the flight number, departure and arrival locations, times of departure and arrival, where and when the problem occurred, a description of the problem, the names of airline employees involved, the names and contact information of witnesses, and the course of corrective action you suggest.

- Often wrongs exist on both sides of a complaint. Take responsibility for your part of the problem, apologize if appropriate, and suggest a mutually beneficial solution whenever possible.

- There are usually several possible solutions to a problem, so be ready to negotiate and compromise.

- Complaint or protest campaigns to political figures and corporations should be made individually; that is, each person should send his or her own letter. Another approach, which may be preferable in some circumstances, is to send one letter or petition with many individual signatures. Check this out before deciding. Also consider other complaint actions such as writing a letter to the editor of your local newspaper, initiating local television and radio station news coverage of the issue, or another type of political action.

- When merchandise arrives damaged by a second-party shipper, you should immediately notify the shipper, and follow their procedure for making a complaint.

- It is often most effective to use a list form and to simply state the facts—what is wrong— in just enough detail so the reader can take action. Include pertinent information like dates and persons involved, and refer to relevant documents by identifying numbers wherever possible.

- If you are angry about a problem, it will be necessary to return to a calm and objective state of mind before you write. Or, you can write your angry letter, read it out loud, tear it into tiny pieces, then toss it. Having fully vented, start over on your real letter of complaint.

- Attach all copies—keep the originals—of any pertinent documents showing the item, situation, date of transaction, place of transaction, cost, sales receipt, invoice, original request, and original inventory certificate. If there are several, reference them in your letter, and number them.

SELECT A FORMAT

- Your complaint or protest should look official. Type it on business letterhead, personal business letterhead, personal letterhead, or quality bond stationery.
- Complaint or claim forms are often required. Type these or print very neatly.
- If your letter must be handwritten, make it neat and clear.

SELECT THE RIGHT WORD

acceptable	accurate	adjust	apparent
appraisal	attention	aware	complain
compromise	damage	defect	desire
dispute	dissatisfied	error	estimate
experience	fault	grievance	guarantee
inaccurate	incident	judge	misrepresent
mistake	negotiate	oversight	protest
quote	reasonable	recompense	register
replace	replacement	resolve	responsible
restore	satisfy	settle	situation
substitute	true	warrant	whole

BUILD EFFECTIVE PHRASES

a satisfactory resolution would be

bring this matter to your attention

does not perform as advertised

I know you will want to correct

I look forward to resuming a

I noticed the error in

I would like to be reimbursed for

I'm sure you will want to correct this

I've enjoyed being a client

not up to your usual customer service standard of

parts were missing from the package

please check your records

please credit me with

please restore my confidence by full restitution

please ship me a replacement immediately

product is defective

restore this item to

resulted in work loss

the order was delayed

this is inconsistent with your usual standard of fine service

uncharacteristic error

was inconvenienced

WRITE STRONG SENTENCES

I am writing regarding your invoice #7556, dated May 17, 2010, for the Model 1664 Adapters.

I suggest you can resolve this problem in one of two ways.

I certainly don't want our working record of five years blemished by such an error.

Please get these parts to me by Friday.

I suggest we simply settle the matter by you issuing Bonders a $500 credit for the broken parts.

Please send a corrected invoice by May 20.

May we please resolve this situation by June 14?

I think you will agree that my request for equipment replacement is a reasonable solution.

I believe this can be easily resolved if you will record a $30 credit in your database, and I'll use it against my next charge.

Your bookkeeper simply charged my account twice.

I'm confident that we can resolve this dispute.

I employed an independent antique appraiser listed on your website to estimate the replacement value of my French leather screen, and a copy of that estimate is attached.

I wish to register my dissatisfaction with your position on this issue.

Your most recent vote in Congress does not reflect the view of your constituency.

This is a violation of basic human rights.

My main objective is to ensure that this doesn't happen again.

There are a number of solutions to the barking problem that you may want to consider.

BUILD EFFECTIVE PARAGRAPHS

I am returning for credit the three dozen ceramic yellow bumble bees that I did not order.

Please refer to my attached order #3210 that lists three ceramic yellow bumble bees and two dozen little foxes.

My fall sale begins September 20. I must have the corrected order by September 15.

This is the fourth time our shipment of paper bags has been late. As you know, we cannot operate our store without them.

I have not received a return telephone call in response to my email of April 10. (Copy attached.)

The assembly line gears supplied by Gears Inc. are not performing to specifications.

I need your immediate response to get this problem solved.

We are losing 20 percent of our production each day.

EDIT, EDIT, EDIT

A cool, clear communication will win the day.

Returning Product for a Refund

Dear Mr. Stark:

I am returning the "Fantastic New Body" kit for a full refund of $49.95, as your advertisement states: "Simply return the unused portion for a full refund if you are not completely satisfied."

After using the products for two weeks, I have experienced no weight loss.

Please send a check for $49.95 to Ellen Worthington, 223 East Drury Lane, Littleton, CO 80223.

Thank you.

Sincerely,

Ellen Worthington

Complaint about Workmanship

SUBJECT: Installation of Exposed Aggregate Walkways, Sun Club Resort, May 15

Dear Mr. Bailey:

When our maintenance man reported a series of cracks in the new exposed aggregate you installed two weeks ago, I asked him to check the thickness. He reported that the sidewalk is 2 inches thick in most places and 3 inches thick in others throughout the 150-yard length.

Since the specifications (see attached, line 15) call for a 6-inch uniform thickness, I must insist this installation be corrected. I suggest either:

1. Maco Concrete completely remove the existing exposed aggregate and reinstall a new walkway according to the specifications and under the supervision of Mr. Ted Walker, our maintenance engineer, or
2. Maco immediately refund the payment of $14,500, plus a removal charge of $8,000.

Please call me by April 15 with your decision, so we may avoid seeking a legal remedy.

Sincerely,

M. B. McDermott

Complaint Offering Two Alternatives

SUBJECT: Cool Daze Air Conditioner,
            Model 1755A,
            Serial No. 3745,
            Purchase Order #6654[1]

Dear Mr. Ricks:

The air conditioner I ordered from Cool Daze on April 1 is not performing according to specifications. (See purchase and delivery documents attached.) After I called your 800 number, your Mr. Wally Cranks came and inspected the unit. He determined the problem is an internal defective seal,[1] and he recommended replacement with a new unit. (See the copy of his report attached.)[2]

When I called your office on April 20, Mr. William Chatter said you have no units in stock, and don't have any scheduled for production until fall. He said you do have several Model 3755As available at $500 more.

Since the weather is already heating up, I suggest we settle this one of two ways:[3]

(1) Cool Daze supply and install the Model 3755A at no additional cost to me, or

(2) You remove the air conditioner from our roof and immediately refund our money.

Please respond by May 15.[4]

Thank you.

Sincerely,

Kim Beerli

(1) Identify problem. (2) Give history and/or facts. (3) Offer solutions. (4) Give response time frame.

Complaint about a Neighborhood Dog

Mr. Backus:

I'm writing after leaving several messages on your telephone answering machine. As I stated, I have a real concern about the safety of our children given the fact that your dog, Bunky, has jumped the fence around your yard several times and displays a vicious nature. My daughter, Karen, who is five years old, is terrified to pass by your yard because of Bunky's ferocious barking and efforts to jump over the fence.

Please call me this evening after 6:30 p.m. to arrange a time to discuss this. I'm sure you'll agree this matter needs our immediate cooperative attention. Surely we can come up with a satisfactory solution.

Sincerely,

Annette Korslund

Overcharge Complaint and Refund Request

Dear Rose:

As we discussed on the phone, the insurance company was overcharged $1,000 on my August 15 annual checkup billing.[1] I have notified the insurance company, and am copying them with this letter.

Thank you for taking care of this immediately, and for refunding the overcharge of $1,000 to Friends' Insurance.[2]

Sincerely,

Carole Sparrow

(1) State the problem. (2) Ask for action.

Incorrect Item Returned for Credit

Dear Teddy:

Shock and awe—as I stated on the telephone—are what I experienced when I opened the parcel I received today. Not only is the silk dress the wrong color (I ordered sage and received saffron), but also it's not a size 8 but a size 18. The real problem, as I stated, is that I must wear the dress next Saturday.

Please immediately ship the dress I ordered at no charge. I'm returning this one today in its original packaging with the provided label.

Thank you.

Sincerely,

Cecilia Shook

Overcharge Complaint and Resolution

Jim:

I believe, as I stated on the telephone, it was a simple error. I came to you as part of the PubClub, and under your agreement to offer members a special website creation fee package of $1,500. So, when I got your invoice for $3,200, I was shocked.

I know I'll be making routine changes to my website, and want to continue working with you. I'm sending a check for the $1,500 payment, as we agreed. And thank you for a great online image.

Sincerely,

Susan Webber

Protesting Erroneous Charge on Billing Statement

REFERENCE: Bank Credit Card
#34-34456-4445

Expiration Date 05/12/09

Dear Customer Service Manager:

The charge #23 for $95 that appears on my current statement (see attached) is in error, and I hereby dispute it.

As you will notice, the next item, #24, is a charge for Scissors Salon services in the amount of $78. The clerk overcharged me for a "sparkle" and hair cut, and then rewrote the charge slip, but obviously failed to destroy the errant one. (The charges are for the same date and time.)

Thank you for contacting Scissors Salon to correct this error and for crediting my account.

Sincerely,

Brenda Schaak

Protesting Credit Denial for Returned Parts

REFERENCE: Account #19778,

Jennifer A. Watts, Watco

Dear Mrs. Calvin:

My monthly statement dated October 30 still shows the item #33 for the three dozen computer parts. These parts were returned on August 10. I'm enclosing another copy of the receipt your Mr. Bill Denson marked and signed when he received the returned parts.

Please send a corrected statement showing that I have been credited with the $89.99 for the parts and I will remit a check for the balance owed.

Thank you.

Sincerely,

Sue Atkinson

Complaint about Damage and Request for Resolution

REFERENCE: Move on September 15, 10:00 a.m. to 5:00 p.m., from 110 West Trinchera Peak to 2340 Sundown Mountain Drive, Littleton, Colorado, for Walt and Mary Downs

Dear Mr. Richman:

As I stated on the telephone today, there were a number of problems with our move by Westward Ho:[1]

1. The packing slips were changed to indicate scratches and dents that were not on the original slips (see the copies of two sets of slips enclosed);
2. A drawer that belongs to the antique credenza (see photo) is missing;
3. The Chinese screen was somehow crushed, ruining the surface; and
4. The white brocade sofa received a number of stains that my cleaning consultant, Mr. Cloudy Oils, says will not come out.[2]

Mr. Richman, as I told you, these damages amount to over $12,000. (See the value, repair, cleaning statements, and estimates listed on the attached sheet, and the estimate copies enclosed.) I have also enclosed statements from two antique authorities who saw the items the day Westward Ho packed them, and have since examined the damage.

Please fax me your damage claim form, and I will immediately complete it and fax it back to you today. I'm sure you will agree that arriving at an equitable settlement by October 15 will be an advantage to both of us.[3]

Thank you.

Sincerely,

May Michelle Riley

(1) State the problem. (2) Present the facts. (3) Ask for action.

(Also see APOLOGY, page 306; REQUEST FOR PAYMENT ADJUSTMENT, page 345; and OPINION EDITORIAL, page 402.)

47 DISAGREEMENT & DISPUTE

Disagreements arise in every relationship. Unsnarling and resolving them before they become major disputes are true tests not only of communication skills, but also of the code of ethics and character of the people involved. The steps to satisfactory resolution are often simple, except when emotions and ego intervene. To defuse the emotional component in a conflict and set the stage for resolution, it's important to communicate calmly and clearly that you are determined to work out a fair and equitable solution. And mean it.

DECIDE TO WRITE

Common areas where disagreements and disputes arise include:

- Written contracts of all kinds (employment, union, client, customer, rentals, home purchase, contractor, subcontractor, literary agent, publishing, etc.)
- Verbal agreements (contracts)
- Orders and sales
- Delivery of services or products
- Schedule of payments
- Employee, employer relations
- Government requirements and policies
- Land use and property lines
- Neighborhood living
- Friendships
- Family issues and inheritance

RESEARCH

- Review the terms of the original agreement.
- Collect any additional information that could have an impact on the agreement (e.g., terms of a preceding contract, relevant laws, current practice, settlements, opinions, and/or resolutions; legal documents, such as property boundaries, etc.).
- Empathize and review the beliefs and opinions held by the other person or party.

THINK ABOUT CONTENT

- Allow yourself to vent in writing if your emotions are elevated.
  - ▸ Sit down, put your pen to a sheet of paper, and without lifting the point, write it all out. Begin with "I'm so upset because . . ." Be sure to include the part about how you feel you've been wronged or injured, and what you're feeling as a result.
  - ▸ In the solitude of your own office, and out of earshot of others, read aloud what you've written (in full voice and expression, if you like).
  - ▸ Tear up your letter after reading it.
  - ▸ Take some deep breaths, and, if you're still feeling less than calm, take a walk or do something fun.
  - ▸ When you feel calm and able to be objective, try to open yourself to the position of the other person's point of view.

- Start over. Communicate, dispassionately, with the other party. State that you are researching and/or considering the matter and will be back in contact on a specific date, if necessary.
- Write your response in a timely manner after your initial emotions have cooled and you are able to be objective.
- Open on a positive note: "Jim, I'm sure we both want to resolve this problem. . . ." or "Dick, I know you to be very fair, and I know you will work with me to resolve this problem. . . ."
- State your points of agreement: "I know we agree that the number of light fixtures originally ordered was . . ." "I'm sure we both want to arrive at the same end result: a fair resolution."
- State your point of view, position, or side of the argument and what you want, complete with relevant supporting facts, documentation, sources, law, and other relevant information. Do it in a calm, factual, and rational manner: "What follows here is my experience . . ."
- Ask the other person for input whenever possible: "This is how I see the matter. Please give me your views . . ."
- Offer a solution—with several alternatives, if possible. This step is likely to find more receptivity if it includes compromise from both sides: "Jane, it seems there are several possible resolutions . . ."
- Allow the reader to save face by stating what you want as an end result in a manner that makes him or her appear generous, powerful, gracious, and willing to negotiate and/or compromise: "With a single word from you, this can be resolved" or "Would you be willing to settle the matter?" or "What, then, do you propose?"
- State when you will contact the reader, or request a response by a certain date: "I'll contact you on Wednesday after you've had the opportunity to consider the alternatives" or "Please get back to me by Wednesday with your decision."
- Conclude with a goodwill statement that includes your wish to have a good relationship in the future: "I'm sure that by putting our two reasonable heads together, we can come to a

negotiated solution that will allow us to pursue our usual mutually beneficial relationship in the future" or "I'm certain you will give this the kind of consideration that has earned you a reputation for working out fair and equitable solutions."

- Test your letter: (1) give it a little breathing time, then reread it aloud to check the tone; and (2) ask a couple of objective experts in the matter to read your letter. (If there are possible legal consequences, ask an attorney to read it and give you an opinion.)

ELIMINATE WRONG MESSAGES

- It's important to remember that your foremost objective is to reach a solution; it is not to seek revenge or get even. Eliminate inflammatory words or phrases such as *outrageous, wrong, ridiculous, unacceptable, insulting, egregious, unfair, no way,* and *resounding no.*
- Refrain from using personal pronouns in an accusatory manner: "You said that the total fee would be . . ." or "You acted unprofessionally." Instead, use positive or neutral statements of fact whenever possible: "On page two, the fee is stated as . . ."
- Concentrate on keeping to objective statements of fact, and solutions. Don't, for example, use "I" or "me" phrases like "I believe this is unfair" or "Others agree with me that I've been treated unjustly."

CONSIDER SPECIAL SITUATIONS

- There are situations where you will not want to compromise or negotiate. In such a case, state your position, then soften it somewhat by appealing to the reader's sense of fairness: "I request a full refund of $550.00. I believe you'll agree that this is a reasonable resolution."
- Because we live in a litigious society, caution must be exercised in writing your letter. Assume that what you write may end up in a court of law, and if you don't want to defend it, don't write it. If there is any possibility that your statements may be actionable, consult legal counsel before sending your letter.
- Red flags that indicate the disagreement is escalating beyond a retractable point include statements of accusation, statements of admission, or threats of legal action. This is the time to seek legal counsel, and/or request arbitration by a third, mutually agreed-upon, independent party. Unfortunately, these situations often involve personal matters, such as the division of a family estate; marriage dissolution; business partnership dissolutions; child custody issues; matters of guardianship of a dependent; or when types of legal action are threatened or initiated by another person.
- Letters to the editor of the newspaper disagreeing with a political position, public policy, proposed law, or social issue will be most effective if you quote the other party's published statement and source, then make your objection in rational, well-documented terms. Often you will be able to post your comments or opinions online directly on the website where the position, policy, or proposed law has been discussed, and/or on a social media website.

- Letters to policy makers expressing your views can be effectively handled if you reference and quote the published policy and source, and clearly state your dissenting view or position objectively and with careful documentation.
- Create your own blog or web page on a social media website, and build an audience of people who share your views. Use these venues and email alerts to inform them of public policy discussions or pending decisions or laws, and request that they join in a letter-writing campaign. This can be effective in giving voice to your shared views and getting public policy changed, or in initiating a group (class) legal action.

SELECT A FORMAT

- Letters of a financial, personal, or personnel nature should be sent by email only when you are responding through an organization's secure online system and there is an established policy to do so. Otherwise, send such communications by registered mail.
- Disagreements and disputes of a personal nature are best handled in a handwritten letter. Whether you use personal stationery, full-sized letterhead, or a personal note card will depend upon the nature and length of your communication. (A note card denotes a more personal and informal communication; a small letterhead an informal one; and a full-sized letterhead one that is a bit more formal in nature.)
- For business or legal disagreements or disputes, type your response on full-sized letterhead (8½ by 11 inches), and send it by registered mail in a legal-sized envelope.

USE POWERFUL WORDS

appeal	compromise	determine	discover
discuss	negotiate	objective	offer
propose	resolve	satisfy	solution

CONSTRUCT EFFECTIVE PHRASES

a win-win solution	accommodate both parties
agree to a compromise	an equitable solution
avoid further disagreement	come to terms with
I do not disclaim the fact that	do please consider the following
I am willing to settle the matter	I estimate the loss to be
in the interest of resolution	in total and complete repayment (settlement)
move toward resolution	my understanding of the matter
our future mutually beneficial relationship	perhaps you were not aware of the fact that
please consider the following facts	the agreed settlement will consist of
the disputed points	the points remaining to be resolved
to resolve the matter completely	we agree to resolve the matter completely
work toward a compromise	your reputation for dealing fairly

WRITE STRONG SENTENCES

I'm sure we can reach a compromise.

I am willing to absorb the cost of the replacement of part of the order.

I can move in the direction of excusing the extra work time involved to complete the replacement.

I know you to be a very reasonable person.

There is no reason we can't settle this matter between us and remain friends.

I refuse to let this cost us our friendship.

I believe we can both agree to move slightly from our current positions in the interest of settling this matter.

I would be very willing to have this matter arbitrated by a mutually approved independent party.

Please let me know if you will accept these terms and agree that the matter is now settled in full.

I can negotiate on three of the items you have listed.

I am willing to settle the matter if you will repay me in the amount of $5,200 for the cost of having the work redone. (My receipt for services is enclosed.)

There are several ways, which I will list here, we may go to resolve this matter.

I have documented what happened with the attached copies.

It seems we have reached an impasse, so I shall now take the matter up with your superior at Tress, Mr. Ralph Suitor.

I believe we have been able to agree on all but one item of your proposed resolution.

CREATE EFFECTIVE PARAGRAPHS

Let's settle this matter immediately. I'll reduce my claim by $5,500 if you'll increase your offer by the same amount, for a total settlement amount of $10,500 to be awarded to me immediately. This isn't just fair; it's also prudent. With this resolution, neither of us will have to engage an attorney, which would, in the end, be much more costly and far less satisfactory. What do you say?

While we can still be friends, I suggest that we agree to chalk up the incident of the wrecked rental car to "one of life's unfortunate accidents," and agree to split the outstanding bill equally between us. That seems to me the only rational way to settle the dispute, since we will never agree on degrees of culpability and who owes the greater amount.

If we can't agree to put the past behind us and act like adults responsible for the care and upbringing of Alicia, neither of us will "win," and she will most definitely lose. So, for her sake, I've decided not to continue to fight for sole custody. Instead, I've come up with a schedule for shared custody that I hope you'll find as fair as I've tried to make it. Please look it over carefully, and let me know if you suggest any adjustments, and if you will agree to it.

Okay, Rachel, as I see it, we can take your approach, and start down the path of legal action, as you suggest, or we can accept the settlement offer, as I prefer, and end the whole matter right here. I've reviewed our situation thoroughly with three leading attorneys who specialize in personal injury cases, and I've attached three transcripts of those discussions. Please review them, and then let's talk about this again. But I must tell you that I think the settlement amount is fair, and I'm unwilling to submit myself to the emotional toll this kind of litigation would require.

Archie, this is crazy. After ten years as business partners, who remembers who brought the pencil sharpener when we went into business? If you think it was you, take it. I suggest we settle the division of the remaining office equipment by having an appraiser come in and put a value on each item. Then we can take turns picking those items we each want (adding values to come out as near equal as possible). For the stuff left over, we can sell and equally split the proceeds.

Let's not let this disagreement escalate. I suggest we ask Jimmy to cast the deciding vote in selecting the investment vehicles for Dad. Jimmy's the expert. I'm totally against dividing the assets at this point and each of us investing half, as you suggest. The capital this money can earn, if properly invested, can be used to take care of Dad for as long as he needs care. What do you say, Billy?

Rose, you said you thought Mom's house should have brought more, and your share should have been more than $65,000. It was your desire that I take charge of selling the house and the contents, and I did that to the best of my ability. I won't haggle about this.

We are all we have left. Please tell me what amount you think your share should be, and I'll write you a check for that amount.

You are absolutely right: your check for $765 was credited to the wrong account. The error has been corrected. Please view the change in your account balance owed online.

We appreciate your help in resolving this dispute quickly. Please accept our apologies for this error and the inconvenience it caused you.

You were right. The books you shipped us were from our warehouse, and the amount of the disputed bill you received has been credited to your account. My apologies for our error in this matter. Please accept the enclosed coupon for $50 off your next purchase from Blunders Books, Inc.

Employment Dispute

Dear Ms. Jitters:

As I stated in my letter disputing the amount of my paycheck for last week, Reddy Boot can confirm that my overtime was authorized and that I am entitled to be paid at the time-and-a-half rate for the additional 30 hours.[1] The total amount still owed is $1,500 ($45 per hour for 30 hours.) Please issue my check for that amount today.[2]

Sincerely,

Jack Boxer

(1) State the dispute clearly. (2) Ask for action.

Rental Payment Dispute

Dear Jack:

As I stated on the telephone, our agreement on the rental lease for the house at 3222 Winchester, Darby, CO, on July 1, 2011, was that we would purchase paint and supply the labor to paint the house interior, and the amount of $1,500 would be returned to us with our security deposit of $2,500—a total of $4,000—at the end of the lease term.

I've enclosed a copy of our agreement, and a copy of the receipt for paint and supplies purchased a year ago. I'm prepared to file a claim in small claims court if we do not receive your check for that amount within the legal period by the end of next week.

Sincerely,

Ginger Scammed

Family Disagreement

Dear Jim Bob,

Thanks for your note expressing concern about Mom and Dad. Yes, now that Dad has been diagnosed with Alzheimer's and his behavior has dictated that he needs to be in a care facility for his and Mom's safety, there will need to be some immediate changes in their living arrangements.

But, while I agree their living situation must be changed, I firmly disagree that we need to step in and make their decisions for them, take over their finances, and move them to an assisted living community.

While Dad is now unable to be involved in the decision making, Mom is fully capable of making these decisions and has expressed her desire to do so. (I believe her direct words were "Butt out.") Our job, as I see it, is to offer as much emotional support and hands-on help as will assist her through this very difficult time. (Difficult for all of us, to be sure.)

Mom and I have surveyed all the suitable facilities for Dad in the area where she wants to live. There are precious few, as it turns out. We selected the best one, and Dad will be admitted to Shady Meadows in Grand Plains tomorrow. Mom will pay for his care from their savings.

Mom wants to sell the house and buy a suitable townhome within a few miles of where Dad will be. I will certainly help her through that process. I will also help Mom arrange for a mover, and help with packing and moving.

I've suggested to Mom that she use several services for home maintenance for things I can't cover from this distance. She has promised that she will take a driver's refresher course since she hasn't been driving. (I'll set that up this week.)

As to her finances, Mom probably is more frugal than we are. We'd probably both benefit from her budget advice.

Please give all this your careful consideration. Mom has promised to ask for help when she needs it, and I firmly believe what I've covered here will work well for the foreseeable future.

All the best,
Cheryl

Failure to Pay Warranty Claim

REFERENCE: B&H Paint Failure, Claim #45562[1]

Dear Sam:

I'm sure we both want to get this dispute settled as quickly as possible, and without further negotiation. We've discussed your response to our initial claim. It isn't acceptable. Here's what we're prepared to do.

First, I'll review the facts as I stated in my call:[2] (1) the pigment on the B&H paint for our home exterior was unstable, so the south-facing exterior wall is discolored and has seriously deteriorated. (2) B&H warranty states (see attached copy, Exhibit 1) that the product and cost of application will be covered completely in the case of paint failure. (3) B&H's representative inspected our home exterior and agreed to supply the paint and cover the labor of repainting the south side of the house only, or a total payment of $2,500. (See Exhibit 2.)

Since the other three sides of the house covered by B&H also failed to hold the color (though the fade and deterioration are considerably less), we requested enough paint for complete coverage and a check from B&H for the total labor cost for repainting of $9,900. (See Exhibit 3.)

The B&H representative, Ron Grinch, told us after his inspection that B&H would pay only $2,500 in labor costs, and would supply enough new paint to cover the entire house. (See Exhibit 4.)

In the interest in getting this resolved, we are prepared to settle the matter for $7,500 for labor and enough replacement paint to cover the entire house with two coats, if this can be settled no later than Friday of next week.[3] We have checked with our homeowners' insurance agent, and he stated that ours is "a generous offer." (See Exhibit 5.)

Please consult with your committee members, as we agreed. I'll call you Tuesday to learn your final decision. If you agree to this, we want to receive your check for $7,500 and 45 gallons of "Tobacco" B&H's Best Exterior Paint by next Friday, April 15, 2011.[4]

Sincerely,
Steve and Susie Swindled

---

(1) Identify dispute. (2) State the problem clearly. (3) Offer resolution. (4) Ask for action and set a time frame.

(Also see APOLOGY, page 306; COMPLAINT & PROTEST, page 282; and REFUSAL, page 274.)

48 NEGOTIATION

While negotiating is often approached with all the transparency of playing a hand of poker, your objective shouldn't be to bluff the other party or parties in order to win the result you want and insure that the other party loses. It's more about win-win. Your objective should be to carefully consider all the factors and to arrive, together, at a solution that will leave all parties as satisfied as possible.

Much of this process will be conducted verbally. Often it's wise to wait to commit the items of a negotiation to writing until: (1) the points of negotiation have been clarified, (2) possible solutions have been identified, (3) possible concessions are offered or requested, and/or (4) final terms and details are being considered, debated, and recorded.

Usually the final discussion will take the form of a letter containing proposed terms (and then counter proposals) spelled out. The final negotiated agreement may be a simple letter stating all the details; a formal agreement; a contract; or a legal document of settlement. (See Disagreement & Dispute, page 291, and Settlement, page 303.)

DECIDE TO WRITE

Skills of negotiation are essential any time two or more people are involved. Some very common situations with important consequences include:

- Contract terms of agreement
- Sales, purchases, and payment terms
- Product orders and delivery schedules
- Working arrangements
- Neighborhood living
- Change orders

RESEARCH

- Gather as many related facts about the other negotiator(s) as possible: strengths, weaknesses, financial standing (if important), past similar negotiations and outcomes, etc.
- Research all aspects of similar transactions to discover how you may best approach your own situation.
- Approach the process with openness and a willingness to compromise.

BEGIN THE PROCESS

- Define—only for your own review at this stage—the optimal list of the elements that you want to achieve; and then create your acceptable list of those elements (or take-aways) that you will accept. Use these headings to create two lists.
- Ask the other negotiator(s) to list the elements she/he wants to achieve. (This may be done verbally or in writing.)
- Propose using a mutually agreed-upon arbitrator (third, independent party) should the negotiations stall or become overly adversarial.
- Listen (or read) the other negotiator(s) list(s) carefully, and always ask for clarification when in doubt.
- Indicate that you've heard (and/or understand) the negotiator(s) by restating his or her elements listed.
- Make a statement of goodwill and your desire for a win-win resolution.
- State your optimal and/or acceptable list of elements. (This is usually best done by starting the process with only your optimal list, unless you have already ascertained that this will stall or stop the process entirely.)
- Engage the other party in a process of creative brainstorming that may open the door to possible new alternatives or solutions.
- Offer your concessions and request concessions from the other negotiator(s) verbally, or in writing.
- Debate areas of non-agreement, maintaining a spirit of give-and-take.
- Close the negotiations with a written list of the compromised elements upon which you've both agreed.
- Give yourself and the other negotiator(s) time to reflect on the compromised elements, if necessary. (Sometimes a letter of agreement, which is signed by all parties, is in order.)

ELIMINATE WRONG MESSAGES

- Early in the process, avoid words that reflect inflexibility, such as *insist*, *non-negotiable*, and *deal-breaker*.
- Using a heavy-handed or negative attack doesn't usually work: "You're not willing to compromise."
- Issuing ultimatums like "This is my final offer" can backfire.
- Avoid, when possible, statements that inflame emotions, like "I'm making all the concessions here" or "You aren't making a good-faith effort."

CONSIDER SPECIAL SITUATIONS

- When emotions become elevated, allow a cooling-off period or time-out of several days or a week before resuming discussions. But be sure to set a restart date.
- When negotiations stall or discussions become incendiary, initiate the use of an arbitrator.

SELECT A FORMAT

- When there is an established policy to do so, emails containing financial, personal, or personnel information should be sent only after proper authorization and only on an organization's secure system.
- Send communications via fax only after agreement by the party(ies) involved.
- Business or legal negotiations should be typed on letterhead stationery (8½ by 11 inches) and sent by registered mail.
- Negotiations of a personal nature may be written on personal and small stationery or full-sized letterhead.

USE CAREFULLY CHOSEN WORDS

accept	agree	alternative	compromise
concession	consider	equal	fair
gain	offer	reasonable	satisfy
solution	substitute	suggest	value

CONSTRUCT EFFECTIVE PHRASES

a better and more satisfactory solution may be

accommodate both parties

both end up satisfied

give the following concessions

offer to negotiate these terms

please give this careful consideration

a win-win solution

an equitable arrangement

come to agreeable terms

of equal value to both of us

please consider this alternative

possible resolutions may include

WRITE STRONG SENTENCES

I believe we can reach an equitable compromise.

Thank you for offering your list of concessions.

I feel your points of concession are most generous.

I believe we are both determined to reach a happy resolution.

I want us both to be satisfied with this agreement.

There remains only an item or two to negotiate.

I think we're almost there.

There are several ways I'll list here to suggest how we may come to an amicable agreement.

CREATE EFFECTIVE PARAGRAPHS

If you can see your way clear to offer me the pick of the litter from your bitch, "Sally," I will forego my usual breeding fee and agree to the deal. Is this agreeable to you?

I do hope you can allow our family to pay for Rachael's lunches each week instead of the required quarterly pre-payment requirement. I believe I've explained why we need to have this alternate agreement in place.

I can't take on the volunteer commitment as required in the agreement you sent. I can, however, commit to drive the after-school program bus for the children every Tuesday and

Thursday. I've made those alterations on the agreement, and I've signed it. Please let me know if Mr. Brown can use me on this basis.

If you can raise your salary offer by $15,000 per year guaranteed, I will accept the expanded territories of New Mexico, Utah, and Arizona. Under this arrangement, I would receive the same bonus percentage payments on total sales volume offered in your original employment contract. If this is agreeable to Master Quirks, I believe we've reached a win-win agreement.

We are willing to be reasonable on this, Jim, but your offer to settle our insurance claim for $500 for the loss of our credenza, desk, and Chinese screen isn't fair. Here are the value estimates (attached) that I received from the appraiser (her qualifications are also attached): credenza replacement value, $4,500; desk, $750; Chinese screen, $9,500. That's a total of $14,750. We are willing to accept the amount of $14,000 as payment in full if we can get a check for this amount by April 15.

Personal Response to Neighbor

Dear Dirk:

Sue and I want to be reasonable and reach an agreement with you, but your demand that we turn off our air conditioner each day at 4:00 p.m. so you and Alice may enjoy sitting on your deck without our air conditioner running just isn't possible.[1] This is the exact time when the heat buildup in our home requires that we run the air conditioner.

After much consideration and discussions with a couple of experts, we'd like to suggest two possibilities: (1) we are willing to install a sound-reducing housing around our air conditioner; and/or (2) we suggest you build a sound barrier on the side of your deck.[2]

I'd be happy to show you the plan for the housing (see attached bid for $500). We are willing to put $500 into this project to try to reduce the present noise level of the unit.

We look forward to hearing your response.[3]

Regards,

Ted and Sue

(1) State your willingness to negotiate. (2) Offer possible solutions.
(3) Close on a positive note.

Shared Fence

Dear Joey and Trix:

We're sure you will agree that the fence between our yards is in need of replacement. We would like to negotiate with you to install a new one.

We have obtained three bids, as I mentioned to you on the telephone, for the total replacement of the fence around our entire yard, and just the section between our two yards will cost $1,200 to replace. (We have samples of the replacement materials, which are exactly like those in the existing fence, and the proposal, if you wish to see either.)

We propose that we pay $700 of the cost since we are requesting the fence, and that you pay $500. This payment would be made directly to the contractor, due on April 1, when the materials are delivered and construction begins.

Please let us know if this is agreeable to you by March 2, so we may get on the installer's schedule.

Sincerely,

Buck and Eddie

Assisted Care for an Elderly Parent

Dear Mr. Soldier:

My mother would like to reserve the two bedroom unit in Restive Acres, if we can arrive at an agreement concerning the following points: (1) each morning between 10:00 and 11:00 a.m., a female personal care assistant will help her with personal hygiene, dressing, medications, and breakfast preparation at no additional charge; (2) Restive Acres will forego the $250 per month unit cleaning fee, as my mother has relatives in the city who will do this for her; and (3) Mother be allowed to have her cat in the unit if she puts down a security deposit of $200.

Additionally, my mother would like to have Restive Acres waive the requirement that she eat one meal each day in the dining room.

We await your response, and hope that we can reach a mutually beneficial agreement.

Regards,

Mason Bent

(Also see DISAGREEMENT & DISPUTE, page 291; and SETTLEMENT, page 303.)

Employment Salary and Benefit Package

Dear Mr. Meech:

I'd like to counter your proposed salary and benefit package offer for the sales manager position with the following, which I believe you will agree allows us both to come out in the winner's circle:

- Squeeze & Company pay me $115,000 per year (instead of the proposed $90,000);
- I will forego enrollment in the company's medical insurance coverage plan;
- I receive an added annual bonus of 2% on net sales.

I believe this will allow both Squeeze & Company and me to receive the maximum benefit from our relationship. I'm hoping you and Rob agree, and we can finalize our employment contract and begin a working relationship.

I, and my family, look forward to hearing your response. I am very eager to join the Squeeze & Company team.

Sincerely,

Mike Glad

49 SETTLEMENT

A settlement agreement or statement is a tidy way to seal a deal and avoid any further discussion or litigation. It often comes after intense negotiations and defines the final payment or division of assets. It simply says the matter has reached a conclusion. Often the phrase "in full and final settlement" or "in full and final payment" is part of the verbiage used to make this fact crystal clear. (Also see Negotiation, page 298.)

DECIDE TO WRITE

This agreement is commonly used to resolve disputes resulting from:

- Cohabitation
- Failed business partnerships
- Family inheritance
- Insurance claims
- Outstanding debt
- Prenuptials
- Real estate transactions (The settlement statement, or the closing statement, is the document that gives a complete breakdown of all the costs in a real estate transaction, and indicates whether the seller or buyer pays them.)

RESEARCH

- Review the original agreement.
- Collect all related information that has an impact on the agreement; for example, relevant laws and restrictions, current practice, legal documents, related financial debts and expenditures, infractions by the other party(ies), and so on.
- Consult an attorney and/or local and state officials concerning any other restrictions and/or requirements involved, and to assess your legal rights and obligations.

THINK ABOUT CONTENT

- Any efforts at settlement should come only after you have taken time to reflect on and assess the situation, and you have allowed yourself to grieve and/or vent any feelings of anger and loss. This is best accomplished by writing out your feelings for your own private review and evaluation.

- Whenever emotions are elevated, be sure to allow a cooling-off period before continuing the drafting of your settlement agreement.
- In our litigious society, you must use caution in writing your settlement agreement. It's important to remember that your statement can end up in a court of law. Consult legal counsel if you are uncertain.
- An equitable settlement requires objectivity and sometimes this is impossible for the parties involved. In this case, a third, impartial party should be consulted to give input and assistance.

ELIMINATE WRONG MESSAGES

- To reach a settlement, it's necessary to renounce revenge. (Remember, if you conclude a very difficult agreement or relationship, you have won!)
- Eliminate inflammatory words that will rekindle conflict.

CONSIDER SPECIAL SITUATIONS

- When you are owed a debt and no longer wish to negotiate, you may be best served by offering to settle the matter for less than the outstanding balance. In this case, initiate the resolution by stating you will forgive interest on the debt and even some of the principal if paid on your schedule or in whole by a stated date. This may allow you to recover something and eliminate further collection costs.
- If you owe a debt you are unable to pay in full, you might propose a settlement. This can have the benefit of stopping further damage to your credit, and it could restore your ability to purchase supplies for your business, for example. It's important in this case to offer the other party something of value, if at all possible.

SELECT A FORMAT

- Use email only when you are communicating on an organization's secure online system, all parties have agreed to do so, and there is an established policy that allows it. Otherwise, send your statement by registered mail.
- Personal settlements may be handwritten on personal stationery or on full-sized letterhead (8½ by 11 inches).
- Business or legal settlements are usually typed on full-sized letterhead or legal sheets (8½ by 13 inches), and are sent by registered mail. They may also be emailed or faxed.

USE POWERFUL WORDS

agree	careful	complete	consideration
dissolve	divide	equitable	final
full	negotiated	resolve	settle

CONSTRUCT EFFECTIVE PHRASES

after in-depth negotiations
the final disposition of
this ends our relationship as
to dissolve the partnership
to equitably divide the assets
to settle the matter in full
we agree not to divulge details of this dispute
we agree to resolve the matter completely and finally
we will not disclose the details of this settlement agreement
with due consideration of

WRITE STRONG SENTENCES

I believe this is a fair and equitable division of the remaining assets.
Each party shall receive an equal amount of the liquidated estate.
All parties shall share equally in the proceeds.
The following list is settlement in full of this dispute.
The final division of remaining assets shall be made on the basis of each party's percentage of ownership in the company.
In full consideration of the initial capital investments of the parties involved, this settlement defines the distribution of the remaining assets of Mickey Motor.
The final settlement can only be made after all outstanding expenses have been paid.
I am willing to settle the matter in full for $4,445 if you will have a certified check for that amount in my office by 8:00 a.m. on Friday, March 24, 2011.

BUILD EFFECTIVE PARAGRAPHS

After our many discussions, here's the settlement statement. The three heirs, William, Cary, and James, will divide equally the 900 shares of Capital stock. Each heir will receive 300 shares.

In full and final settlement of the outstanding debt of $10,500 incurred by Squeakers, Charles Baker will repay the amount of $6,500 to Checkers Corp.; and Joan Dithers will repay the amount of $4,000 to Racey Inc.

The following listing is a complete and final settlement statement for the disposition of the remaining equipment at Dolly's Deli.

Personal Cohabitation Dissolution Settlement Statement: With the signatures of both parties, Ruth Ann Bittles, and Bobby Ray Effel, the attached list of the items and designated distribution is hereby agreed to by both. This represents the total claims and assets subject to consideration in this dissolution. [Complete listing of the property items to be awarded to each of these people follows.]

50 APOLOGY

Writing an apology takes a pen, a contrite and brave heart, and a desire to make a positive change in your behavior. Civilized society is based on the agreement to not harm each other. But sometimes we do harm those around us—by acts of omission or commission. Opening the door to healing those hurts and restoring a relationship requires that we effectively apologize.

A true apology is an act of moral courage. It takes strength of character. You must demonstrate remorse, take responsibility for the offense, show empathy for the person harmed, and be willing to remedy the wrong you did to another. Apologizing may mean you admit such things as a personal weakness, a failure, a mistake and/or an act of wrongdoing. It may also require that you express your guilt, shame, and remorse in order to create the possibility for true forgiveness.

A written apology can be more effective than a verbal apology because it allows both you (the offender) and the reader (the offended) to reflect upon, absorb, and react after careful consideration. It underscores your sincerity. It can help to diffuse heightened emotions, and it can allow you the opportunity to be completely heard.

DECIDE TO WRITE

Offenses that require apologies may range from trivial to very serious. They may be personal, social, or of a business or public nature. Some require legal action.

Some common everyday offenses include such things as:

- Not responding to an invitation or request in a timely manner
- Taking for granted the opinions or views of another person
- Treating someone unfairly (consciously or unconsciously)
- Making an error that affects someone else (billing, credit, shipping, accounting, etc.)
- Causing damage to someone's property
- Acting in a boorish or offensive manner
- Disseminating incorrect information that affects another person
- Making a statement that discredits another person
- Making insulting or insensitive comments
- Falsely accusing someone
- Exceeding personal boundaries
- Acting inappropriately or in an abusive manner toward another person: verbally, physically, sexually, etc.
- Lying to someone

THINK ABOUT HOW AND WHEN TO COMMUNICATE

- If you've offended someone, the apology process must start with a real sense of remorse and the desire on your part to make things right.

- Apologize in a timely manner—usually immediately—to avoid the possibility of a small offense growing into a long-lasting grudge. But there are times when waiting for a period of time is necessary to give your apology the weight it needs for the offense involved. Or, it may be necessary to wait to first allow the offended person an opportunity to express how the offense affected him or her, so you completely understand before writing your apology.

- Be sure your apology measures up to the offense and its consequences.

- For minor offenses, like failing to introduce a friend during a conversation, bumping into someone on the sidewalk, failing to offer the courtesy of allowing an elderly person to precede you in line, or interrupting when someone else is talking, an immediate verbal apology is usually best and adequate.

- For social and business situations, like forgetting (and missing) a dinner party, breaking an item while a guest in someone's home, or making a customer billing error or credit mistake, a handwritten or typed (for business offenses) apology needs to be accompanied by a restorative act. If you missed a dinner party, for example, you may want to deliver a bouquet of flowers with your handwritten apology. If you have broken a vase while a guest, you need to replace it with one of equal value or work out another way to repay the debt.

- In business, when you have failed to issue a credit when one is due, you need to send a typewritten apology and include the credit issue. You may also need or want to call the person immediately to admit and correct the error, and/or offer the customer a token of recompense or goodwill, like a discount on a future purchase.

- For a serious offense, the apology needs to include something to restore the person. For example, if a banking customer's account was shorted years earlier, not only should the amount be restored to the account, but the customer also is due the interest the funds would have earned during that period. Perhaps other restorative steps are needed, too, depending on the circumstances.

- Sometimes apologizing in writing may seem cowardly because it allows you to avoid facing an embarrassing situation in person. If this is the case, it may be necessary to apologize face to face. And, perhaps, follow the verbal apology with a written one.

- It's important to remember that the measure of the apology needs to be in proper proportion to the offense. Not smaller, not bigger.

THINK ABOUT CONTENT

Offending someone robs the person of power or diminishes him or her. Apologizing gives that power back. It's this second exchange that allows the healing process to begin.

- **Write out your apology.** This allows you to examine why and how you offended someone, and to experience remorse. Writing words that express your regret and desire to make amends is an opportunity for real character growth. Reading your written apology allows the other person to process the offense.

- A genuine apology can also be a solution; it can eliminate the problem, and it can offer the opportunity to restore your relationship with the other person.
- **Acknowledge the offense** and accept responsibility for it.
  - ▸ State the offense and how you violated a moral code: "Lexy, yesterday Jim gave me credit for doing the Chase brochure you created. I should have corrected him immediately, but I didn't. . . ."
  - ▸ Accept responsibility without excusing yourself: "That was wrong of me."
  - ▸ Acknowledge how you injured the person. (This sometimes must be accompanied by an invitation for the person to express her injury and how it affected her.) Show empathy with the offended person: "Not correcting Jim immediately robbed you of the credit you deserve for such fine work."
- **Explain.** Give any extenuating but valid circumstances, if they exist, but don't create excuses for yourself: "Here's how it happened. Jim and I were talking in his office while he waited to be connected to Roger Graham in Chicago. Immediately after he credited me with your work, Roger came on the line . . ."
- **Communicate your regret.** This is key. Be sure to include a statement of your emotions of anxiety, sadness, guilt, and shame: "I'm ashamed of myself for not immediately emailing or phoning Jim to correct his impression. I didn't realize, of course, that he would put a credit in the employee newsletter. I believe that on some level I envied the great job you did, and when it was assumed that I'd done the brochure, I just didn't correct it. Lexy, I've called Jim and told him you deserve all the credit because it was totally your creative concept, copywriting, and execution. I also wrote a correction for the newsletter that will come out next week."
- **Make reparations.** An offense creates a debt that needs to be repaid. Often such repayment is symbolic, and the apology itself is the reparation—in part or in whole. But sometimes, to even the score, you need to replace what was lost or otherwise make amends: "Lexy, please also accept this bouquet as a token of my heartfelt apology. I've also recommended that you get the Leaf job, as you requested, because your work on the Chase brochure demonstrates that you have the right balance of creative talent and product knowledge needed to do the job."
- For major offenses—infidelity, chronic alcoholism, abuse, theft, etc.—a very strict plan for change in behavior and **restitution** must be part of the apology. This includes such things as a step-by-step plan by the offender and an organized plan by the offended (injured). Both plans need to include the corrective steps the offender must take before complete reconciliation can take place, if reconciliation ever does take place. This includes demonstrated behavior changes over time that must be achieved before a relationship is restored.
- **Offer an olive branch.** Reestablishing a relationship after an apology has been made and accepted may begin by the offender initiating an act of friendship. Restart communication

with a new or neutral topic, or offer an invitation to an event. Either of these approaches can help eliminate any remaining awkwardness. Sometimes a period of time is needed, too, before the relationship can be resumed.

ELIMINATE WRONG MESSAGES

- Don't make excuses. This detracts from your apology, or eliminates its effectiveness altogether.
- Don't offer a false apology that shifts responsibility to another (or the other) person. Here are some examples:
    - "Sorry." This tells the offended person you want to end the discussion, and/or close the subject immediately without really taking responsibility.
    - "I'm sorry you're upset" or "I'm sorry you feel that way" avoids taking responsibility, these statements place responsibility squarely back on the offended person. It infers the offended person is obviously too sensitive.
    - "You know I didn't mean it" and/or "You're trying to make me feel guilty" are statements that attempt to make the offended person feel responsible.
    - "I regard you as a friend. I would never intentionally hurt you." The offended person is left to conclude it is her fault she feels injured. She's obviously too thin-skinned, she misunderstood, or she attributed a mean or wrong motive where there was none.
    - "I wouldn't have done it if you hadn't . . ." This excuse aims at escaping responsibility and placing blame on the offended person.
    - "I know how you feel," "I see where you're coming from," or "I'm working to correct the situation . . ." When glibly offered, these statements avoid taking responsibility.
- Don't deny, trivialize, or dismiss your behavior if someone tells you he or she was offended. Offer, instead, to hear him or her out, and then offer your apology if you are culpable.
- Don't over-apologize, or apologize inappropriately. If you apologize automatically or when you are not responsible, you devalue your apology. You may be trying to please or placate. In business relationships, over-apologizing can brand you as incompetent.

CONSIDER SPECIAL SITUATIONS

- The process of apologizing for a personal offense is a dynamic transaction between two people. There's no guarantee of a particular outcome, and sometimes apologizing takes negotiation. It takes a commitment to the process to see it through to resolution.
- When your actions or words affect (or are heard by) more than one person, your apology needs to be made to all those involved: "Tim, I know you overheard my boorish comment criticizing the way Giles handled the Fisher problem. That was wrong of me, and I feel terrible about voicing such a criticism. I apologize both for the comment I made, and also because I neglected to first get all the facts. In the future, I promise to be far less critical and much more circumspect."

- In business situations, an apology that includes a complete written explanation is often needed to provide an accurate record of what happened.
- Sometimes, in situations that involve customer relations, it's important to apologize when you don't bear nearly as much responsibility for an error as the customer. For example, if an irate customer complains that she received five polka-dot dresses, instead of one, and you determine that the error occurred because the customer placed her order five times, you may need to write: "I'm sorry that an error occurred in your order. You are right; I should have called you to check the quantity of dresses you intended to purchase." In such a case, you may want to follow your apology with an explanation of proper ordering procedure, and close with a goodwill statement like "We look forward to continuing to serve you in supplying the latest-trend solutions to all your wardrobe needs."
- For customer apologies, effective use of discount coupons, gifts with purchase, entrance to special sales, valued-customer premiums, or other things may be included with your apology: "Along with our apology, please do accept the enclosed coupon for 20 percent off your next purchase."
- When your child offends, injures, or damages someone's property, apologies need to come both from you, as the responsible parent, and from your child (in an age-appropriate and situation-appropriate fashion): "Mr. Winters, I am so sorry that Nicky rode her bike through your flowerbed. She's not yet quite in control of her training wheels, and I was several steps behind her when I realized she was unable to stay on the sidewalk. I've tried to telephone you, but I have been unable to reach you. May we come over Friday at 3:30 p.m. with the replacement petunias, and so that Nicky can apologize in person?"
- When a major offense includes apologizing for a legally actionable offense, e.g., driving while drinking, causing an accident, theft, remarks that may be interrupted as sexual harassment, etc., you should first consult an attorney who specializes in the area of offense before writing your apology. It's important in such cases to carefully word your apology and include statements that indicate you are not only sorry for such behavior, but you will take corrective steps so that the behavior will not be repeated.

Ask for an Apology
- If you've been offended, and you want to heal and restore a relationship with the offender, you may need to ask for an apology.
  - ▸ First, give yourself some time to reflect or cool off if you're angry.
  - ▸ Write how you feel to the other person. (Don't accuse.)
  - ▸ Ask for an explanation or an apology: "I value our friendship, and I would like to resolve this" or "Would you think about this, and discuss it with me?" or "I believe you owe me an apology" or "I'd like to discuss the matter and learn how this happened in case I have misinterpreted something. . . ."
  - ▸ Don't avoid asking an offender for an apology. Allowing someone to continue to offend you tells the person you are weak. Instead, tactfully state how you feel: "I felt

insulted when you said . . ." or "Your statement troubled me. What did you mean when you said . . ."

 ▸ If the offender doesn't apologize and won't discuss the offense and try to work it out, you may decide to discontinue the relationship. Remember, the most common reasons people don't apologize are: (1) pride (fear of shame), (2) egocentricity, (3) fear of the offended person's retaliation, (4) fear of being rejected, and/or (5) fear there will be requirements to make amends.

 ▸ Act honorably and respectfully, and be compassionate and fair.

SELECT A FORMAT

• Business apologies are best typed on business letterhead when the letter is going to a customer, employee, client, or business colleague or associate.
• For personal apologies, use a personal note card or stationery, and handwrite your apology. Apology greeting cards are available, too, and may be appropriate for some situations, but don't fail to write your apology in your own words inside the card.

CHOOSE THE RIGHT WORD

accept	acknowledge	admit	apologize
callous	committed	conclude	confess
determine	failed	fault	mistake
offended	rectify	repair	repay
responsible	restore	tactless	thoughtless

BUILD EFFECTIVE PHRASES

am guilty of	bear the shame of it
can offer no explanation	can you find it in your heart
can't believe my own actions	cannot offer a viable explanation
correct the situation	distressed by my behavior
given the same situation again	I admit
I am responsible	I am so contrite
I can offer no excuse	I regret to inform you that
I reproach myself for	I take responsibility
I wish to apologize	I've offended you by
if do-overs were allowed	if it's any consolation
make amends	my intent was
never again will I	offer you this recompense
owe you an apology for	please allow me to make this right
promise to act very differently	repair the damage
sincerely regret	there is no logical reason for such behavior
will always live with the regret of	will compensate you for
will correct the matter by	wish to completely replace

WRITE STRONG SENTENCES

I apologize for my bad behavior.

I know I offended you, and I am so very sorry.

Please accept my apology.

There is no excuse for such boorishness.

Yes, if I had been in your shoes I would feel offended; I'm so sorry.

I'm so sorry I neglected to see the matter from your point of view.

I would like very much to hear how my insensitivity made you feel, if you care to tell me.

I know I hurt you, and I am thoroughly ashamed of myself.

I sincerely apologize.

I so regret my actions.

I can't explain with any reasonable explanation why I didn't respond better in the situation.

I'm so sorry my actions caused you such pain.

The error was completely my fault, and I apologize.

May I please have the opportunity to make things right?

If only I had acted honorably, things would have turned out much differently.

I know a simple "I'm sorry" may seem too easy, too weak.

Please don't give up on me.

I do promise to be more sensitive to your feelings in the future.

I can make this right, and I will.

I acted completely inappropriately.

The error was completely mine.

I certainly don't blame you for being angry with me for such behavior.

I do pledge to right this wrong.

I won't ever let you down by not allowing you to offer your opinion again.

I do hope you can forgive me for being so dense.

Yes, you are correct, the amount of the bill should have been $534.

It was wrong of me to take the credit.

Your complaint won't go unnoticed.

I'm sorry you were treated in such a rude manner, and I plan to correct the situation.

Yes, my son was completely out of line, and I apologize.

I will certainly correct our error, and restore the funds owed you.

We do apologize, and ask you to give us another chance to serve you better in the future.

Here's my plan for correcting the error.

I'm intent upon righting this injustice done to you.

With a contrite heart, I seek your forgiveness.

I acted completely out of jealousy; I apologize.

I owe you my sincere apology.

BUILD EFFECTIVE PARAGRAPHS

Most apologies are only a few sentences. Often saying more is less effective; few words can have more impact. The following paragraphs could be most or all of the apology:

Yes, Alycia, I did make that boorish comment. It was completely insensitive of me, I admit. I can only imagine how it hurt you, and I feel terrible about it. Please accept my sincere apology and my promise to be more sensitive in the future. (I've also apologized to Teddy, who I'm sure overheard it.)

Your complaint didn't go unnoticed. After careful research, I agree that we didn't meet our guarantee to replace any item damaged in shipment. I sincerely apologize for this failure, and want to assure you that the new tub will be delivered tomorrow morning between 9:00 a.m. and 11:00 a.m.

Please accept our sincere apology for this blatant error. This does not reflect our committed standard for delivery of services, and we will work with you to correct the situation to your satisfaction.

Roger, this is very difficult for me, as I'm sure you realize, but I wish to apologize from the bottom of my heart for not showing up for the ski trip at the designated time and place. I simply hit the snooze alarm, rolled over, and then didn't awaken until 9:30 a.m., long after everyone had returned home. I know I ruined the trip for all four of you, and I feel terrible about this. I've certainly learned my lesson: redemption doesn't hit the snooze button. (I'm sending a note to each of the other guys, too.) I know I can't entirely make this right, but please let me try to redeem myself by both driving and buying the lift tickets for all of you next Saturday.

Yes, you are due the contractor discount of 33 percent off the retail price. I apologize for this billing error. I forgot to inform accounting that you get that rate. Please accept my apology with this refund check of $987.

Trudy, my comments at yesterday's luncheon were petty, and I'm truly sorry. (Thank you for telling me exactly how you felt.) Please accept my apology.

I know there's only one chance to make a great first impression, and I blew it. Ben, I'm so sorry. I feel like a complete louse. I know you were looking forward to introducing me to Julia, and I still have no clue as to why I acted so badly. I apologize, and ask for your forgiveness. You have my promise, too, that such behavior won't ever be repeated by your big (and yesterday feckless) brother. (Please pass the enclosed apology note along to Julia.)

First of all, I must take responsibility for the error. I sent you the order before carefully reviewing my spec sheet and making sure I'd included all the parts we'll need. (I'd be happy to tell anyone else in your organization, if that will help, or please feel free to pass this letter on to others who were inconvenienced.) I apologize, and request that you order the drain assembly, Part #453A.

EDIT, EDIT, EDIT

- If in doubt, write your apology out in a rough draft first.
- Reread your apology and make any changes.
- Let it rest for a period of time.
- Reread it aloud to make a final check for tone before you send it.
- Give it verbally, then send it by mail unless there is a compelling reason that it must be emailed.

For an Error on the Op-Ed Page

Dear Miss Elder:

My sincere apology for the omission of your name after your insightful op-ed piece that appeared in Sunday's Sun. As editor, I certainly failed in my job of catching the error before press time. The error was a simple one of fitting copy to the available space and inadvertently dropping off your name.

We will run our apology for this error next Sunday, and credit you for the evocative piece.

We invite you to again submit your opinions on the school issue, or any other issue. We look forward to receiving them, and will make every effort to make sure they appear without any such error.

Sincerely,
Woody Beaner

For Offensive Remarks

Dearest Cricket,

There's no fool like an old fool, unless it's an old fool who shoots off his mouth at his niece's bridge luncheon. I realize now (too late) that you were mortified, and I'm so sorry.

I apologize for sharing my (apparently unpopular) political views (in full voice) with your genteel ladies' bridge group. Reflecting now on the horrified faces I saw after I stated I'm in favor of returning to the law of the sword makes me realize that I was out of line and out of touch with where I was. (It doesn't raise an eyebrow in my neighborhood pub.)

Please forgive me for such an outburst. If ever again you need a bridge substitute, and your Aunt Ruth isn't available, I hope you'll trust me enough to ask me. I promise to keep all such heretical views to myself. (I've enclosed copies of my apology for each of the ladies.)

Please accept this floral bouquet as a symbol of my contriteness. (And, if you can find it in your heart, would you please tell your Aunt Ruth that it's OK to resume speaking to me?)

Your chastised Uncle Browsard

For a Shipping Error

Dear Mr. Crispy:

Thank you for calling to inform us that you did not receive the overnight shipment of our Model 433A sterilizer. You are correct; it should have arrived at your place of business, 445 Walker, Suite 334, Orlando, FL 32808, at 8:30 a.m. this morning.

I have researched the matter thoroughly and can only conclude that the sterilizer was stolen around midnight from our loading dock. We have reported the situation to the police, and an investigation has begun.

I want to thank you for contacting me immediately. Your call gives us a head start in locating the missing machine.

I do apologize that your machine hasn't arrived. We are shipping you a replacement today, as I stated on the telephone, and it will arrive at your office tomorrow morning. It will not have the customized features that you ordered, but we will have an installer add those on site within two days.

We look forward to continuing the great relationship we have enjoyed with your company for five years now. And I personally look forward to serving you in the future.

Sincerely,

Robert Wild

For Job Performance Failure

David:

I know I committed to have the Bennett progress report complete and to you by Friday at 2:00 p.m. I realize, too, that this impacted your ability to make your report to Sattersfield. I then compounded the failure by not letting you know Friday morning that I'd be unable to complete the report. I'm sure this put you in an awkward position, and I'm truly sorry. (Please forward this to Sattersfield, if you like.)

I should have notified you as early Friday as possible that I couldn't get all the numbers together until today. The storms in Raleigh made things impossible for the field guys to get their counts complete. I have, in fact, just gotten the final figures, and I'll have my report to you by the end of today.

In the future, I will let you know immediately if there is a problem with keeping my commitment. If there is any other way I can right this wrong, please let me know.

Sincerely,
George

For a Family Rift

My Dearest Sister:

I'm writing this in the hope that, even if you aren't speaking to me, you'll read this note and reflect on my heartfelt apology.

I'm totally ashamed of myself, Bebe, for not complying with your wishes that all the attendants wear full-length dresses to your rehearsal dinner. My short dress was a selfish and reactionary decision on my part, one rooted in some leftover envy from early childhood. I know I wounded you, and I am so sorry. (I didn't realize there was going to be a photo shoot of the wedding party; and it wasn't until I saw the photographs that I realized the wisdom of your request; I'm the only person in a cocktail-length dress.) I'm totally ashamed of myself.

I know there is no way I can make amends for being so obstinate after you made your wishes clear; but I hope that you'll find it in your heart to forgive me.

I would love to host a smallish reception here in Denver for you and Mahesh after you return from your honeymoon. I'd invite those on the enclosed guest list at our country club or, if you prefer, in our home. But I'm happy (this time) to comply with any other plan you'd prefer.

Please reflect on this, and let me know. You are most precious to me, Bebe, and I want more than anything for our sisterhood to be restored to its loving best.

Sonia

For Betraying a Trust

Dearest Rita:

It is with a truly contrite heart that I sit down to write you this note of apology. Yes, it is true: I did betray a trust by repeating very personal information you told me in strictest confidence. As I stated last night, I know you must feel betrayed, and I'd like for you to tell me whatever you'd care to about how you feel.[1]

I have no plausible explanation for my behavior. I was talking with Squibb in confidence and just blurted it out, completely without thought.[2]

I know it may take time for you to absorb this betrayal and to be willing to talk to me about it; but I do want you to know how very, very sorry I am. I also regret my transgression to Squibb, and am repeating my request that she not share this information with anyone else.[3]

I do hope you can find it in your heart to forgive me. I want to restore our relationship and will happily do anything you wish to make amends for breaking your confidence.[4]

I'd like to take you to lunch and discuss any aspect of this you may feel is needed—or just let you unload on me. Please do give me a call whenever you are ready.[5]

Remorsefully,
Katie

(1) Accept responsibility. (2) Explain, if possible. (3) Apologize. (4) Ask for forgiveness, if necessary. (5) Offer recompense, if appropriate.

For Failure to RSVP

Ginny:

As I said on the telephone, I'm so sorry I didn't RSVP on time to the invitation to the Grand Pooh Bah Ball.

I do know better. I've actually done your job and know what a hassle it is to have to call people to find out if invitees will be coming so the number of reservations can be made to the caterer on time. I'm so sorry you had to call me to check. It was inexcusably rude of me.

Thank you for letting me do the rest of the follow-up calls as a token of my contriteness. As we agreed, I'll email a list of RSVP responses to you by Wednesday.

All the best,
Rachel

For Rude Behavior

My Dear Cherie:

I just want to repeat what I said on the telephone. Please do forgive me for my rudeness this morning in rushing in and rushing out without a civil greeting, or taking the time to meet your interior decorator.[1] I know you wanted me to see the choices she was presenting and give you my advice.[2] Selfishly, I was completely preoccupied with the schedule of getting to three more places before the clock struck twelve! I feel very badly about my rude behavior. Again, please forgive me.

Will you please come to a leisurely tea on Thursday, and show me all the possibilities for changes you'll be making in your home? I promise to pay full attention and to offer any advice you'd like.[3]

Sincerely,
Max

(1) Take responsibility. (2) Empathize with the offended. (3) Make things right.

(Also see COMPLAINT & PROTEST, page 282; DISAGREEMENT & DISPUTE, page 291; FORGIVENESS, page 317; NEGOTIATION, page 298; RESPONSE, page 257; and SETTLEMENT, page 303.)

Pet Apology

Dear Nigel:

As I said on the telephone, we are so sorry that Nipper bit your cat, Claws, this afternoon. I can only imagine how distressed you were.

We have never had such an incident, and Bobbi Anne has walked Nipper on his leash every day for a year. We felt confident that she was able to control him, but she has never faced the situation of a cat approaching him.

We will, of course, pay the veterinarian bill if you decide to take Claws for a checkup. Nipper is current on all his shots, as I said, and Ben Wright at Animals R Us on Grove St. is the vet we use (312-555-0123). Nipper sustained a serious cornea scratch and several bites we are treating.

In the future, Bobbi Anne will not be allowed to walk Nipper on your side of the street. Hopefully, that will avoid any further potential for conflicts.

Sincerely,
Mavis Moore

Confessing a White Lie

Dear Pet:

My sin, to be sure, has found me out. Well, actually, it's the weight of guilt for telling you a "white lie" that had me pacing the floor at three this morning.

I share your passion for the truth, yet I've lied to you (of all people) about the silliest and most mundane thing. I'm very ashamed of myself. I didn't attend the Roscoe party simply because I didn't want to. And, no, I wasn't in San Francisco for the weekend.

I'm at a loss to say exactly why I lied. I know we'd talked about seeing each other at the party. I hope my actions didn't cause you any discomfort, but I just wasn't up for going out. I wasn't in a party mood and was just feeling generally deflated.

Please do forgive me. I do promise in the future to keep our shared standard of truth.

Yours,
Griggs

51 FORGIVENESS

Although we often think of forgiveness in religious terms, it is true that we need to forgive one another when someone injures us. Forgiveness is usually linked to the apology process (see Apology, page 306) as the last step before reconciliation.

When you've been hurt by another person, the natural responses are denial, anger, and/or even the desire for revenge. The decision to dispense with these responses (or pass through them without getting stuck there), and instead to forgive your offender, requires a change of heart and mind. That usually doesn't happen immediately.

Choosing forgiveness is a dynamic way of canceling a debt owed to you (created by an offense). While you offer the gift of forgiveness to your offender, you are the one who realizes the benefits of increased health: the reduction of anger, stress, and even physical problems like headaches, backaches, colds, and other maladies.

Writing out your message of forgiveness—either asking for or offering it—will benefit both you and the reader by allowing you both to process the offense, have a change of heart, change undesirable behavior, and/or begin to work toward reconciliation.

DECIDE TO WRITE

The Offender

- When you've injured someone, you may want to apologize and ask for forgiveness immediately: "Buzz, I did say Dad prefers to spend his time at Jimmie's. I didn't think how that comment might hurt you, and, to be clear, Dad never said that. Now, of course, I realize how it did hurt you. Thank you for speaking up. Please forgive me for such a thoughtless and callous remark. I promise to never do it again."
- When someone doesn't respond to your calls, letters, or emails, or responds with anger or acts upset, you may want to ask if there is a problem. Or, ask if you have offended the person in some way in order that you might consider the matter, apologize, and ask for forgiveness, if that's appropriate.
- If another person says you have offended him or her, ask for an explanation so that you may properly consider the matter, apologize, and ask for forgiveness, if appropriate.

The Offended

- When you are harboring angry thoughts toward someone, you may want to examine your feelings to learn exactly why you feel as you do. Isolate the reason for your anger. Be able to state exactly what it is that distresses you.

- When you value your relationship with the offender more than you value your feelings of hurt and you want the relationship to prosper, ask the offender to discuss the problem with you so you may consider all the facts. If it's appropriate, ask for an apology so that you may forgive.
- Start with a statement about how you're feeling: "Jane, I felt hurt when you said my report didn't measure up to the established standard. I'd like to privately discuss with you why you felt my report was substandard." "Jennifer, I'm feeling very disappointed, or did I misunderstand you? I thought you said I'd have my check for the Jazz Session performance last week."

THINK ABOUT CONTENT

The Offender

- Consider your actions. Write them down to more thoroughly understand them.
- Write out your apology in order to consider it. (You may, or may not, decide to send a written apology.) Make your apology (see Apology, page 306).
- Ask the offended person(s) for forgiveness.

The Offended

- Calm down.
- Examine your anger and its effect on you. Writing it out can be very helpful (though you'll probably not let anyone else read it).
- Decide not to pursue revenge but to take the path of forgiveness.
- Take stock and ask yourself: Can I talk about the hurt with the offender without attacking? Will the other person be objective and not defensive?
- Empathize with the offender, and reframe your thinking about him or her. Allow for his or her weaknesses. Ask yourself: "What was going on in his or her life at the time?" and "Was he or she under stress?"
- Accept what happened without tossing it back at the person who offended you or displacing it onto someone else.
- Move forward. You may decide to try to work with the offender (if he or she is willing) toward resolution and reconciliation. Or, you may decide to limit or discontinue your relationship. Either way, forgive the offender in your heart.
- Realize your own full release in the act of forgiving.

ELIMINATE WRONG MESSAGES

- Don't expect to forget the offense, and don't ask for the other person to forget. You will undoubtedly always remember the offense. Forgetting isn't a part of the forgiving process, nor is it a goal.

- Don't immediately seek reconciliation when a serious offense is involved (abuse, betrayal, etc.). Reconciling is not a good idea until the offender has undergone extensive therapy and has established a long record of reformed behavior.
- Don't excuse or condone the offender's bad behavior. The offender is still responsible for his or her misdeed; you (the offended) have just canceled his or her debt to you.
- Making amends doesn't mean you are weak. On the contrary, it's a sign of strength and moral courage.
- Don't expect an instant resolution. Keep your commitment to resolve the issue, and know that it may take time. Exercise patience.

CONSIDER SPECIAL SITUATIONS

- Anger, a natural response to another's offense, is initially energizing. But it can grow into a debilitating grudge that holds you captive. Use forgiveness to eliminate the grudge and free yourself from its control.
- The process of forgiving is a dynamic and complex one. It often takes time to work through anger, loss, and grief. When very serious abuses, death, and/or legally criminal acts are involved, the steps of forgiveness can and must happen independently of the offender paying any legal debt to society.
- Each person must come to forgiveness. True forgiveness is possible only when you are ready to forgive.
- Sometimes two people offend each other, or one overreacts to an offense with a greater (revengeful) offense. It's especially helpful in these situations, after both people can approach it calmly, to discuss the offense(s) and each person's roles. Each person needs to accept responsibility for his or her own part. Writing out your apology, even if you don't give it to the other person, can be very helpful in working through to forgiveness.
- After the offender has apologized to you, even though you know he or she is sorry, your pride and stubbornness may keep you from offering forgiveness. It's important to recognize this and make a commitment to forgive for your own sake. You don't even have to tell the offender.

SELECT A FORMAT

- There are some greeting cards created for things like a missed birthday, a personal injury, etc. These may be used if you also write your own personal message asking for forgiveness and taking responsibility for your actions or inactions.
- Use a note card and matching envelope for personal short notes of forgiveness.
- Use personal stationery for longer letters of forgiveness.
- Business matters of forgiveness may require the use of business letterhead, or may need to be sent by secure corporate email.

USE STRONG WORDS

admit	anger	beg	believe
change	commit(ted)	courage	decide
express	forgive	pardon	reconcile
regret	repent	responsible	trust

CONSTRUCT EFFECTIVE PHRASES

acted very badly	blame no one but myself
committed an offense	conduct was wrong
genuinely sorry for	I alone am to blame
need to come clean	no excuse for
responsible for	should never have said
will not repeat	wish to confess

BUILD STRONG SENTENCES

The Offender

I need to ask you for your forgiveness.

I accept the responsibility for offending you.

I promise I will never repeat my offense.

There is no excuse for my rude behavior.

I acted badly, and I'm sorry; please forgive me.

I can only tell you how sorry I am, and ask for your forgiveness.

Please forgive me.

You have every right to be angry with me for my offensive remark, but I do hope you will consider my apology, and forgive me.

Yes, my response was wrong; I do apologize for offending you, and I ask for your forgiveness.

The Offended

Yes, I do forgive you.

Like you, I don't want this to come between us. Let's discuss this matter so that we may both come to an understanding and work toward forgiveness.

I believe you owe me an apology for your statement at the meeting today. Your apology will help me greatly in coming to the point of forgiving you.

I need to tell you that your remark was very offensive to me. But after our discussion, I want to say I do forgive you and wish to move forward.

You totally misrepresented the facts, and I need to discuss this with you before I can take the step of forgiveness.

Please review your actions, which I found very offensive.

I must ask you for an apology, so that I may forgive you.

I've tried to understand why you chose to lie about the matter, and I need to discuss this with you in order to take the next step.

I've chosen to forgive you, but at the same time I've elected not to continue our relationship.

I did carry a grudge over your betrayal, but I have chosen to forgive you and, in that act, to release myself from the anger that held me prisoner for so long.

BUILD EFFECTIVE PARAGRAPHS

The Offender

Thank you for reinforcing the fact that my bad behavior doesn't mean I'm a bad person. And thank you for the gift of forgiveness. I do promise to be more considerate in the future.

Please forgive me for my lack of understanding during Dad's illness. You are the one who carried the primary burden for his care. I could have been, and should have been, much more help. I was not. I finally realize how much of a burden I left on your shoulders, and I'm truly ashamed of myself. It's too late to help more with Dad, but I will be a much more participating, and caring, sister in the future.

I hope that over time, you will forgive me.

Please do forgive me. In the heat of the moment I called you some very unkind—and all untrue—names. I feel like a complete heel. And I repent. In the future, when faced with a point upon which we disagree, I do promise to make my statements in terms of the idea I object to, and refrain from letting it inappropriately become a personal attack.

Jamie, please consider my humble appeal for us to sit down together so you can tell me exactly how my behavior hurt you. I am so desperately sorry, but I believe if I completely understand how it affected you, I will be more certain never to repeat it.

The Offended

I can't offer forgiveness at this moment. I'm still processing the offense. But I'll call you in a couple of days to arrange a time to sit down and discuss it.

Yes, of course I forgive you. I do want us to be "safe friends," knowing we can go to each other with anything and feel certain we'll each be heard.

I'm not finding forgiveness is coming that easily this time. I know we've been over this ground before, and I can only say I need a bit more time to process the injury. I'll get back to you as soon as I can.

We've come to the age when we must forgive each other speedily. We don't have time or energy to harbor hurt or ill feelings toward each other. I know the stress you've been under, and I appreciate the fact that at times such pressure results in unkind words. I love you, and I do forgive you.

EDIT, EDIT, EDIT

The great thing about writing out your forgiveness message is that this helps you to process the offense and work toward forgiveness. Be sure you give your message breathing time, and then reread and edit it before sending. Or, you may choose to write out your message and reread it just for your own benefit, and not send it. Either way, writing will help you get to the healing power of forgiveness.

Forgiveness Granted for Thoughtless Remarks

Mort,

Can I forgive you? Are you kidding? How many times have I had to beg you for forgiveness? Many more than either of us wants to remember. You are my dear brother, and I shall always have forgiveness for you.

Al

Forgiveness Granted for Damage at a Party

Dear Mark,

Yes, I do believe the guests enjoyed the party. (A highlight for many who've called or written was seeing you in that lampshade.)

I do accept your apology. You are forgiven for dropping the lamp while trying to reattach the shade. The check for $257.50 does cover the repair.

Alice

Forgiveness Request for Breaking a Promise

Dearest Buckie:

I betrayed a sacred promise I'd made to you, and I am so sorry.

I've told you why, and I am thoroughly ashamed. I can only say I'm devastated at the thought that I so wounded you. And I can only plead that if you'll forgive me, I will never do such a thing again.

Can you ever forgive me? Please do consider it, though I don't deserve it.

Your Cousin,
Ruth

Forgiveness Request for Online Personal Attack

[After face-to-face apology]

Dear Raz,

As I said today, I had to apologize face to face after I reviewed my post (to the group) and realized I'd allowed the anonymity of email to release me from the bonds of normal civility. My remarks were undeservedly harsh. There is no excuse for my personal attack on you, calling you a "twit" for your expressed views. It was your idea and not you that I should have addressed. I'm truly sorry for this ad hominem.

I'm sure you've read my online apology; and have considered my in-person apology. I don't view you as a twit, and I certainly should not have made that statement.

In the future, I promise to direct my comments only toward the ideas expressed. Please do forgive me.

Remorsefully,
Chaz

Forgiveness Request an Angry Outburst

[After verbal apology]

Dear Bonzi:

Again, I must ask for your forgiveness for flying off the handle when you brought up your stance about drinking. We don't share the same views, obviously, but a gentleman has a long fuse and a generous tolerance of other views. I displayed a lack of both, and I'm deeply sorry.

Please accept this bouquet as a symbol of my remorse, and consider forgiving me my red-faced rant. I promise not to repeat such behavior.

With true remorse,
Ivan

Forgiveness Request for Challenging an Employee

Dear Raylene:

I improperly challenged your numbers on your report at the department meeting this morning. I shouldn't have done that, and what's more, your numbers are correct. I was wrong. (I'm copying all staff members at the meeting.) Please forgive my mistake.

In the future, I'll do the proper research first, and contact you privately if I have a question.

Sincerely,

Frankie

Forgiveness Request for Bad Manners

Dear Sis:

Yes, my lack of gentility was on complete and boorish display at your dinner party. I didn't realize how uncouth my question about money was until I saw the slack jaws and the shocked expressions, and heard the gasps followed by resounding silence around the table.

I'll gladly submit to your etiquette class 101A if you'll forgive me. (And, if you'll ever invite me again, I'll agree to wear a placard that reads: "This is the feckless lout of a brother—a black and cloddish sheep—of the hostess. Please disregard any inappropriate bleating.") I'll also submit to any other recompense you feel is appropriate.

My dear sister, can you ever find it in your heart to forgive me?

Contritely,
Lenny

Forgiveness Request for Failing to Keep an Agreement

Dear Antoine,

There's no excuse—none—for discussing our book idea with Jennifer after we'd agreed to keep any word of it completely to ourselves, yet I did exactly that. And the stupid irony is that I did so only after carefully making her commit not to discuss or reveal the idea to anyone else. (Of course, she kept that promise for exactly what—three minutes, five minutes? I don't introduce this fact to detract from my culpability and guilt for breaking our agreement. I only do it to point out the absurdity of my flawed rationale as well as my wrong-headed and wrong-heartedness.)

As I explained to you in my confession and apology, I followed up with Jennifer (after the fact) by having her sign a nondisclosure agreement, primarily to reinforce the terms of her commitment. In fairness to her, she didn't discuss it (she says) with anyone else, but only called you to discuss it because I wasn't available.

I do understand your anger. I empathize completely. I would have reacted exactly as you did, had the situation been reversed.

The only feeble explanation I can offer is that I found myself in the position of having the opportunity to try our idea out on a senior editor at Catherine Publishing and couldn't at that moment get in touch with you to get your consent. (You'll remember I did leave a message to that effect on your cell phone.) I shouldn't have gone ahead without your agreement. But I rationalized that you would certainly want me to take the opportunity presented. (In retrospect, I could have asked Jennifer if we could contact her together on a conference call to discuss the idea. At that moment, this idea didn't occur to me.)

Please forgive me. I do take my commitments seriously, and will never break our agreement again.

Sincerely,
Dutch

Forgiveness Request for Repeating a Rumor

Dear Hoda:

Yes, I am guilty of passing on the rumor that you were seen interviewing for a job at Mathers. I do know better. It was both unethical of me—by my own standards too—and demonstrates vividly to me just how damaging idle chatter can be.[1]

I've searched my heart, and I don't believe I bear you any ill will. But I did harm you, and I am so sorry.[2]

I have gone to those six people, including your boss, James Wright, and confessed my role in spreading a completely false rumor.

I know, when I reflect upon it as I have, how angry you must be. And I also know such an injury isn't easy to forgive. Yet I do ask you to consider forgiving me after your initial anger has cooled, and you are able to do so.[3]

And please allow me to make any other amends that are appropriate. May I start by taking you to lunch so you can administer 20 lashes with a wet Vietnamese noodle?[4]

Sincerely,
Joni

(1) Admit your behavior. (2) Express remorse. (3) Acknowledge how you injured someone. (4) Ask for forgiveness. (4) Offer recompense.

Forgiveness Request for Long-Term Abuse

My Dearest Daughter,

If I were to list—and over the next six months of intense therapy I shall—all the ways I've sinned against you and injured you with my abuse of alcohol, I would—and will—undoubtedly fill the pages of your diary many times over.

Why did I do all those horrible things? I'm determined to learn the answers myself in order to change and reclaim my life completely. I'm only desperately sorry that I subjected you to so much suffering. Please be clear: none of what I have done is in any way your fault or your responsibility.

I know it would be improper of me to ask you to reconcile with me immediately. Improper and completely wrong. I must—and I will—demonstrate over time that I have repented of my past and that I have changed, not instantly and miraculously, but by being sober from now on.

Please do forgive me so that you may move on to the healing and happiness you deserve. And I would like to ask you if you are willing to start a correspondence dialogue wherein I can repent of each injury I've caused you over the past 20 years. Consider it, and let me know.

I do look forward to reconciling with you when I've earned the right to do so.

With all my love,
Dad

(Also see APOLOGY, page 306.)

VIII

ORDERS, CREDIT & COLLECTIONS

Reason is the mistress and
queen of all things.

—*Cicero*

52 ORDER

An order, whether it is placed electronically, over the telephone, on a printed order form, or face to face with a salesperson, requires specific and clear information. There may still be occasions when it's necessary to submit an order letter for items you wish to purchase. The keys to a successful order: be concise, include complete information about what you want and how you will pay for it, list any order conditions, and provide a contact name and shipping information.

After an order is placed, any number of problems may require you to compose a letter. Using concise, clear, and complete information is always the best approach for resolving problems and keeping a customer informed about the status of his or her order.

DECIDE TO WRITE

Use this communication to:

- Order
- Confirm an order received
- Explain procedures, change in product, unavailability, issues of payment
- Request additional information
- Make adjustments
- Cancel or change an order
- Inquire about the status of an order
- Clarify payment questions/problems
- Accept or refuse changes
- Refuse or return an order

THINK ABOUT CONTENT

- Cut to the chase when placing an order: "Please send me," or "This is an order for" is the clearest way to start.
- Arrange items with identifying information: number, catalog identification code or number, name, description, unit price, color, dimensions, special information (engraving or monogramming), and total price.
- Set the order out by indenting if you're not using an online form:

  3 copies
  Melvin Batcher, Clear Thinking, 2nd edition, 2010 @ $29.95 each
  Total: $89.85

- State any conditions of your order clearly. If you must have the order by a certain date, for example, or if you will accept no substitutions, these conditions must be part of your order.
- Cover tax, shipping information, timeframe, any special instructions, and method of payment.
- Make sure your contact information is complete: full name, mailing address, shipping address, telephone number(s), email address, and fax number.
- Conclude with a friendly comment, if possible.

ELIMINATE WRONG MESSAGES

- Don't confuse the order with unnecessary information.
- Be singular in purpose; don't include other business.
- Don't bury the order in a paragraph.
- Don't order special items without first talking with someone at the organization and confirming it can be done.

CONSIDER SPECIAL SITUATIONS

- If you will accept substitutions, state these clearly.
- Emphasize any deal-breaking information. For example, if your order is only good if the product can be delivered by the 15th, say so: "Order good only if products will arrive by January 15."
- If your order has been lost, emphasize you are submitting a duplicate order in the event the first is found.
- When writing about an order that was placed, always completely identify it by order date and your purchase order number, and/or tracking number and confirmation number, if possible. Also transmit a copy of the order, if you have one.
- If you want to cancel your order, first state clearly that you are canceling your order. Make your contact by telephone, and be sure to get the name of the person who records your cancellation. Repeat all identifying information. If you paid for by check, ask for a refund; if you charged the item, ask to have your credit card or account credited. Follow up with an email or letter of cancellation.
- If you must change your order, start by stating you are issuing an order change. Include the original order information. This should be telephoned in and followed by faxing or emailing the change.
- Get confirmation. Telephone orders, especially complex ones over a certain dollar amount, should be confirmed by the supplying organization. If orders will be delayed or must be back-ordered, the supplier should call the customer, and should send a letter that states this fact. A back-order letter should include an apology for the inconvenience, and end with a brief statement of goodwill. More and more these are sent by email, or are faxed.

SELECT A FORMAT

- Official, printed order forms are best. If an online order is used, you should print out a copy. If a letter is used for your order, be sure to include customer name (with title), business name, shipping and billing addresses, zip codes, purchase order number (if you have one), customer number (if you have one), contact telephone numbers, and fax numbers. Order information should include a catalog number (if available), description of the items ordered, catalog page number (if available), size, color, type (design, motif, etc.), quantity, unit price, and total price. Where applicable, sales, shipping and handling, place and method of delivery, payment information—charge, COD, credit card payment, or payment by check—should all be noted. Include and emphasize any conditions or restrictions, such as delivery deadline, and the acceptability of substitutions.
- When online or mail orders are made, always request a return confirmation. This ensures your order was received and processed.
- Type letters concerning orders on organization letterhead or personal stationery. A legible handwritten letter is also acceptable.

Supplier Notification to Customer of Product Arrival

[Date]

Dear Mr. Kowaleski:

It's a beauty! The BMW 735i you purchased through our Munich European Delivery Program has arrived, it has been prepped and serviced, and is ready for pickup. Please call me at 310-555-0123 so I can arrange a time for you to complete the paperwork. My hours are 9 a.m. to 6 p.m. Monday through Saturday.

It will take about 20 minutes to complete the transaction and make any adjustments you may request. You will need to bring the folder of paperwork you received in Munich at the time of purchase and your photo ID (driver's license).

I look forward to hearing from you. You'll be the envy of Englewood.

Sincerely,

George Crawford

Customer Service Manager

Supplier Notification to Customer on Back-Ordered Shipment

[Date]

Dear Dr. Hanson:

We have received the autoclave you ordered (your purchase order #9984) on January 10, which was on back order. I am shipping it to you by air service (shipment #44-C-1390), and it will arrive in your office on the 13th.[1]

Thank you for being so patient, and as I said on the telephone, our service representative will call you to arrange a time to come by and check the unit thoroughly.

We look forward to serving you in the future.[2]

Sincerely,

Ronald D. Servos

(1) Give complete identifying information. (2) Conclude with a friendly comment.

Customer Ordering Supplies

[Date]

Jasmine Flowers, Sales Manager

Dear Ms. Flowers:

I am ordering the following from your June 15 price list:

20 boxes	Neenah Parchment bond paper, Dove Gray, 25% rag, 8½ by 11 inches, 20-pound, @ $15.50	$310.00
14 boxes	Neenah Parchment bond envelopes, Dove Gray, 25% rag, 20-pound, size 10, @ $35.00	$490.00
5 dozen	Printer cartridges, #20A, black @ $22.50/box	$112.50
5 each	Stanza computer stands, #1233, Model K in black @ $298.99	$1,494.95
	TOTAL	$2,407.45

Please ship by prepaid parcel post to:
540 East Bayaud, Suite 7
Lincoln, Nebraska 68514
and charge the amount on the usual 2/20, net 60 terms to The Barker Account #34456.

I'm nearly out of these supplies and would appreciate you getting these out ASAP.

With sincere thanks,
Joan Thrush

Supplier Filling a Partial Order

[Date]

Dear Ms. Trout:

Thank you for your order (PO #3455), which we can fill within the next 48 hours, except for 32 of the 65 pairs of Deep Freeze mittens, which we will back-order and ship to you in two weeks.

You will receive your first shipment of the items on the attached invoice within five days; the remainder within three weeks. Thank you again. We look forward to serving you in the future.

Sincerely,

Nighthorse Walker

Customer Ordering Services

[Date]

Martin Schine, President

Dear Martin:

I would like to order these items from your December 15 proposal:

1)	Prepare the site, including, but not limited to: a. remove and dispose of existing junipers b. grind out pear tree stumps c. remove lowest branches on existing Austrian pines	$935
2)	Furnish and install 5 yards compost	440
3)	Furnish and install 110' steel edging	145
4)	Rebuild rock wall at west of garage	430
5)	Remove and dispose of existing exposed aggregate	460
6)	Remove and dispose of existing cobblestone	460
7)	Furnish and install flagstone step stones	290
	TOTAL	$3,160

I agree to the terms of payment in your proposal: 50 percent upon starting, and the balance on satisfactory completion. Your "General Conditions" for performance will also be part of our contractual agreement. I do wish to take advantage of your winter discount of 10 percent, or $316, that you offered for beginning the work immediately.

Our agreed completion date is February 15, after which there will be a penalty of $25 per day taken off the price.

I look forward to having your company complete this project. Please call me if you have any remaining questions.

Sincerely,

Gladys Poundstone

Customer Order Confirmation

[Date]

MaryLou Manners, Sales Manager

Dear MaryLou:

This confirms my telephone order, our purchase order #44556, for 435 five-gallon Happy Juniper Shrubs, @ $20.00 each . . . $8,700.00

As agreed, you will guarantee that any shrubs that die or fail to thrive within the first year will be replaced free of charge.

Also as agreed, this order is conditional upon these shrubs being delivered by March 15 to:
    8220 East Dartmouth Avenue, #55.

No substitutes will be accepted.

Thank you for your help on this.

Sincerely,

Henry Wilkins

Author to Bookstore on Back-Ordered Books

[Date]

Julie:

When I appeared at the Big Dog Bookstore in Chicago for the book signing on May 16, I was told by Janet Jones, who purchases books, that the books had been on back order for months, and she has been unable to get copies from Ingram, the distributor.

I checked six different times between March 1 and May 10, and was assured that books were shipped directly from the St. James warehouse on April 1, and would arrive on May 15.

I need to know how this all went so terribly wrong. Please check and call me by tomorrow at noon, so we can get this resolved before my next book signing, May 29.

Regards,

Melville Bounder

Customer Received Broken Merchandise

[Date]

Richard Munch, Customer Service

Dear Mr. Munch:

I just opened the two custom speakers, Model ZZXs, that Stereo Parts made and shipped to me July 2. The membranes over both speaker openings are punctured. As you directed over the telephone, today I am returning the damaged speakers to you for repair or replacement.

I will expect the speakers returned to me by July 15, as agreed. Thank you for your attention to this problem.

Sincerely,

Jack Reynolds

Order Quantities for Building Project Reversed

[Date]

Jerry:

The shipment of "Durango" tumbled travertine tiles arrived today, and we are delighted with the appearance. The condition seems fine. But, as I stated on the telephone, the quantities in the order have been reversed: there are 500 sq. ft. of 18-inch tiles and 1,500 sq. ft. of 4-inch tiles, which is the reverse of what we ordered.

As we agreed, Caps Inc. will deliver the missing 1,000 sq. ft. of 18-inch tiles to, and pick up the 1,000 sq. ft. of 4-inch tile from the construction site, without charge, no later than Monday, April 5. And we will incur no other charges for this error.

Thank you for expediting this.

Best,

Charlie Fiddle

Also see COLLECTION LETTER, page 354; COMPLAINT & PROTEST, page 282; ACKNOWLEDGMENT & CONFIRMATION, page 264; OFFERING AN ADJUSTMENT, page 350.)

CREDIT INQUIRY & PROVIDING CREDIT INFORMATION

Credit information—your own and others'—must be handled in a straightforward, diplomatic, and confidential manner. While computer records are fast and efficient, they also present unprecedented new challenges to credit security and confidentiality. Both your ability and that of those with whom you do business may be impaired if credit information is mishandled. Exercise every precaution to safeguard your own and others' credit information.

DECIDE TO WRITE

Use the credit inquiry to:

- Routinely check your credit rating and records
- Learn why credit has been denied
- Obtain credit information on a business or person
- Clear up a credit blemish
- Correct credit report misinformation or mistakes

THINK ABOUT CONTENT

When requesting credit information:

- Call first to learn why credit was denied and to determine the agency that issued the credit report.
- Contact the credit bureau (see page 332), and obtain a copy of your credit report.
- Be direct and to the point.
- Give all the necessary identifying information: name, address, telephone number, purchase dates, item, purchase amount, account number, place of purchase, etc.
- For another person's or organization's credit information, reference the request of the party involved, give any identifying background information, state that all remarks will be kept confidential, and conclude with a statement of goodwill and an expression of appreciation.
- For a copy of your personal credit report, write to the bureau that issued it. There are three major bureaus:

Experian
PO Box 2002
Allen, TX 75013-0036
(888) 397-3742
www.experian.com

TransUnion Corp.
Consumer Relations
PO Box 2000
2 Baldwin Place
Chester, PA 19022
(800) 916-8800
www.transunion.com

Equifax Credit Information Services
Consumer Assistance
1600 Peachtree St. NW
PO Box 105069
Atlanta, GA 30374-0241
(800) 685-1111
www.equifax.com

The FACT Act allows you to obtain one free credit report each year from these three credit bureaus. Make your request through a central source: www.AnnualCreditReport.com (for more information visit www.ftc.gov). Cost for additional reports is $5.95 for one or $25 for all three. Be sure to use the official, secure websites.

You are also entitled to a free credit report copy within 60 days after you have been refused credit. Call the toll-free number if you have questions, then mail a copy of the refusal letter along with your request. Make it a practice to obtain a copy of your credit report at least once a year, preferably more often—problems or not—to check that your credit record is accurate. Enclose a self-addressed, stamped envelope if you're inquiring by mail.

SELECT STRONG WORDS

application	approve	balance	character
collateral	credit	debt	deny
establish	extend	funds	lend
loan	paid	payment (repayment)	rating
record	references	satisfactory	savings
substantiate	verify	vouch	welcome

BUILD EFFECTIVE PHRASES

after careful consideration	all payments on time
application has been received	apply for credit in the amount of
can establish a credit line of	cash basis only
current outstanding balance	delinquent payment record
due to your current credit status	excellent repayment history

lists past-due amounts

no delinquent payments

please reapply after

present economic conditions

repayment record indicates

restricted line of credit

to verify employment

wish to open the account with

your credit policy

my credit record shows delinquencies due to

our current credit policy requires

pleased to approve your application

record of repayment

request a credit report

substantiate the repayment record

will be happy to consider a credit line in the amount

your credit background

BUILD STRONG SENTENCES

I wish to apply for a line of credit in the amount of $200,000.

Please accept my application for a short-term loan in the amount of $125,000.

Mr. Saurabh Beta has listed you as a credit reference.

We are inquiring about the repayment record of Susie Ort's loan to First Federal.

I request to meet with a small business loan officer to establish a business account and line of credit.

Ignacious Dorifo has an excellent credit history with this company, and we would recommend him as a credit customer.

The repayment record of Mark Putz shows five payments over 30 days late.

We would appreciate any credit information you may give us on your customer Matthew Mathers.

SELECT A FORMAT

- For all Internet inquiries and responses, be sure to strictly comply with federal, state, and organizational security requirements in all your communications.

- For mailed inquiries, type your request on personal stationery or letterhead. A neatly hand-written personal letter with return address may also be used for your personal credit report.

- Develop standard (boilerplate) statements consistent for approved credit inquiries and responses. This will allow you to quickly request information, or check off and return a response to credit inquiries.

EDIT, EDIT, EDIT

Your challenge here is to include all the necessary information in a very clear, straightforward, and legally acceptable manner.

Company Credit Inquiry

[Date]

Allen Alexrod, Credit Manager

Dear Allen:

As I explained on the telephone, High Country Duds has just placed a large order, requesting delivery the first of the month. Their purchasing director, Bob Adler, gave your company as a credit reference.

I realize this company is new, but I'd appreciate any information you have as well as your recommendation regarding an extension of credit.[1] Your comments will be kept strictly confidential.[2]

I appreciate your help.[3]

Cordially,

Nathan Spratt, Sales Manger

---

(1) Make your request. (2) Give needed information. (3) Express thanks.

Requesting a Credit Report on Another Person

[Date]

Delbert Donavan
Manager, Credit Department

Dear Mr. Donavan:

Regina Merriweather, account #4456, listed your store as a credit reference on her application for a More Credit account. Would you please supply your creditor information on Ms. Merriweather regarding:

• length of credit relationship
• monthly and annual billed amounts
• payment record

We will keep the information confidential.

An envelope is enclosed for your response. I appreciate your prompt attention to this request.

Sincerely,

Harold M. Miser
Credit Manager

Standard Credit Inquiry Form

[Date]

Reference: Credit Report for _____

Dear _____:

In order to complete a credit application for the above individual/organization, we request the following credit information:

____ Record of loan repayment history

____ Standard Credit Response Form

Sincerely,

Joseph Wright

Requesting a Copy of Your Credit Report

[Date]

Mr. B. Kind, Credit Manager

Dear Mr. Kind:

On September 21, I applied to open a bank account at 1st Bank, 540 West Applegate in Dallas. I was told that there are three negative items on my credit report, and Mr. Jim Bob Aires in the customer service department refused to open the account.[1] (Letter of refusal attached.)

I have lived at my present address at 540 Locust in Dallas for five years. Prior to that I resided at 434 East Windsom Drive in Dallas for nine years. I have worked for Lone Star Graphics, 200 Long Horn Trail in Dallas since 2002.[2]

Please send me a copy of my credit report. If you have any questions, I may be reached at 214-555-0123.[3]

Sincerely,

Suzanne Richardson

---

(1) Be direct and to the point. (2) Include all necessary information. (3) Ask for what you want.

Requesting a Company Credit Reference

[Date]

Mr. Milfred Brookfield, Credit Manager

Dear Mr. Brookfield:

Silvers, Inc., located at 500 Silversmith Way in Springfield, has applied for an account with us and has listed your company as a reference.

Their initial order is for $64,500. Can you supply us with information concerning this company's account with you, especially the credit terms, lending limits, and payment history?

We will keep all information you provide in the strictest confidence. Please use the enclosed envelope and it will get directly to me.

Thank you for your help.

Evelyn Smith, New Accounts

Renewing a Credit Relationship with a Former Customer

[Date]

Ms. Mable Bugg, President

Dear Ms. Bugg:

I'm preparing my confidential credit file on your company for extension of a line of credit with us before our visit to your plant next week. I noticed that your financial statements and references date back two years. Our policy for increasing credit lines requires that all such information be current.

Please supply me with these items of updated information:

- last quarter's profit-and-loss statement
- five current credit references
- current banking affiliation

All information will be kept confidential.

Please fax your response or overnight mail it to my attention by Wednesday so we can keep our appointment for next week.

We look forward to again working actively with Grasshopper, as we did in the past. Thank you, and please call me if you have any questions.

Sincerely,

Mable Karing

Requesting Credit References from a Company

[Date]

Mr. Malcolm Meeker, President

Dear Mr. Meeker:

Thank you for your purchase order for our Model SXZ computer system. Before we can finalize the sale, we will need some additional information. Please fax or overnight mail the following information to my attention:

- last quarter's profit-and-loss statement
- copy of certificate of incorporation
- a listing of corporate officers
- the completed attached Form A-345 listing credit references and banking affiliations

All information will, of course, remain confidential.

When your information arrives, we will review your entire application file, and make a determination on your line of credit.

We look forward to processing your application. Thank you for your interest in Diccy Systems.

Sincerely,

Jack Hammer

(Also see COLLECTION LETTER, page 354; OFFERING AN ADJUSTMENT, page 350; CREDIT APPROVAL, page 337; and CREDIT DENIAL, page 340.)

Positive Credit Reference

[Date]

David Jensen

Credit Manager

Dear David:

In response to Bob Adams's request of July 8 to supply you with credit information on BYK, 870 Adair St., Detroit: we have enjoyed a mutually beneficial relationship with BYK for seven years.

All the company's payments have been received on time, and we have extended our credit line with the company from an initial $5,000 monthly limit to a present $25,000 per month line. Annual purchases by BYK have increased from approximately $4,500 to $225,000.

If you require any additional information, please call me.

Sincerely,

Jim Backus
Credit Manager

Negative and Positive Credit Response

[Date]

Mr. Simpson Alexander

Credit Manager

Dear Mr. Alexander:

Here is the reference requested by Jon Robb, your credit applicant, of Flatlanders, 777 West Aberdine, Fort Worth:

- Customer from June, 1997.
- High credit balance: $4,520.
- Payments were slow from June to December of last year.
- Comments: The company underwent a loss of customers and cash flow during that period, but has resumed prompt payment.

We are currently doing business with Flatlanders in a satisfactory manner.

Sincerely,

Joyce Evers, Credit Manager

Positive Reference

[Date]

Jeremy Handler

Credit Manager

Dear Mr. Handler:

Our business relationship with Whitcomb Packaging has been excellent over the seven years they have been purchasing our products. They have always paid invoices within 30 days whether they were $2,500 or $17,500 (as our records indicate they were).

We value Whitcomb's business, and have, in fact, just raised their credit limit to $25,000 per month.

I hope this is helpful. Please contact me if you need additional information.

Sincerely,

Raymond Q. Featherlight

When the decision to extend credit is made—after all the credit information has been collected, checked, analyzed, and the applicant has been approved—you are sending a good news message to announce the fact to the individual or organization. Write it with a welcoming and enthusiastic tone.

THINK ABOUT CONTENT

- State the good news immediately, and cordially welcome the credit customer.
- Define any limitations, and follow that with a brief statement about expanding credit limits.
- Close with a goodwill statement about the future of the relationship.

ELIMINATE WRONG MESSAGES

- Do not include doomsday or negative statements about possible delinquency, late payments, or credit exceptions. If this information has not been conveyed, enclose an explanation and reference it in the letter. Or, to personalize the relationship, invite the reader in for a face-to-face meeting.
- Do not omit a complete statement about immediate credit limits and terms. This could get the relationship off to a bad start.

SELECT A FORMAT

- Use a business letterhead, typewritten.
- Secure internet communications may be used if organization policy permits.

SELECT STRONG WORDS

accept	approve	balance	extend
funds	receipt	receive	welcome

USE EFFECTIVE PHRASES

accept your application	appreciate your business
approve a line of credit	as a valued customer
become a valued customer	begin a relationship
establish a relationship with you	excellent credit references

extend premier services

good payment history

introduce you to our bank officer

make available to you

open a line of credit

outstanding credit record

welcome to our banking family

find us easy to work with

happy to establish

join your business team

new small business customer

opening an account in the amount

realize business reward in working with us

wish to welcome you

WRITE STRONG SENTENCES

We believe you will become one of our valued customers.

We are pleased to open a Dollars account for you with a beginning line of credit in the amount of $50,000.

We would like to welcome you to our preferred customer group.

Here is a list of the services you will enjoy as a preferred bank customer.

We look forward to working with you for all your widget needs.

Your application has been approved.

You will be happy to learn that your application has been approved for an opening line of credit in the amount of $100,000.

Please check our online services to learn the many ways we are prepared to help you with your business financial needs.

Ordering from Snoopy's was just made a whole lot easier with the approval of your request for a line of credit.

Your small business loan has been approved.

We welcome the opportunity to do business with you as a credit customer.

BUILD EFFECTIVE PARAGRAPHS

We are pleased to report that your loan has been approved for the requested amount of $225,000. Please call my office to arrange an appointment time to complete the necessary loan documents and to receive the check.

After careful evaluation, we are prepared to open a line of credit for Scampy's in the amount of $50,000 for a period of one year. At the end of that period of time, we will reevaluate the line of credit. If your record of repayments has been satisfactory, we will increase the line to your requested $150,000.

Jim, I'll be happy to loan you and Elise the $20,000 toward the down payment on your house. As we agreed, you will repay the loan in $5,000 increments next year on the following dates: June 1, September 1, December 1, and March 1. (If you don't meet this payment schedule, Sarah and I take immediate possession of the basset hound, Ralph.) Please countersign on the line below, and this will become our loan agreement. (I was just kidding about the dog; it's the kids we want.)

EDIT, EDIT, EDIT

Because of the legal implications, be sure your letter and agreement terms are reviewed by an attorney. If in doubt, give your letter some reflective time, and then reread it aloud a bit later to make sure you've said exactly what you intended.

Individual Approval for Department Store Credit

[Date]

Sarah Wasserstein

Dear Ms. Wasserstein:

It is with pleasure that I welcome you as a preferred credit customer at Oren's Department Store. As a new credit customer, you will have an immediate credit limit of $500.

We believe you will enjoy the convenience and value of our products and services, as well as the special benefits of being a preferred credit customer who is entitled to special sales and discounts.

Please validate your new enclosed Oren's charge card by signing the back. It is good in any of our stores or for any of our services. Enclosed is a copy of our credit terms specifying how you will be billed each month.

Again, we welcome you as one of Oren's preferred charge-card customers.

Sincerely,

Marilyn H. Houser

(Also see CREDIT DENIAL, page 340, and CREDIT INQUIRY & PROVIDING CREDIT INFORMATION, page 331.)

Customer Service Organization Credit Approval

[Date]

Mr. Harold Appleton

President

Dear Mr. Appleton:

After reviewing replies to all the references listed on your application, we are happy to extend to Harold's Way a $75,000 line of credit on a 30-day billing cycle (2 percent, 10 days). You may order online at Squids.com any quantities you need throughout the month (no minimum order). Just identify the account with your company name and password. We will provide you with free, same-day delivery.

We know you'll find an account with Squid's both convenient and economical, and we look forward to serving you.

Sincerely,

Horacio Blackhorn
Account Services

Offering Limited Credit

[Date]

Lucille M. Foster

President

Dear Ms. Foster:

We appreciate your credit application, and are happy to report that we have now received and reviewed all the responses from the creditors you listed. We would like to offer The Silver Slipper an immediate line of credit for $25,000 based upon our present credit policy. (See the policy statement enclosed for details.)

We will certainly be happy to review and raise this limit to the amount you requested after one year.

We look forward to being of service, and I shall await your first order.

Cordially,

Samuel R. Wright

55 CREDIT DENIAL

Writing a letter denying credit is a very difficult and delicate task, because this sensitive area is closely tied to character, integrity, and social acceptance. Deliver the bad news in an objective matter-of-fact manner, while trying not to injure the applicant further. Both an indirect approach (see Refusal, page 274) and an extremely tactful tone are necessary.

Your final strategy will depend to a certain degree on why you are denying credit. If the economy or the segment of the economy that affects the applicant's ability to repay are weak, the job is not as difficult as a refusal based on an unexplained nonpayment of debts. End with a good-will statement.

DECIDE TO WRITE

Use this response to inform an individual or organization that credit cannot be extended.

THINK ABOUT CONTENT

- There may be local, industry, state, or federal regulations and standards that apply to your statements. Follow them closely.
- Respond to the exact information requested.
- Begin by being direct:
  - ► Identify the request you are responding to.
  - ► If the response is one simple answer, give it.
  - ► If the response consists of more than one answer, start with the major answer. Be tactful, but truthful. Give the points of information with appropriate emphasis.
  - ► Arrange your answer logically.
  - ► Make clear, concise statements, visually setting them off, if possible.
- Offer the applicant an alternative plan or hope for a future credit relationship, if either is feasible. People or businesses with weak credit often become good credit risks at a later date.
- End, if possible, with a statement of goodwill.

ELIMINATE WRONG MESSAGES

- Do not supply unsolicited information.
- Don't cite exact "bad" credit references. It is far better to ask the applicant to set up an appointment to discuss these, if he or she desires.

- Don't offer statements you can't back up with facts.
- Do not give confidential information or unnecessary details.
- Don't make promises about the future.

SELECT A FORMAT

Use standard forms where appropriate, or type your response on company letterhead.

USE STRONG WORDS

analyze	build	consider	creditworthy
demonstrate	deny	establish	evaluate
future	policy	reconsider	record
reevaluate	review	risk	successful

CONSTRUCT USEFUL PHRASES

a review of your debt load	after careful review
demonstrating a successful repayment record	financial review committee concludes
in order to build a credit record	loan committee decision
our analysis indicates	past performance indicates
please review the enclosed schedule	to extend further credit
upon further review	we are not authorized

BUILD EFFECTIVE SENTENCES

Our loan committee has carefully reviewed your application for a small business loan.

We have analyzed the profit-and-loss statement you submitted.

Unfortunately our current bank policy requires that a small business loan applicant demonstrate a two-year successful credit relationship with suppliers in order to establish a line of credit in the amount of $250,000.

While we are unable to offer you a line of credit at this time, we do encourage you to reapply in 14 months, and submit a record of the missing financial statements at that time.

We must deny your credit application at this time.

In order to offer you the line of credit you desire, we will need to see a track record of five years of successful operation.

In order to have your application for a line of credit approved, you will need to have the signature of a personal guarantor.

Please reapply once you have completed the items checked on the enclosed form.

We look forward to serving you as your loan institution in the future.

We have every confidence that you will be able to complete the requirements.

EDIT, EDIT, EDIT

Limit the information you give, keeping it as objective as possible. Always be sure you have complied with local and state credit-reporting regulations.

Line of Credit Denied

Dear Ms. Deloy:

Reference: Loan Application #20344

Your loan application for a second mortgage is denied because the home appraisal completed (see attached) indicates a market value below the present loan balance. We understand you are interested in selling the home, and would encourage you to contact James Bonder at 202-555-0123 to discuss how you might make some simple and inexpensive improvements that would create a higher market value.

We are all hoping that house market conditions will turn around soon, and Jim will also be able to share with you the most recent forecasts.

Sincerely,

Tu Ryse

Loss of Credit Privileges

Dear Ms. Annoy:

Due to the disuse of your Bonwitt Credit Card (last purchase December, 1999), we are rescinding your credit privileges effective immediately. This means, of course, that you will no longer enjoy the benefits of a Bonwitt customer: flight insurance in the amount of $500,000 for airline tickets charged on the account; insurance against theft of any item purchased on the card; and discounts on 350 major hotels, motels, car rentals, and restaurants.

Should you wish to renew your account with Bonwitt, please complete a new application during your next visit to any of our fine department stores across the country.

Sincerely yours,

Darius Drommett

Denial of Loan Application

Dear Sharon Shine:

Thank you for considering Foremost Bank as your banking resource for your new women's apparel store. After a careful review of your submitted financial package for a small business loan, the loan committee has declined your application, citing the need for a stronger equity to debt ratio.

We would like to see you qualify for the small business loan and develop a successful retail venture. Therefore, we would like to offer to enroll you in a series of small business seminars that could help build a stronger financial loan package. If this interests you, please call me. I've also enclosed a copy of the loan committee's report that outlines the areas where you may wish to focus your attention.

Sincerely,

Joan Saltz

Personal Retail Credit Denial—Residency Requirement

Dear Ms. Longfellow:

Thank you for your interest in a Homestead House credit account. We are pleased that you find the quality and variety of home furnishings fit your lifestyle.

Our policy on new accounts requires that applicants have lived in the area for one year, so we are not able to open an account for you at this time. As a newcomer, however, we would like to welcome you to the community with the enclosed certificate. It gives you a ten percent discount on your next purchase in one of our seven area stores.

We certainly hope you will continue to shop at Homestead House, and we would welcome the opportunity to reconsider you as a credit customer next summer. Please submit an application at that time.

Sincerely,

Rhonda Weaver, Customer Service

Commercial Credit Denial—Lack of References

Dick Chancey, President

Dear Mr. Chancey:

Thank you for your order and application for credit. Woods Supplies has long been a friend of new businesses.

We do, however, require five credit references of over two years duration in order to open a charge account for over $50,000. If you have established the additional two references, please submit them to me.

If not, Woods Supplies will be pleased to reconsider a credit arrangement with New Waves after you have been a cash customer with us for one year. Cash orders at Woods Supplies have one great advantage: we offer a five percent discount. Please indicate on the enclosed order form if you would like to place a cash order.

I look forward to receiving your additional credit references, and will keep your application open for four months. We look forward to working with you and wish you great success in your new endeavor.

Yours truly,

Roger Crocker, Credit Manager

Personal Credit Denial—Slow Pay

Jerald Pearlmutter

Dear Mr. Pearlmutter:

Thank you for applying for a Bullock's credit card. A careful review of your credit references precludes us from offering you credit at this time.

We would like to encourage you to resubmit your application when your credit record indicates timely payments on your present debts over an eight-month period.

We look forward to the possibility of serving you now with cash sales, and in the future by offering you a credit card.

Sincerely,

Jack Bolden, Credit Manager

Corporate Refusal—Bad Credit Risk

Marshall Feedler, Controller

Dear Mr. Feedler:

We appreciate your interest in establishing an account and line of credit with Whimple and Sons.

We have now completed our review of your application, and have made the credit checks you authorized. We have determined that we can offer Wild Things only a cash arrangement at this time. But, as you realize, cash purchases save money by giving you an additional five-percent discount.

We hope you continue as a Whimple and Sons customer, and we look forward to serving you.

Yours truly,

Marvel White

Credit Manager

Corporate Credit Cancellation

Mr. Sheldon Ryder, Credit Manager

Dear Mr. Ryder:

Our records show that during the past 12 months your account balance has remained above our agreed credit terms. As of today, your balance is $2,100.54, and the 60-day, past-due portion of that amount is $1,143.56.

In keeping with our credit policy, we must convert our arrangement to a cash basis. Please make an appointment with Mr. Alex Stitwell this week to review your account and work out a more suitable payment schedule.

If our records are in error, please bring your documentation to your meeting with Mr. Stitwell. We look forward to getting this satisfactorily resolved.

Yours truly,

Norman Nicely, Credit Manager

Commercial Credit Denial— Additional Information Needed

Kevin Doerr, President

Dear Mr. Doerr:

Thank you for your interest in RayGlows and your application for a line of credit. We have now thoroughly reviewed it.

Our policy requires three more references than you have supplied. If you have these references and current financial statements, please return them to me. We will be pleased to reprocess your application.

In the meantime, we welcome your business on a cash basis and offer you a standard five percent discount on all product lines.

Sincerely,
Lane West, Credit Manager

Personal Credit Denial—Lack of Work Reference

Mr. Raymond Wayward

Dear Mr. Wayward:

Thank you for your interest in Bowland's and your application for a personal credit card.

Our policy on issuing credit cards requires that applicants have been employed full-time for a minimum of one year at their present place of employment. Your six months of part-time work at Shelby's prevents us from issuing you a credit card at this time, but we will be happy to reconsider your application if you will resubmit it when you meet this requirement.

Thank you again for your interest in Bowland's. Enclosed is a certificate that entitles you to 15 percent off when you make your next purchase.

Yours truly,
Charlene Childs, Credit Manager

(Also see CREDIT APPROVAL, page 337; CREDIT INQUIRY & PROVIDING CREDIT INFORMATION, page 331; and RESPONSE, page 257.)

Corporate Credit Denial— Offering Alternate Payment Methods

Doris Misewire, President

Dear Ms. Misewire:

Thank you for your interest in using Formed Container's new line of pop-up packaging for your products. It does make an extremely handsome and marketable combination.

We share your enthusiasm about this venture, and after extensively investigating the credit references you provided in your application, we can offer you two initial alternatives for beginning a credit relationship:

- you may pay for the containers in advance of shipping, or
- we will ship containers to you COD.

With either arrangement, we will offer you a five percent cash discount. After six months of a successful relationship, we will reconsider establishing the requested line of credit.

We hope to have the opportunity of working with you to fulfill your packaging needs.

Sincerely,
Stanley Shakely, Credit Manager

Corporate Credit Termination

Sidney Boyer, President

Dear Mr. Boyer:

A review of your account indicates that you have an outstanding balance of $5,678.20, and that no payment has been made on your account in 60 days. We must therefore cancel your line of credit, effective immediately.

Please submit your check for the overdue amount, or contact me to discuss alternate arrangements. We hope you will bring your account current so we can reinstate your line of credit.

Yours truly,
Archie Bufford, Credit Manager

56 REQUEST FOR PAYMENT ADJUSTMENT

When you cannot meet a payment schedule, or a repayment commitment cannot be met as agreed, it is vitally important that you take the initiative, immediately, and contact the creditor or loan institution. Usually face-to-face or telephone contact is the best first course of action. At that time, or immediately afterward, make a written request for—even suggest and outline—an alternative plan for payment.

Remember that the creditor holds the power to damage your credit record. Be as tactful as possible. Be realistic about the plan you propose. Think carefully before you suggest an altered payment plan. Enclose some payment with your letter. And by all means, honor your altered schedule of payment.

DECIDE TO WRITE

Use this communication:

- As soon as you know you will be unable to keep the original agreement
- To renegotiate your payment agreement
- To request and/or notify the lender about late payment

THINK ABOUT CONTENT

- Examine every aspect of your agreement and find out everything you can about the practices of the creditor before deciding on your altered repayment proposal.
- Refer to any appropriate account or customer numbers.
- Use the indirect (bad news) approach: make a positive statement that sets up the problem.
- State the problem, and, as succinctly as possible, give the explanation for the necessity to alter the payment schedule.
- Give the proposed altered plan details.
- Assure the reader you will pay the bill in total.
- Remind the reader of your past positive performance, if possible.
- State the fact that you have enclosed a check, and list the amount of the partial payment enclosed. (Always enclose at least a partial payment.)

- End with a goodwill statement about a continued positive relationship, and ask for the lender's cooperation.

ELIMINATE WRONG MESSAGES

- Do not start with a negative statement.
- Do not fail to include an altered plan for payment.
- Do not fail to enclose a check as a statement of your good intentions.

START WITH A STRONG WORD

adjust	agreement	alter	amend
arrangement	consideration	cooperation	extend
necessary	patience	regret	renewed
repay	reset	restructure	satisfactory

USE EFFECTIVE PHRASES

adjust the present payment schedule	after careful analysis
alter our present agreement	appreciate your cooperation
circumstances dictate a change in payments	considering these new developments
have performed satisfactorily in the past	hope this is agreeable
keep my credit record unblemished	lower the payment amount
meet both of our objectives	propose this new schedule of payments
regret that I'm unable	request your cooperation
restructure the payment plan	resume regular payment schedule
trust you can work with me	unable to meet
will be able to pay	will keep the new plan

BUILD STRONG SENTENCES

I request that my present payment schedule be altered.

I need to request an extension on the payment schedule.

I need to restructure the repayment plan to the modified schedule below.

Since making our original loan agreement, we have experienced several financial changes that require us to request a repayment adjustment.

We will be unable to meet our agreed payment schedule.

Our June and July payments will be late.

I will make up the missed payments in the month of December when I will pay off the loan in full.

Please allow us to complete our loan agreement without incurring any late fees or a negative credit report.

We look forward to continuing our banking relationship in the future without further interruptions in the payment schedule.

I believe you will find us worthy credit partners in the future.

Thank you for your consideration of our request.

SELECT A FORMAT

- Use a business letterhead; or, for a personal loan, use a standard 8½ by 11–inch sheet with return address.
- For communicating by email, use a secure website for all financial matters.
- Type for business; type or use neat handwriting for a personal letter.

EDIT, EDIT, EDIT

Reread your letter to be sure it is correct in tone as well as clear and concise in content.

Request for Repayment Extension

Ms. Sudi Bastra, Vice President

Dear Sudi:

As you know, I suffered a back injury in an auto accident on July 1, and have been unable to work for two months due to acute back pain. This has resulted in my loss of the Thompson account and several smaller accounts with project due dates in July, August, and early September.

I'm now greatly improved and shall resume a full-time work schedule next week. But, as a self-employed writer, the loss of income over ten weeks has left me temporarily financially stretched.

I have just signed a new agreement with Phillips in the amount of $150,000 for the completion of two books, and an agreement with Leopard for $75,000 for copywriting on their Williams and Courtesy accounts, so the future looks bright once again.

I request that you extend my repayment schedule for September, October, November, and December (a total of $6,000), and allow me to make these payments in one total payment on January 1 to coincide with installments I will receive on the Phillips and Leopard contracts. (I have enclosed the payment for August in the amount of $1,500.) I will, of course, expect to pay interest on the payments for the additional time at the current preferred loan rate. I also request that no negative note be made to my credit rating.

Thank you for your consideration of my situation. I look forward to continuing our banking relationship, and to being a valued bank customer long into the future.

Sincerely,

Bebe Rice

Request to Restructure Payments

[After face-to-face or phone discussion]

Mr. Fred Aster
Accounts Receivable Manager

RE: Account TR-4578

Dear Mr. Aster:

Following our discussion, I am enclosing a check for $450 to be applied toward our account number TR-4578. This is, of course, less than the scheduled payment of $1,800 designated in our payment booklet. As I stated, we have had a temporary but marked downturn in business because our farmer customers have experienced severe flooding, as I'm sure you've heard on the news.

We will need to adjust our payments to $450 a month for the next 12 months, since farmers will not be purchasing seed or planting this season. We plan to be able to pay our account in full in April of next year; plus, of course, the incurred interest on the loan extension.

We have enjoyed a long and satisfactory relationship with your company; and we look forward to resuming a mutually profitable one next season.

We will greatly appreciate your cooperation and patience in this difficult time.

Sincerely,

Jacob Stern

Request for 30-Day Extension—Slow Receivables

[After telephone discussion]

Alexander Fishbein
Collections

Dear Alex:

I'm enclosing a check for $200 instead of the $1,300 balance due because, as I detailed in our conversation yesterday, we have unfortunately had a delay on several large units. Those have now been shipped, but the accounts receivable pipeline hasn't been replenished.

I am sorry about this reduced payment and certainly do not want to blemish our 10-year, excellent credit record. We'll be back on track and pay this in full in 30 days, bringing our account current.

We ask for your patience with this delay.
Thank you.

Best,

George Buckingham

Payment Withheld Due to Creditor Error

[After telephone discussion]

Suzie Stith

President

Dear Suzie:

I'd like to pay the outstanding balance on our account RR-440, but I haven't received a response to my letter of March 10 requesting that you check the balance and correct the error in your bill dated February 15. (See copies attached.)

I will gladly pay the corrected balance of $765.20 in full when I receive a corrected statement. Thank you.

Sincerely,

Jennie Garrison

Applying Credit to Accounts Payable

[After telephone discussion]

Jesse Choice
Accounts Receivable

Dear Jesse:

As we discussed, I've shipped the valves that are missing seals back to you. You will have them this morning. The total charge for these (your invoice #12221) is $5,455.23.

I've reduced our outstanding invoice #122554 for July of $15,897 by the refund credit amount of $5,455.23 we paid for the valves; and I've enclosed a check for the balance of $3,866.23.

Sincerely,

Pablo Martinez

Request Concerning Late Payment

[After telephone discussion]

Sherri Grove
Accounts Payable

Dear Sherri:

As I explained on the telephone, I inadvertently left my mortgage payment for October in the amount of $1,564 in my purse for more than three weeks. (Yes, I must clean out my purse more frequently. In my defense, I changed purses, and just pulled this one out of the closet to use again.)

I would like to avoid having this appear as a late payment on my record, if possible, and request your consideration. I'll also promise not to let it happen again. Please do initiate the automatic withdrawal of the mortgage payment from my account to start with my next payment.

Thank you for your help with this.

Sincerely,

Jade Jewell

Request for Return for Credit

[After telephone discussion]

Esmeralda Squat
Customer Service

Dear Esmeralda:

As discussed on the telephone, I wish to return 50 boxes of the 18 by 18–inch "Durango" travertine stone tiles (priced at $8.76 per sq. ft.) for full credit in the amount of $1,292, including tax. I understand that this was a special order, but it is a frequently ordered product and the local supplier, Quido, has stated that they will accept the return of the tile for full credit without a restocking charge.

If you prefer, I would be happy to have a store credit in the amount of $1,292 rather than a refund.

Thank you for your cooperation in this matter. I shall return the tile on Wednesday if you give me a call today with approval.

Sincerely,

Rachel Chance

(See also ORDER, page 326, and OFFERING AN ADJUSTMENT, page 350.)

57 OFFERING AN ADJUSTMENT

When you are offering a product or service and something goes wrong, you'll want to take the necessary corrective steps to maintain the goodwill of your customer.

Quick action increases your chances of maintaining a positive relationship and the esteem of the other party. In the ideal situation, of course, your follow-up is so impeccable that you are aware of a problem before the customer has registered a complaint. This often is not the case, of course. But do act immediately. This is when your efforts will be most effective.

Communicate directly, accept proper responsibility, resolve the problem fairly, and work toward complete customer satisfaction, if possible. The critical factors in the adjustment letter are the tone of the letter and the emphasis. Be both respectful and positive, regardless of the factors involved, and emphasize customer satisfaction.

DECIDE TO WRITE

Timing is vital. Write this communication immediately when:

- An error has been made in the delivery of your services or products
- A customer registers a complaint
- A damaged product has been received
- An exchange is requested
- A refund is requested
- There has been a change in payment terms or amounts
- There has been a billing error

THINK ABOUT CONTENT

- Open with the good news the customer or other party will want to hear. Focus on a positive solution. This may be the granting of an adjustment, or it may be acknowledging the customer was right. Sometimes it's both.
- Quickly identify the complaint you are responding to. Do not go into a lengthy explanation of the negative aspects of the complaint or problem.
- Briefly, and in positive terms, explain what caused the problem if this is essential to restoring the reader's confidence in you and your organization.
- Explain exactly how you will correct the problem. Make your statement sound eager, not begrudging.

- Give any steps you will take to prevent the problem from recurring, if this is appropriate.
- Thank the customer for bringing the situation to your attention.
- Close with a friendly, positive statement that will help to reestablish rapport, but don't apologize again.

ELIMINATE WRONG MESSAGES

- If the customer or other party was at fault, do not state this outright. Rather, let it be known by implication or understatement.
- Do not over-apologize or over-emphasize the problem.
- Do not make statements that could be construed as you accepting liability beyond the scope of your responsibility, or admitting that you acted in a negligent manner.
- Do not place blame. Keep your statements, whenever possible, objective, brief, and simple.

CONSIDER SPECIAL SITUATIONS

- In all situations where there are serious issues of neglect or liability, consult your attorney on how your letter should be worded.
- If the problem has resulted in a loss of income or other consequences for the customer, try to arrive at a solution that will rectify the situation. Perhaps something such as a future discount that allows the customer to recoup lost revenue could be proposed.

SELECT A FORMAT

Use a standard letterhead, typewritten, or send by email.

EDIT, EDIT, EDIT

Make your letter factual, brief, and concise.

Supplier Sent the Wrong Product

[Date]

Ms. Vivian Waverly

Dear Ms. Waverly:

I was sorry to learn that an error was made, and that you received the wrong fabric color on the sofa you ordered from us May 15. Our source at the factory has located your sofa, and it is being shipped to you tomorrow. It will arrive on Thursday, and someone will telephone you on Wednesday to arrange an exact delivery time. The delivery people will pick up the burgundy sofa at that time.

I am enclosing a brochure on a pair of chairs the manufacturer is showing with your sofa. If you wish to order these, we would be happy to offer you a 10 percent discount. Just show the salesperson this letter.

Sincerely,

Janice Placid, Customer Service

Delayed Shipment Due to Strike

[Date]

Nigel Redenbacker
President

Dear Mr. Redenbacker:

Thank you for your call today. I will keep you updated on your shipment (order #4456) of April 14. The dockworkers' strike in New York persists; however, we have heard that a settlement is expected this week.

In the meantime, I'm enclosing pictures I took this morning of some great rugs we have in house that I can ship to you immediately if you need them to fill out your inventory for your upcoming sale. I am willing to offer you a 5 percent discount on the prices listed.

The minute the strike is settled I will be in contact. Meanwhile, if you decide to order any of the rugs pictured, please call Ann at (617) 555-0123.

Sincerely,

Hasan Raheeb
President

Damaged Merchandise

[Date]

Sophie Stit

Dear Ms. Stit:

Thank you for informing us of the damaged drapery rods.

As I stated on the phone, we are shipping replacements to you and you will have them tomorrow morning. Please give the delivery person the damaged rods.

We look forward to your continued business.

Sincerely,

Carly Smith

Data Entry Error

[Date]

Mr. Edward Fishwhacker
President

Dear Mr. Fishwhacker:

Thank you for your call this morning concerning the error in your bill dated April 12 for $2,456. In investigating, as I stated in my return telephone call, I found that due to a data entry error, your check #8998 was credited to the wrong account.[1]

Please accept our apology. The correction has been made showing your account paid in full. (Copy enclosed.)

Would you please review your company listing below to ensure that we have complete and correct information?[2]

Customer:	Whaler's Cove
Address:	Worthy, MA 01075
Telephone:	(617) 555-0123
Account #:	55420-98

I'm enclosing a 15 percent discount certificate for your use on any products you purchase before September 1. We look forward to serving you in the future.[3]

Sincerely,

Stan Swinebuckle
Customer Service

---

(1) Offer information. (2) Prevent further problems. (3) Close on a positive note.

Negative Response to Request to Return Merchandise

[Date]

Mr. Charles Reeves

Dear Mr. Reeves:

Thank you for your letter of March 19. I was sorry to hear that sales of the custom-made hutches did not go as you expected. The question of returning the 32 remaining miniature hutches you still have in stock is a difficult one. Because you ordered these 16 months ago and we had them made to your specifications and delivered them to your stores 11 months ago, any return policies have long expired.[1]

I have checked with the manufacturer and with other retailers. Bill Hornblower at Country Way in Boston (617) 555-0123 and Henry Hopewell at Repasts in Rhapsody (213) 555-0124 both offered to discuss with you some ideas for selling them.[2]

Additionally, we have received a few calls from interior decorators in your area for similar pieces: Ted Booker at Draper Designs (555-0125) and Hillary Groves at Design Works, Inc. (555-0126).

I hope this is helpful, and I look forward to serving you in the future.[3]

Sincerely,

Sherman Taylor
Customer Accounts

(1) State your response as simply as possible. (2) Offer additional help, if possible. (3) End on a positive note.

Replacement of Damaged Goods—Problem Unknown

[Date]

Mr. Arthur Knight

Dear Mr. Knight:

I am enclosing a check for $553.12, the amount you paid for the custom-made Wright suit. We are very sorry this unfortunate accident occurred.[1]

My investigation did not turn up the exact source of the stains on the suit. Our laboratory determined that the stains were made by an acid of the kind used in automobile batteries. Evidently something was spilled on the package during shipment. In 18 years, we have never had such an incident.[2]

I am also enclosing a certificate for a 15 percent discount should you want to order another suit.[3] We would be happy for the opportunity to serve you.[4]

Sincerely,

Frank Fong
President

(1) Apologize. (2) Give any explanation. (3) Make a positive gesture. (4) End on a positive note

Overcharge

[Date]

Arnie Ruff

Dear Mr. Ruff:

Yes, you were charged the wrong price. My apologies for the mistake.

You are entitled to the 20 percent volume discount, and I've attached a corrected invoice.

Thank you for your business and for keeping us on our toes.

Sincerely,

Dusty Weiner, Customer Service

58 COLLECTION LETTER

Unpaid debts are growing losses to the seller. The goal here is to collect money owed as soon as possible, while at the same time retaining customer or borrower goodwill. But in times of economic hardship, being sensitive to the debtor's situation is critical.

Don't bypass the friendly reminder telephone call. This is often the first and best approach in collecting. (But do check, first, all call restrictions.) In writing the first collection letter, use an indirect approach (see Refusal, page 274) and write the letter in a persuasive tone. Collection letters to individuals should take an empathetic "you" attitude, and business-to-business letters should also ring with sensitivity to the reader.

Most organizations develop a series of four stages of progressively stronger collection letters. They must be well timed to be effective, and although the computer makes this process very easy, you must carefully monitor it. (Any emails with financial subject matter must be made on secure servers.)

The first-stage letter is usually a *reminder*, the next an *inquiry*, followed by an *appeal*, and finally a *demand*. The wording and timing depend on whether the customer is a person or a business, the balance owed, your type of business, the debtor's situation, and a number of other financial and industry factors. All stages should be completed in a courteous manner.

There are local, industry, state, and federal standards and regulations concerning collection practices. These must be carefully followed.

THINK ABOUT CONTENT

- Let the reader know in the first sentence that this is a collection letter.
- You can then ask him or her to act.
- Put the responsibility to communicate or explain on the reader. You may even ask the reader for an explanation on the back or bottom of the letter or statement or by return email.
- In each letter, state the total amounts owed, the original due date, suggest an alternate plan, and invite the reader to call and discuss it.
- Make it easy for the reader to respond. Enclose an envelope and provide a telephone contact name and number.
- Be flexible and as generous as possible in trying to work out terms for repayment, especially if the debtor expresses that difficult circumstances have caused nonpayment. This, of course, can be easily checked out.
- Use a polite tone in the first series of letters and gradually make it stronger.

Early or Reminder Letter

- Begin by identifying with the reader, then remind the reader of the past-due bill.
- Include a statement that shows confidence the reader will pay.
- End with a goodwill comment, or a statement about your future relationship.

Inquiry or Stronger Reminder Letter

- Following the steps for the early reminder (above), start with a neutral inquiry in an effort to begin a dialogue, but follow it with a stronger statement about the necessity of paying the overdue bill.
- Assume circumstances are preventing invoice payment, and ask directly for payment.
- Inquire about problems, and suggest alternatives like partial or installment payment plans, if you can offer this.
- Offer a toll-free telephone number, a fax number, and/or a web address where payment may be made with a credit card.
- Mention the importance of good credit, and remind the creditor that he or she has received considerate treatment from you.
- Make it easy for the customer to respond by including a toll-free telephone number; an email address; and/or a stamped, addressed envelope.

Middle or Appeal Letter

There may be a number of graduated letters in this stage, starting with ones with lots of goodwill statements to ones with fewer goodwill statements. In all these letters, you should do the following:

- Begin with an attention-getting statement that sets up your appeal.
- State your appeal using the second-person ("you") viewpoint and persuasive language.
- Ask for payment.
- Optionally, repeat the appeal.

Develop a persuasive strategy that will appeal to your particular reader:

- The pride approach appeals to the reader's self-respect and desire for social acceptance.
- The ethics approach appeals to the reader's moral standards of honor, character, integrity, and "doing what's right."
- The self-interest appeal stresses the importance to the reader of keeping his or her credit rating and buying power.
- The fear approach is the flip side of self-interest: the consequences of not paying, such as legal action, and not being able to buy on credit, etc.

Final or Demand Letters

- You must first consider any federal, state, and local laws governing collection procedures, business practices in your industry, and the image you wish to convey about your organization. Your objective is to get the debtor to take action and pay the delinquent account. It is not to harangue or demean.

- In most cases, you have three courses of action if payment is not made:
  1. Report the delinquent account to a credit interchange group such as a credit bureau.
  2. Turn it over to a collection agency.
  3. Take the debtor to court.

Decide which alternative(s) you will take, then write your letter accordingly.

- Begin by stating which course of action you are taking and why.
- Explain the effects of this action in a matter-of-fact statement.
- Offer the reader one last chance to pay by setting a deadline and urging that it be met.
- Optionally, end with a statement that the reader can stop the action, or the reader will cause the action by his/her inaction.

ELIMINATE WRONG MESSAGES

- Never write an angry letter.
- Don't apologize.
- Do not use stilted language.
- Never repeat an appeal made in a previous letter.
- Never imply that your customer is not an honest person.
- Do not lapse into abuse or threats.
- Do not use inflammatory or demeaning words or phrases such as *demand, failure, repeated failure to respond,* or *failure to pay.*
- Don't use sanctimonious, coercive, or false reverse psychological terms or phrases in an effort to manipulate.
- Do not include any statements that could be considered libelous.
- Do not violate an individual's right to privacy. Do not send statements or make collection telephone calls to his or her place of employment, for example.

CONSIDER SPECIAL SITUATIONS

Handle collection of personal loans to friends or relatives with pleasantness but with firmness:

> Dear Jill: Did you forget? My records indicate we agreed you would repay the loan ($5,000) on January 15 . . ." Or use humor if it's appropriate: "I've reached that scary stage of not being able to remember if I remembered! Didn't we agree the loan of $5,000 would be repaid on June 1?

USE CAREFULLY SELECTED WORDS

agree	alter	alternate	amount
arrive	balance	check	contact
cooperate	due	eliminate	outstanding
overdue	partial	reimburse	remember
reminder	repayment	resolve	terms

BUILD EFFECTIVE PHRASES

according to our agreement

do not wish to discontinue deliveries

due the first of the month

find a delinquency

invite your call to discuss

let's discuss alternatives

please contact us immediately

request partial payment

show your account overdue

did you forget

don't want to disrupt

experiencing financial difficulties

friendly reminder

let us know your plan to repay

payment now due

preferred customer

review our records

use our convenient website

CREATE STRONG SENTENCES

Please call me to discuss your payment schedule.

Please go to our convenient website and make your payment to immediately resolve this matter.

Perhaps a simple accounting error has been made.

We wish to discuss with you how you may bring your account up to date.

This is a reminder that your June 1 payment has not been received.

Alice, please give me a call to discuss the matter.

I know there is a simple explanation as to why the payment has not been received

Have you somehow overlooked paying the August invoice?

By sending a check today, you will preserve your excellent credit standing.

We are concerned because we have not heard from you.

Partial payment arrangements can be made if you will call me today.

Please use the enclosed envelope to send in your November check, or call me at 888-555-0123.

We will work with you in every way possible to bring your account up to date.

Your account in the amount of $5,650 is now 120 days overdue.

Because you have not responded to our reminders and notices, we must turn your account over to Credit Mongers Inc. for collection of the outstanding balance of $6,322.

You can easily avoid the nonpayment status by calling me today at 800-555-0123.

Don't endanger your fine credit standing by ignoring this notice.

You can easily resolve this problem by sending in your payment or calling today.

SELECT A FORMAT

Use a business letterhead.

EDIT, EDIT, EDIT

In addition to verifying the facts in your letter, be sure to eliminate any grammar and spelling errors. But most important, check the tone of your letter to ensure that it promotes cooperation and ends with a goodwill statement.

Initial Corporate Reminder Letter

[Date]

Antiqua Brookner
Accounts Payable

Dear Ms. Brookner:

Just a reminder that your account balance of
$1,545.24 at Highlands' Ranch is now overdue.
Please mail your payment today, or if your check
has crossed this letter in the mail, please accept
our thanks.

Yours truly,

Charles DeVoe
Accounting

Intensified Business-to-Business Reminder Letter

[After telephone call]

(Date)

Melissa Beale
Accounts Payable

Dear Ms. Beale:

This is a follow-up to our telephone conversation
regarding your order #5443 of April 30 for seven
chandeliers, totaling $7,540.76. We invoiced you
on May 7, the day the chandeliers were shipped.
They were received by you on May 15. (See copies
attached.)

We agreed that you would send a check for the
chandeliers upon receipt, but that was 60 days ago.

Please remit payment immediately so we can get
this resolved and ship your present order sitting
in our warehouse.

Sincerely,

Jeannie Dickson
Account Services

Personal Reminder Letter

[Date]

Jeena Bucarra

Dear Jeena:

This is to remind you that we've not received your
payment for April's club fees of $185. Please mail
your payment today to avoid overdue charges in
the amount of $20, which will be added to your
account balance on the 15th. Or, you can simply
go to our website, www.fitforaction.com, and
make your payment with a credit card.

Jeena, you may wish to initiate our automatic
withdrawal payment plan for future use and
eliminate the monthly check-writing exercise
altogether. To initiate this, give me a call at
213-555-0123, return the enclosed form, or go to
our website.

I've also enclosed our monthly specials for June.
I hope you will again be joining us for the weekly
tennis drills program.

Sincerely,

Rafael Truss

Appeal for Further Business Communication

[Date]

Derek Dietz
Controller

Dear Derek:

Concerning your nonpayment of our invoice #8990
for consulting services in the amount of $1,425,
presented on April 17: I'm again asking you to call
me or Eleanor Jeffries at 529-555-0123 to discuss
any details you still have unresolved.

Perhaps if we talk, we can arrange an alternate
payment schedule. Please call by Friday so we
can get this settled.

Sincerely,

Sharron Decker
Accountant

Appeal for Payment

[Date]

Vadi Kroft
Accounts Payment

Dear Vadi:

I'm concerned that I haven't heard from you concerning the outstanding invoice #32222 in the amount of $4,520 even though I've sent three reminders over a 90-day period. We've had a mutually rewarding credit relationship over the past five years, and this is quite out of character. I'm wondering what extraordinary circumstances have caused this delay of payment.

Please do send in your check today, or call me at 729-555-0123 to arrange a payment plan. I'm certain that if we put our heads together, we can satisfactorily resolve this.

I've enclosed an envelope for return of payment. Or, you may always pay by credit card through our website, www.cycle.com. I look forward to talking with you, and getting the issue of your line of credit resolved.

Sincerely,

Yuri Stern

Informal Demand before Credit Collection

[Date]

Dizzy Foote

Dear Ms. Foote:

Would you please give me a call to see if we can work out a payment plan on your outstanding balance of $7,520 to avoid the collection process?

Surely we can work this out.

Sincerely,

Stan Musale

Appeal for Action to a Customer with Financial Problems

[Date]

Mr. Kirk Foster
President

Dear Kirk:

We understand the trials and tribulations of a rotten season for retailers, but we still need to hear from you on the overdue payment of invoice #4559 for $4,650. (Copy enclosed.)

We'll work with you to reschedule payments so when things pick up in the next couple of months you won't be without a supplier.

Please call me today. I'm going to be in Steamboat on Tuesday, and I can stop by to resolve this.

Sincerely,

Joan Dickson
President

Demand Letter

[Date]

Asa Blizzaard
Sun Thongs

Dear Asa:

Your outstanding balance of $3,200 is now 120 days overdue (pull up your account and take a look), and we can no longer extend additional time for bringing the account current.

Since we haven't heard from you, we will have to turn your account over to our attorney for collection if we don't receive payment in full by Friday. This may, of course, adversely affect your credit.

Please do take care of this by issuing your check for the balance, and sending it today; or by going to the website, www.reflections.com, and paying by credit card. You may also call me at 800-555-0123 to discuss the matter.

Sincerely,

Jorge Ruff

IX.

MARKETING, PUBLIC RELATIONS & SALES COMMUNICATION

The Internet has brought dramatic changes to effective marketing and public relations. You can now communicate directly with your audience to tell them your story, engage your audience in immediate dialogue, and get immediate feedback.

The old techniques for marketing included lots of one-way strategic planning, competitive analysis, targeting market segments, branding, positioning and differentiating your product from the competition, etc. While these skills are still useful, and the old methods of one-way advertising to mass and targeted markets are still effective, the Web now offers easy access to effectively and cost-efficiently get your message directly to those people who want and need it.

The old approach to public relations was to get the media interested in your story, so they would retell it to a wide or targeted audience. This is still true. But now, using the Web, you can also send news releases, blogs, online videos, and even your comments on websites to communicate directly with your audience. It's a whole new venue for not only one-way, but interactive exchanges with your audience.

59 DIRECT MAIL

While it's true that nearly every letter you write has some sales message, the direct-mail sales letter is designed and written with the sole purpose of persuading the reader. The number of these direct mail printed pieces sent through the mail has diminished dramatically with the rise of the use of the Internet and sending such ads via email. In fact, Borrell Associates predicts a 39 percent decline in printed direct mail over the next several years. Although many organizations still find using printed and mailed pieces effective tools to persuade their audiences, more are switching to sending their direct mail through emails. This approach, says Borrell, is very effective for the small business when it is directed at the local market.

The term *direct mail* means that the letter or piece is sent out directly to the target market instead of being sent in response to an inquiry. It may promote a product, service, concept, or even a person. It often includes the use of coupons to get the customer to buy.

In order to sell, the effective piece must (1) get the reader's attention, (2) appeal to the reader's interest by relating to his or her needs or desires, (3) explain the product or service in terms of reader benefits, and (4) motivate the reader to take the directed action.

First you must identify the selling points of your product or service. With these in mind, you must select the right recipients or target audience. This can be scientifically done by using a variety of marketing techniques and data to select the names of people most likely to be interested in what you're selling. There are a great number of firms that do this. Or, with some work, you can develop your own mailing lists.

Many products or services have more than one target audience. But each audience will undoubtedly need its own specially-tailored direct mail piece. If you are selling a new product, your first mailing list is almost always your present customers, and the next list is your current prospects. You have already established a positive relationship with the first group, and are well on your way with the second.

To tailor your letter (or piece) to these readers, learn as much about them as possible. If your mailing list hasn't designated it, learn the sex, age, marital status, vocation, income level, geographical location, interests, hobbies, etc., that will help define your readers in terms of people most likely to buy your products or services.

Write your letter (or piece) to fit this individual target audience, emphasizing how your product or service can benefit the reader. When possible, phrase these benefits in the second-person viewpoint. Remember to test your letter for any overstatement, and check it for any possible liability statements.

End on a note aimed at bringing the reader to the point of the desired action. In the case of big ticket or complex-concept sales, this will probably mean leaving the door open to make, or setting up, the next contact. So instead of ending with "Give me a call for more information," you will write, "I will call you on Friday morning at about nine o'clock to give you the details."

In our electronic age of computer mail-merge, it is easy to "personalize" a letter's inside address and salutation. With the present wide use of email, the direct-mail piece can be instantly and cost-effectively electronically delivered to your target market. (The key to email marketing is a tantalizing subject line that gets readers to open your email, and appealing content to keep the recipient reading.)

DECIDE TO WRITE

Use this letter to:

- Introduce a new product, service, or candidate
- Sell to known prospects
- Invite customers to a grand opening
- Announce a special sale or promotion
- Announce a business closing

THINK ABOUT CONTENT

- Collect direct-mail sales letters or pieces. Test your own reaction to the messages. Examine what the writer (and graphic designer) did well and what he did poorly. Look especially at letters concerning the type of product or service you have to offer.
- Direct mail has become so commonplace that only the very best will be read. Be sure to make yours as brief and complete as possible to give it the best chance. This includes having something unique to say, keeping sentences and paragraphs short, using white space to make the letter appear easy to read, and using visuals to attract attention.
- Consider writing a series of letters. This will affect the letter content and approach.
- Look at the length of the messages. It's best to keep your letter shorter than a single page, or screen length for email, if possible. There are certainly exceptions, but not many. If your letter is over one page, ask yourself if the sales process should be broken into more steps. Maybe the letter should have the goal of setting up a face-to-face meeting, participation in a seminar, or a personal sales call, rather than a "sale-in-one."
- The Internet and social media networks have revolutionized the approach for many products and steps of building an audience. Very short messages, and the use of posted videos, comments, and blogs that direct traffic to your website are limited only by your imagination. These new tools can be a huge boon to your cost-effective marketing and sales efforts.

Get Your Reader's Attention

- When you are ready to write, outline the points you want to make.
- You'll want to lead with a statement to get the reader's positive attention. Use what you've decided is your strongest psychological sales point that's keyed in to a benefit to your reader.

Build your message around it. Open with your strongest psychological point and use your best creative efforts. Think your lead all the way through to the follow-up sales letter and the final sale. An announcement letter telling the reader about a new home loan interest rate of 3.5 percent in a 6 percent market, especially if the letter was mailed to a special list of targeted new-home shoppers, would get the reader's attention, preparing the reader for your loan message, your follow-up telephone call, and your sales presentation and closing statement.

- A statement or question opening that introduces a need the reader has that the product will satisfy works well. These are based upon a rational appeal:

A Capital Loan can save you $125,000 in house payments.
You can qualify for a 3.5 percent home loan.

Or try a question:

Will you pay too much for your new home loan?
Would you like to save $420 each month on house payments?
How can you pay $225,000 less for your new home?
How can you get $175,000 more house and pay $95 less each month?

Or your opening may be based on an emotional appeal, like this letter for aid to children:

Pablo is seven years old today. As he sits inside the darkening hut that is his home, an old pot sits on the dirt floor beside him to catch rain dripping from the tin roof. He's very hungry. But he knows there will be no dinner tonight.

- Select an approach appropriate to your product or service and your audience. Often there will be both rational and emotional elements in the same opening. The use of gimmicks in conjunction with the opening can work well if the gimmick supports the theme.

Select the Right Viewpoint
- Use the second-person ("you") viewpoint whenever possible to make the reader a participant in your appeal. This works well in the home loan example. The second example ("Pablo") relies on the narrative, or "story," technique to draw the reader in.
- The second-person viewpoint or the reader-benefit approach helps focus the message and keep it direct and to the point.

Develop Your Strategy
After the "grabber" first sentence, you must make the transition to telling your reader how your product or service will fulfill his or her need or desire. This must logically follow, of course, from your opening statement. In the example of the home loan, you would follow this rational opening with, perhaps, a true example that your targeted reader can relate to: "Lynne and David Ross pay $2,157 each month on their home loan. . . ."

Choose Your Voice
Make your writing conversational, fast paced, and assertive. You must gain and hold the reader's interest very quickly. To perfect your style, you must write and rewrite.

Select Your Words Carefully

Shades and nuances of words are very important. Strive for words that enliven your sentences. Check the difference in the effect of these words:

Instead of	Try one of these
Hot	sweltering, steaming, fiery, sizzling
Cold	freezing, frigid, frosty, icy
Delicious	sumptuous, delectable, feast, ambrosia

Very important here, too, is selecting positive words of persuasion. Negative words or statements are seldom the best choice:

Negative Wording	Positive Wording
Reduce downtime by 10 percent.	Increase your production by 10 percent.
Less than 2 percent of our clients do not get a new career.	We place over 98 percent of our clients in new careers.
Easy Press eliminates wrinkles.	You get a wrinkle-free shirt all day long.

Enliven Your Text

Use visual techniques to add interest. Consider using bold-faced type of various sizes, italics, color, and graphics.

Give the Reader the Necessary Information

- You must accomplish two things: (1) answer the reader's questions and overcome his or her objections, and (2) supply enough convincing information and facts to motivate the reader to take the next step. This requires a careful balancing act. You must include enough information without bogging the reader down. The fine details of most sales presentations require that you enclose supplementary collateral pieces. But again, this is a balancing act. Too many pieces and the reader will toss the letter and the supplements into the wastebasket.
- So keep supplemental materials to a minimum, and coordinate them with the letter by referencing them: "Price details are covered on page two of the enclosed brochure." Another good example of this might be a cruise with a whole variety of price possibilities. Your letter could include a statement like: ". . . from $434," or "Prices begin at $434."
- There are many visual possibilities when you deliver your direct mail piece via email. But remember that many of the same rules apply: keep it simple; use visuals whenever they promote, but do not detract from, the message.

The Action Step

There are several ways you can bring the reader to the point of taking action. Select the one consistent with your product, and audience, but be sure to make your close clear and specific, preferably with only one course of action to take. Here are the best ways to initiate the last step:

- Call for action. If you offer an incentive to act now, this step makes sense:

  To get your free sample, mail in the enclosed card.
  Just hit 'reply' to sign up for our free newsletter.
  Order your GlowBright bulbs now, in time for Christmas.
  Order now, online, and receive a 20 percent off coupon to be used on your next restaurant visit.
  Order your original print now, before they are gone.

- Complete the circle. Take the reader back to your opening. This is sometimes referred to as the pay-off on your teaser lead:

  Start saving $295 each month on your home mortgage payments now.

- In the case of the narrative story, end with the possible happy ending:

  With your help, Pablo can eat three meals a day, go to school.

- Add "postscript punch." Sometimes overused, but often effective, is the added postscript (P.S.) that makes one last pitch for the reader to act. This should be short, punchy, and call for a precise action. It is usually done in script, or what at least looks like a handwritten note:

  Call now. Offer expires . . .
  Only $9.95 if you order before January 5.
  To take advantage of this offer, place your call now.

Take the Final Steps

- Double-check your letter to be sure you have included all the information the reader needs in order to act, and make sure it is easy for him or her to respond.
- Hand-address the envelopes, if practical, and affix with stamps (make them commemorative). This is more appealing to readers than envelopes with address labels and metered postage marks.

ELIMINATE WRONG MESSAGES

- Avoid "hard sell" pushy techniques. Most readers find these a turnoff.
- Eliminate negative pitches unless they are the strongest.
- Do not give too much information or a fragmented message in your letter.
- Don't be too familiar. Many readers who are strangers don't want to be instant "friends."

CONSIDER ALL YOUR MAIL-OUTS

- It is important to think of the direct-mail sales letter as part of the family of letters you send to customers and clients. It is also important to think of the sales aspects of other letters and pieces you send. Make sure they will fit together and reinforce your message.
- Create a complete family of letters or pieces. This is part of building an identity for your organization.

- Don't miss an opportunity to get the word out about your product or service. Think of everyone you do business with in terms of whether they can be customers.
- Think about creating specials for valued customers to build loyalty. This is usually easily done by offering special discounts or pre-sale access to merchandise.

SELECT A FORMAT

- Use a format consistent with the product and audience. Two-color embossed letterhead isn't the best choice for catalog sales, but it usually is for announcing new banking services, investments financial service, and life insurance.
- Computer-generated letters make personalizing a simple task.
- Email offers are a great way to give a special class of customers a special deal, and coupons can be easily printed out for use in redemption.

EDIT, EDIT, EDIT

Double- and triple-check the facts in your direct-mail piece. Then check for typos and have at least several reviewers (preferably people like your target reader) review your piece before sending it. Make sure, too, the tone is right.

Charter Membership Offer

Dear Charles:

Congratulations! You are nominated for membership as an honored Charter Member of the Regional Air and Space Museum to be opened at the spectacular George Q. Queezy Center. This magnificent center will be constructed entirely with private funds, and, as a noted pilot, you qualify for recognition as a Charter Member. All Charter Members will have a bronze plaque on the entry wall to the museum.

We cannot accomplish this without your support. Will you join my wife, Gertie, and me in choosing to make a contribution and bequest in commemoration of the Century of Flight?

If you want to create your legacy for the Regional Air and Space Museum, please complete the back of this card, and we will send you a contribution and bequest agreement form. Or, you may call or email for more information from the Office of Development's Gift Planning Department either at 800-555-0123 or at legacy@flight.com

Thank you for considering the Regional Air and Space Museum in your estate planning. With your help, we will be able to construct and operate this as one of the leading museums worldwide.

Best regards,

General Dizzy Daft

Special Customer Offer

Dear Janice:

This is your special preferred customer invitation to Cricket's "Pre-Season Preferred Customer Sale." This year our Spring Trunk Show and Sale includes the hottest new fashions that will flatter your figure.

As usual, it's one day only, January 15, from 2:00 p.m. to 8:00 p.m., and our doors will be closed to all other customers.

Print out the coupon below, and come on in for our best preview ever. We've even upped the preferred customer discount to 25 percent off your total purchases.

High tea will be served, and your favorite models from the Junior League will be modeling the latest hot designs. A 10 percent contribution of all sales for the afternoon will be donated to the Junior League Little Miss Scholarship Fund.

See you on the 15th!

Best regards,

Betty Gossamar

Seminar Promotion

SUBJECT: How to Make Your Book a Best Seller in Just 21 Days!

On Tuesday, January 15 you can learn how to hit the bestseller list and sell up to $200,000 in books, even if you're a first-time author and a marketing and sales novice.

Dagwood Dugan and Greer Slough have perfected a simple, four-step formula that you can use to achieve this kind of book sales success. Rob Chock used it to hit four regional bestseller lists and sell $500,000 in books. The cost to implement the formula is less than a good meal out. And it works for all authors—fiction or nonfiction—and all subjects.

Here's your pass to success: tune in for the 45-minute FREE telephone seminar on Tuesday, January 15 at 6:00 p.m. EST.

To register, go to www.bookbust.com, or call toll-free 800-555-0123.

Bike Promotion

Subject: Your Invitation to Ride the Rockies!

There are only 90 days until you'll be meeting at the Park Meadows Roundup! Are you ready? How about your bike?

Print out this coupon, and bring in your bike for our special customer tune-up for only $39.95. That includes a total Mountain High rework of the brakes, tires, lights, chains, all moving parts, and frame integrity.

The offer's good from April 15 through May 15. Give us a call now at 303-555-0123 to subscribe to our free online "Readiness Teleseminar" and to make an appointment to get your bike in. Or, click here to set up your appointment now.

PR Company

Dear Archie:

Over the past five years, Scream Communications has served as King Sausage's public relations agency, netting your company a market share increased by 150 percent each consecutive year. That's a record your competition has openly coveted!

Now that representation for your corporation is coming up for review and bid, we would like the opportunity to again make a presentation to your marketing committee on how we feel we can improve—even more—on our past outstanding record.

We have some new and exciting ideas for King Sausage, including plans that will appeal to three new market areas. I will call your office next week to set up a presentation meeting with your selection committee. We look forward to sharing our dynamic ideas with you.

Sincerely,

Manning Trace

(Also see ANNOUNCEMENT, page 18; CONGRATULATIONS, page 28; INVITATION, page 63; PRESS RELEASE, page 385; THANK-YOU, page 75; and WELCOME, page 57.)

60 SALES FOLLOW-UP

A follow-up sales letter follows an initial contact and has a sales motivation. A number of studies have shown that sending a follow-up sales letter to a prospective customer can net as good or better results as the initial sales letter (see Direct Mail, page 361).

In fact, the first sales letter or sales contact seldom produces enough results from readers to eliminate them from your follow-up sales list. You may want to plan a series of sales letters, often four to six, as part of your total sales campaign. This, of course, also applies to the number of email follow-ups sent.

Follow-up sales letters should contain some of the same vital information as the initial sales letter to build on the message already given. Making this reference helps to build your sales effort.

A progressive number of follow-up sales letters—a sales-letter ladder—is actually required by some audiences. Probably some of the best examples are those involving ideas readers are initially opposed to, such as buying an insurance plan for an extended-care facility or buying a new product that uses brand-new technology.

Many follow-up sales letters also wear other labels: *thank-you, congratulations, response, invitation,* and *request.*

DECIDE TO WRITE

Use this letter:

- After an initial direct-sales letter has introduced a concept
- In response to an inquiry
- After a sales call
- As part of a planned, multi-contact sales campaign
- After receiving a sales referral
- With new customers

THINK ABOUT CONTENT

- Reference how the reader has come to your attention. If he or she is a referral, name the person. If you are following up after a sales call or a telemarketing call, thank the reader for his or her time. If you met the reader at a meeting, say so. This information establishes a relationship and may increase the reader's receptivity to your message.
- Describe the product or service you are offering. Refer to the first letter or email, if appropriate.

- Stress the customer benefits.
- Back up your lead with facts and information. Make statements that will overcome the reader's objections, and answer needs and desires.
- Give new or additional information that may arouse the reader's interest.
- Make a strong close by tying a special offer or incentive to your lead.
- End by leaving an opening for your next contact.
- Follow up by thanking those who give you leads. Write a thank-you letter and report your progress, if appropriate. As a point of courtesy, always let your referral source know if you make the sale.

ELIMINATE WRONG MESSAGES

- Don't send the exact letter you used for the first mailing if it got little or no results. Try to determine why there was little response and make some changes.
- Don't close the door to future contact. Close with a statement that you will make the next contact and/or that invites the reader to contact you.

SELECT A FORMAT

Match or coordinate the look of this letter with any others you have sent the reader. You want to build recognition of your organization's name and products or services.

EDIT, EDIT, EDIT

Transforming your letter into an arresting, clear, and concise form is your challenge. Reread your letter to make sure it (1) gets the reader's attention, (2) creates interest, (3) convinces the reader your product or service meets his or her need or desire, and (4) asks him or her to take the next action you suggest.

Follow-Up to Returned Postcard

Hi, Brad,

Yes, you are registered for the FREE teleseminar on Wednesday, June 15 at 6:30 p.m. EDT.
You'll want to be prepared to take notes, as the information Randy and Ralph will share is truly phenomenal.

Ginger Rogers

Follow-Up to Inquiry

Dear Sudi:

Thank you for your inquiry concerning Freddie's Hand-Printed Wallpaper. The design you're inquiring about may be seen by going to our website FreddiePrints.com, and searching by the design name "Landscapes."

Orders may be placed through the website. We look forward to supplying you with the world's best hand-printed wallpapers.

Best regards,

Ara Glibb

Follow-Up after Direct-Mail Letter

Richard Munson, Photographer

Dear Mr. Munson:

I'm glad you and four of your staff are considering attending our Fifth Annual Shoot 'Em Up Seminar October 20–22. We will cover the latest advanced photo techniques and high-tech photographing in several hours of instruction on each of the three days. I have marked these sessions on the enclosed brochure.

International expert Flash Weasel will teach three of these sessions, and Edsel Redeye will teach the other three.

I've enclosed six applications for your staff to use. If you return the completed applications with tuition payments before Friday, your staff will be assured of getting places, and you will save $25 on each tuition fee. I will call you Wednesday to see if you have any additional questions.

Sincerely,

Miriam Foil
Program Coordinator

Follow-Up on Request for Samples

Dear Mavis:

Here are the Prestige silk shantung samples you requested in both the silver fox and the pewter blue. We also produce a wonderful embossed and corded shantung in coordinating colors, and I've included samples of those, too. Any combination of these fabrics will provide the elegance you are seeking.

Our shipping schedule is enclosed for your reference. Quantities for the draperies, pillows, bedcover, and chaise are available.

If you place your order this week, we can offer you a 7 percent discount on these fabrics. Please call me if you have any additional questions.

Sincerely,

Rachel Trapp

Follow-Up to Set Sales Presentation Appointment

Sybil Snidvider, Marketing Director

Dear Sybil:

It was a pleasure talking to you today. Yes, Marketing Communications is a full-service marketing, advertising, and public relations agency. We specialize in technical accounts and have been able to get great results for our clients using a personalized program emphasizing public relations. Our capabilities statement and a list of some of our clients are enclosed.

I will be in Orlando on the 21st, and would like to talk with you about the possibility of LiveWire using us on a per-project basis. As I mentioned, you may call Roy Bender of B/PAA and discuss with him how we have helped that organization gain a 74 percent market share—an increase of over 50 percent.

Your new energy products sound very exciting, and I'm already percolating some great, low-cost promotion ideas. Would you be able to give me 30 minutes from 1:30 to 2:00 p.m. on the 21st for a brief presentation? I'll call your office on Friday to see if I may schedule that time.

Sincerely,

Eric Muskgrove, Account Manager

Follow-Up to Request for Information

Dear Ryan:

Yes, you can get the Roadster Rabbit Model X2 in carmine red in time for Christmas—if you order this week.

There's more good news: we are offering you a Model X2A, an upgrade that includes two new features this year, for the same dealer-plus price.

If this is the automobile you've had your heart set on, now's the best time ever to make the decision to purchase.

I've put a hold on this particular car for 48 hours. Give me a call today, and I'll run through the pricing and payment structure with you.

All the best,

Rudy Rotor

Follow-Up to Request for Search

Dear Ruby:

I'm amazed. I've actually located two lemon-yellow Model 77s in vintage condition and have attached photo files so you may take a look.

My advice: if you love one or both, please authorize me to make an offer. On the File A bike, I suggest offering $11,500, and I'd try for this one first; and on the File B bike, I think the seller will let it go for $13,000, though as you'll see, it's slightly less desirable.

All the relevant stats are in the photo files.

Best,

Mike

Thank-You to New Customer / Sales Follow-Up

Darrel Covey

Dear Mr. Covey:

Thank you for your order for the Bridgestone Model AS-34.

I was happy to hear about your increase in production with this fine machine. As I mentioned to you on the telephone, I believe you will be interested in the two Bridgestone grinders, Models RE-34 and RE-50. These will replace your present machines, and offer the efficiency and increased production you desire. I've enclosed the spec sheets for both.

I will be demonstrating these grinders during our open house on the 15th, and you could see all the benefits to your present operation with this hands-on opportunity. I will also have a complete sequence of machinery set up to demonstrate an operation similar to yours. You're welcome to bring some of your own parts and try these new machines.

I'll call you later this week to see if I can sign you up for this session (it's free), or exactly how I can help you with your next step.

Sincerely,

Frank Sharpe
Customer Sales

Follow-Up to Sales Call

Alexander and Elle Callan

Dear Mr. and Mrs. Callan:

It was a pleasure meeting you last evening. Thank you for the opportunity to introduce our insurance plan. I believe Plan D in the brochure is ideal for your first goal of sending Derek to college. The other elements of the plan will meet your family protection, retirement income, and other education goals.

I will be conducting a luncheon workshop on Thursday for about 20 people. I'd like to invite you to attend because I will be covering the plan elements in depth. Or, I would be happy to meet with you again on Thursday evening to answer any additional questions. I will call you on Tuesday evening to discuss which you would prefer.

Sincerely,

Charlie Sellwell, Personal Wealth Manager

Follow-Up Sales Letter

Johnathan G. and Louise Kettering

Dear Mr. and Mrs. Kettering:

Welcome to Tucson. Thank you for requesting our brochure from the Welcome Wagon. I've enclosed it along with several photos you requested in our telephone conversation. These are five of the homes we have landscaped in your area.

We have been giving Tucson homeowners the best of the desert Southwest for over 25 years. Please feel free to check with a few of those customers from the enclosed list.

We do have a small welcome gift for you, which I will bring by after I call you next week to set up a time to give you a landscaping estimate.

Sincerely,

James Morningflower

(Also see DIRECT MAIL, page 361; REQUEST & INQUIRY, page 246; RESPONSE, page 257; THANK-YOU, page 75; and WELCOME, page 57.)

X.

MEDIA RELATIONS, PUBLICITY & PUBLICATION

On the Internet, the exclusive focus on media relations to get your story out to your audience has been turned on its head. Now it's possible to communicate directly with your audience through social media, and also connect with many others who have a web voice: bloggers, online news sites, micro-publications, etc. It makes the job of telling your story both easier and more difficult.

It's still important to contact those editors, writers, and reporters and interest them in retelling your story; and it's also important to hone your story carefully with content-rich information and get it out directly to your audience(s). This requires careful strategies, extensive market research, and lots more knowledge of processes and paradigms.

Cast your bread upon the water,
and it may come back to you with
peanut butter and jelly.

—*Anonymous*

61 PITCH LETTER

When you wish to promote an idea to be covered by the media, you'll "pitch" the editor, TV reporter, movie producer, or other appropriate person. This is done either verbally or in written form, and it's best to find out the form preferred by each of the individuals you wish to convince. (Sometimes to get your story covered, you'll want to offer a single member of the media an "exclusive.") You will want to carefully develop and hone your pitch, a sales tool cut to its most concise and persuasive best.

Most editors at magazines and newspapers, online or printed, will insist you send a pitch letter—usually transmitted by email—explaining your idea or the subject you are requesting they cover. But sometimes you will get the opportunity to make a pitch over the telephone.

A good pitch message must not only suggest a newsworthy idea, or an idea with human interest, it should also offer the editor a bit of background information, and sometimes the opportunity to set up an interview (if you are suggesting the editor cover the story rather than you writing the piece). When appropriate, also include a product sample (like a book, if you have a new book out). Include all the ingredients that will make it convincing and easy for your reader to make a decision to cover your story. (The pitch is usually a short version of the query letter, but the terms are often used interchangeably.)

THINK ABOUT CONTENT

- Be sure you understand the subject or product thoroughly so you can explain newsworthy aspects well.
- Know the target media and appeal to their particular interests.
- Make sure you target the right editor.
- Call the person—editor, reporter, or interviewer—and, if appropriate, make a verbal pitch, stating you will follow up with a letter.
- Determine how the person prefers you submit your pitch letter: mail, email, or fax. It may be necessary to offer an "exclusive" on the story. If there are competitive newspapers, for example, try to get one to do a feature by using this approach.
- Check the spelling of the person's name, title, and address.
- Personalize your letter to your reader, offering a "slant" for his or her readership.
- Use an intriguing first sentence to hook the reader immediately. This "hook" can be a news angle or something the reader needs or wants.
- Use a professional but friendly tone.

- Keep the pitch short—no more than a single page or one computer screen in length—pithy, and full of information.
- Conclude with a statement taking the initiative to make the next contact; for example, "I'll call you on Thursday to see if this will work for you."
- Follow up exactly as you promised to increase your credibility.

ELIMINATE WRONG MESSAGES

- Do not use a first name in the salutation unless the reader is a personal friend, or you know it will be okay.
- Gimmicks are high risk. Don't use them unless you've tested them on a substantial market sample and know they fit the reader well.
- Avoid overused adjectives like *unique, fantastic, greatest, incredible,* and *best.*

CONSIDER SPECIAL SITUATIONS

- If you are pitching a product, single out the most newsworthy and interesting aspect of the product and make that the first sentence.
- If you are pitching the results of a survey or a personality for an interview, use a provocative opening, either a statement or a question:

   Did you know that over 97 percent of husbands are unfaithful?
   Today nine accidents will happen within 25 feet of your desk.
   The job market for sports editors is drying up.
   Did you know that 93 percent of working mothers will only get six hours sleep tonight?

- Back up your first sentence with facts, an explanation, and/or an expansion on the lead.
- Put the facts in the middle of your pitch, but keep it short and snappy.
- Use bullets and indentations to make important points.
- Keep your purpose in mind: to get the reader to agree to do an interview, take a tour, assign a feature for you to write, or some other request.
- Be sure you close asking for what you want:

   Will this work for you?
   I'll call you Wednesday to answer any additional questions.
   May I write this in 1,500 words?

SAMPLE OPENING PITCH LINES

   Robert Wright had no idea that the chimp, Axel, he'd raised from a two-month-old orphan would try to kill him.
   Jason Quit had no idea as he ate his Cheerios Tuesday at 7:45 a.m. that he would face death not once, but twice, before dinner time.
   The candy craze now accounts for a quadrupling of your family's dentist bills.
   You can save $10,000 per year on your son or daughter's college tuition.
   Would you buy this car if it promised to save you $15,000 this year on gasoline?

SELECT STRONG WORDS

act	assign	exclusive	feature
first	fresh	learn	new
now	only	please	readers
research	results	survey	unknown

BUILD EFFECTIVE PHRASES

findings revealed	first timenew facts	new research indicates
new survey	recent research	research results
secrets revealed	survey results	budding trend

CREATE STRONG SENTENCES

New research indicates medical treatment for AIDS is near a cure.

Mom learns how to raise thankful kids.

Is this the cure for breast cancer?

More than 100 pounds lost in just 20 weeks with this diet.

Lifting cans of soup results in strong bones.

Will the new transit system eliminate the brown cloud?

Free zoo day for kids is Tuesday.

Do you have the kind of blood that will save a child's life?

You can give the gift of life on your lunch hour.

Do you know how to apologize?

Forgiveness isn't about forgetting.

Pitch Letter

April Meehan, Senior Editor

Dear April:

I suggest a feature story on Blanchard Banks of Detroit, who, at the age of sixty-four, has just read his first book ever to his granddaughter, Jasmine, age four. "It's a miracle," the silver-haired man explains.

Blanchard began life as a farm worker in Mississippi and migrated to Detroit as a young man in 1950. Working in a factory, he managed to get by without reading, by meticulously following instructions and occasionally asking someone to "clarify" written communications.

When Marks Industries, where Blanchard works, joined the fight for literacy, Blanchard signed up for the after-work tutoring program offered at his local library. In June he will graduate in a special ceremony to be attended by several members of the U.S. Congress.

In the Marks Industries program alone, fifty people have already been able to experience the joy of learning to read. It wasn't easy for Blanchard and the others to admit their reading deficiencies; it wasn't easy to overcome the obstacles of getting enough volunteer instructors and a suitable meeting place; but the Marks program is making a big difference. In fact, there are now plans to expand it into a fifteen-state partnership with local community organizations.

I believe your readers would be inspired by Blanchard's story. There are great photo opportunities here. I'll give you a call in a few days to discuss your interest.

Sincerely,

Samantha Gerkins

62 FUNDRAISING

The fundraising letter is a sales letter with a heart tug. But it must be tempered with the kind of persuasive and cogent writing that brings results without broadcasting that it is selling the reader something.

Many charities compete for the same dollars, and unsolicited direct mail has gone beyond the saturation point. Frustrated, people often toss requests for donations after only a cursory glance, or less. To be successful, a fundraising letter must be part of a larger campaign that has established the organization as one with worthy goals and a demonstrated accountability for donations. It helps a great deal if the charity is immediately recognized as a good cause.

For economy, the letter or email recipients should be people who have demonstrated interest in the charity's work or who have track records of giving to similar charities. Then the letter must deliver a simple, concise, and convincing message.

All these factors make the fundraising letter very difficult to master.

DECIDE TO WRITE

You'll use this special communication to:

- Elicit monetary or other contributions
- Request volunteers
- Invite contributors to a fundraising event (also see Invitation, page 63)

THINK ABOUT CONTENT

- Grab the attention of the reader in the opening sentence.
- Identify the charity and its purpose.
- Convince the reader of the need to contribute.
- Define exactly how the reader's contribution will be used.
- Explain the benefits of the reader's contribution to charity recipients.
- Explain the benefits the reader will receive by contributing.
- Make the act of contributing as easy as possible.
- Use language and a tone that indicate that you expect the reader to help.
- Tune your message to your reader as closely as possible.
- Use positive, clear, and concise language that focuses on benefits to the reader. Rather than writing "Jose Perez won't eat tonight unless you give," write "Helping children like Jose

Perez feels good" or "You can make sure Jose Perez eats tonight" to make your statement reflect reader benefits.

- Define specifically your contribution request:

    There are several ways you can help:
        Return a check for $15 or more.
        Check the box that says "I volunteer to be a telephone operator one hour a week."
        Call 555-0123 and tell the operator you have an item to be picked up Tuesday for the auction.

- Remember, your message should entice the reader to act immediately: "Return your contribution in this envelope now to help." Statistics indicate there's a dramatic drop in response if action is delayed by the reader.

- Construct your letter using informal language, including contractions, some short sentences (but don't make it choppy or staccato), questions, and perhaps even acceptable slang to achieve a conversational tone. Contractions are useful: isn't, don't, can't, won't, and we're. But don't overdo it. Some short, useful sentences include these:

    We're almost there!
    Just $50,000 more and we'll start building.
    Can you believe it?
    You've been wonderful!
    And now for the final lap!
    We need your help.

- Include a mission statement. Briefly and exactly tell the reader what you want to accomplish: "In just three months, we have raised $500,000 of the $5 million needed to build the new Lily Women's Center."

- Expect the reader to fulfill his or her commitment. If this is a letter in a series that follows a pledge on the part of the reader, you might say, "Your pledge is important to finishing the job."

- Remind the reader of his or her pledge, but don't let your letter slip into a harping, pressuring, or threatening tone.

- Use a postscript to attract additional attention. By placing a punchy, handwritten (script) point outside the body of the letter (perhaps even in colored ink), you may create a strong emphasis.

ELIMINATE WRONG MESSAGES

- Don't let your letter take on negative, moralizing, or guilt-inducing tones. Givers want to feel their motivation is prompted by their own best intentions.

- Be sure your letter doesn't have a slick or patronizing tone. Test it on a number of readers to be sure it rings genuine and sincere.

- Don't include more than two inserts. Too many inserts dilute and clutter your message, prompting the reader to classify your letter as junk mail.

- Avoid creating undue pressure, but make it easy for the reader to respond.

- Don't use gimmicks that will detract from or cheapen your message.
- Don't pressure contributors to give you the names of friends and associates.

CONSIDER SPECIAL SITUATIONS

- Target your letter to a specific audience. If a form letter is sent, be sure it is tailored to a carefully selected audience to increase your response. Change it and tailor it to another audience.
- Computers make it possible to personalize form letters to recipients. Use this approach, if possible.
- Email fundraising can easily be viewed as spam, and therefore isn't usually effective as a first communication plan. However, it can work nicely as a follow-up plan, after responders have indicated they want to be contacted by email. You may want to create a newsletter or progress email memo or blog approach to keep contributors involved.
- Successful direct-mail solicitation receives a 2.5 percent positive response. A 5 percent response is excellent. This illustrates how important it is to be very selective about the people to whom you send a fundraising letter. And it also makes a vital statement about the necessity to write an effective letter.
- It's important to have contributors feel good about giving, even if it involves a dozen mailings.
- Enfranchise contributors, bringing them into the action. Make sure they feel a part of the fundraising: "With your help, we've almost met our goal."
- Fundraising requires a multifaceted approach to be successful. Appealing for contributions through direct mail is only a small part of it. Many other parts of your campaign, like effective public relations efforts, will be needed to help make your fundraising letters successful. (See Announcement, page 18; Opinion Editorial, page 402; and Press Release, page 385.)
- Fundraising often involves functions like luncheons, gala events, dinners, dances, and the like. Use the appropriate invitations for contributors. (See Invitation, page 63.)

SELECT A FORMAT

- Invite readership with an appealing letter layout. Select a typeface that is easy to read and has space between the lines of type. Indenting also creates an impression of being attractive, open, and easy to read as does lots of white space.
- Individualize your letter, if possible, by using the reader's name in the inside address and salutation. This is true, too, of memos and other updates you send by email. Personalize them whenever it's practical.
- Have the letter signed by the highest and/or most recognized official of the charity organization. Respected celebrity endorsements can also be helpful.
- Consider using a postscript to attract additional attention and get action.

- Design and create a website where contributors can always go to respond with a contribution. This, too, will give you a venue to keep fresh information flowing to contributors, and to help build interest and participation. One example might be to show the donations building toward the goal. Another might be an update on research for a cure. Posted informational videos, and interviews with experts, and also with victims, are effective. Blog posts that keep fresh information flowing and reader interest high are also useful.

SELECT POWER WORDS

assist	benefit	build	change
charity	construct	contribute	cooperate
difference	donate	drive	encourage
endow	generous	goal	grant
gratitude	heartfelt	help	participate
partner	plan	power	prosper
receive	reconstruct	relief	rescue
reward	share	sponsor	survive
thanks	tribute	urgent	volunteer

WRITE EFFECTIVE PHRASES

almost complete	continue to work
count on you	direct help
donate what you can	give a helping hand
help is needed	here's how you
join with us	lend your support
make a difference	meeting the need
near our goal	only need three more contributions of
open your heart	plan to contribute
respond today	send your donation
three-fourths complete	volunteer to make
will you commit	you can help
your contribution	your generosity

WRITE STRONG SENTENCES

Start with an action verb and then construct lean sentences with a strong message:

Let's all work together to eliminate this devastating disease.

Only $500,000 remains to be contributed before we can begin work.

Your contribution can help send 50 underprivileged children to Cower's Camp for a week.

Please use the enclosed, stamped envelope to return your check, and thank you for your help.

Share your love of animals.

Help make a difference.

Contributors of $5,000 or more will become listed in next year's program under Patrons of the Library.

Friends of the Library enjoy several special privileges.

Why not send your contribution today?

Books are a wonderful thing to contribute!

BUILD EFFECTIVE PARAGRAPHS

Let's eradicate this debilitating disease. Researchers believe one more year at a cost of $1,500,000 will produce the needed vaccine. We're that close to a solution. Won't you help with a contribution of $25 or more?

You can help now in two ways: (1) write Senator Allen Dirkson and congressional representative Alice Schroeder, and state your objection to the legislation, and (2) return your check for $25 today.

Operating Angel's Kitchen takes $3,500 and 400 volunteer hours each week. You can help by signing up to serve for one or more of the time slots indicated below, and by returning your contribution of $25, $50, or $75.

United Foundation will be canvassing neighborhoods again this year for contributions. Will you help?

The Sisters Against Crime meeting to organize for this year's campaign will be Tuesday, September 10, at 7:30 p.m., in the Logan School Auditorium. Please call Sarah Crimpton, 555-0123, and tell her you'll be on hand to help.

It's spring again and time to get our after-school program organized. Without your volunteer efforts, the children of Burton Township will not have this enriching experience.

Your contribution to the Dempster Project has made it possible to make the recreation program a reality. Thank you.

EDIT, EDIT, EDIT

Fine-tuning this communication will increase your response. If possible, have several other people read your communication and check for tone and typos. Always run your spell-check, and read the communication aloud to hear any words that don't ring true to your message.

Request for Volunteers and Donations

Dear Sally:

High Achievers has turned the lives of 79 children around in just two years. The first year we sponsored the program, school officials reported that the 79 children who attended were at high risk of dropping out of school. The second year the number was only 20 of those children. This year all 79 are performing far above average, and are committed to completing their high school studies.

You can thank yourself and all the volunteers from Chambers Corporation who dedicated after-school hours to be tutors at Elbert Middle School.

This year we're taking on an even bigger challenge. In order to purchase needed supplies and operate a store where students can purchase things with their "achievement dollars," we are asking for money contributions. Chamber Corporation's president, Robert Elliot, has pledged a matching $35,000 for the program if we raise that amount and enlist volunteers for 4,000 tutoring hours.

Please make a difference in a child's life and put your commitment on the enclosed card and return it today.

Yours truly,

Angel Martin

P.S. Production has already pledged $2,000 and 600 tutoring hours. Can your department top that?

Community Fundraiser

Dear Alice:

This Holiday Season we will again sponsor the Noel House Tour to benefit the Opera Society. Since last year's tour raised $650,000, which went directly and completely to the opera, we felt it was extremely profitable. Our contribution paid for the renovation work that's been done to the Opera House. A complete breakdown of how the money was spent is itemized on the enclosed sheet.

This year our goal is $675,000 for enlarging the stage area and providing two new sets. We believe we can meet this goal with all our members' help. Contributions from florists, designers, and interior decorators are already rolling in.

The Tour Committee is requesting that eight members of the Park Hill neighborhood volunteer their homes for the tour, 50 members volunteer to function as tour guides and receptionists, and 225 members volunteer to serve on the preparation subcommittees.

We know you'll want to help. Please return the volunteer card indicating your choices, or go to the website, COC.com, and sign up.

Sincerely,

Roger Wagner

Special Invitation to Fundraising Event

Dear Andrea:

The North Bay Arthritis Foundation counts on you. In fact, if it weren't for you and our other 500 members, the Foundation would have been unable to fund the Remus Research Project last year. Your help meant that we got much closer to finding a cure for this debilitating disease.

Our goal for this year is to again fund the Remus Research Project. (See the encouraging progress report enclosed, and check the "Progress" column on the website, RemusResearch.org.) We will all need to work together like last year—but even harder—to achieve our goal of $500,000.

This year's art show, Contemporary Artists of America, will include 200 pieces of art by regional artists. It's the second largest show of its type in the country. A blind-drawing, fixed-price sale will be conducted at the opening gala at the Historical Society Hall on September 15. Works not sold that night will be available on a first-come basis starting the following day.

Tickets for the gala will be $125. The fee will include a cocktail party, a souvenir medallion designed by Hugo Halsey of Santa Fe, admission to a private preview of the exhibit, and a seminar at the downtown Chilcott on September 12.

Please call 708-555-0123 to order your group tickets today and sign up online at CAA.org to contribute in a number of other ways.

Sincerely,

Horatio Gailbladder

P.S. This year we will have 75 of the artists attending the gala.

Plea for Food Contributions

Dear Alice:

Channel 4 is starting its Fifth Annual Holiday Basket Drive on Thursday, October 17. Trucks will be parked at convenient locations listed on the back of this letter.

Your help last year meant that 1,900 families throughout the metro area got holiday baskets. This year you and other captains requested we make our appeal to clubs, schools, and businesses, as well as to the general public. And that's why you're getting this letter.

Won't you organize the efforts of your club to make sure the drive receives enough canned foods for 2,500 families? That's our goal.

Please list your club name and number of members on the enclosed card, selecting the type of participation you'd like to volunteer for.

Let's make this the city's brightest holiday season yet.

Sincerely,

Levitt Lighthorse

Call for Pledge of Time and Commitment

Dear Jim:

Little League time is here! And we need to get organized!

We already have enough kids to field 14 teams. That means, of course, we will need another $3,500 for equipment and supplies, and a total of 60 coaching volunteers. At this moment, we have $1,250 and 10 head-coach volunteers.

The team families committee feels it can raise over $3,500 at the bake sale next weekend, so that leaves the coaching volunteers.

This promises to be Little League's best year ever. But we'll need your help. Please call Joe Baker at 415-555-0123 by March 15 to sign up.

Yours truly,

Sparky Henderson

Alumni-Related Fundraiser

Dear Manny Lester:

The Hi Phis are again sponsoring the "Gifts for Children" program this Holiday Season. Last year your generous gift helped provide a party and an individual gift for all 90 children hospitalized on Ward B at Children's Hospital.

Can we count on you this season?

Please indicate your contribution, and return the enclosed card now so the preparations can begin. Thank you.

Sincerely,

Sally Strutter, Chair

Scholarship Fundraiser

Dear Press Club Members:

It's that time of year again! Gather up those gently used books and bring them to the club by September 6, so they'll be ready for our Fall Book Sale Bonanza on September 10.

This year we'd like to create three Young Writer Scholarships for $2,500 each. It's possible with your help.

If you can't get your books in, call Bob Bittle at 502-1234, and he'll arrange a pick up.

Best,

Susie Snivels

Church Fundraiser

Dear Sarah and Ted Ellis:

Isn't it exciting that our church has taken the step of faith to increase our outreach by 50 percent for the coming year? On Thursday, October 10 at 7:30 p.m. we will discuss how we can exercise our faith.

Please plan to be there. Both the outreach and the increased youth activities will mean a commitment of $50,000. Split among us, each member will need to pledge to help meet this goal by helping in the planned fundraisers, or making a donation commitment.

Please consider the choices on the enclosed pledge card, fill it out, and bring it to the meeting.

Yes, this is an exciting time to be a member of our church and have the opportunity to exercise and increase our faith.

Sincerely,

Dollie Parish

Garage Sale Fundraiser

Neighbors:

It's all set—June 10, 8 a.m. to noon, the Annual Neighborhood Garage Sale.

So clean out those cupboards and closets and empty out those attics and basements. All funds raised will go toward decorating the clubhouse.

Marge Hood will be around with coffee and donuts. See you in your driveway.

Reggie Diggs, Association President

63 | MEDIA KIT

The media (press) kit is a carefully designed set of written pieces placed together in a folder to give editors, reporters, interviewers, and other media people background information on a subject. The kits are made available to media people at large-scale, newsworthy events, or are viewable online at the organization's website. They may be put on flash drives, or on disks, too. The most common pieces include: news releases; biographies of speakers; bibliographies of publications authored by or featuring someone or something of import; brochure; a copy of a speech delivered at the event; and/or Q&A, FAQ, or talking points. (See specific chapters.)

Sometimes other pieces, described below, may be used to help tell the complete story: a backgrounder; fact sheet; timeline; media alert; and photo opportunity alert. Carefully think about what you need to most effectively and succinctly tell your story, and stay with a few comprehensive pieces to maximize impact. Avoid cluttering your media kit with nonessentials.

- The **backgrounder** is used to help readers understand the subject in terms of developmental steps, functions, size, structure, and operation. It also covers topics of objectives, goals, priorities, new areas, and research.
- The **fact sheet** breaks down complex information into related sections the reader can quickly understand. It is often organized in bullet form, and accompanies a news release. Outline the information under headings. For a fact sheet for international visitors to a city, for example, include subheadings: population, employment, government, number of residents, climate, history, hotel accommodations, cultural attractions, sightseeing spots, meeting and convention facilities, restaurants, and special events. Also include notes about customs, dress, formalities, visas, and inoculation requirements.
- A **timeline,** organized chronologically by dates, can be useful to help the reader quickly understand the sequence of events. Organize the material under date headings and subheadings.
- A **media alert** and/or **photo opportunity alert** are used as short-notice invitations to the media when there are opportunities to ask a subject questions, and/or take photos or get video coverage of a subject or event for television, podcast, or other broadcasting outlets. Include the essential information: event or subject, time, place, special visuals (like demonstrations or product introduction), and any other information or restrictions the media will need to know to participate. Always include a contact person and information.

(Also see BIBLIOGRAPHY, page 396; BIOGRAPHY, page 394; BROCHURE, page 406; PRESS RELEASE, page 385; QUESTIONS & ANSWERS, page 391.)

The press release is a vital tool—the workhorse of any personal promotion, or organization's public relations program. Used properly, it can raise your visibility in the public eye, help create a positive image, and assist you in marketing your own or your organization's services or products.

A press release should describe an event or new facts of importance: a personnel appointment or promotion; the release of a new product or service; a new business opening, major expansion, reorganization, new direction; an achievement; or a change in management or philosophy.

Write releases in journalistic style, answering *who, what, when, where, why*, and *how*. Present the information in order from the most important to least important, from the central idea to specific facts. Imagine that an editor will take a pair of scissors and clip from the bottom of your release. To keep the essential facts in place, include all critical information in the first paragraph—the first sentence, if possible. The press release should be objective, clear, and easy to read, and it should not include extra words or superlatives. Photos, if used, should be carefully identified. Or, if the press release is emailed, the photo may be sent as an attached file.

No cover letter is necessary when mailing the press release, and the format described in this chapter should be strictly adhered to. When your press release is emailed, you may want to preface it by a very short personal message to help distinguish it from spam.

THINK ABOUT CONTENT

- Determine what is newsworthy—offering new information. Ask yourself:
  - Who will care?
  - Will the release answer the questions it will undoubtedly raise?
  - Will it advance my objectives?
  - Have I gathered all the facts and double-checked them for accuracy?

- Determine if the release is hard news (personnel appointments, new products, company openings, new services, events, research, or survey results), or soft or feature news (human-interest items, business trends, ongoing research, or projects).
- Create an outline to ensure a logical and clear flow of information. Answer the five questions: *what, who, where, when*, and *why*, and then answer *how*.
- Use the journalistic style of the inverted pyramid; the most vital information should come first. The rest of the information should follow in order of its importance. Include all critical information in the first paragraph—the first sentence, if possible.
- The lead is all-important. It should read like the lead of a news story.

- The personnel appointment should focus first on the responsibilities of the appointee. Then it should give the appointee's background.
  - ▸ State the appointee's title and credit the announcement to the proper organization official.
  - ▸ Give the name of the person to whom the appointee will report and the start date.
  - ▸ State the appointee's responsibilities. (In the second paragraph, you may want to use a quote by the organization official.)
  - ▸ Describe the appointee's professional experience and educational background. Social and personal information like marital status, professional affiliation, charity, and/or social affiliations is sometimes included.
  - ▸ State if the position is new. You may also want to give the name of the person being replaced if the circumstances are positive.
- Rewrite and edit for clarity, trying to keep your release to one or two pages, or one computer screen in length. Make sure your copy is clear and concise.
- Define any technical terms.
- Quotations add interest and lend personal authority. Use some, if possible, but only those that provide relevant information. If you use a quotation—and be sure to quote the correct official/authority here—check it with that person for approval. If you obtained a direct quote in an interview, you should still get the person's approval to quote before using.
- Samples, photos, and review copies (books, CDs, DVDs, etc.) add interest to your release, so include them when it's practical. If not, make an event, press conference, or interview available to the editor.

CONSIDER SPECIAL SITUATIONS

- Send the release to a specific person, if possible. If you cannot, address the news release to a particular editor, for example, business editor, social editor, sports editor. It is worth calling major media such as daily newspapers or television stations to learn the correct person's name, title, department, and specific address (4th floor, Department 4-A) or email address. It's often worth a telephone call to that editor stating you are sending a press release.
- The official statement, for use in crisis situations or when controversial situations arise, should be developed and distributed to the press and internal organization representatives to help control rumors and eliminate misinformation. Timeliness and the frequency of these reports are key to keeping the media informed, eliminating the start or growth of false reports, and preventing public anxiety caused by misinformation. Obviously, these are most often sent by email to provide the fastest means to keep the media informed.
- It is extremely helpful to have a crisis public relations team ready to act in emergencies like a flood, fire, earthquake, or other natural disaster. This team should draw up and have in place a crisis plan. Preparations for disasters should allow you to create and send releases from another location on official letterhead, if faxing or mail is also necessary. Email is usually the best way to send these.

- Use electronic distribution of releases and updates when the editor or reporter makes subsequent communication requests.
- Check and note publicity policies of the particular media. Some organizations do not welcome unsolicited emails, faxes, or other electronically transmitted information.
- Consider these additional factors in crisis situations:
  - ▹ Estimate the audience scope and send releases to local, state, regional, national, and international media as appropriate.
  - ▹ Write in a brief, concise style, using bullets so the facts can be easily pulled out.
  - ▹ Type in the time after the date on page one, and put the date and time on every page. (Exceptions to this rule are press releases that aren't time-sensitive such as new-book press releases.)
  - ▹ Add "Issued by: [person's name]" or "Contact: [person's name]" with a telephone number, a cell phone number, and an email address.
  - ▹ Include contact names and all contact information for a 24-hour basis.
  - ▹ Issue updates as frequently as new information is available.
  - ▹ Get legal approval, if possible, before releasing.
  - ▹ Keep a release log covering when, and to whom, releases were made.
  - ▹ Use recorded telephone messages and update them, if possible, for incoming calls.
  - ▹ Set up a schedule of briefings.
  - ▹ Make videotapes and/or live reports from the disaster scene available on a website and social media, if possible.
  - ▹ Use audiotaped official statements for radio, if possible.
  - ▹ Have press kits with background information about the organization available, if possible. Have all this information available on a website.

USE THE CORRECT FORMAT

- All releases must be consistent, be sent on official letterhead, and look professional. For those emailed, use standard format.
- For mailed or faxed press releases, leave the top third of the first page blank for the editor to write his or her headline.
- Although emailed press releases have changed the traditional format a bit, press releases should still have six key elements. For printed press releases, follow the placement of these elements as shown in the samples.
  1. A *date* to indicate when the release was issued. Indicate when the information should be made public: "FOR IMMEDIATE RELEASE" or "FOR RELEASE ON [or AFTER] (date) and/or (time)."
  2. A press release should have a *title*. Type "NEWS RELEASE" in capitals at the center of the first page or in the lefthand margin.
  3. A *contact* appears two lines below the title; type "CONTACT" flush left with the margin (or as illustrated in the samples). Include the name of the contact person for

the release along with a telephone number or email address, or both. The name of the organization may also be included. For emailed press releases, this information may be at the end of the press release.

4. A *headline* (subject line) appears two lines below the contact, centered, and usually in caps. If possible, include the company's business and the subject of the release: "DOODLE'S HAIR SALON NOW OPEN." Try to catch the reader's attention. This is your chance to advertise your story to the editor so he or she will decide to print it. If the story is complicated, use a subhead as well: "Free Styling on January 10 by New York's Best."

5. The location and the *dateline* appears two lines below the subject line and is usually indented two spaces. It is composed of the city (and, if necessary, the state, in caps). The date may appear in upper and lower case, followed by a double dash.

6. The *copy* begins on the same line, immediately after the dateline.

- The release should be typed on a single side of 8½ by 11–inch paper, double-spaced with a minimum of one inch margins all around. Exceptions to this rule do exist. In some industries, like publishing, an 8½ by 14–inch paper is used. Emailed press releases often appear single-spaced.
- If more than one page is required, center and type "(MORE)" or "(CONTINUED)" in capitals at the bottom of page one, and begin the next page flush left on the margin with a one-word title and page number: "Doodles 2."
- Short paragraphs are best.
- Use capitalization sparingly.
- Be consistent.
- Use the active voice if possible.
- Write in an objective tone.
- Use simple, clear, and concise sentences.
- Edit. Eliminate all unnecessary words.
- Include the same, complete information when sending by email. Standards of spacing and arrangement are, of course, not as prescribed.
- At the end of the news release, center one of the following to indicate the end: # # # or (END).

Hotel Summer Rates

FOR IMMEDIATE RELEASE

Media Contact: Andria Zee
Best Choice Public Relations
212-555-0123
andria@bestchoice.com

MEXICO RARE HOTELS ANNOUNCE SUMMER SAVINGS

PUERTO VALLARTA, MEXICO July 15, 2006—Mexico Rare Hotels, a collection of 23 small, boutique hotels in 24 destinations throughout the Mexican Republic, announces Sizzling Summer Savings at one of its eclectic lodgings within the collection by calling 1-800-555-0123 or online at www.mexicorarehotels.com.

EL CASSANTOS (Savings of 45%)

El CASSANTOS is a remarkable getaway that combines unique architecture inspired by Mexican masters with adventure, artistry, and the tranquility of nature. Spacious and luxurious accommodations include a freeform swimming pool and a variety of leisure activities, including horseback riding, water sports, and a luscious spa facility. Rates range from $250 per room, per night for a resort-view room to $1,500 per room, per night for a 3-bedroom casita.

This special is valid for travel from June 30 to September 30, 2011. For an additional person, add $25 USD to the rate (breakfast included), 17% tax and 5% services charge not included, subject to availability. The Bed & Breakfast Special is for a minimum stay of two nights and includes a full breakfast for two (adults only) and a massage (pay for one; get one free).

All rates and information can be found at www.mexicorarehotels.com where travelers and travel professionals can research and reserve the new hotels immediately and get extensive destination information, rates, and packages. Personal assistance is available in the U.S. and Canada toll-free: 1-800-555-0123; Mexico toll-free 01-150-0123; or calling from other countries to +(00)-444-555-0123. Mexico Rare Hotels can also be reached by email at info@mexicorarehotels.com or via fax at +(00) 445-555-0123. The hotels are presented in the company's full-color directory, which is available on request.

# # #

PHOTOS AVAILABLE

For additional information, contact Andria Zee
Choice Public Relations, 212-555-0123
andria@choicespr.com

New Website Service

CONTACT: Mark Little
mark@marklittlepr.com
202-555-0123

FOR IMMEDIATE RELEASE

YOURTRAVEL.COM, TOP HOTEL RESERVATIONS AGGREGATOR, ADDS AMENITIES FILTERS TO WEBSITE

BOSTON, MASSACHUSETTS (July 15, 2011)—Internet hotel room shoppers just got a boost with a new user-friendly tool with seven new amenities filters to search its popular website, including:

- Dataport
- Wireless Internet
- High Speed Internet
- Indoor Pool
- Outdoor Pool
- Fitness Facilities
- Pets Allowed

"These are now in place in Orlando, Phoenix, Dallas, San Francisco, and Chicago," said Manuel Casca, president of YourTravel of Minneapolis, Minnesota, the world's largest aggregators of hotel reservations and one of the world's fastest growing aggregators of hotel reservation information.

These new amenities filters join six basic search filters—distance, hotel, name (keywords), price, hotel rating, and preferred websites.

In addition to the new amenities filters, YourTravel has expanded the room and rate information when the user clicks the BookIt button. This expanded feature allows the customer to view all room and rates available from each website, not just the lowest, creating more booking flexibility.

"As more Americans are traveling in a market with increasing room rates, getting the right price at the right hotel is more and more important," adds Casca. "These new filters will make the customer's job much easier."

- YourTravel.com provides the only online, side-by-side hotel price comparison.
- The customer is able to search the best price from more than 20 different travel websites.
- The ease of use and the ability to locate the best price benefit both the business and leisure traveler, saving time and stretching their travel budget.
- The four-year-old company serves business and leisure travelers with hotel information for 3,250 cities in 104 countries, from Albania to Zimbabwe. Information from more than 20 different travel websites has been compiled into unbiased price comparisons with the lowest price highlighted. While YourTravel highlights the lowest price for each hotel, the user is able to select any travel website to book a room. Casca adds, "We don't just return the lowest rate, we return the most options in one search and then leave it in the hands of the consumer to make the choice."

#

Contact:
Mark Little
mark@marklittlepr.com
212-555-0123

65 QUESTIONS & ANSWERS (Q&A) & FREQUENTLY ASKED QUESTIONS (FAQ)

The Q&A, or Questions and Answers; and the FAQ, or Frequently Asked Questions, are designed to promote understanding of a topic. They anticipate questions editors or general readers may have, state them, and provide the answers or explanations. Either of these commonly accompanies a complicated press release, and is also an effective tool for distribution within an organization to help personnel deal consistently with questions.

In a number of forms the Q&A is distributed to radio or television talk-show hosts or interviewers to interest them in interviewing a person and to help direct the interview into comprehensive areas of public interest.

The key to an effective Q&A is doing the proper research to learn what your public wants to know and what information the issuer wants to disseminate. The FAQ is often used in the same manner on websites, or in printed form.

When you are interested in proposing a topic of potential interest for a radio or television interview, e.g., to propose an author be interviewed about his new book or to reveal findings of a research project, use a modified form called "Talking Points." Instead of using only questions and answers, the "Talking Points" format may also highlight salient issues and then list the supporting points below them.

DECIDE TO WRITE

Use this communication to:

- Suggest questions of general interest to an interviewer
- Promote an author of a book, play, research finding, etc.
- Stimulate reporters' interest
- Simplify and address common questions of a complicated news release

THINK ABOUT CONTENT

- Use a thought-provoking title to capture interest.

- Develop a list of the questions most likely to be asked about the topic. For an advanced personal computer, for example, the questions might include:
  - ▸ What advantages does it offer over other products now available?
  - ▸ When will it be available?
  - ▸ Where can it be purchased in our area?
  - ▸ How easy will it be to operate?
  - ▸ What kind of setup, instruction, etc., will it require?
  - ▸ What will the price be?
  - ▸ Who will buy it?
  - ▸ Are other companies making a competitive product?
  - ▸ What are the company's first-year sales projections?
  - ▸ How long did it take to develop this product?
  - ▸ How will this make consumers' lives better?
- Write short yet comprehensive answers to the questions for the people who will be interviewed.
- Be sure to have both questions and answers approved by the appropriate individual or organization officials before you distribute them to the media.

ELIMINATE WRONG MESSAGES

- Do not include technical terms without defining them.
- Remove all jargon.

CONSIDER SPECIAL SITUATIONS

Be sure the people who will be interviewed are prepared. Rehearse with them.

SELECT A FORMAT

- If the Q&A, FAQ, or Talking Points are sent with a press release, the design of the two documents should be complementary. They should be on matching or coordinating 8½ by 11–inch letterhead in the same format, with the same typeface.
- If the Q&A, FAQ, or Talking Points document is sent by email, it should be included within the email, and not as an attachment (unless requested). This increases the chances it will be read.
- Many other formats for explaining or distilling information may be used to create interest. Oversized postcards printed in glossy four-color ink might be used for a list of interview questions, for example.

Author Interview Talking Points

CONTACT: Sandra E. Lamb
(303) 555-0123 or Email: sandylamb@email.com
(Please state "Interview Request" in the email subject line.)

SUGGESTED TOPICS

Sandra E. Lamb, author of *Personal Notes: How to Write from the Heart for Any Occasion,* enjoys outstanding reviews for bringing fresh wisdom and wit in answers radio and television audiences love. Perhaps your audience would be interested in hearing some of her "pithy," "excellent," and "knowledgeable" takes on one of these subjects:

Topic #1: How and what do you write to a friend or coworker who suffered a loss?

Talking Points
1. Write as soon as you hear and have confirmed the bad news, but if time has lapsed since the loss, write anyway.
2. Open with a simple, strong sentence expressing how sorry you are, naming the person, loss, or event you're writing about: "I was so sorry to hear that you lost your dear Harry, and my thoughts are with you at this time of sorrow," or "I was sorry to hear you are no longer director of operations."
3. Relate a fond memory in the case of a deceased person, if possible.
4. Offer specific help: "May I take over the Adams project until you get back to the office? I'll call on Thursday, to see what would be helpful, and if you have any special instructions."
5. Close on a warm note.

Topic #2: Is your employer reading your email?

Talking Points
1. Your personal emails written at work can be read by your employer. The courts have usually found in favor of the employer owning emails sent from the workplace.
2. Personal emails written anywhere are not private. This is a very public forum, and messages may float forever in cyberspace.
3. Know and follow your organization's rules for email use. Every organization should establish rules, and make those rules known to all employees.
4. Never violate someone's copyright by forwarding his or her email, or cutting-and-pasting from his or her email to send to someone else. You must have permission to use parts or all of someone else's email.
5. Follow my 10 Golden Rules of Email to stay out of email interpersonal conflicts. Go to www.Sandra Lamb.com to review. Recognize when a message requires a human moment, and therefore a face-to-face meeting. Understand the communication bandwidth, and where email fits. Follow my rules of Netiquette.

Here are some other topics Sandra is prepared to talk about:

T: Why don't people RSVP? What should I do?
T: No one writes thank-yous anymore. Why should I?
T: How can I teach my child to write thank-yous?
T: How do I put real power in my resume?
T: How do I keep negativity out of my bad-news letter?
T: How do I write an attention-getting resume cover letter?
T: How do I say I'm sorry in writing?
T: How do I write a red-hot love letter?

###

66 BIOGRAPHY (BIO)

The biography or "bio" is an explanatory piece designed to give background information on a person. There are basically two forms to follow. The first is simple and comprehensive. The second form, a feature biography, gives information more as a personality profile. Either piece may be accompanied by a fact sheet or timeline.

DECIDE TO WRITE

Use this piece:

- To get special media coverage
- As part of a media kit
- To give information to someone who will introduce the person for a speech
- With a book the person has authored

THINK ABOUT CONTENT

- Develop a logical outline.
- Write a commanding lead.
- Flesh out your ideas.
- Vary and simplify sentence structure and language.
- Craft for logical flow and comprehensive coverage.
- Back up all your claims, and pay off on your lead.
- Include some human interest facts.

FOR THE NEWSPAPER-STYLE BIO:

- Open by identifying the person by name, title, and achievements relevant to the biography's point.
- State the person's educational and professional background.
- Include or exclude personal information, such as marital status, children, and academic standing, depending upon the audience.

FOR THE FEATURE-STYLE BIO:

- Use a more relaxed writing style, similar to that used for a magazine profile feature.
- Add human-interest details.
- Include quotes from the person.

SELECT A FORMAT

Use standard letterhead. If the biography is to be part of a media kit or mailing, use a typeface consistent with other pieces sent at the same time. If the bio is to be emailed, it may best go as an attachment file.

EDIT, EDIT, EDIT

Check for consistent verb and person tenses. Proofread, proofread, proofread.

Biography

John Frisk, CHE
President and CEO
Good Samaritan Hospital

John Frisk is the president and CEO of Good Samaritan Hospital of Kearney, NE, one of Nebraska's largest healthcare providers. The Catholic Health Initiative–affiliated Good Samaritan has been serving the central Nebraska-northern Kansas region for 80 years. Frisk was appointed president and CEO in July 2011.

Frisk most recently served as the president and CEO of Spencer Hospital in Spencer, IA. Previously, he served as senior vice president for administration at Indiana Hospital in Indiana, Penn.; vice president of general services at Central Vermont Hospital in Barre, VT; and administrator of Olmsted Community Hospital in Rochester, MN.

Frisk holds master's degrees in hospital administration and industrial relations from the University of Minnesota and Iowa State University, respectively, and a bachelor's in sociology from the University of Kansas.

Frisk and his wife, Sue, reside in Kearney. They have two grown children.

(Also see ANNOUNCEMENT, page 18; MEDIA KIT, page 384; PITCH LETTER, page 373; and PRESS RELEASE, page 385.)

67 BIBLIOGRAPHY

A bibliography is a useful accompaniment to a biography (bio), or a resume (to list what the person has authored or written). A bibliography may list articles and books that have been published by or about the subject. When this piece is part of a media kit or is attached to a press release, the reporter, editor, or interviewer can quickly retrieve any additional information he or she needs. When the bibliography is part of a report, document, or book, it functions to list relevant sources for further study on the subject.

A bibliography lists sources; an annotated bibliography also includes a succinct description of the contents of the listings.

DECIDE TO WRITE

Use this piece:

- As part of a person's credentials or credits
- To accompany a resume
- As background information if a person is going to be introduced
- As part of a media kit
- To document relevant sources for a report, article, or book
- Book example: Author's last name, first name, and middle initial. Book title (in italics). City of publisher: name of publisher, year of publication.
- Magazine example: Author's last name, first name, and middle initial. "Title of Article." Name of publication (in italics), month and year of publication.

THINK ABOUT CONTENT

- Use a standard format, such as one described in the current edition of the *Chicago Manual of Style*, for your listings.
- Be consistent throughout.

(Also see BIOGRAPHY, page 394; MEDIA KIT, page 384; PRESS RELEASE, page 385; and RESUME, page 126.)

Public speaking is an effective way to gain recognition and demonstrate leadership. It is a powerful tool for informing, inspiring, persuading, helping to set policy, and initiating action. A speech must be easily understood to be effective. Customize to fit the audience, the speaker, and the occasion. The best speeches go beyond spoken words; they make a connection between the speaker and the audience.

In speech writing, use the rules for spoken, conversational English.

THINK ABOUT CONTENT

- Before starting, consider the audience composition, needs, and educational background.
- Learn all you can about the time and setting for the speech.
- Focus on a single theme.
- Research the subject thoroughly.
- Rehearse—on site, if possible—and make adjustments and corrections as needed.

WRITE THE SPEECH

Preparing to Write

- Consider the audience and the speaker's relationship to it:
  - How much background will audience members have; and what are their ages?
  - What will the audience's reference points, interests, and attitudes be?

- If you are writing the speech for someone else, take some additional preparatory steps:
  - Interview the person who will deliver the speech, acting like a reporter.
  - Record the session and take notes.
  - Pay attention to how the person speaks, his or her style, manner, range, pronunciation, and delivery. Note if he or she is aggressive, soft-spoken, loud, or mild-mannered.
  - Listen for natural speech patterns, colloquialisms, expressions, and mannerisms.
  - Learn any apprehensions or fears the speaker may have.
  - Select possible topic areas, considering any ideas the speaker may have. Include issues facing your industry, anecdotes, the speaker's areas of expertise, and special concerns.
  - Calculate the length of the speech. (A typewritten, double-spaced page takes between one minute and one-and-a-half minutes to deliver.)
  - Interview the organizers of the event to learn every detail: the setting, time of day, other speeches and speakers, presentations, awards, and other activities. Ask what the

audience will be doing during the speech: Will people be eating, drinking, standing, or sitting? If possible, visit the site and examine the setup.

- ▶ Select the specific topic of the speech. Now the speechwriter must become an ideas person. Review other speeches from other such events, perhaps from previous years, if this is an annual event. Sometimes the event will dictate the speech topic and content.
- ▶ Present the ideas for approval, if necessary.
- ▶ Research the subject. Gather all the material you can, making sure your references are the most comprehensive and current. Use the library as well as any organization files. Interview organization officials and other experts. Review other speeches the speaker has made on this or related topics.

The Speechwriting Process

- Outline the speech. Within the basic format of **introduction**, **body**, and **summary**, carefully detail the points. Here, for example, is an outline for a speech for a corporation's annual sales meeting:
    1. Opening remarks and welcome: Recognition of sales managers; purpose of the meeting
    2. How are we growing? Last year's sales figures; this year's sales figures; next year's sales projections
    3. How are you growing as a salesperson? Looking at the numbers; great accomplishments; new goals
    4. Conclusion: New challenges ahead; this is how we will DO IT!

- Write out the speech. Make it conversational. Include interesting details and anecdotes, and points of review. Keep the speech simple with logical points of progression:
    - ▶ The **lead** should get the audience's attention with a compelling statement, humorous anecdote (be careful using jokes), thought-provoking question, quotation, or human-interest story. The opening must lead into the theme and set up the message.
    - ▶ The **body** of the speech should be easy to follow, progress logically, and emphasize and review major points. It must also be personalized to the audience and contain emotional content that will get them involved and make them care.
    - ▶ The **conclusion** should reiterate the major points, summarize, and tie the end to the beginning—pay off on your lead. Leave the audience optimistically challenged.

- Repetition can help make a speech successful by emphasizing important points.
- Use solid transitions to keep the audience's attention.
- Repeat nouns instead of using pronouns.
- Use parallel phrases for clarity and emphasis: "a government of the people, by the people, for the people."
- Stick to simple words and simple, declarative sentences.
- Construct sentences with the subject and verb together. Instead of "He, with fear and trepidation, crept . . ." use "He crept . . ." or "With fear and trepidation, he crept . . ."

- Limit subordinate phrases and clauses. These become tedious and will lose your audience.
- Build in flexibility so the speaker can make adjustments during the speech, if necessary.
- Incorporate visuals to add interest and keep the audience's attention. They should be keyed to the points of emphasis in the speech in order to reinforce and illustrate the message.
- Include cues in parentheses: (Slide #4. Pause.)
- Make sure your visuals will work well with the size, arrangement, and composition of the audience. Emphasize them with action words.

Before Speaking
- Practice the speech in front of a mirror and, if possible, in the setting with the visuals that will be used. Practice until the delivery is smooth and the speaker is comfortable.
- Rehearse the speech and change any problem areas.
- Test the speech on an audience sample and, if possible, at the speech site. Make sure all the details are in place. (Speeches have failed because of a bad electrical cord, failure of a Power-Point visual, or a screeching microphone.)

ELIMINATE WRONG MESSAGES

- Do not try to include more than one central idea or theme in a speech. Be sure you can explain the speech in one sentence.
- Don't trust an outline if you are not a practiced speaker, or if you are writing a speech for someone else. Type it out, double-spaced, underlining points for emphasis. (Some speakers like all capital letters and large type size.)
- Do not exaggerate the facts or overdramatize.
- Do not include jokes that are not germane to the audience, occasion, and subject. The same applies to quotes.
- Do not plagiarize. If you use a quote, give full credit to the author and source.
- Watch out for homophones that can be misunderstood: scene or seen; sew, so, or sow, etc.
- Eliminate things that don't work with the speaker's skill level or presentation manner, and limit any elements that are difficult for the speaker to deliver, such as words ending in *s*.

CONSIDER SPECIAL SITUATIONS

- If the media will attend, make copies of the speech available.
- Recycle the speech by using excerpts for press releases, magazine articles, newsletters, etc.

69 PUBLIC SERVICE ANNOUNCEMENT (PSA)

The public service announcement, or PSA, is to broadcast public relations what the press release is to print public relations. It's the basic tool used to get broadcast coverage of an event or product.

The Federal Communications Commission (FCC) requires radio and television stations to serve the community and public interest. Part of their obligation is interpreted as broadcasting brief announcements of nonprofit events. While these were historically events sponsored by nonprofit organizations, they are increasingly becoming nonprofit events sponsored by for-profit organizations.

PSAs range from ten to sixty seconds in length, and may be written in either release or script form and produced in audiotape for radio or videotape for television. PSAs can lead to radio or television interviews of official representatives of the event, or to coverage of the event in a special feature segment.

Some PSAs feature health information or safety tips. All kinds of PSAs are opportunities for positive publicity.

DECIDE TO WRITE

Use this vehicle to offer information on:

- Public health discussions
- New health, safety, or product information
- Health, welfare, and/or enrichment services offered to the public

THINK ABOUT CONTENT

- Write as a news release, starting with an arresting lead, usually in the form of a teaser—a catchy phrase, question, or term—that gets the attention of the audience.
- Use action verbs and short, declarative sentences.
- State the facts.
- List any photo opportunities, audiotapes, videotapes, or interviewing sessions that are available.
- List any authorities or celebrities available for interviews.

- In writing the broadcast script, you must write for the eye as well as the ear, and your script must include all the instructions and clues for production of how to create the end product. Start with your idea, then visualize how it should appear.
- Topics must have general public interest, a consumer angle, or an element of current news.
- Events with a news angle, products with a release date (books, new telephone service, a charity race, a new drug), and human-interest or consumer topics all provide possibilities for PSAs.
- Hard news releases are based on factual current events, and soft news releases are based on entertainment topics and celebrities. Know which you are doing, so you can direct it to the proper producer, editor, or director.
- It is often best to telephone a radio or television producer and very briefly pitch your idea first. Be sure you have it boiled down to a very interesting 20 to 30 second statement or two to grab his attention. Present it in one of these media categories, and be sure to suggest the audiotape or videotape opportunities:
  - Natural disaster or crisis
  - Health, medical, safety, or well-being
  - Economics that affect the public
  - Good Samaritans—personal stories about people who have done something for the community
  - Humor or special human-interest stories

CONSIDER SPECIAL SITUATIONS

- For television, suggest ways to make the information or event visually interesting.
- Suggest ideas for interviews, filming, or audio recording.
- Make videotapes and audiotapes available, if possible.
- Suggest writing the broadcast script, if necessary. If you write the script, use the standard abbreviations used by the broadcast organization (Visit www.sandralamb.com for script examples.).

SELECT A FORMAT

- Use 8½ by 11–inch sheets, type title in caps at the top of the first page. Under the title center and list the script time.
- Divide the pages vertically with video directions on the left-hand side and audio script on the right-hand side.

70 OPINION EDITORIAL (OP-ED) & LETTER TO THE EDITOR

The opinion editorial (or op-ed), letter to the editor, or guest editorial column is a mainstay of many newspapers and magazines, appearing—as the name suggests—on editorial pages opposite pieces written by the publication's reporters and editors. In magazines these usually appear in a special section called "mail," "from our readers," etc.

Pieces selected to appear here reflect the personal viewpoint of readers and include letters to the editor, contributing editorials, and articles with bylines.

While the op-ed by nature offers substantial latitude, it is important to study the particular publication you wish to write for, and then follow that specific publication's guidelines.

DECIDE TO WRITE

Use this venue to:

- Influence public opinion about a major political issue, societal ill, crisis, or current event
- Respond to or correct incorrect or inaccurate information presented in the publication
- Promote a particular point of view
- Point out that relevant information was omitted from an article
- Congratulate the editor or author on a position or piece

THINK ABOUT CONTENT

- Inquire before writing to learn the policy of a publication and its editorial requirements about these pieces.
- Letters to the editor offer the opportunity for publicity and visibility. Keep that connection in mind when writing.
- Write to the requirements, specifications, or guidelines of the particular publication.
- Be sure to get the approval of organization officials if your letter represents your organization.
- Take a positive approach and upbeat tone whenever possible.
- If you are refuting an editorial, reference the editorial title and date. State your position and support it with hard data and facts, giving the sources and authorities, but use only one or two sources. Stick to the point and be as clear, objective, and brief as possible. Be passionate, but don't go overboard.

- In responding to mistakes or inaccuracies, refer to the publication date and page of the piece you are responding to. Quote the incorrect statement and then state the correct information. Make sure you document your statement with one or two sources. Finally, sign your letter with your name and, if applicable, title.
- Keep letters or articles brief and to the point. Most publications allow a maximum of 500 to 800 words per piece. Check with the publication.

ELIMINATE WRONG MESSAGES

- Don't fire off an immediate response to a negative article without reflection. Carefully weigh the decision, and try to determine if a response is likely to fuel more negative press.
- Stay away from inflammatory or derogatory remarks.
- Do not threaten legal action.
- Unless you are doing a humorous piece or parody, refrain from hyperbole.

SELECT A FORMAT

Type your piece double-spaced with a minimum of one-inch margins; or submit by email to the proper editor.

CONSIDER SPECIAL SITUATIONS

Use the correct name and title of the editor, and address your op-ed piece directly to that person.

Op Ed

Dear Editor:

Concerning your Tuesday piece about more alcohol on our public beaches, I must ask: More drinking allowed on our beaches? Really? Why would this possibly be a good idea?

Yesterday I was sitting on the beach next to a trio of inebriated, out-of-control beer drinkers who were horrifying at least six families with small children. The trio was intermittently operating wave runners from shore—a grave danger to both themselves and many others. Imagine what they could do with hard liquor. I called a park ranger in an effort to avoid certain disaster, but it took an hour and a half for one to appear.

And, of course, these happy "bathers" had to leave the beach in automobiles to drive our highways. Approving more alcohol use on our beaches is a completely insane idea! Vote NO!

Keep Our Beaches Happy, Safe, and Sober.

Sadie Bath

Op Ed

Dear Editor:

Regarding Sunday's piece about Governor Brown, I say bring on the moonbeams and quirks and "out there" philosophical bent if they come with Brown's veteran, sane, and solid plan for pulling this once great state back from the abyss, restoring fiscal sanity, and righting inequities for hundreds of thousands of its citizens who've lost pensions and benefits. And much more.

You go, Governor Brown! May the force of all we citizens be fully and solidly behind you.

A Proud Californian Once Again

A newsletter is a publication for a defined and specific audience. Most are written for an "in" group, such as employees, neighbors, club, and association members—people with a common interest. They are generally written in an informal journalistic style as news or features.

STUDY TYPES OF NEWSLETTERS

- Employee newsletters are produced by the organization to help create a sense of community. They usually include a mix of employee information and organization news.
- Community newsletters are usually directed at geographical neighbors to create unity by addressing common concerns and issues, and for the purpose of disseminating information.
- Association, club, or group newsletters exist to keep members of an identified group in touch. For example, the Rotarians, Toastmasters, Book-of-the-Month Club, Mystery Writers of America, and all sorts of small common-interest groups for runners, tennis players, health-club members, and genre writers use the newsletter to inspire, inform, and create camaraderie among their members.
- Publicity newsletters exist to create their own publics. Hotels, vacation clubs, fan clubs, and politicians create newsletters to promote themselves.
- Self-interest newsletters make a profit by offering common-interest information, advice, and solutions to problems for a fee. Such newsletters exist for financial investors, public relations personnel, public speakers, bargain shoppers, writers, and many other kinds and groups of people.

THINK ABOUT CONTENT

- Know the audience thoroughly so the newsletter can be focused appropriately.
- Use a journalistic style of writing. There is no need to write in the inverted pyramid style of putting all the facts in the first sentence or paragraph.
- Informal writing is best for most readers.
- Article length depends upon the audience, although business-related newsletters tend to keep article length from 200 to 600 words.

- Create a mix of informational and entertaining pieces. Features should have a beginning, middle, and end. Make the lead a hook for the readers, and follow it in logical order, explaining and elaborating on the lead.
- Give feature pieces more human interest than news pieces, and more color.

SELECT A FORMAT

- Almost any size may be used, but the major consideration here will be the cost of the paper you select. Newsletters are often only available to be read online, eliminating paper entirely.
- Computer-generated type or table-top publishing may be used for printed newsletters. A banner on the front page and line art or photos will give the newsletter character, but keep it simple.
- Balance pages, taking care to not place all the photos or illustrations on one side of the page, or all in the center where they will seem to be falling into the fold. Consult Graphic Design & Layout, page 14, for information on and examples of desirable arrangements.
- Place the most important items in the upper left-hand or lower right-hand positions on the page, since the eye falls to these spots first.
- Use white space to add interest and create an open, easy, and quick-to-read feel.
- Online newsletters are becoming very popular because of their cost-saving character. Study many before creating one. This medium requires writing in a more concise manner.

72 BROCHURE

A brochure is a sales piece used in sales efforts, promotion, and media kits. It should present a description of the organization, its capabilities, product line, and goals.

The brochure should answer the questions:

- What is the organization?
- Where did it come from (background)?
- What does it have to offer (product or service)?

It should also tell the reader where the organization is located, its representatives, complete contact information, and why it is unique or special. Include information on the organization's mission, its benefits to members, and how they can join.

THINK ABOUT CONTENT

- Research, review, and collect scores of brochures, then note what you like or don't like about them.
- Decide what and how much you want to say.
- Identify the message in terms of features and benefits. Features are the nitty-gritty of the services or products; benefit statements describe what's in it for the reader.
- It's also important to be as economical with words as possible. The most effective brochures are often the shortest.
- Decide how you want your brochure to look. The visual appearance of your brochure must promote the message.
- Decide how many to produce, estimating what the shelf life of the brochure will be and how much you have to spend. You may want or need to get the professional help of a designer and printer to make these decisions.
- Write the copy, then review and rewrite it.
- Select a desktop publisher and/or printer and work with him or her to fit your copy into a finished brochure size allowing for photos, visuals, and displays.
- Edit the copy, collect any photos or artwork, and rough out a layout indicating the size and placement of the headings, graphics, and photos.
- Select a paper with the right look, feel, color, and durability. The cost of the stock may limit your choice, but select one that will work best with your type style, graphics, and color choices.

XI

ELECTRONIC COMMUNICATION

Nothing is more simple than greatness;
indeed, to be simple is to be great.

—*Ralph Waldo Emerson*

73 | EMAIL

We wonder how we ever managed our business and personal lives without email. It allows us instant communication, keeps us from prolonged telephone encounters (or frustrating telephone tag), and lets us communicate seamlessly with specific groups to exchange information, pass along reports, get input, and make requests. It can make us much more productive and save us time. But managing our email has also added a considerable workload to our day. Surveys indicate that people spend from thirty minutes to four hours each day emailing. We send about 200 billion emails each day. And wireless email users are expanding that number exponentially by the minute.

To do it right, this revolution in communication requires that we learn to write and edit better, and that we learn how to effectively use and manage this medium to avoid the possibility for serious errors. So, be sure to scrupulously follow all the principles of writing clear, focused, brief, timely, and precise email communications.

WHEN TO EMAIL

Before you email, first consider your message content and response requirements, and all the possibilities for communicating; then select the best vehicle:

- If what you have to communicate requires a human moment (it's high in either emotional or personal content), requires dialogue, negotiation, or if the content is of a personnel, confidential, or financial nature, a face-to-face exchange is still best.
- The telephone is a good choice when you need an immediate answer, if the person you want to communicate with prefers voice contact, and/or if your message will benefit from the nuance of voice inflection (even leaving a voice message).
- To send a very personal message of praise, comfort, or support, a handwritten letter or note is best because writing it down adds the weight of care, contemplation, and a permanent record.
- Email is the best choice for informal interoffice, business to business, and informational messages and memos; or when speed, large distribution numbers, and creation of a permanent record are requirements of your message.

EMAIL MESSAGE CAUTIONS

Remember these important things about email communications:

- Never send a message (or reply) when emotions are high. Calm down, reconsider, and re-evaluate before you hit "send."

- You will be judged on the basis of your workplace email writing skills.
- All email that is generated from an organization or company (desktop, laptop, company mail server) is owned by that organization or company.
- Emails can be intercepted (and forwarded) to an unintended recipient.
- Emails aren't ever truly deleted. So don't fill in the "To:" until your email has been completed to your satisfaction, and only hit "Send:" after you have thoroughly checked and edited it.
- You can best manage your email if you designate specific times of the day to process and respond to the messages in your inbox.
- Email creates an invaluable audit trail for documents, contracts, and correspondence.

EMAIL TERMS

It's helpful to know some of the basic terms of email and internet use:

Archive	Emails stored for later access.
Attachment	File of any type that is appended to and sent with an email.
Autoresponder	Prewritten reply that is sent in response to a received email.
BCC	Blind carbon copy (allows the sender to email a copy of the message to recipients without their addresses being revealed).
Blog	Serialized features written expressly to share with others and foster the building of a community or audience.
Bounced message	An email that returns undelivered to the sender.
Browser	Software program (Explorer, Netscape, Safari) that allows the user to view websites.
CC	Carbon copy, which (the sender copy the email to more recipients. The recipients' addresses appear in the email header field).
Challenge-Response	Used to authenticate emails as coming from an individual. Sender must respond to an email challenge before message is delivered.
Chat rooms	Online meeting places where people discuss topics of mutual interest.
Digital Signature	Unique encrypted digital code that is attached to messages to guarantee the authenticity of the sender.
Distribution List	A list of email addresses saved as a single recipient.
Download	Transferring a file from a sender to the recipient's harddrive.
Emoticon	Symbols and punctuation marks used to make facial expressions (smiley face, wink, sad face) within emails.
Encryption	Encoding within email that allows only a recipient with the code to read it.
FAQ	Frequently asked questions.
Filter	Sorts emails automatically, usually to eliminate SPAM.
Firewall	Safety software or hardware that prevents unauthorized access to or from a network or computer.
Flame	A personal attack sent by email.

Hard Copy	A printout of the email.
Header	The address and subject part of the email.
Host	Supplies services of applications, web pages, etc., to a network of computers and their users.
HTML	Hypertext Mark-Up Language, which is used to create web pages. Used with most email.
Hyperlinks	(Or links) are elements in an electronic document that will connect you to another place or document when you click on them.
IM	Instant Messaging.
Intranet	Private network of computers inside an organization.
IP Address	Internet Protocol Address (a computer's unique address that identifies it to the internet to direct information).
Junk Mail	Unsolicited email.
Listservs	Allows the sending of messages to a collection of members (similar to chat rooms).
Netiquette	Etiquette online, the unwritten rules of using email and the internet to promote civility.
PDA	Personal digital assistant (formerly used on Palm Pilots and similar devices; now they are blended with cell phones in the class of "smart phones" such as iPhone, Blackberry, etc.)
Phishing	Identity theft that uses email to "bait" and "hook" users into giving them private information, such as credit card numbers, social security numbers, etc.
Plain Text	Uses no formatting elements so any email program can read it.
Protocol	The rules that two computers must follow to exchange messages.
Q&A	Questions and answers.
Search Engine	System that finds information on the Web.
Signature Line	Automatically attached signature that appears on messages.
Snail Mail	Written mail sent through the postal service.
Social Networks	Websites like Facebook, MySpace, LinkedIn, and Twitter where people create a community of "friends" and share ideas.
SPAM	Unsolicited junk email.
SPAM Block	The text inserted between the @ symbol and the domain name in an email address to prevent the collection of the actual email address.
Surf	Navigate or peruse the Web.
Texting	Messages sent on WiFi cell phones and tablets. Communication between iPhone or PDAs sends a message, which may not be immediate (the recipient may not get the text for seconds or minutes after it is sent). Larger mobile devices, such as tablets, can have more robust applications, so WiFi is becoming more prevalent, allowing for immediate communication. The lines are blurring functionally, but IM and TEXTING use different technologies.
Thread	An ongoing string of messages; an email conversation.
Tweets	Posts of 140 characters sent on your Twitter account.
URL	Uniform Resource Locator.

Virus	A potentially infective software program that can spread through your system when you open email attachments.
WiFi	Wireless Fidelity (broadband wireless access; a play on words from Hi-Fi meaning high-fidelity stereo).
Wikis	Websites anyone can edit and update.
Worm	A self-contained software system that replicates itself as it spreads from one computer to another clogging networks and information systems. It can enter your system through email and attachments.
Zip Files	Files that have been compressed to save storage space and to download more quickly.

THINK ABOUT CONTENT

- See Memo, page 170, and/or other communication chapters, and use the general rules presented in those chapters. Emails are informal memos, and sometimes much more formal letters, cover letters, or even proposals, reports, and requests.
- Know your organization's rules for email use. If no policy is in place, create a well-thought-out one.
- Begin by answering these questions:
  - Does the organization limit employee email and online use?
  - In your organization, are messages confidential and owned by the sender, or are they organization-owned as part of the system? That is, is the sender the "custodian" or the "owner" of the email messages he or she sends?
  - Does the organization reserve the right to monitor, as owner of the system, all email?
- Use your organization's rules of netiquette, technical terms, approved abbreviations, and symbols where they exist.
- Remember, correct capitalization, spelling, and punctuation are part of a proper message, and all capitals equals a shout.
- Use email only for business messages in your business setting, if appropriate.
- Restrict your email message to one subject whenever possible. Multiple subjects impede the receiver's response and create a filing problem.
- State the subject briefly, clearly, and precisely in the subject line.
- Copy or highlight only the point of a received message you are responding to, when appropriate.
- Respond promptly, or use an acknowledgment message if your response will take you over 24 hours: "I got your message, and I'll get a response back tomorrow morning."
- Make sure your recipient can accept and open your attachments before you send them.
- Limit messages to one screen length whenever possible.

ELIMINATE WRONG EMAIL MESSAGES

- Do not write confidential or sensitive messages that you do not want people other than the intended recipient to read.
- Do not fire off messages without thoroughly thinking them through.
- Do not forward messages without the permission of the sender/author.
- Don't copy and paste copyrighted material into your messages without the author's permission. Copyrighted material includes any original material someone has emailed you.
- Don't use acronyms (BTW, FWIW, LOL, IMO) or emoticons (keyboard characters to create "faces" showing emotions) in business emails; and use them sparingly in personal emails.
- Don't forward jokes and other materials in business email. Ask personal friends and associates if they wish to receive them before sending to avoid becoming viewed as a SPAM-er.
- Don't send urgent messages by email unless you know the recipient is online.
- Be sure to check to whom your response email is being sent; sometimes in groups the "reply all" function will be on.
- Never send an angry (flame) message, or make a personal attack. Take time to cool down before emailing.
- Beware of posting personal information that could result in identity theft.

SELECT AN EMAIL FORMAT

- Use a business salutation to start your email for business communications, or follow your organization's established format. Because this is an informal communication, it's usually acceptable to use "Hi," or "Hello," and/or the first name of the person you're emailing, if you know the person even casually.
- Learn and use your organization's special abbreviations and symbols, if any.

USING LISTSERVS, ELECTRONIC BULLETIN BOARDS, CHAT ROOMS

Electronic email groups and bulletin boards where messages on a wide variety of subjects are posted are common worldwide. Posting and discussion rules should be in place. You may be required to agree to comply with online group rules in order to participate. Carefully review, then observe these rules at all times.

THINK ABOUT ONLINE GROUP MESSAGE CONTENT

- Tune in for a period of time before posting on an online group so you can learn the language, rules for participating, culture, and symbols.
- Think in terms of writing a value-added message.
- Give your message some reflection before sending.
- Evaluate your message before you send it to be sure it adds new information or ideas. "Me too" messages usually waste a lot of people's time.

- Phrase your posts in objective, positive terms whenever possible. Online messages can easily be misinterpreted, and offense can easily be taken.
- Always address the idea, and not the person who expressed it.
- Online levity is an art form that's difficult to master. Become very familiar with the particular culture before you try it. Even then, consider that self-deprecating humor is always safest.

SELECT A FORMAT

- Email form, typeface, line lengths, etc., are affected by the systems used, so make your sentences brief.
- Use short paragraphs with a space between. Indenting isn't necessary.
- Use lists with bullets whenever possible.
- Use a salutation consistent with your relationship with the recipient and your organization's policy. An informal greeting is fine for recipients you know.
- Your closing needs to tell the reader that he has reached the end, and give him a way to contact you. Use of the automatic signature lines here is helpful.

USE POWER WORDS

act	announce	answer	attached
assign	confirm	conclude	correct
deadline	eliminate	explain	guidelines
information	initiate	instruct	input
list	meet	notice	order
propose	progress	proposal	purpose
remind	renew	review	reply
report	response	revise	start
status	summary	thanks	

BUILD EFFECTIVE PHRASES

ask for your input	request a change
announce a new policy	revise the procedure
in response to	review the attached
submit your comments	change the time
thank you for	please note changes
here's my response	I'm answering your question
the deadline is	ask for your help
here's the decision	listed below
summarized here	note these points

WRITE STRONG SENTENCES

I'm attaching the report you requested.

There are several changes in the policy, which are listed here.

Here's the requested document.

Please give me your input.

The deadline is Tuesday.

Thank you for your comments.

It was so good to hear from you.

Here's the latest update.

You can find the information at this website.

Please apply by March 10.

I'll finish my report by June 4.

Our deadline is approaching.

It's a beautiful spring day here.

Now for the news!

I couldn't wait to tell you.

BUILD EFFECTIVE PARAGRAPHS

There won't be time for any additional changes. So, please submit your final recommendations by Tuesday.

I'm on deadline at the moment. I'll get back to you on Saturday.

Whew! I've just finished a marathon project. Now for two more assignments that are due by next Wednesday. Can we delay lunch another week?

The lunch policy will change to: all hourly employees take the 12:30 p.m. to 1:15 p.m. timeframe. This will insure all production is covered.

Thank you. I appreciate your comments. They are both insightful and informative.

Your efforts on this report are outstanding! I will ask you to take a bow and present your findings at next week's meeting.

How is the Jones family handling this cold blast? We had temperatures of -20 degrees last night and slept in our wool socks and sweaters.

I'll bring the lantern and backpacks. Would you please put in a dozen of those protein bars?

In response to your question: yes, we are still interviewing for the production manager position. And, yes, you are still at the top of the candidate list.

I'll get back to you with more information on the trip next week. We haven't decided how to work out our timing yet.

EDIT, EDIT, EDIT

Use powerful words, brief sentences, and very short paragraphs. Edit for brevity and clarity.

EMAIL SAMPLES

Often the paragraph is the entire email. Think and write short. Remember Shakespeare's words: brevity is the soul of wit. Because the heading material is prescribed, and the subject line should contain a concise, attention-getting distilled idea of the email content, those elements aren't included in the following samples.

> I'm attaching the new report. Please review and send your comments to me by June 1.

> Thank you for such a great team effort. It's evident that Marketing will hold the trophy for another year.

> Please be sure to review the company email guidelines. In the last week we have had some serious infractions of the rules of netiquette. Personal attacks will not be tolerated.

> The attached report points out three areas where we need to improve:
> - Third shift production output
> - Reduction of Line 4 rejects
> - Model 104A quality

> Please carefully read the entire attached report, and come to Monday's meeting with your ideas for making the necessary changes.

APPENDIX

Forms of Address		
Person	**Title for Envelope/Inside Address**	**Salutation**
Ambassador, American	The Honorable [Name] American Ambassador/ Ambassador from the United States City, Country	Sir/Madam: Dear Mr./Madam Ambassador:
Ambassador, foreign	His/Her Excellency [Name] Ambassador of [Country] Washington, DC	Excellency: Dear Mr./Madame Ambassador: My dear Mr./Madame [Name]:
Archbishop, Roman Catholic	The Most Reverend [Name] Archbishop of [City] City, State	Dear Archbishop [Name]: Most Reverend and dear Sir: Your Excellency: Reverend Sir:
Bishop, Episcopal	The Right Reverend [Name] Bishop of [Diocese] City, State	Right Reverend Sir: Dear Bishop [Name]:
Bishop, Methodist	Bishop [Name] City, State	Your Excellency: Dear Bishop [Name]:
Bishop, Roman Catholic	The Most Reverend [Name] Bishop of [Diocese] City, State	Your Excellency: Most Reverend Sir: Dear Bishop [Name]:
Brother	Brother [Name] Address City, State	Dear Brother [Name]: Dear Brother:
Cabinet member, United States	The Honorable [Name] The Secretary of [Dept.] Washington, DC	Sir/Madam: Dear Mr./Madam Secretary: Dear Mr./Mrs. [Name]:
Cardinal, Roman Catholic	His Eminence [First Name] Cardinal [Last Name] Archbishop of [City] City, State	Your Eminence: My dear Cardinal: Dear Cardinal [Name]:
Clergyman, Protestant [except Episcopal]	The Reverend [or with a doctorate, Reverend Dr.] [Name] Address City, State	My dear Mr./Mrs./Ms. [or Dr.]: Dear Mr./Mrs./Ms.: Dear Pastor [Name]:
Consul	[Full Name], Esq. [Country] Consul City, State	Sir/Madam [*Madame* if foreign consul]: Dear Mr./Mrs./Ms. Consul:
Dean, college	Dean [or Dr.] [Name] College or University City, State	Sir/Madam: Dear Dean [Name]: Dear Dr. [Name]:
Doctor	Dr. [Name] [or Full Name], M.D. or Ph.D. or D.D. Address City, State	Dear Dr. [Name]:
Governor	The Honorable [Name] Governor of [State] City, State	Sir/Madam: My dear Governor [Name]: Dear Governor [Name]:

Person	Title for Envelope/Inside Address	Salutation
Judge	The Honorable [Name] Name of Court City, State	Sir/Madam: My dear Judge [Name]: Dear Judge [Name]:
Legislator	The Honorable [Name] Name of Legislative Body City, State	Sir/Madam: Dear Senator [Name]: My dear Mr./Ms./Mrs.: Dear Mr./Ms./Mrs.:
Mayor	The Honorable [Name] Mayor of [City] City, State	Sir/Madam: Dear Mayor [Name]:
Military officer	[Full or abbreviated rank] [Full Name], [Abbreviation for Service] Address City, State	Sir/Madam: Dear Major/Captain/General/Admiral [Name]:
Monsignor	The Reverend Monsignor [Name], or The Rev. Msgr. [Name] City, State	Dear Monsignor [Name]: Monsignor [Name]: Reverend and dear Monsignor [Name]:
Nun	Sister [Name], [Initials of Order] Address City, State	Dear Sister [Name]: Dear Sister:
Patriarch, Eastern Orthodox	His Beatitude the Patriarch of [Diocese] Address City, State	Most Reverend Lord: Your Beatitude:
The Pope	His Holiness Pope [Name], or His Holiness the Pope Vatican City Rome, Italy	Your Holiness: Most Holy Father:
President, college or university	President [Full Name], or Dr. [Full Name] College or University City, State	Sir/Madam: Dear Dr. [Name]: Dear President [Name]:
President, Prime Minister [foreign country]	President [Name], or Prime Minister [Name] City, Country	Excellency His/Her [Title and Name]: Mr./Madame Prime Minister:
President, United States	The President The White House Washington, DC 20500	Mr. President: President: Dear President [Name]:
Priest, Roman Catholic, Episcopal	The Reverend [Dr.] [Name] Address City, State	Reverend Father:
Professor	Prof. [Name] Department of [Subject] College or University City, State	Dear Sir/Madam: Dear Professor [Name]: Dear Dr. [Name]:
Rabbi	Rabbi [Name] Address City, State	Dear Rabbi [Name]: Dear Dr. [Name]:
Representative	The Honorable [Name] The United States House of Representatives Washington, DC 20515	Sir/Madam: Dear Mr./Ms./Mrs. [Name]: Dear Representative [Name]:
Secretary-General of the United Nations	His [or Her] Excellency [Name] United Nations United Nations Plaza New York, NY 10017	Excellency: Dear Mr./Ms./Mrs. Secretary-General:

Person	Title for Envelope/Inside Address	Salutation
Senator	The Honorable [Name] United States Senate Washington, DC 20510	Sir/Madam: Dear Senator [Name]:
Speaker of the House	The Honorable [Name] The United States House of Representatives Washington, DC 20515	Dear Mr./Madam Speaker:
Supreme Court Justice	The Honorable [Name], Associate [or Chief] Justice of the United States Supreme Court Washington, DC 20543	Sir/Madam: Dear Justice [Last Name]: Dear Mr./Ms./Mrs. Justice [Last Name]:
United Nations Representative	His/Her Excellency [Country] Representative to the United Nations United Nations New York, NY 10017	Excellency: Ambassador: Sir/Madam [*Madame* if foreign]: Mr./Ms./Mrs. [Name]:
Vice President, United States	Vice President of the United States, or The Vice President of the United States Washington, DC	Dear Mr./Ms./Mrs.: Vice President [Name]:
Baron/Baroness	The Right Honorable Lord/Lady [Name]	My Lord/Lady: Dear Lord/Lady [Name]:
Baronet	Sir [Name], Bt.	Dear Sir: Dear Sir [Name]:
Wife of baronet	Lady [Name]	Dear Madame: Dear Lady [Name]:
Duke/Duchess	His/Her Grace, the Duke/Duchess of [Duchy]	My Lord Duke/Madame: Dear Duke of [Duchy]: Dear Duchess:
Earl/Countess	The Right Honorable The Earl/Countess of [Place]	My Lord/Madame: Dear Lord [Name]: Dear Countess:
Knight	Sir [Name]	Dear Sir: Dear Sir [Name]:
Wife of knight	Lady [Name]	Dear Madame: Dear Lady [Name]:
Marquess/ Marchioness	The Most Honorable The Marquess/Marchioness of [Place]	My Lord/Madame:
Viscount/ Viscountess	The Right Honorable The Viscount/Viscountess of [Place]	My Lord/Lady:
Other royalty	His/Her Royal Highness The Prince/Princess of [Place]	Your Royal Highness:

Abbreviating Titles

Educational degrees, memberships, military or civil honors, and titles that follow a name include these:

Abbreviation	Title
A.A.	associate of arts
A.B.	bachelor of arts (artium baccalaureus)
A.M.	master of arts (artium magister)
B.A.	bachelor of arts
B.D.	bachelor of divinity
B.F.A.	bachelor of fine arts
B.S.	bachelor of science
CEO	chief executive officer
CFO	chief financial officer
CPA	certified public accountant
D.B.	bachelor of divinity (divinitatis baccalaureus)
D.D.	doctor of divinity (divinitatis doctor)
D.D.S.	doctor of dental surgery
D.O.	doctor of osteopathy
D.S.O.	Distinguished Service Order
D.V.M.	doctor of veterinary medicine
Esq.	esquire
F.R.S.	fellow of the Royal Society
Hon.	the honorable
J.D.	doctor of law (juris doctor)
J.P.	justice of the peace
Kt.	knight
L.H.D.	doctor of humanities (litterarum humaniorum doctor)
Litt.D.	doctor of letters (litterarum doctor)
LL.B.	bachelor of laws (legum baccalaureus)
LL.D.	doctor of laws (legum doctor)
L.P.N.	licensed practical nurse
M.A.	master of arts

Abbreviation	Title
M.B.A.	master of business administration
M.H.A.	master of hospital administration
M.D.	doctor of medicine (medicinae doctor)
M.P.	member of parliament
MP	military police
M.P.H.	master of public health
M.S.	master of science
M.S.W.	master of social work
Ph.B.	bachelor of philosophy (philosophiae baccalaureus)
Ph.D.	doctor of philosophy (philosophiae doctor)
Ph.G.	graduate in pharmacy
PM	prime minister
Psy.D.	doctor of psychology
R.N.	registered nurse
Rev.	reverend
S.B.	bachelor of science (scientiae baccalaureus)
S.J.	Society of Jesus
S.M.	master of science (scientiae magister)
S.T.B.	bachelor of sacred theology (sacrae theologiae baccalaureus)
VP	vice president

Abbreviating U.S. military Branches*

Abbreviation	Title
USAF	United States Air Force
USCG	United States Coast Guard
USMC	United States Marine Corps.
USN	United States Navy
USA	United States Army

* Add an "R" suffix to indicate reserve status.

INDEX